Cynthia A. Ruder is Associate Professor of Russian Studies at the University of Kentucky. She received her PhD from Cornell University and has previously published *Making History for Stalin*, which focused on the 1933 construction of the Belomor Canal. She has also contributed to peer-reviewed journals and edited collections and was the only non-Russian citizen who participated in the conference to commemorate the 70th anniversary of the Moscow Canal's opening in 1937.

"The history of a canal-building project might be thought in some quarters as an unpromising subject for a good read, but it is some years since I have found myself so drawn into a book as I was reading *Building Stalinism: The Moscow Canal and the Creation of Soviet Space*. In five meticulously researched and elegantly crafted chapters, Cynthia Ruder excavates the multiple layers of meaning embedded in the landscape of the Moscow–Volga canal. The canal was the centerpiece engineering project of the second five-year plan that transformed Moscow into a 'port of five seas' and supplied the city with water and electricity, but did so at the cost of tens of thousands of lives of Gulag victims. This book is not a conventional history of a Gulag camp (although the discussion of Dmitlag is a valuable addition to the literature) because throughout, it is the canal and the water in it that is center stage. The originality of the book is in its combination of different conceptions of space – representational, discursive and socio-political – to reveal the role that the canal played in securing Moscow as the very epicenter of the USSR's mythic landscape. It does this by taking the reader on a journey along the canal, with pauses to explain how the natural environment was reworked in a particular place or to give a detailed history of an architectural monument, loch or statue, or to note the place where bones were uncovered by a twenty-first-century digger. And we learn also of the music, writing and art and other cultural productions that told the canal's story from the point of view of the people who built it. Much of the book is about memory and it is obvious that Cynthia Ruder cares very deeply that the canal's origins in one of the harshest camps of the Gulag will not be forgotten under the new layer of meanings associated with the elite homes and yacht clubs that now line its banks. This thought-provoking and moving historical-geography will help guarantee that this will not happen."

Judith Pallot, Professor Emeritus, University of Oxford and President, British Association for Slavonic and East European Studies (BASEES)

"This is a deeply researched and beautifully written book that will be read by scholars and non-scholars alike. In accessible, flowing prose, Cynthia Ruder explains through the lens of the inception and building of the Moscow Canal what Stalinism looked like, felt like and how it worked in the 1930s Soviet Union. Upon reading this book with its wonderful details, character studies, plates and illustrations, the reader comes away with a deep understanding of 'the triumph of Soviet over Russian culture and the shift from Russian to Soviet spaces,' and the social, psychic, political and economic impacts of the Moscow Canal that still reverberate in today's Russia. Beautifully written and researched, this book profoundly enhances our understanding of Stalinism and the workings of Soviet communism."

Deborah Kaple, Research Scholar and Lecturer, Princeton University

"A highly original work, *Building Stalinism* examines the way human lives were reforged in order for Stalinist culture to succeed. Focusing on artistic representations of the Moscow Canal, Cynthia Ruder brilliantly illustrates the way space could be shaped to fit an ultimately destructive ideology."

Olga M. Cooke, Associate Professor of Russian, Texas A&M University and editor of *Gulag Studies*

"An extremely well-researched and original book that sheds new light on the ideology and operation of Stalinism by bringing together myriad rare or unknown sources, including new voices both from the Gulag and from contemporary Russia. Ruder uses the Moscow Canal as a powerful vantage point from which to study Stalinism and the memory of Stalinism today, as well as questions of landscape, environment, and water policy."

Karen Petrone, Professor of History, University of Kentucky

Library of Modern Russia

Building on I.B.Tauris' established record publishing Russian studies titles for both academic and general readers, the Library of Modern Russia will showcase the work of emerging and established writers who are setting new agendas in the field.

At a time when potentially dangerous misconceptions and misunderstandings about Russia abound, titles in the series will shed fresh light and nuance on Russian history. Volumes will take the idea of 'Russia' in its broadest, cultural sense and cover the entirety of the multi-ethnic lands that made up imperial Russia and the Soviet Union. Ranging in chronological scope from the Romanovs to the present day, the books will foster a community of scholars and readers devoted to a sharper understanding of the Russian experience, past and present.

New and forthcoming

Building Stalinism: The Moscow Canal and the Creation of Soviet Space, Cynthia A. Ruder
Criminal Subculture in the Gulag: Prisoner Society in the Stalinist Labour Camps, Mark Vincent
Dissident Histories in the Soviet Union: From De-Stalinization to Perestroika, Barbara Martin
Fascism in Manchuria: The Soviet–China Encounter in the 1930s, Susanne Hohler
Ideology and the Arts in the Soviet Union: The Establishment of Censorship and Control, Steven Richmond
Myth Making in the Soviet Union and Modern Russia: Remembering World War II in Brezhnev's Hero City, Vicky Davis
Nomads and Soviet Rule: Central Asia under Lenin and Stalin, Alun Thomas
Power and Conflict in Russia's Borderlands: The Post-Soviet Geopolitics of Dispute Resolution, Helena Rytövuori-Apunen
Power and Politics in Modern Chechnya: Ramzan Kadyrov and the New Digital Authoritarianism, Karena Avedissian
Russia in the Time of Cholera: Disease under Romanovs and Soviets, John P. Davis
Russian Pilgrimage to the Holy Land: Piety and Travel from the Middle Ages to the Revolution, Nikolaos Chrissidis
Science City, Siberia: Akademgorodok and the Late Soviet Politics of Expertise, Ksenia Tartachenko
Soviet Americana: The Cultural History of Russian and Ukrainian Americanists, Sergei I. Zhuk
Stalin's Economic Advisors: The Varga Institute and the Making of Soviet Foreign Policy, Kyung Deok Roh
The Communist Party in the Russian Civil War: A Political History, Gayle Lonergan
The Idea of Russia: The Life and Work of Dmitry Likhachev, Vladislav Zubok
The Politics of Football in Soviet Russia: Sport and Society after Stalin, Manfred Zeller
The Russian State and the People: Power, Corruption and the Individual in Putin's Russia, Geir Hønneland *et al.* (eds)
The Tsar's Armenians: A Minority in Late Imperial Russia, Onur Önol

BUILDING STALINISM

The Moscow Canal and the Creation of Soviet Space

CYNTHIA A. RUDER

I.B. TAURIS
LONDON · NEW YORK

Published in 2018 by
I.B.Tauris & Co. Ltd
London • New York
www.ibtauris.com

Library of Modern Russia 2

ISBN: 978 1 78453 947 4
eISBN: 978 1 78672 356 7
ePDF: 978 1 78673 356 6

A full CIP record for this book is available from the British Library
A full CIP record is available from the Library of Congress

Library of Congress Catalog Card Number: available

Typeset in Garamond Three by OKS Prepress Services, Chennai, India
Printed and bound in Great Britain by CPI Group (UK) Ltd, Croydon CR0 4YY

FSC www.fsc.org
MIX
Paper from responsible sources
FSC® C013604

For Igor

CONTENTS

LIST OF FIGURES

LIST OF PLATES

ACKNOWLEDGEMENTS

This book has been *years* in the making. It took me longer to research and write it than the Dmitlag forced laborers took to build the Moscow Canal, a fact not lost on the many people and organizations that supported me throughout this project.

Financial support for my research trips to Russia was generously provided by three organizations. A research grant from the National Council of East Europe, Eurasia, and Russia (NCEEER) and the Department of State Title VIII Program allowed me to spend 2007 doing research for the book in the US and Russia. I am particularly indebted to the late Bob Huber, as well as to the NCEEER staff, for their support and patience as I completed the requirements for my grant. In addition, the American Councils for International Education (ACTR/ACCELS) consistently provided travel and visa support for my trips to Russia. Maria Lekic, Carole Gibran, Jon Smith, and Jeanette Owen in particular deserve my thanks. None of these research trips would have been possible without the support of my College and Department. The University of Kentucky College of Arts & Sciences generously provided me with successive grants for international travel. Former A&S Dean Steve Hoch made it possible for me to take a year of research leave in order to make full use of my NCEEER grant. Current A&S Dean Mark Kornbluh has continued to support my international travel to research collections and conferences, for which I am most grateful. The Department of Modern & Classical Languages, Literatures & Cultures consistently encouraged my research and provided additional travel funds when possible. I am grateful to former chair Ted Fiedler for his support. Current chair, and friend, Jeanmarie Rouhier-Willoughby has enthusiastically continued that support, which I deeply appreciate; I thank her for that.

Permission to use some of the material that has been published elsewhere previously has been kindly provided by Olga Cooke, editor of *Gulag Studies* and the journal's publisher Charles Schlacks; Routledge Publishers along with Jane Costlow and Arja Rosenholm, editors of *Meanings and Values of Water in Russian Culture*; and David Patton and Dana Ponte at the National Council of East Europe, Eurasia, and Russia (NCEEER) and the Department of State Title VIII Program NCEEER. In addition, the phenomenal staff in the University of Kentucky Young Library Interlibrary Loan Department efficiently supplied all the materials I requested; they are remarkable. Also worthy of note is librarian Gordon Hogg, who managed to find in the depths of the University of Kentucky Library a copy of a Lopatin book on the Moscow Canal. He also generously gave of his time to help me review the proofs of this book. Thanks, Gordo.

Just as the construction of the Moscow Canal was a collective enterprise, so too was the production of this book. This project would not have come to fruition had it not been for the organizations and individuals in Russia that were instrumental in assisting me. I am always amazed and humbled by the dedication and wealth of knowledge these colleagues possess, especially given how little they are paid to curate such treasure troves of information. At the State Archive of the Russian Federation (GARF) the late A. I. Kokurin and many other staff members in reading rooms and the GARF Library consistently and courteously provided me with the materials and support I needed. At the Central State Archive of the Moscow Region (TsGAMO) I. V. Ryzhova supplied archival materials, especially the personal file of M. B. Granovsky, which were especially helpful in visualizing the Moscow Canal construction process. As always, the librarians at the Russian State Library and the State Historical Public Library efficiently retrieved necessary materials and offered helpful advice. Elena Ovcharenko and Natalia Krupina at MGU readily assisted me as well. Moscow Memorial permitted me to work with the archive of Konstantin Sobolevsky and to copy reams of material, thanks to the efforts of Dima, who fulfilled all my requests with professionalism and good humor, as did Boris Bileikin in the Memorial Library. To all of them I extend my deepest thanks and appreciation.

At the Moscow Canal headquarters I first met V. S. Barkovsky through the assistance of the former chief engineer of the Moscow Canal, A. Y. Kirillov. I also had the pleasure of conferring with N. N. Ermakova, G. A. Gerke and G. I. Yurchenko. They graciously supplied information and materials that would otherwise have been unobtainable. Both Gerke and Yurchenko spent a great deal of time with me at the Moscow Canal Museum; their commentary and anecdotes about the waterway were insightful and highly valued. I was deeply impressed by the dedication these individuals display to the Moscow Canal, its history, current operation, and future viability, as well as their desire to openly and honestly discuss the waterway; for all their help I am especially grateful.

At the Dmitrov Kremlin Museum-Preserve, N. V. Tabunova welcomed my inquiries and shared images of many of the paintings from the Museum's collection that are discussed in this book. She extended an invitation to me to attend the conference held at the Museum in May 2007, from which I collected valuable information and contacts. I thank her very much for including me. In Dmitrov I also had the very great pleasure and privilege to work with Nina Lvovna Elovskaya at the Dmitrov Regional Public Library. As the former curator of the Dmitrov Ethnography room, Nina Lvovna offered me access to a wide variety of print materials that helped immensely in understanding the reception of the Moscow Canal subsequent to its construction. It is thanks to Nina Lvovna, who served as my tour guide, that I was able to visit and photograph the remnants of the Dmitlag camp in Dmitrov. She has also kept me informed of recent publications about the Moscow Canal. She was able to secure for me a copy of the Maslov book that has been extremely useful in preparing this study. I treasure our collegiality and friendship and owe Nina Lvovna eternal gratitude for all her help and support.

Most recently the authors of the site Moskva-volga.ru, especially in the person of Igor Kuvyrkov, have been incredibly helpful in sharing information, answering questions, and providing resources that have benefitted this study immensely. Their determination to keep the memory and discussion of the Moscow Canal alive is inspiring. Because of Igor Kuvyrkov's help I was able to secure permission from Vasily Elkin's grandson to use his grandfather's poster, which graces the cover of this book. To Igor K. my sincerest thanks.

Sadly, just as some of the people most helpful in the writing of my Belomor book did not live to see its publication, the same is true of this book. The late Valentin Sergeevich Barkovsky, Mikhail Ivanovich Bulanov and Aleksandr Ivanovich Kokurin generously shared with me their time, knowledge, and resources. No detail was too small, no question was too insignificant. Valentin Sergeevich gave me a copy of his book and materials from his personal archive that have figured prominently in my work; his kindness and hospitality are not forgotten. Both in Dubna and Moscow, Mikhail Ivanovich readily and enthusiastically mentored my work and offered encouragement and advice, as well as materials to help complete this study, including a signed copy of his book. His warm collegiality, ready smile, and utter devotion to the topic are sorely missed. Aleksandr Ivanovich tracked down all my requests, introduced me to the *Library of Re-Forging* materials in the GARF Library, and secured for me a copy of the *maquette* of the unpublished *Kanal Moskva-Volga*. My project would not be what it is without those resources. All three colleagues patiently and doggedly helped me whenever and however I needed their assistance; I sincerely regret that they are unable to see the result of their labors on my behalf, and I offer to them my deepest gratitude.

Many colleagues, friends and family members have offered support and encouragement as this project has trudged along. Unbeknownst to them a number of colleagues have inspired and mentored me: Olga Cooke, Jehanne Gheith, Deborah Kaple, Judy Pallot, Kelly Smith, and Lynne Viola. Their scholarship models the kind of writing and research that I have tried to emulate; I hope I have lived up to their unfailing belief in my abilities. Their collegiality, friendly support and kind words have meant a great deal. I am honored to know them and thank them most sincerely.

I extend my warm thanks as well to the wonderful Molly Thomasy Blasing and Anna Voskresensky, who patiently and generously permitted me to absent myself from program events and responsibilities to complete my manuscript, while offering unfailing good cheer and kind words; to Donna Brigaman, Donna Medich, K. Andrea Rusnock, and Bonnie Sikes who through their e-mails, phone calls and much-needed conversations supplied good humor, wisdom and encouragement; and to Lew, Steve, George, and Joe Ruder, who lent their expertise to help me understand how the Moscow Canal was engineered, thereby enabling me to explain it clearly to readers. The many breakfasts that Sadia Zoubir-Shaw and I shared while we worked on our projects provided the perfect opportunity to release frustration, share strategies, and encourage each other; for this I thank her very much. We did it!

My editor at I.B.Tauris, Tom Stottor, sought me out to publish this book. His steady energy and enthusiasm for the project, as well as his professionalism, unstinting patience and perceptive comments contributed mightily to its completion. For all this and his generous support I thank him. Sincere thanks as well to production editor, Arub Ahmed, whose astute comments and professionalism were greatly appreciated. My sincere thanks as well to the manuscript reviewers who offered cogent suggestions and comments that improved the book and pushed me to think in new and different ways. I hope they see the results of their work here. Keith Blasing, my copy editor, has been a gift. His own work as a professional translator, his fluency in Russian and his great editorial skill provided the polish the manuscript needed. I am most grateful for his help. Sincere thanks to Rick Spencer who helped proofread the manuscript. His sharp eye and willingness to help at a moment's notice are truly appreciated.

This book would not exist had it not been for Karen Petrone, whose wisdom and keen intellect helped shaped its form and content. Karen's patience and insights, as well as her willingness to be a sounding board for my ideas, are deeply appreciated, as is her unfailing encouragement. I am blessed and grateful that she is a colleague and a friend. It is impossible to overstate her contribution to this book. To her I offer my deep and most humble thanks.

Likewise, this book would not exist had it not been for my kind, patient, unfailingly supportive friend Mary Nicholas. When I needed a good laugh (sometimes through tears), she was there; when I needed to talk through my ideas or wade through particularly turgid theoretical material, she was there; when I presented excerpts of my work at conferences, she was there. She is always there. And she was the first person (after my husband) whom I called to share my jubilation when this book was accepted for publication. Mare, you are the best friend a girl could have. There is not enough dark chocolate and Prosecco in the world to repay you for all you have done for me. So I suppose my deepest and most heartfelt thanks will have to do. Please accept them with my love, respect, and friendship.

I would not continue to exist were it not for my wonderful, supportive husband Igor V. Sopronenko. Through thick and thin, for better and for worse Ig has been with me every step of the way over the many years it took to write this book. From translating difficult-to-understand Russian sources to cooking dinner every night; from listening to my complaints and frustrations to making me laugh when I was low; from insisting that I finish this book to making me believe that I actually could, he has done it all. His infuriating ability to be right most of the time, his technical expertise as a first-rate photographer and one-man video production operation, his great sense of humor and unstinting love and affection have kept me going, especially when the going was rough. His faith in my abilities and commitment to our life partnership continue to amaze. I would be lost without him. I cannot thank him enough for absolutely everything. Thank you, Iggy.

I apologize to anyone who I have forgotten to mention and I offer my sincere thanks to them. Unless otherwise noted, all the translations from Russian into English are mine. I have followed the Library of Congress system of transliteration except in those instances when a more common spelling seemed appropriate, i.e. Mogilianskaya instead of Mogilianskaia. I alone am responsible for the content of this book. I apologize for any errors found herein.

INTRODUCTION

SURVEYING THE SITE: HISTORICAL FRAMEWORK AND SPATIAL PARAMETERS

> We might describe the history of the Soviet Union as the history of the production of a new space, a "Soviet space".[1]

Why write about the Moscow Canal? What significance can there be for contemporary scholars, students, and policymakers in the history of a waterway that is now used more for pleasure boating and swimming than for cargo transport and naval security? The answer, of course, is water, the very stuff of life. It is no exaggeration to say that Moscow would not exist as it does today without the Moscow Canal. In fact, the Moscow Canal provides metropolitan Moscow with more than 60 percent of its potable water supply, as well as electricity for the city and its region. Indeed, just as Moscow needed a reliable source of water during the city's reconstruction in the 1930s, so too does it now rely on that source to support the city's expansion and continued vibrancy.

No less important, the Moscow Canal constituted identifiable, influential, unmistakably *Soviet* space. By space here we mean not only a physical area, but the psyche and imagination as well.[2] The Soviet enterprise to create a "single, unified 'national' space" emerged as the "key Soviet project" in the 1920s and 1930s, as Emma Widdis argues.[3] Likewise, control over that space demonstrated that Soviet power possessed the ideology, human capital, and natural resources to accomplish the task.[4] There could be no argument against the claim that the USSR was the largest country on earth, an honor that resulted from both historical circumstances and geographical reality. The totalizing effect of creating, defining, and altering space, be it metaphorical or physical (and all points in between), upheld Stalinist construction in particular and Soviet power in general.[5] The need to fill a space, to mark one's territory, carried with it both the burden and responsibility of demarcating space such that it became redolent with the Soviet ethos.

In the instance of the Moscow Canal this space needed to be claimed before it could be fully Sovietized. The only way to accomplish this feat was to create the rhetoric first and then fill that rhetorical space with the physical features that embodied and reinforced it. This in turn eliminated any "neutral" space susceptible to forces other than Soviet power; any space created would be unmistakably a politicized, controlled, ideologically laden Soviet space.[6] Equally important was the idea that Soviet power could control water – an element both vital to life and difficult to confine or dominate. The Moscow Canal, in its appropriation of this elemental power, thus became the life blood of Moscow and the USSR as a whole.

As the present study illustrates, the process of creating Soviet space through the construction of the Moscow Canal necessitated the domination of spatial parameters both in the imagination of Soviet citizens and on the ground in both the city and the countryside.[7] It should come as no surprise then that articles dedicated to the completion of the Moscow Canal bore titles such as "The Whole Country Built the Canal!" At the Moscow Canal the center and the periphery converged in both actual and imagined space.

A history of the Moscow–Volga Canal, or the Moscow Canal as it was known after 1947, offers contemporary readers a glimpse of life in Stalin's Soviet Union.[8] Metaphorically and rhetorically reconstructing the Moscow Canal allows us to reassess how the Stalinist system attempted to tame nature through the mastery of its waters, build an empire that would rival its Western foes, and meld its population into an obedient, focused citizenry ready to support the Soviet Union no matter what the future might hold. Likewise, as the first full examination in English of the Moscow Canal, this study offers readers the opportunity to explore a variety of cultural products – sculptures, paintings and drawings, literary works, documentary prose, and architecture – that have been unknown or rarely seen by anyone outside of Russia or without knowledge of Russian. These cultural artifacts are fascinating in and of themselves but acquire even greater meaning when situated in the Stalinist context that produced them. Consequently, this understanding can help us better comprehend contemporary Russian policies and attitudes regarding not only water resources but also the history behind them.

This study also addresses the importance of waterways to contemporary societies regardless of the fraught past in which the infrastructure was built. Like the Suez and Panama Canals, the Moscow Canal serves a vital function based on its location and the resources it provides, such as recreational areas and shoreline land use. How the Moscow Canal is exploited today reveals significance lost or gained since its construction. With the increase of consumer wealth in contemporary Russia, the Moscow Canal offers opportunities as a conduit for expensive yachts to sail beyond Moscow; as a territory for the facilities of sailing clubs such as "The Cape of Joy" (reputedly built on a Dmitlag prisoner gravesite);[9] and as land for suburban and vacation homes. Yet the modern Moscow Canal is limited precisely by its location and landscape unlike, for example, the Panama Canal, whose recent multi-billion-dollar expansion has enabled it to accommodate mammoth cargo ships laden with Chinese goods. Thus the future of the Moscow Canal and its potential as a cultural and historical artifact gain in significance, even as its viability as a shipping route deteriorates. Moreover, as the main source of potable water for Moscow, in an age when water resources remain crucial in an increasingly thirsty world, the Moscow Canal story serves to inform contemporary readers about the ways in which water is both metaphor and resource in Russia and beyond.

Critical to the Moscow Canal endeavor was the philosophy that all elements of society and culture could be marshaled in service to the state to implement large construction projects that would reflect Soviet-Stalinist ideology. Art, architecture, literature, documentary prose, and music were deployed in the Soviet Union's battle to conquer nature and channel it in the direction determined by Stalinist ideology. That the Moscow Canal still exists and functions testifies to the tenacity of its builders, the ingenuity of its engineers, and the "brute force technology," as Paul Josephson calls it, that the Stalinist state applied in order to achieve its goals.[10]

A Brief History of the Canal

The notion of land-locked Moscow gaining access to major bodies of water was not a new one. Even before the time of Peter the Great, Russian rulers had sought to connect Moscow to the Volga River and beyond to exploit the rich natural resources of the Russian interior, link the city with the wider world through the Caspian, Baltic, and White Seas, and provide a reliable channel to move goods, services, and military hardware and troops to and from Moscow via the upper and lower reaches of the Volga. This project was as metaphorical as it was physical, for the canal not only brought the Volga's waters to the Kremlin steps, but also brought the world to Moscow, inevitably changing the views of the city's inhabitants about its place in the global context.

The Moscow Canal project was one of many NKVD-supervised construction sites in the Gulag economy,[11] a system that by its very nature demanded large and continuous infusions of human capital.[12] At the behest of the Soviet of People's Commissars of the USSR, the NKVD established the Dmitrovskii Correctional Labor Camp, or Dmitlag (1932–8), to undertake canal construction. The canal project was also included in the second five-year plan (1933–7),[13] establishing it within the larger context of the Soviet economy. The Moscow Canal, like its sister canals Belomor and Volga-Don, garnered official approbation for the engineering feats achieved with minimal mechanization, maximum exploitation of the local natural resources, and tightly regulated monetary support.

Like its predecessor Belomor,[14] the Moscow Canal project took thousands of lives, flooded villages out of existence, and forcibly resettled peasants in order to construct a reliable transportation route, a series of hydroelectric stations, and a supply canal to bring potable water to Moscow. Conventional wisdom argued that such a canal between the Volga River and Moscow would bring the Russian interior closer to its capital. Engineers (many of whom had worked on Belomor) designed a project that was built as economically as possible through the use of forced labor (considered by many to have been slave labor), as well as natural materials – rock, timber, peat, sand and dirt – found along the construction route. Concrete and mechanized construction equipment were used sparingly. Natural waterways, such as the Dubna, Sestra, and Khimki Rivers, were incorporated for further efficiency.[15] The Ivan'kovo

Reservoir/Moscow Sea was created by damming and rechanneling the Volga River such that it splits into the Moscow Canal, which heads southward to Moscow, and downstream through the first lock of the Moscow Canal, which provides the only access through which vessels can continue toward Yaroslavl', Nizhny Novgorod, and points beyond.

The Moscow Canal officially opened on 15 July 1937. Dmitlag was headquartered in the ancient Russian city of Dmitrov, the halfway point between Moscow, the canal's terminus, and Dubna, the canal's starting point at its confluence with the Volga River. At its peak (1 April 1935) the inmate population of Dmitlag was almost 196,000 (it was officially organized on 14 September 1932 and dissolved on 31 January 1938). Official statistics cite 22,842 inmate deaths in Dmitlag from 1933–8, although it is widely thought that the actual death toll was much higher.[16]

Over the course of four years, eight months (Fall 1932–Summer 1937) canal workers produced a waterway 128 km long with a minimum width of 85.5 m at the water's surface and 46 m on the bottom of the channel with a minimum depth of 5.5 m (Figure I.1). The waterway is replete with 240 man-made structures, including nine single and two double-chamber locks, 14 dams, five pumping stations, eight hydro-electric stations, several railway and highway bridges, and two tunnels – one in Dubna under Lock 1, and the other where Moscow's Volokolamsk Highway passes under the canal at Lock 8. The lock junctions along the canal are especially notable due to the architects who designed them. Each lock was assigned to a particular architect, often highly esteemed practitioners, who subsequently also oversaw its construction. Work on the canal included the erection of the Northern River Station on the Khimki Reservoir, the main terminal for passengers traveling to and from Moscow. Six reservoirs were constructed along the canal route, as well as a separate channel at the Akulovo Reservoir in order to direct water to the Stalin Water Works and Filtration Plant in far eastern Moscow. Most significantly, the Volga River was rerouted through the creation of the Ivan'kovo hydro-electric station, dam, and attendant reservoir, with a surface area of 327 km^2. Just as impressive a feat, the canal's builders managed to negotiate the change in elevation between the Volga River and Moscow by constructing the first five locks of the canal, traversing the Yakhroma heights, in a "staircase" pattern that permitted vessels to move from 124 m above sea level to 162 m

Figure I.1 Map of the Moscow Canal clipped from a Soviet newspaper. Moscow is at the bottom, Dmitrov in the middle, and the Dubna/Volga Junction at the top. Each lock, reservoir, and dam on the canal is marked on the map. The upper caption reads "The Moscow–Volga Canal."[17]

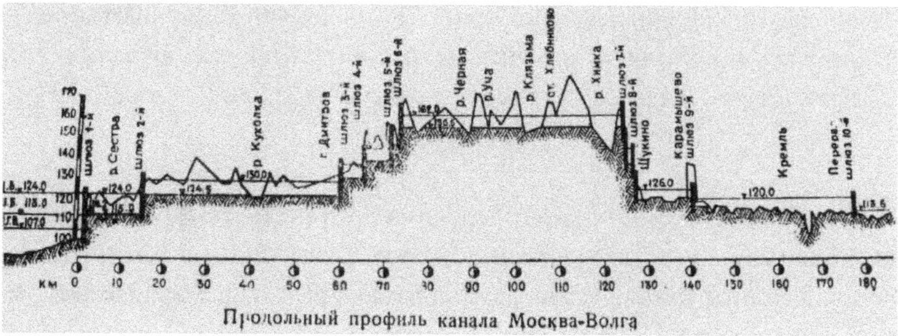

Figure I.2 The topographical profile of the Moscow Canal. At left is the Volga River level and at right the level of the Moscow River at the Kremlin.[18]

between Locks 6 and 7 (Figure I.2). Having passed through Lock 7, vessels then descend to 120 m above sea level at the Moscow River. Clearly, the size and variety of discrete construction projects along the waterway's route both tested its builders and designers and testified to their skills and the intensity of their labor.

The Moscow Canal reduced the travel distance between Moscow and Nizhny Novgorod to the east by 109 km and between Moscow and St. Petersburg to the north by more than 965 km. According to official Soviet rhetoric of the time, "At the initiative of the great Stalin, the city of Moscow, which was formerly far removed from 'big water,' has thus been transformed into a port of three seas: the White Sea, the Baltic, and the Caspian Sea."[19] It is notable here that Moscow is cast as the port of *three* seas, a metaphor that would soon disappear from official and unofficial discourse. More importantly, the Moscow Canal provided and continues to supply more than 60 percent of the potable water and significant amounts of electricity that keep Moscow's thirst slaked and its lights on.[20]

Theoretical Issues

In her illuminating study of the reformulation of Russian identity as seen through the image of the periphery in writing culture, Edith Clowes notes that:

> In the Soviet era official identity relied on images of time, of belonging to the "radiant future," the image of the train of history

> or the rocket blasting into space. Post-Soviet public discourse, whether conservative or liberal, has preferred the alliance of Russianness with concepts of geographical and geopolitical space.[21]

This formulation is only partly true, however, for it would be a mistake to underplay issues of geography, space, place and landscape in the construction of the Soviet state in general and in the Stalinist state in particular. Indeed, in building the empire of Stalinism, geographical concepts and images were woven into the physical and metaphorical fabric of the empire. Often the dual concepts of space and place functioned in tandem, and how could it be otherwise? In constructing the physical landscape of Stalinism, the state was not only bringing to bear the complex network of meaning in a landscape or hardscape,[22] but also situating that place in historical time as an exemplar of the movement toward the "radiant future." Places – be they natural or manmade – served as emblems of ideology, contemporary aesthetic practice, political decision making and cultural production. The Stalinist state displayed great interest in the geographical space it inhabited. How else to explain the profusion of maps on postage stamps, posters, and book jackets, as well as the movement in the 1920s and 1930s to "map" and conquer the periphery through writers' brigades on the cultural front, prison camps on the political front, and construction projects on the ideological front?[23] Space – how it was structured, constructed, situated, and apprehended – played a dominant role in the development and promulgation of Stalinist culture. Arguably no other physical landmark visually and metaphorically demonstrates this better than the Moscow Canal.

The Moscow Canal functions as a concentration of the main issues of space/place relevant to the development of the Stalinist state. The 128-km canal was literally carved out of the earth in an effort to provide not only a built environment that physically embodied Soviet power, but also to bring life to Moscow through the diversion of Volga water to the capital. The Moscow Canal project affords rich territory for the application of the current theoretical approaches that focus on reading landscapes, determining the location of culture, and teasing meaning on multiple levels out of a place. In particular, this discussion examines the spatial relationship of the Moscow Canal vis-à-vis its physical presence in the landscape (including works of architecture and sculpture), its ideological underpinnings (the Dmitlag camp and forced labor), its metaphorical space as conveyed in works of visual art and literature, and its "imagined geography" as the site where the monumental and the memorial collide both physically and psychologically.

Naturally, the spatial relationships within and among these discrete "places" overlap with and infiltrate each other, which means that certain assumptions about the function of landscape and the relationship of space and place are common to them all. First, the control of landscape and space is a function of power and power relationships. He who controls the land likely controls everything within that land. The more land you have, the more powerful you are. Consequently, mapping the land is likewise a power relationship in which choices about how to draw one's empire and what to illustrate within it convey meaning and ideological priorities. These visual manifestations of the control of space and place send a message to outsiders as to the hierarchy of values and ideological precepts adhered to in producing the space and modifying the landscape. How a state chooses to situate itself in a landscape reveals not only its sense of self, but also the image it seeks to project to outsiders.

A related issue, of course, is whether or not a landscape can be identified with the power that produced it. That is, how can we determine the difference between essentially Russian and Soviet landscapes? Is it not probable that a so-called Soviet landscape nonetheless bears the marks, be they physical or metaphorical, of the Russian empire that preceded it? Yes and no. What is important here is not so much the land itself – the natural world that exists regardless of what political entity controls it – but rather how a given ideological system reshapes, repurposes or redefines the landscape in order to reflect its values and priorities. No less vital is the notion that just as an agent, human or natural, affects a landscape, so too does the landscape affect the agent. Although this mutual relationship is not always in a state of equilibrium, it is essential to understand the interplay of these forces with each other and the resulting spatial relationship.

Within this context it makes sense to explore the political and ideological space that the Moscow Canal replaced and created through both its physical presence and the ideology it sought to promote by its existence. The act of physically inscribing a landscape – literally reconfiguring, digging into, and displacing the land – is an overtly political act, for the motivation behind such inscriptions stems from a particular ideological stance that seeks to control, reconfigure, renew or destroy one landscape in the service of another. In the case of the Moscow Canal, the physical embodiment of the waterway provided tangible proof that a landscape could be made Soviet. This premise is, of course, posited on the fact that a landscape can reflect the values and ideology of the system in which it is situated. In the case of the Moscow Canal, Stalinist ideology was made visible in four especially important ways: the creation of the Dmitlag Labor camp, the establishment of Moscow as the "Port of Five Seas,"[24] the seeming control over the uncontrollable force of water, and the strategic placement of structures laden with ideological significance. Each of these moments, supported by and physically embodying discrete elements of Stalinist ideology, enabled the Moscow Canal to exist as Stalinist ideology made real, thereby creating a Soviet space that demarcated the might and right of Soviet power. If we consider the construction of the Moscow Canal as part of the larger program to construct a singularly Soviet space, albeit essentially on the backs of slave laborers, then the consequences and subsequent apprehension of the construction process take on even greater significance. Indeed, in building this canal and other structures, the Gulag constructed Soviet space. And this Gulag space may have been the most Soviet space of all.

Some idiosyncrasies of the historical context must be kept in mind as this study unfolds. First, the rhetoric of the Stalinist period is redolent with recurrent hyperbole and superlatives that often stretch the bounds of veracity. Any project or achievement completed during this time, including the Moscow Canal, was described and depicted in the strongest possible terms to enhance, energize, and aggrandize it, even if in reality such a treatment was unwarranted. In the repetition of the same metaphors, photographs, illustrations, and captions lurk two apparent contradictions. On the one hand, the repeated use of certain phrases, descriptions, or images ultimately limits the usefulness of those rhetorical strategies by making them commonplace or depleting the power that they supposedly convey. On the other hand, the very plasticity of word and image makes it flexible and adaptable to a variety of projects and achievements. This plasticity presents a seemingly unified picture of the triumphs and successes of Stalinism, and contributes to its ubiquity and forcefulness. That some projects undertaken to build the Stalinist Soviet state were successful is without question. Proof is seen in any of the structures that still stand and serve the contemporary Russian state, not least among them the Moscow Canal. Yet the over-the-top method of enshrining these projects in the Stalinist canon might seem to some readers as empty posturing. To this I would counter that in every hyperbolic aggrandizement of a Stalinist achievement there is a drop (or more) of truth, to borrow from a common Russian saying.

In addition, since this study purports to reveal how the Moscow Canal helped build Stalinism, it bears stating that "Stalinism" as a system, ideology, and historical era cannot be described with a single, neat definition. Rather, the narrative of this study regards Stalinism as a multi-faceted, shape-changing phenomenon that had at its core certain firm ideas that remained throughout its existence. Among these were the construction – rhetorically, politically, socially and culturally – of a new Soviet state greater than any capitalist state; the primacy of the State in policy making, policy-breaking and governance; the utility of central control emanating from a strong leader; and the ability to use any means to control citizens and remove perceived enemies.

Given this multi-layered system, an approach that examines the spaces, places, and landscapes created during Stalin's regime offers a way to trace how one significant project – the Moscow Canal – created and emended Stalinism. Indeed, one of the most pervasive tropes of the era holds that the creation of the Soviet state was foremost a program of capturing space, taming nature and making it all Soviet, regardless of region, nationality, or geography. One efficient and highly visible way to achieve this goal privileges construction projects and their physical presence. If bending nature to the will of the Soviet state and remaking social miscreants into model Soviet citizens become part of the bargain, then so much the better.

Methodology

To understand and contextualize the nexus of ideas and ideologies that form part of the Moscow Canal requires the methodology of cultural geographers, as well as the theoretical work of philosophers, historians and cultural critics of space and place, many of whom have heretofore been applied to the Stalinist enterprise minimally, if at all. Recent relevant works in this area include Eric Naiman and Evgeny Dobrenko's edited volume *The Landscape of Stalinism*, Vladimir Paperny's *Architecture in the Age of Stalinism* (*Kul'tura dva* in Russian), Emma Widdis's *Visions of a New Land*, Mark Bassin, Christopher Ely, and Melissa Stockdale's *Space, Place, and Power in Modern Russia: Essays in the New Spatial History*, the volume *Beyond the Limits: The Concept of Space in Russian History and Culture* edited by Jeremy Smith, as well as some of the essays in Mark Bassin and Catriona Kelly's *Soviet and Post-Soviet Identities.* All of these volumes apply theoretical models of the study of space and place to examine questions of national identity, "high" and "low" cultural production and politics in the Soviet and post-Soviet eras.[25]

Equally valuable within the context of Soviet culture is Katerina Clark's *Moscow, the Fourth Rome*, especially her discussions of Moscow as a "lettered city." Her theoretical formulation in regard to Stalinist aesthetics and her application of the theory of the "imperial sublime" figure substantially in my treatment of Soviet architecture and landscape. As she notes, "The new vogue for dramatic landscapes was not just a matter of taste. The sublime provided inspiring tropes for allegories of national identity." As she later adds, "More, I am proposing the sublime as a dominant that structures these tropes and narratives in a poetics of space."[26]

In addition, the pioneering work of Gaston Bachelard in his study *The Poetics of Space*, as well as Henri Lefebvre's *The Production of Space* have been instrumental in providing a fundamental understanding of issues of space – its function, form, ideological underpinnings, and philosophical ramifications – as well as shaping the approach to space and place that this book takes. Simon Schama's penetrating and perceptive study *Landscape and Memory* serves as a model for discussing the connections between a given landscape and the historical and personal memories it provokes upon closer observation.[27]

Seminal works on cultural geography, foremost among them Yi-Fu Tuan's *Space and Place*, Edward W. Soja's *Postmodern Geographies*, Don Mitchell's *Cultural Geography: A Critical Introduction*, and Cosgrove and Daniel's edited volume *The Iconography of Landscape* have similarly provided the language and framework necessary for adequately and meaningfully parsing out the space, place, and landscapes that the construction of the Moscow Canal destroyed and created.[28] However, this historical and geographical approach to space, which relies heavily on the methodology and interpretive tools regularly deployed by cultural geographers, has rarely been applied to Stalinist landscapes in general and Gulag landscapes in particular. The present study seeks to fill this gap.

Structure

To examine more closely how the Moscow Canal was constructed, this narrative charts a virtual journey along the Moscow Canal that focuses on space, be it physical, metaphorical, monumental, artistic, abstract, absolute, constructed, or imagined. Because the construction and existence of the Moscow Canal is first and foremost about water, it makes sense to begin the discussion in Chapter One: Water as Power: Real and Imagined with an examination of water as a symbol of power. As Schama, Paperny, Wittfogel, and other scholars have argued, hydraulic societies like the former USSR and their water despots, in this case Stalin, perceived water as not only life-giving, but also power-granting. Any society that could control water would conceivably control life itself, a goal consonant with Stalinist ideology. The paradox, of course, is that it is impossible to truly control water. Hence, the first part of this chapter will discuss the theory and practice of water as power, water's symbolic role, and its place within the larger Soviet context. For further illustration, this chapter will examine two elements of the Moscow Canal that best represent the issue of water and power: the creation of the Moscow Sea/rerouting of the Volga River and the crowning of Moscow as the "Port of Five Seas."

No discussion of the Moscow Canal would be acceptable without a discussion of the Dmitlag camp and the forced laborers, both skilled and unskilled, who built it, and this is the focus of Chapter Two: How the Gulag Built the Moscow Canal. This chapter addresses how the largest camp in the Gulag system managed to construct a waterway, built with little mechanization but much back-breaking labor and ingenuity, that still serves Moscow. Because remnants of the camp remain in Dmitrov, the camp's headquarters, this chapter has a dual focus on the past and the present, with the bulk of the discussion dedicated to Dmitlag and its workers: who built the canal and how did they do it. Just as important to this discussion is an analysis of some of the cultural production in which the Gulag inmates engaged. Foremost among them is the long-hidden *Biblioteka Perekovki* (*Library of Re-forging*), a series of booklets written by and for Dmitlag inmates. These priceless works, along with camp newspapers and the journal *Na shturm trassy* (*Storming the Worksite*) provide a rare, fascinating, and often sobering view of how inmates were marshaled into the campaign to promote the very project that was meant to re-forge them into new Soviet citizens, yet often killed them.

The discussion of the *Library of Re-forging* in Chapter Two lays the foundation for Chapter Three, entitled Creating Metaphorical and Ideological Space: Cultural Production and the Moscow Canal. This chapter examines cultural production undertaken both within and outside the Dmitlag camp that celebrates and documents the construction of the Moscow Canal. Three key areas of cultural production are analyzed: the sculptures adorning the canal route, the paintings crafted by official and inmate artists, and two unpublished literary works conceived as laudatory histories of the Moscow Canal. These cultural artifacts were intended to construct an imagined, idealized space extolling the viability and wisdom of Stalinist ideology. Of particular interest here are the two unpublished literary works, one of which was ready for release until the 1937 purges intervened. Since most of the upper echelon of the Dmitlag directorate was killed or imprisoned, the work was not destined to see the light of day; it would be impossible to glorify the canal while vilifying those who directed its construction. This volume was meant to serve as a companion to the *History of the Construction of the Stalin White Sea–Baltic Canal*, written to document the Belomor Canal. Replete with original inmate artwork and a portrait of Stalin, the Moscow Canal volume was instead relegated to the shelves of the Russian State Archive, where it was discovered by the archivist and Gulag scholar A.I. Kokurin in 2004.[29] The conclusion drawn from this analysis contends that the metaphorical, imagined space created by these cultural products was just as potent as the physical space the canal still occupies.

No less significant in the construction of Soviet space are the monumental and the memorial, two distinct yet often related concepts. Chapter Four: Monuments, Monumentality, and Memory: Forgetting and Remembering explores the structures from which monumentality emanated: the canal's lock configurations (constructed 1932–7), the Moscow Canal Museum and its attendant chapel (opened 2007), and the two 37-m tall monuments to Stalin and Lenin (erected 1937), all of which claim vertical space along the canal route. Distinct architectural styles grace each lock on the Moscow Canal. This diversity of ornamentation and structure strove to impress travelers and onlookers, as well as to glorify the skill and imagination of Soviet architects. It is no accident that architecture serves as the instrument by which monumental space on the canal is created. It alone permits both the horizontal and vertical occupation of space, while simultaneously creating metaphorical and ideological space through its style and size. This is especially true of the Northern River Port (built 1937), which was designed in the shape of a ship, with a mast that rises and falls and windows shaped like portholes. After all, this building welcomed ship passengers to the capital and bade them farewell from it. Although firmly planted on land, the Northern River Port implies motion, adventure and travel, all of which could be attained through a voyage on the Moscow Canal.

However, the most imposing monumental structures to adorn the canal route were the twin 37-meter monuments on the canal's banks (statues seems an inadequate word to capture their massiveness). These enormous images of Lenin and Stalin, facing each other across the channel, greeted passengers as they entered and exited the canal at the first lock. The monument to Lenin still stands, while the monument to Stalin met its fate on a dark night in the early 1960s. With the post-Stalinist Thaw in full swing, the 240-ton statue was destroyed and fell into the very canal that Stalin promoted, so that to this day ships sail over it, unbeknownst to their occupants. It is this lack of knowing that undermines the impulse to memorialize how and why the Moscow Canal was built. Yet efforts to do so remain, most strikingly in the steel cross erected in 1997 on the banks of the canal in Dmitrov, the chapel along the channel at Dedenevo with its golden onion dome, and the Moscow Canal Museum on the first floor of the Yakhroma Divisional headquarters. In their modest ways, these three sites create spaces of memory and remembrance. That they stand at all testifies to the insistence by those who created them that nothing about the Moscow Canal saga should be forgotten, least of all the terror used to create it.

Finally, Chapter Five: The Present and Future of the Moscow Canal examines the contemporary reception of the Moscow Canal and posits future outcomes for its structures and history. Thousands of travelers use the canal daily on their way in and out of Moscow to the north and yet remain oblivious to its history. However, efforts are underway to address that situation, partly through the memorial spaces discussed in Chapter Four, and partly through the work of dedicated professional and amateur scholars who believe that the canal still affords an opportunity to make sense of the past and shape the future. Even the canal administration sees the waterway as a valuable asset for national and economic security. The administration organized a gala celebration in honor of the canal's 70th anniversary in 2007, which sought to reinstate the importance of the canal as a structure worthy of praise and admiration, regardless of its difficult history. Interestingly, no such grand celebration was held in 2012 to mark the canal's 75th anniversary. The canal's 80th anniversary in 2017, coinciding with the 100th anniversary of the October Revolution, was marked by a scholarly conference held at the Dmitrov Kremlin Museum-Preserve on 12 May 2017. Presenters included scholars and enthusiasts, who continue to study various aspects of the Moscow Canal's history, legacy and contemporary importance.

In addition, contested spaces along the canal route have emerged as key issues pitting the canal administration, the city of Moscow, and property owners against one another. Conflicts over the rights of owners to develop land along the canal, which some consider a sacred burial ground, reveal that the legacy of the Moscow Canal is still being constructed and contested. This situation ultimately suggests that the apprehension of a space shifts according to the prevailing ideology and leaves us with the question as to whether the Soviet space created by the Moscow Canal has been transformed into a Russian space, and what that might imply.

Sources

To tell this story I have relied on archival materials from the State Archive of the Russian Federation (GARF), the State Archive of the Moscow Oblast, the Archive of the City of Moscow, the ethnographic section of the Dmitrov Regional Library, and the Russian State

Library.[30] Russian sources on the Moscow Canal are relatively plentiful, although most studies were authored during and shortly after the canal's construction and therefore advance an ideologically biased view that fully supports the Stalinist regime and the canal's currency within the context of the 1930s. Since that time only a few Russian scholars have made it their mission to reveal the often painful details of the canal's construction. This was not due to a lack of interest in the canal itself, but rather the exigencies of life in the former Soviet Union that dictated what could be written about the Moscow Canal. As with so many other topics, the break-up of the Soviet Union and the subsequent wider access to archival materials enabled those interested in the Moscow Canal's history to write about it openly and honestly for the first time.

Foremost among these researchers is the late Dmitrov newspaper editor and author Nikolai Fedorov, who undertook the first systematic study of the history of the Moscow Canal, especially the reliance on the Dmitlag camp for its construction. Fedorov's numerous newspaper articles, most in his local newspaper *Dmitrovskii Vestnik* [*Dmitrov Herald*], as well as his monograph (one of five contemporary books in Russian on the topic), *Byla li tachka u ministra?* [*Did the Minister Have a Wheelbarrow?*] opened the discussion. It was then continued by the late Mikhail Ivanovich Bulanov, who investigated the construction of the Moscow Canal in general and its influence upon the Dubna region in particular. His monograph *Kanal Moskva-Volga: Khronika Volzhskogo raiona gidrosooruzhenii* [*The Moscow–Volga Canal: A Chronicle of the Hydraulic Projects of the Volga Region*] examines the building of the Ivan'kovo Dam and hydroelectric station, the Moscow Sea, the entrance and first two locks of the canal, and the gigantic sculptures of Lenin and Stalin at the entrance of the canal, as well as the personalities central to the completion of these projects. Valentin Sergeevich Barkovsky, a retired hydraulic engineer for the Moscow Canal, authored the third monograph, *Tainy Moskva-volgostroia* [*The Secrets of Moskva-Volgostroi*], outlining the entire history of the canal's construction with special attention paid to its Gulag builders. Barkovsky's narrative relies on materials obtained from the closed Moscow Canal Authority (FGBU-KiM) archive,[31] but his slim volume is the least scholarly of the current extant works on the Moscow Canal.

While each author took a different approach to the material, their motivations for researching the topic were uniform: to reveal how and why the Moscow Canal was constructed and the price that was paid in human lives to achieve it. All these authors agree that the construction of the Moscow Canal remains a sore spot in the collective memory of Russia, an echo of the lasting effect of this mammoth Stalinist construction project on those who rely on the canal for their livelihoods and indeed their survival.

In addition to these sources, the volume *Stalinskie stroiki GULAGA, 1930–1953* [*Stalinist Construction Projects of the Gulag, 1930–1953*], the first chapter of which discusses the canals built by the Gulag: Belomor, Moscow–Volga, and Volga–Don, remains the most extensively researched nuts-and-bolts account of the construction of the Moscow Canal based exclusively on archival materials from GARF. The book's compilers, the late Yu. N. Morukov and A. I. Kokurin, examined hundreds of files in order to reconstruct the political and practical concerns related to the canal projects, as well as to provide statistical evidence regarding the manpower exploited to build these structures. The documents that they collected present a timeline of construction edicts, orders, and analyses of the Moscow Canal project.[32]

The most recent volume that traces the history and construction of the Moscow Canal was produced in conjunction with the canal's 75th anniversary in 2012. *Kanal imeni Moskvy: Stroika veka. Sud'by liudei* [*The Moscow Canal: the Construction Project of the Century. The Fates of People*] was written by a retired mechanical engineer, Valentin Ivanovich Maslov, whose interest in the ethnography and history of the Mytishchinsky area near Moscow (and which a 30-km segment of the Moscow Canal traverses) was documented in a series of newspaper articles. Maslov's account presents to readers a narrative that tries to bridge the gap between the canal's fraught history and its current reception. The present study is unquestionably indebted to the work of these Russian historians and writers.

Sources in English about the Moscow Canal are scarce and usually take the form of passing references or short descriptions of the Moscow–Volga Canal project in the 1930s. Aside from short mentions in books dedicated to Soviet industrialization, exploitation of natural resources, or general discussions of the Gulag system, the only recent specific treatment is a chapter in Dorothy Zeisler-Vralsted's 2015 book *Rivers, Memory, and Nation-Building: A History of the Volga and Mississippi Rivers*. Zeisler-Vralsted's comparative study of these two great rivers analyzes the Moscow Canal project as a companion undertaking to the Mississippi River Channel project. As she notes, "Both projects, regardless of political ideology, were born out of a faith in modernity and a need to industrialize," a statement that captures at least something of the essence of the Moscow Canal project.[33]

In his masterpiece *Moscow 1937* Karl Schloegel dedicates a chapter and other assorted references to the Moscow–Volga Canal.[34] He offers a brief history of construction by examining how the canal came to be, how the Gulag built the canal, and how the canal was framed as a *Gesamtkunstwerk* ("total artwork"). He examines political, historical, and aesthetic issues with an eye toward contextualizing the opening of the Moscow–Volga Canal in the riveting and bloody history of Moscow in the pivotal year 1937, the height of the Great Terror. Likewise, in his recent book *In Space We Read Time: On the History of Civilization and Geopolitics*, Schloegel offers additional insights into Stalinist conceptions of space and place that figure into this discussion. The present study moves beyond and expands on the work of Zeisler-Vralsted and Schloegel, for it is the single work in English that analyzes the entire Moscow Canal project as illustrative of a faith in a precisely Stalinist modernity.

In view of this challenge, the detailed examination of the spaces that the Moscow Canal created must begin with water, not only as it was understood within the Soviet context, but also as it was used to create physical and rhetorical spaces whose mere mention would immediately conjure up images of the new topography that Stalinism was creating. Hence the discussion now turns to water as an instrument of power, especially as it was conceived in the creation of the Moscow Sea and Moscow as the Port of Five Seas.

CHAPTER 1

WATER AS POWER: REAL AND IMAGINED

> The variations and contradictions of metaphors reflect the fact that humans' relationships with water differ both in space and time and that water plays central though different roles in people's lives.[1]

It is impossible to overestimate the importance of water in both practical and metaphorical terms to the construction and promulgation of Stalinism, especially during the pre-World War II period. Water, as a natural resource, a symbol of national prosperity, an element for Stalinist ideology to conquer, a metaphor expressing a host of cultural signs and meanings, served as an ideal medium for the promotion of Stalinism as a way of life. Of course, the varied symbolism that water promoted was not limited to Soviet ideology. However, the metaphorical flexibility and universality that the image of water conveys served not only to accentuate the success and correctness of the Stalinist way, but also linked the construction of the USSR, especially in the 1930s, with the larger world beyond its borders. Indeed, the emphasis on water and hydraulic projects allowed high Stalinism to comfortably, even legitimately, insert itself in the continuum of world history, thereby securing for itself a place within the narrative of the most powerful nations of the twentieth century.

Within the Stalinist context the fascination with and desire to control water emerged both out of necessity and as a product of Marxist ideology. Lenin's oft-quoted formula: "Communism is Soviet power plus the electrification of the whole country" particularly resonates here, given that Soviet water projects epitomized both the literal production of power and symbolic power in the form of hydro-electricity.[2] As Simon Schama notes:

> A long tradition of sociologists, from Karl Marx to Karl Wittfogel, has seen "hydraulic societies" and despotism as functionally connected. In naturally arid regions, they argued, only an absolutely obedient, virtually enslaved regime could possibly have mobilized the concentrations of labor needed to man and maintain the irrigation canals and dikes on which intensive agriculture depended.[3]

Although the Moscow Canal (like Belomor before it and Volga–Don after it) was not constructed to enhance agricultural production through irrigation, Schama's description nonetheless applies to how water projects were implemented in Stalin's USSR due to the regime's ability, through the Gulag, to harness the labor resources required. While massive water projects, regardless of their ideological bases, uniformly gain recognition and are touted as monuments to the systems that produced them, according to Schama "[Wittfogel] saw in the Chinese and Soviet regimes further evidence that it was as the arbiters of water that tyrannies anointed themselves as legitimate."[4] This legitimacy through water differentiated Stalinist water projects from the Tennessee Valley Authority, Grand Coulee Dam, and the Hoover Dam (among other projects) in the US and the Panama and Suez Canals. These undertakings shared the same qualities of technological innovation, size, scale, and monumentality, but the governments that sponsored them did not need these projects to prove their legitimacy. Their existence and power as states had already been justified, unlike the relatively young Soviet state, which felt compelled to prove its viability just as did Stalin himself. As Schama comments, "Steaming along the Volga–Don canal to which countless thousands of slave laborers had been sacrificed, Stalin could proclaim himself the master of the waters."[5] While Schama focuses on the later Volga–Don Canal, his observations are perhaps even more applicable to the Moscow Canal, because it was constructed in the mid-1930s, a time when socialist construction and Stalin's vision were advancing rapidly to prove that the USSR was a worthy competitor with its capitalist enemies in the West.

Likewise, if every large-scale hydro-project ultimately marks a victory of man over nature, then the Soviet projects differ fundamentally from their counterparts in other systems because of the Marxist edict that "in changing nature man changes himself." The Soviet enterprise was fully committed to the notion that nature was not to be admired, but exploited as fully as possible in the quest for power and domination. As Paul Josephson persuasively argues, through brute force technologies such as dam and canal building "we have gained extraordinary power to transform nature into something increasingly orderly, rational, and machine-like – in a word, industrial."[6] This is not to imply that other political systems have avoided brute force technology in order to pursue a kinder, gentler approach to massive building projects. But what sets this Soviet context apart from this is Stalin's contention that "only under socialism had the worker mastered the laws of nature to direct them for the good of society – through electrification, irrigation, recreation, reclamation, elimination of erosion, drainage of swamps, and the creation of green zones around cities and industrial centers, along rivers, canals, and reservoirs, and so forth."[7] This was the approach that sustained the Moscow Canal project. Stalin's ambitions demanded that water be inducted into the service of the Soviet state, for "he wanted tangible concrete temples attesting to the glory of his leadership – the hero projects of the century, such as the seven gaudy neoclassical wedding-cake skyscrapers, that dot Moscow's horizon. The biggest monument to Stalin's enlightened rule, built in the same architectural style as his skyscrapers, was the 2.1 million kW Kuibyshev station,"[8] whose dam's capacity was far higher than the Grand Coulee dam in the US. Stalin tied part of his legacy and political fortunes specifically to water projects because of their size and grandiosity, utility in providing both water and electricity to assist industrialization, and physical presence that occupied spaces thought to be off limits.

Consequently, water is important in the context of Stalinist projects because the (perceived) conquest of water demonstrated Soviet power over nature. Water manifested or could be imbued with key elements of Soviet ideology, philosophy, culture, and power, made even more striking by the fact that the water was, seemingly, controlled. This perceived control over the ultimately uncontrollable thereby suggested a greater legitimacy for the regime and its policies. Even more importantly, unlike air, water is visible and therefore lends itself to being propagandized. Finally, the Soviet Union's rich natural resources in general, and its abundant water supplies in particular, ostensibly remained static and meaningless until acted upon by Soviet power.

Hence water eloquently demarcates the space that the Moscow Canal occupies. It literally brought life to the center of the country and, most importantly, to the center of power, the Kremlin. Similarly, the Moscow Canal physically and rhetorically joined Moscow not only to the rest of the Soviet Union, but to the rest of the world. The Moscow Canal cut through the landscape, and now it continues to cut through time and space, linking the landscape's and the country's past, present, and future. The contradictions inherent in the metaphor of water are as evident today as when the Moscow Canal was constructed: water is life-affirming and life-taking; it simultaneously nourishes and destroys; it is impossible to live without it, yet also impossible to control it completely; it can be deceptively calm or blatantly raging. This list of opposites suggests a certain strange equilibrium not unlike that which defined Soviet space, for the waters of the Moscow Canal were a source of both immense pleasure and great sorrow.

In his seminal work, *Architecture in the Age of Stalin: Culture Two*, Vladimir Paperny argues that Culture One represents pre-Revolutionary Russian culture and Soviet culture up to roughly 1930. He juxtaposes this with Culture Two, which represents Stalinist-Soviet culture from 1932–54. He discusses the importance of water to Soviet culture:

> There is a possible connection between the development of the culture and the special attitude toward water that appeared in the early 1930s. Of all the architectural endeavors of Culture Two,[9] the canals were always given top priority. The White Sea–Baltic canal was the first to be built (1931–3). It was followed by the Volga–Moscow canal in 1932–7 and the Volga–Don canal in 1949–52. The idea of water – understood by Culture Two almost as it is by truly "hydraulic" societies, which view water as the basis of existence – was gradually superimposed onto the idea of the city, which in turn was understood archaically, that is as the center of the world. As a result of that superimposition, the

> project for the Volga–Moscow canal and the General Plan for the Reconstruction of Moscow mutually penetrated and enriched each other.[10]

Paperny's observation is perceptive given that Moscow was imagined as the center not only of the Soviet universe, in spite of its physical location far from the actual geographic center of the country, but also as the center of the world Marxist revolution. The actual star on the map that represented Moscow was beside the point; more important was the metaphor of Moscow as the heart of the country, with its main life-giving artery (both actual and figurative), the Moscow Canal, fed in a straight line south from the Volga, the mother of Russian rivers, to the capital, and conversely from the capital north to the Volga and onward to the rest of the USSR and the world. Nevertheless, the notion of "hydraulic despotism" does not sufficiently explain the importance that Stalinism attached to water and water projects. Within the Stalinist system water was more than just an element of nature; it was also an ideological tool, a social construct and a cultural artifact that both supported and celebrated Stalinist power and society.

In this regard, the analytical approach that Terje Tvedt advances, which he calls the "water-system approach," resonates especially clearly. Tvedt posits three conceptual layers that comprise a productive examination of the function of water within a society. According to Tvedt, "The first layer is water's natural (physical and chemical) form and behavior."[11] This layer covers not only the hydrological cycles of a given waterscape, but also the physical and chemical properties that make it such a unique natural element. As Tvedt suggests, "An analytical focus on the physical, natural aspects of the water system highlights another very interesting theoretical and empirical aspect of water: it is both exogenous and a part of the society at the same time."[12]

Yet this "hydro-historical approach," as Tvedt terms it, fails to fully capture the interaction between water and society. He therefore proposes a further analytical tier that addresses another important part of this interaction: "The second layer of the analytical approach here called the water-system approach captures and highlights the anthropogenic changes in the way water flows through the landscape."[13] Here Tvedt has in mind the human intervention that acts on water so as to engineer it to meet human needs. Such projects include irrigation systems, potable water supplies, sewage systems, and the regulatory administration of shared water resources. Coupling the physical properties of water with its appropriation by human agents permits a more nuanced reading of the interaction between water and society. Yet these two analytical constructs still lack a significant element – that of water and culture.

To fill this gap Tvedt proposes a third layer, one that "recognizes and focuses on how water as an element of nature and society – as a natural resource and a social good – will always be culturally constructed and filtered. It is concerned with how water is ascribed different meanings and has symbolized different things, from time to time and place to place for different actors."[14] This analytical layer addresses the aforementioned contradictions inherent in the study of water, and consequently waterways. As Tvedt notes, "The special character of water makes it a unique medium for cultural constructions and metaphorical traditions."[15] Tvedt's framework differs from prior approaches to the analysis of water within a social, political, and cultural system because it relies neither on a purely ecological approach, nor on a singularly political approach, nor on an analysis of water as a symbol central to any number of religious and cultural beliefs and rituals. Tvedt's water-system approach instead underscores the complexity of any relationship between a landscape and its water, a social system and its water, and a cultural system and its water. All these elements must be brought to bear on any investigation of how a society reacts to and exploits water. Within the framework of Stalinist society, this three-layered approach seems an especially profitable way of making sense of the importance of water in general and the Moscow Canal project in particular. The water-system approach likewise proposes a more sophisticated method of understanding the singlemindedness with which the Stalinist system invested in and promoted water projects, be they canals, reservoirs, or hydro-electric projects.

In terms of the Moscow Canal project Tvedt's three-layer water-system approach yields especially fruitful results when applied to two signature landscapes that were created by and with water: The Moscow Sea, known officially as the Ivan'kovo Reservoir, and Moscow the "Port of Five Seas." The intersection of the physical properties of water, water as a social good (both a benefit and a commodity), and water as a cultural construct obtain in these two signature landscapes that occupy the physical spaces that denote the entry and terminus of the Moscow Canal.

These two spaces, both imagined and real, also denote the linking of Moscow with the Volga River, thereby situating Moscow within and connecting it to the long history of reverence for the Volga and the image of the Volga that has been lodged in the Russian cultural imagination for centuries. With this background in mind, it makes sense to start the detailed examination of the Moscow Canal and the attendant trope of water in Moscow itself with a description of how Moscow came to be the "Port of Five Seas."

Moscow: Port of Five Seas[16]

Simon Schama discusses "rivers ... as lines of power."[17] Such natural advantages lend authority and influence to the government that can harness the inherent power of these resources and thus display its ability to control nature. This kind of dominance emerges even more clearly from canal building, itself an exercise in power and a method of control. Political systems build canals to demonstrate their capacity to achieve various goals, including, most importantly, the wielding and display of power in the broadest sense. To manage a large-scale construction project, the state must mobilize its fiscal resources, reveal its capacity for intelligent engineering and planning, and supply considerable physical labor, usually coupled with expensive heavy equipment. Earth must be moved, water channeled, physical barriers removed, and people displaced. The state that manages such a project wins an ideological victory by demonstrating its capacity to overcome any obstacle due largely to its ideology.[18] The physical structures that adorn waterways – the locks, dams, dikes, reservoirs, pumping stations, and control towers – exude power through the very fact of their existence.

This context frames the construction of the Moscow Canal, along with its "sister" canals, Belomor and Volga–Don, and illustrates how this waterway celebrated, personified, and implied Soviet power. This was achieved most notably through a trope that emblematized the significance of the Moscow Canal not only to Moscow and the USSR, but to the world: Moscow as the "Port of Five Seas."[19] Contemporary and recent treatments of this label offer valuable insights into the causes and effects of its use. Especially evocative are the materials produced by and for the Gulag that integrated the trope of Moscow as the "Port of Five Seas" into a broader discussion grounded in pronouncements that operated outside the parameters of popular culture.[20] In a system that prided itself on its ability to harness nature to serve man, the canals provided a rich ideological opportunity and a practical solution to transportation issues. These projects were intended to show that the political system responsible for them was strong, ideologically sound, and superior to nature. When such structures successfully performed the tasks for which they were designed, their physical existence would provide physical proof of the validity of the ideology and the wisdom of the state. The metaphor of land-locked Moscow as a port reaching five seas was irresistible to a system intent on proving its legitimacy as a world power and viable alternative to the capitalist system. Likewise, the Moscow port of five seas trope served as a nexus where the landscape, social environment, cultural system, and their water created a rhetorical space and an imagined space that persist to this day.

In an article from the 6 January 1935 issue of *Pravda* Lazar' Kogan (NKVD officer and head of construction of the Moscow–Volga Canal project) asserted that:

> Under the leadership of the Party this attractive canal is growing. It grows not by the day, but by the hour. In 1937 Moscow will become the Port of *Three* Seas [Emphasis added – CR]: the Caspian, Baltic, and the White Seas. And in a few years, then the Volga–Don Canal will be built, and Moscow will become the "Port of Five Seas": The Caspian, Black, Azov, Baltic, and White Seas.[21]

As soon as Kogan first pronounced the phrase "Moscow . . . Port of Five Seas" in *Pravda*, the descriptor became one of the most oft-repeated and potent tropes in the context of the construction of the Moscow–Volga Canal. Moscow magically became the "Port of Five Seas," as though uttering those words aloud made it so.[22]

That Moscow so effortlessly assumed the mantle of the "Port of Five Seas" when other Soviet cities, including Leningrad, Gorky, Stalingrad, Kazan, and Saratov, had better claims to the title lays bare the ideological nature of the term. Any city situated on the banks of these connected waterways could have made this same claim.[23] The epithet itself is a misnomer of sorts, since Moscow does not stand on the shore of any sea. Like most of the cities noted above, Moscow is a river port, landlocked and only reachable via a system of waterways that includes canals, lakes, and rivers, but no bodies of water that rival the size of any major sea. Yet Moscow emerged as the "PPM" because it was Moscow: the ideological, cultural, political, and economic center of the Soviet universe. Hence in preparation for the 1937 May Day celebration P. German, a Dmitlag inmate about whom little is known, composed a song entitled "Moscow Will be the Port of Five Seas,"[24] printed in an NKVD booklet produced at the camp. The song's refrain proclaims:

> That, about which the people have sung,
> That which echoed in [their words]
> Has become today's reality.
> It is ready, our Canal! Soon our Moscow
> Will be the "Port of Five Seas!"[25]

The combination of verb tenses here is especially revealing. While the refrain starts with the past tense, a transition occurs with "Has become today's reality,"[26] which simultaneously denotes a past action, yet moves to the present. In turn, the use of the present tense in "It is ready" brings the action fully to the present, while German uses the future tense "will be" to denote Moscow's impending, although not-yet-realized, status as a "Port of Five Seas."

Similar examples of the exploitation of this trope appear in the work of Dmitlag inmates who contributed to *The Library of Re-forging* booklet series published by the NKVD and distributed mainly within the confines of the Dmitlag camp.[27] The "Port of Five Seas" trope resonated both within and outside the Gulag, thereby securing its rhetorical importance for the entire USSR. Gulag inmates (unlike those outside the camp system) could access both internal and external pronouncements of Moscow as the "PPM" through wall-newspapers and at sector cultural centers on the canal work site, as well as through *The Library of Re-forging*.

Foremost among the Gulag treatments of the "Port of Five Seas" trope stands Veniamin Riumin's 1935 booklet *PPM. Stories*.[28] The initials PPM here stand for "Port of Five Seas" (*Port Piati Morei*), a sobriquet that also serves as the name for the first cycle of six stories in the work. The sixth story, entitled "The Port of Moscow" narrates the voyage of a ship that has traversed the Moscow–Volga Canal and triumphantly arrives at Moscow, referred to not by its proper name, but as "PPM. Port of Five Seas."[29] Another Dmitlag contributor to *The Library of Re-forging* series, Sergei Riabonon, sets the scene in his 1936 poem "Tomorrow" as: "Here, at the 'Port of Five Seas'."[30] Riumin and Riabonon were writing in 1935 and 1936 respectively, one to two years prior to the completion of the Moscow Canal, which suggests that the description of Moscow as the "Port of Five Seas" was aggressively promoted on the canal work site and in the Gulag press.

Moscow as the "Port of Five Seas" also illustrates various deceptive rhetorical practices that prevailed in the construction of the Soviet-Stalinist state. This status was not actually realized by the Moscow–Volga Canal.[31] Rather, the completion of the canal meant that Moscow gained access to only three seas – the Baltic, Caspian, and White – just as they gained access to Moscow. Not until the completion of the Volga–Don Canal in 1952 would Moscow fill the imagined rhetorical space created by the "PPM" trope by having access to the Sea of Azov and the Black Sea.

References to Moscow as the "Port of Five Seas" were not limited to the 1930s, but also appear in subsequent official publications about the Moscow Canal. A large-scale brochure, including a map of the Moscow Canal and an abundance of color photographs, was published in 1987 to mark the canal's 50th anniversary. The first page notes:

> "Moscow – the Port of Five Seas." This epithet appeared after the creation of the Moscow Canal, thanks to which the European part of the USSR turned into a single deep-water river system. Snow-white passenger ships depart from Moscow to Gorky, Leningrad, and Astrakhan and to many other cities in our Motherland. Freight ships ... carry out international non-stop freight hauling along these river and sea routes to ports in Europe, North Africa, and the Near East.[32]

The author of these lines, like his predecessors, mistakenly proclaims that Moscow became the "Port of Five Seas" upon the completion of the Moscow Canal. The repetition of this mistaken claim signals the standard, rote deployment of this trope from the 1930s onward.

Even more recently, in 2007 this label was applied in materials that celebrated the Moscow Canal's 70th anniversary.[33] In honor of this occasion, the Moscow Canal Authority (FGBU-KiM) produced a softbound 22-page booklet with articles about the history and operation of the Moscow Canal. One particular article, "Moscow: Port of Five Seas" guilelessly discusses Moscow's place as a major port. With language clearly lifted from the 1987 article, the text begins, "This epithet appeared after the creation of the Moscow canal, thanks to which the European part of the USSR turned into a single deep-water river system."[34] After an abbreviated history of the canal's evolution from Peter the Great's dream to Stalin's reality, the article notes that, "To this day the canal responds to all contemporary technological demands and is a deep-water transport artery that guarantees the linkage of the capital with Russia's main river, the Volga, and provides an outlet for the capital to five seas: The Baltic, Azov, Black, White, and Caspian Seas."[35] The resilience and longevity of the original Stalinist idea and the canal itself resonate in this recent description. The descriptor links the two eras historically, while ignoring the ethical and moral dilemmas the Moscow Canal continues to pose, namely the human cost exacted by the project on its Gulag builders.

Most recently the Museum of Moscow staged an exhibition from 29 March–23 April 2017 entitled "Moscow – Port of Five Seas."[36] The exhibit, curated by the composer V. I. Martynov, brought together from the Museum's collection photographs taken during the 1940s and 1950s and inspired by this trope. Visitors viewed the photographs while listening to music from the era, as well as the composer's original music. As the announcement for the exhibit notes, "In Martynov's project Moscow in the middle of the twentieth century is 'scanned' and moves into a special dimension – the culture of cyberspace. Its topography and landmarks are woven in an infinite variety of meanings and connections."[37] Without seeing the exhibit it is difficult to comprehend how Martynov achieved these stated goals and to assess his success. Nonetheless, of note are the specific spatial metaphors that the Museum uses to advertise the event: the narrative describes the claiming of new territory in cyberspace and it weaves Moscow's topography and landmarks into the overall experience. That the description of Moscow as the "Port of Five Seas" persists speaks to its enduring quality as a trope that creates and defines space well beyond its initial context.

Upon completion of the Moscow–Volga Canal, the reality of whether or not Moscow in fact became the "Port of Five Seas" was not as important as the imagined space this created as a metaphor. Because feats of engineering within the Soviet context were conceived as manifestations of totalitarian art and culture, the Moscow Canal physically demonstrated socialist realism in practice. In other words, the Moscow Canal, and consequently Moscow itself, simultaneously existed while in the process of becoming, a chief tenet of the aesthetic method of Socialist Realism. Socialist Realism held, among other ideas, that Soviet art in its many forms had to capture the "bright future" of the Soviet state both as it should be and as it was being realized through actual practice. This metaphor triumphed over time and space by promising that, even though Moscow physically, in 1937, was not a "Port of Five Seas," it should be thought of as one. Its future was being realized as its reality was unfolding. This was the dictum of imagining life as it *ought to be* and living in this imagined future.

This is not unexpected given the tendency of totalitarian regimes to occupy their spaces as fully as possible so that no physical feature and no geographical location remain untouched by their power. Even sites that were not yet realized became part of the Soviet enterprise, as ideologues, engineers, and construction crews rushed to claim spaces that had not yet been placed on the map. Indeed, a map from Pavel Lopatin's 1938 book *The Volga Goes to Moscow* (*Volga idet v Moskvu*) (a title that emphasizes the motion of the Volga *toward* Moscow) convincingly illustrates this point. The map is labeled "Moscow: 'Port of Five Seas'."[38] As the map illustrates, the title does not fully align with reality. The legend at the bottom of the page notes that the map features both *completed* and *proposed* canal routes. The only completed canals in this proposed system of five seas were the Belomor and Moscow–Volga Canals. The Volga–Don Canal, and lesser waterways, are merely projected, but not completed.

As one of the more prolific chroniclers of the Moscow Canal, Lopatin addressed the notion of Moscow as a port city in all of his works, but with telling variations. Whereas in his children's book *Moscow–Volga* Lopatin initially notes that "Moscow must be the central port for Soviet seas,"[39] he also declares that "according to the idea of the great Stalin, arid Moscow, hundreds and thousands of kilometers from 'big water,' will turn into the port of three seas – the White, Baltic, and Caspian."[40] Later in the same work, however, Lopatin discusses the future plans for the Volga–Don Canal and explicitly concludes that "in the center of this new route, as the crossroads of these waterways, stands Moscow, the port of five seas."[41] In both *The Volga Goes to Moscow* and his 1937 work

Canal Moscow–Volga, Lopatin wavers between identifying Moscow as a port of three or five seas. In *Canal Moscow–Volga*, Lopatin initially notes that a placard at the Northern River port should identify Moscow as "The port of three seas – the White, Baltic, and Caspian."[42] Later in the same work Lopatin includes a map entitled "Moscow Port of Five Seas," which predates the one included in *The Volga Goes to Moscow*, but includes the same notations for existing and proposed canal routes. Lopatin's vacillating description of Moscow as the port of either three or five seas reflects a palpable confusion. The system hoped to substantiate the notion that the imagined reality of Moscow as a port of five seas was equal to – if not stronger than – the actual reality of Moscow as a port of three seas when the Moscow Canal was completed.

Indeed, the illustration (Figure 1.1) featured in the magazine *The USSR in Construction* in a 1938 issue devoted to the Moscow–Volga Canal insists that Moscow had already become a "Port of Five Seas," despite the reality of the situation. However, this illustration captures exactly the "rhetoric before reality" approach that was taken with the canal project. Not only does the illustration prematurely celebrate Moscow as a port of five seas, it also provides captioned pictures of the main cities on those bodies of water, their topographical outlines embedded within the rays of the ubiquitous Kremlin star, and most importantly encircling the Kremlin as emblematic of Moscow. Symbolically, all points on this "map" revolve around and lead to Moscow, just as the city reaches all the points on the map. Here the pictorial depiction of water, coupled with the carefully chosen shorelines that feature industry, leisure, and transport (all because of the water) not only celebrates the success of Stalinism in deploying water in service to the state, but also the close connection between the center and the periphery. In fact, this illustration demonstrates Tvedt's contention that the complexity of the relationship between a landscape and its water, a social system and its water, and a cultural system and its water all figure into how both the water (here the five seas and by extension the Moscow Canal) and the system that created it are presented, interpreted, and judged.

The rhetoric of the "Port of Five Seas" captured the notion of motion and energy, images prevalent throughout the flurry of construction projects undertaken during the first three five-year plans. A canal is a conduit that connects geographical locations that would otherwise not be linked (as Figure 1.1 also suggests). Like a river, a canal sustains two-directional transport. As such it not only links geographical map

Figure 1.1 "Moscow – Port of Five Seas" from *The USSR in Construction*, No. 2 (February 1938).[43]

points, but it also carries cargo and passengers from one place to another. The cargo and passengers can be both real and symbolic. In the case of the Moscow Canal during the 1930s, the tangible cargo comprised building materials, foodstuffs, and tourists traveling to and from Moscow. This could be a pleasure trip from Moscow to Kalinin (now Tver') to the north, as Lopatin describes in *Canal Moscow–Volga*, grain from the lower Volga, fruit from Central Asia, or building materials from Siberia. More significant was the symbolic cargo, composed of Soviet Stalinist ideology and the image of Moscow as the beacon of Soviet power for the world. This was personified in the passengers themselves, as well as in the names of the steamships that plied the canal's waters – the *In Memory of Kirov*, the *Dynamic*, and the *Sergo Ordzhonikidze*, among others – that recall the honored Soviet dead, but certainly not the heroes of the Gulag.[44] The crews of cargo ships and the happy tourists enjoying shipboard entertainment and the sights along the canal, such as sculptures and natural landscapes, likely failed to sense (or did not openly acknowledge), either then or now, the heavy emotional cargo that the canal carries with every voyage: the memory of those who suffered and died building it.

A different kind of cargo sailed along the Moscow Canal in 2007 during the commemoration of the 70th anniversary of the Great Purges. A barge laden with a cross embarked from the Solovki Islands Monastery, sailed through the White Sea, along the Belomor Canal, reached the Volga River, and sailed down the Moscow Canal to Butovo in southern Moscow. There this cross was erected in honor of the believers – referred to as "new martyrs" – who perished during the Great Purges at the Butovo shooting range, one of the NKVD's bloodiest killing fields.[45] It is fitting that this barge reached its destination by sailing, given that waterways, by their very nature as constantly flowing conduits, embody the notion of the ceaseless current of time and space. As this barge plied the waters, it cut through time and space to link past events with contemporary reality, while churning up memories in the process. In a general sense, this episode illustrates the metaphor of the "river of life," which in this case symbolically and actually was also a "river of death." In particular, the event organizers were keenly aware of the history of the Moscow Canal's construction and the victims it produced, so that the cross as cargo served as a potent, meaningful counterweight to the typical 1930s cargo.

Moscow's primacy as the "Port of Five Seas" was literally and figuratively inscribed into the landscape, just as the elaborate Northern River Station and the monumental statues of Lenin and Stalin at the canal's confluence with the Volga further inscribed symbols of Soviet power into the landscape.[46] These inscriptions created a new Soviet geography that physically and visually manifested Soviet ideology. Indeed, one commentator noted that not only was Moscow the "Port of Five Seas," but that the Moscow Canal itself was the "main connector for five seas."[47]

In characterizing Moscow's reach in such an exaggerated way, Soviet rhetorical practice created imagined space in which Moscow actually extended to the very borders of the USSR. This rhetorical strategy was not limited to the Moscow Canal, but also reverberates in the imagery in the *Song of the Motherland* from the 1936 film *Circus*. As the second stanza states:

From Moscow to the borders,
From the southern mountains to the northern seas
Man stands as a master
Over his vast Motherland.[48]

Moscow metaphorically subsumed the entire Soviet land mass so that, although the city's shores touched no seas or oceans, land-locked Moscow's reach extended to the very edges of the country. Its power reached from shore to shore. Moscow became the metaphor for the nexus of Soviet power, just as the "Port of Five Seas" became the metaphor for Moscow's political and ideological reach.[49] There would be no "neutral" space that was susceptible to forces other than Soviet power; any space created would be unmistakably politicized, controlled, ideologically laden Soviet space.[50]

The official pronouncement of Moscow's status as the port of five seas fell to Lazar' Kaganovich. He delivered a speech on 10 July 1935 on adoption of the "Resolution Concerning the General Plan for the Development and Reconstruction of Moscow."[51] It was generally held that any development in Moscow required a more stable water supply, especially if tall buildings were to be constructed.[52] Without a steady water supply, plumbing systems in high-rises would fail due to insufficient water pressure. The flow of the Moscow River, which often ran dry at the banks of the Kremlin, needed to be stabilized in order to help support further growth in the city's population, infrastructure, and shipping industry. Kaganovich's speech repeatedly emphasizes the importance of water as a resource and a tool in the further development of Moscow as a world capital at least on the level of cities such as London, Paris, New York, and Chicago, all of which are located on water. The speech is redolent with spatial metaphors and images of the Moscow that was in the process of becoming. Kaganovich cites the pressing need for more water in Moscow:

> The Moscow–Volga Canal, having created the shortest water throughways between the country's seas and most important water basins, will come on line in 1937 and will solve the problem of Moscow's water supply for many years and open the way for the unprecedented improvement and beautification of the city.[53]

Kaganovich continues by stressing that water will not only enhance Moscow's footprint, but will also grow industry and agriculture in the region, as well as furnishing the city with green space, fresh air, and recreational opportunities. He proceeds to note that:

> All the great waterways will intersect in Moscow. Moscow will be turned into the port of five seas . . . Refreshed rivers will intersect in Moscow. These will be new rivers, waterways unified and supported by power plants. Moscow will be the capital of five seas: the five seas will become part of a single system connected by the rivers. In the third five-year-plan it will be possible to travel from Moscow to the Baltic, White, Caspian and Black Seas, to the Kola Bay of the Arctic Ocean; to reach the basins of the Northern Dvina, Dnepr and Ob without once having to leave the steamship.[54]

Throughout his speech Kaganovich stresses the integral part played by water in changing the face of Moscow from a large capitalist city/village to a modern, world-class metropolis by means of "water and greenery." Moscow will become a "city-park" filled with trees, landscaping, and open spaces all for the benefit of its inhabitants, especially its workers.

Kaganovich's vision of Moscow is not only a space graced by greenery and fed by water, but also a majestic capital lined with broad asphalt roads, large, elegant buildings and abundant nature. Almost rapturous in tone, Kaganovich concludes by saying that "skylarks will happily sing; bees will quietly fly for honey to Yauzsky Boulevard. And people will say that here the line between the city and the countryside is erased. We are approaching the epoch of Communism."[55] Indeed, Kaganovich sketches an imagined map that encompasses vast swathes of Soviet territory, from the far north to the south, from the west to the Siberian interior.

This speech captures the interplay between water and landscape, water and social environment, and water and cultural system, for it insists on the unification of all those elements in the new Moscow. The literally and figuratively revitalized Moscow, thanks wholly to the sustainable water supply via the Moscow Canal, would not only occupy more physical space, but would also create new spaces, both imagined and real. In so doing, at least in the space that Kaganovich creates for Moscow, Communism would reach fruition.[56] The creation of the Moscow Sea further promoted the use of water to create a new Sovietized space that physically and metaphorically inundated the traditional Russian space.

The Moscow Sea[57]

> The will of the Bolsheviks and their leader turned the Volga toward the red capital.[58]

The epoch of Communism to which Kaganovich referred in his speech could not be achieved, however, without rerouting the Volga River and creating a reservoir that both provided a sustainable source of water for the Moscow Canal and generated electricity for Moscow and the cities and towns at the canal's northern end. This element of canal construction was the first in a series of proposed improvements to the upper Volga to provide better navigational channels from Kalinin/Tver' downstream, to afford Moscow a sustainable water supply, and to generate electricity for the burgeoning Soviet economy. Later projects would include building the Uglich and Rybinsk reservoirs and power stations, but in the early 1930s the pre-eminent project was the construction of the Volga Junction, whose main features were the Ivan'kovo Reservoir and dam. As section chief Kripaitis noted,[59] "We are standing at the head of the canal ... from whence will start the greatest structure of our epoch."[60]

Decree No. 2640 of the Council of People's Commissars, dated 7 December 1933, proclaimed that "It is considered necessary to quickly begin the construction of the Ivan'kovo Dam on the Volga River ... At the Ivan'kovo Dam on the Volga River a hydro-electric station with a capacity of 60,000 kilowatts will be built."[61] The dam's reservoir, known officially as the Ivan'kovo Reservoir, is more commonly referred to as the Moscow Sea. Its creation marked one of the most ambitious construction projects on the Moscow Canal, and even more than the creation of Moscow as the port of five seas reveals the integration of a landscape, a social environment, and a cultural system with their water, as posited in Tvedt's water-system approach. At the Moscow Sea the industry of Gulag laborers, the literal and figurative inundation of one culture by another with water, the ingenuity of Soviet engineers, and the unbending will of the authorities coalesced to create an emblematic space that still shapes our perception of its creation. As Maslov contends, the entire idea of the Moscow Canal depended on the construction of the Ivan'kovo Dam and its accompanying reservoir, the Moscow Sea, which was the largest reservoir constructed on the canal.[62]

Of special note here are the draft plans for the Moscow Canal project produced by the NKVD, in particular the *Techno-Economic Note* issued in Dmitrov in October 1934 as an appendix to the schematic draft design of the canal.[63] This *Note* provides not only detailed information on the geological and hydrological specifics of the project, but also includes projections as to the amount of labor and materials required for each segment of the waterway, as well as detailed plans, backed up with measurements and dimensions for all of the objects that were to be built along the waterway. Concerning the Volga Junction (as elsewhere) the *Note* stated that

> The Volga Junction, at the headwaters of the Moscow–Volga Canal, provides that water is diverted from the Volga River into the canal. At the same time, it is the first link in the reconstruction of the Upper Volga. Therefore, the Volga Junction must not only feed

> [water] into the canal from the Volga River and provide convenient access for ships to the canal, but also form a deep-water route on the section of the Volga above the [Ivan'kovo] dam.[64]

Also crucial in the site selection was the physical landscape into which the Volga Junction would be inscribed. According to the *Note* the location of the Volga Junction was especially favorable given the bedrock and the sturdy river banks that could support a heavy structure such as a dam. The high and steep right bank of the Volga River was composed of rock and soil that would permit the joining of the canal and river without a full-blown excavation. The lower left bank of the Volga was characterized by alluvial loam and sand resting on the lower moraine, thereby creating propitious conditions to construct the earthen dam that would abut the concrete structure. Soil and sand excavated for the dam's foundation pit would be used either to construct the left bank of the dam (loam and inferior-quality sand), with superior-quality sand used in the production of the concrete to build the dam.[65] The *Note* provides a photograph of a Kovrovets excavator at work on the dam site,[66] as well as estimates for the volume of work in cubic meters that the complex would entail.[67] Significantly, throughout the discussion, no mention was made of the labor force required to achieve these projected goals. Labor was discussed not in terms of input, but rather in terms of output: how much concrete would be laid and earth moved. This is not surprising, given the low regard of the canal administration for its labor camp workforce and the extremely difficult conditions in which they were forced to work. As the *Note* attests, the central factors in the undertaking were the plans and technical specifics, not human beings.

Hence, to understand the importance of the Moscow Sea to any discussion of the spatial parameters of Stalinism, we must first examine how it was built so as to appreciate not only what was created, but what was destroyed. When the first party of supervisory personnel arrived at the site in September 1933, the Volga Junction's Sector Two boss Kripaitis noted:

> There were seven of us. What was here? The village of Ivan'kovo and forest all around. In the village we were not met so warmly. We created an approach ramp, talked about the construction.

> They didn't believe us and said that nothing would come of this project. We arrived at an empty site. There was no railroad. Work had already begun on the canal, and here we just needed to start.[68]

The first squad of forced laborers appeared at the site on 25 September 1933. Initially they lived in the former dachas of the industrialist Mamontov, and then the camp was constructed on the right river bank of the Volga where the town of Bol'shaya Volga is now situated.[69] From this seemingly inauspicious start the construction site began to emerge near the ancient Russian city of Dubna.

The city of Dubna (population 67,800) is perched at the junction of the Moscow Canal and the Volga River, and has enjoyed a rich history, most notably as a center for theoretical and nuclear physics in the USSR and Russia. This worldwide scientific fame developed after World War II, and has continued to make Dubna a destination for foreign scientists. As the home of some of Russia's premier scientists and research institutes, it occupies a special place in the world of Russian science and has earned the nickname "science-city."

Founded in the twelfth century, the city's first claim to fame was its position as a trading center. Dubna is now home to the Joint Institute for Nuclear Physics (JINR),[70] as well as a Satellite Communications Center, and the Scientific Research Institute for Applied Acoustics.[71] Dubna's close proximity to Moscow and location at the northern edge of the Moscow region provide easy access to visitors, aided largely by the direct highway between Moscow and Dubna, as well as the rail line that links the two cities with regular service.

Within the context of the history of the Moscow Canal, Dubna is significant in that it functions as the nexus at which the Moscow Canal begins and ends. Dubna and its immediate environs witnessed one of the greatest construction achievements of the Moscow Canal: the construction of the Ivan'kovo Dam and power station that succeeded in rerouting the flow of the Volga River, channeling Volga water into the Moscow Canal toward the capital, and creating the Moscow Sea. At the Volga Junction the settlement of Bol'shaya Volga was created, including its own railway station. Fifty-five buildings were constructed, of which 36 were designated as housing for the workers who would manage and maintain the Ivan'kovo Dam, reservoir, and hydro-electric station, and first lock of the canal. This is in addition to any enhancements that were made to the city of Dubna, located just beyond Bol'shaya Volga. Indeed, the construction of the *avant-port* at Bol'shaya Volga brought additional visitors to Dubna, as did the resituated Moscow–Savelov rail line. The enhanced production of electricity and the improved transportation and communication links supported Dubna's growth into the scientific center it is today. Indeed Bol'shaya Volga and Dubna profited from the construction of the Volga Junction and the Moscow Canal in ways that other populated areas did not.

These feats rival any of the other construction triumphs along the canal and were pivotal to ensuring the success of the entire Moscow Canal project. Had the Ivan'kovo Dam not succeeded, it is questionable whether the waters of the Volga would even today flow to Moscow. Presently, the adjacent Dubna "suburb" of Bol'shaya Volga marks the spot where workers who built the canal's first lock, the dam, and the Moscow Sea lived during construction. Thus the following discussion focuses on two key moments that make the Dubna site such an important element of the Moscow Canal story: the construction of the Ivan'kovo Dam and related flooding of nearby villages to create the Moscow Sea, and the rerouting of the Volga River through the first lock of the Moscow Canal.

Prior to the construction of the Ivan'kovo Dam, the area around Dubna was dotted with numerous small towns and villages that had existed for centuries. Among them, the village of Ivan'kovo was situated on the Volga's right bank prior to the construction of the canal, while the town of Korcheva served as a regional administrative center slightly farther upstream. They, along with 108 other settlements that stood within the area designated for the future Moscow Sea and Ivan'kovo Dam, were uprooted and moved to new locations, while their original geographic footprints were erased forever by the deluge of water. When it was decided to use the Dubna River as a feeder into the canal and to begin the canal at Dubna, these villages found themselves in the crosshairs of the plan to dam the Volga. In order to generate the amount of water necessary to provide Moscow with both an adequate supply of potable water and a sufficiently deep channel for all manner of river traffic, it was vital to control the flow of the Volga. The Ivan'kovo Dam could do this, aided in its effort by an earthen dike that was built as a continuation of the dam to fully block and reroute the flow of the Volga. The first lock has additional significance in that it is one of two locks (the other being Lock 7 over Volokolamsk Highway in Moscow) on the canal that flows above a road that was built underneath it to re-connect Dubna with the northern shore of the Volga. This engineering feat, along with the construction of the dam itself, highlights the labor and skill that went into the erection of these structures.

In its initial incarnation as a stopping point on the canal, the plans positioned Dubna as the gateway to the canal and the Volga River. As such, the area between the first lock and the entrance to the waterway's main channel featured an *avant-port* that served as an embarkation point for those traveling via either waterway. The *avant-port*, essentially a ship that was anchored to shore, provided waiting rooms and cafes that allowed passengers to comfortably pass the time before their passage.[72]

When examining the course of the Volga River prior to the construction of the Moscow Sea, it becomes clear just how limited a water source the river would be without the intervention of engineering. Figure 1.2

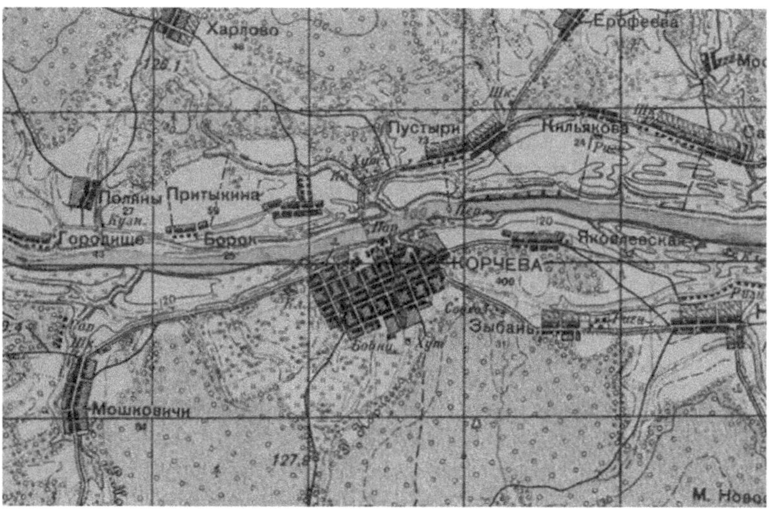

Figure 1.2 Original channel of the Volga River past Korcheva in the center of the map and moving toward the proposed Volga Junction at the right edge of the map.[73]

shows a segment of the Volga by the old Russian town of Korcheva that is slightly upstream from the future Moscow–Volga Junction (on the right edge of the map). While the river is sizeable, the volume of water required to replenish and refresh Moscow was inadequate based solely on the river's flow through this channel. Thus it was decided that a reservoir would be built in order to maintain a sufficient supply of water for both the canal and for the 60,000 kilowatt power station/dam that would breach the Volga. This plan also required that the Volga be rerouted so that beyond the Ivan'kovo Reservoir the Volga would continue to flow downstream through the first lock of the Moscow Canal, as well as through the Ivan'kovo Dam itself, thereby generating power and ensuring an adequate flow for the Volga further downstream.

As with any dam project, the construction site needed to be dry in order to permit the reliable assembly of the concrete dam and its attendant earthen dams that would extend to create the left and right banks of the reservoir. In early 1934 canal workers began building coffer dams around the dam's foundation pit that would prevent the Volga from overrunning its banks and flooding the pit. In February 1934 workers began constructing the coffer dam on the Volga's left bank as well. This effort required removing 150,000 cubic meters of material from the pit and building an embankment with 85,000 cubic meters of fill.[74] This coffer dam was 1.5 km long and 120 meters high by 1 April 1934. Yet from the start the Volga Junction, the most complicated segment of construction, was faced with shortages of material and manpower. As Lazar' Kogan's Order No. 3 dated 9 January 1934 noted, "What general tone and pace can there be on the construction site with kerosene lamps if there is not a consistently guaranteed supply of kerosene?"[75] The completion of a new rail line to Ivan'kovo permitted the transfer of more prisoners to the site. Only in 1935 did supplies become more stable and additional workers were brought to the site to maintain the necessary speed to complete the project by spring 1937.

In 1934 one of the most celebrated inmate workers, Anushevan Lazareev, organized his brigade into an excavating powerhouse.[76] They routinely fulfilled and over-fulfilled their work quotas, in part because of Lazareev's innovation to ensure the smooth movement of wheelbarrows: he constructed wooden plank "pathways" that were laid end-to-end with no drop-offs. Thus the wheelbarrows never got stuck in the mud or ran off course. This improved the ability of workers to haul out earth and redeposit it to build both the coffer dams and the permanent earthen dams and dikes that abutted the concrete dam and proscribed the river's and canal's channels. In this manner the earthen barriers continued to take shape.

Likewise, in 1934 the first Soviet Kovrovets excavator arrived at the construction site to assist in the digging work. The year 1935 witnessed an increase in the production of Soviet excavators, as 135 were produced at the Kovrov Excavator Plant. In 1936 some of these excavators were brought to the Volga site to support construction efforts, but the bulk of the work had already been carried out by the canal workers using spades, wheelbarrows, their bare hands, and the single Kovrov excavator that had been on site since 1934.

Two other technical innovations assisted canal builders in their back-breaking work: hydraulic earth removal and local cement factories. In hydraulic earth removal, workers deploy industrial-sized hoses through which a powerful stream of water is directed at the earth to be moved. The force of the water dissolves the earth into a pulp that is then removed by large vacuum pumps and put into railcars and trucks that then transport the pulp to areas where it was redeposited to build earthen dams and dikes. The water gradually drains out of the pulp and what remains is soil that settles into a solid mass, thereby creating the dike or dam.[77]

In addition, at the Volga Junction as elsewhere on the canal construction site, concrete factories were erected to provide a stable local supply for the builders. The initial primitive concrete factory enabled workers to lay the first cubic meter of concrete at the dam site on 16 August 1934.[78] Subsequently, from January to May 1935, a larger, more complex concrete factory was built that started production on 1 May and provided round-the-clock supplies of concrete. This meant that the concreters likewise worked around the clock to build the foundation and gates of the Ivan'kovo Dam. By means of these machines, excavators, shovels, and wheelbarrows canal laborers were able to create the structures that formed the new landscape of the Volga Junction.

Engineers and laborers were charged with building simultaneously a reservoir, a concrete dam, and earthen dikes on either side of the new dam, while rerouting the Volga River through a new channel controlled by the canal's first lock, as well as erecting both the entrance to the

Moscow Canal and the first lock, whose channel passed over a tunnel they constructed to connect the right bank of the Volga with the power station/dam complex. Complicating matters were both the weather conditions and the spring thaw on the Volga, which promised ice floes and accelerated currents, especially given that the coffer dams were further limiting the Volga's flow. The illustration of the Volga Junction (Figure 1.3) best demonstrates the combination of engineering and construction feats that the canal workers accomplished.

This plan shows the original flow of the Volga in solid parallel lines, with the future channels through the dam (above the old channel), the protective barriers, and Lock 1 (below the old channel) in segmented lines. The Volga's flow would be cut into three parts: one part would flow downstream through the dam at controlled intervals, one part would flow due south through the Moscow Canal, and one part would flow downstream through Lock 1, the portal through which all vessels would need to travel.

Figure 1.4 shows a more complete view of the Volga Junction, including the location of the *avant-port*, as well as the sites for the monuments to Lenin and Stalin. The flashing lighthouse at the beginning of the canal is sited at the bottom of the illustration.

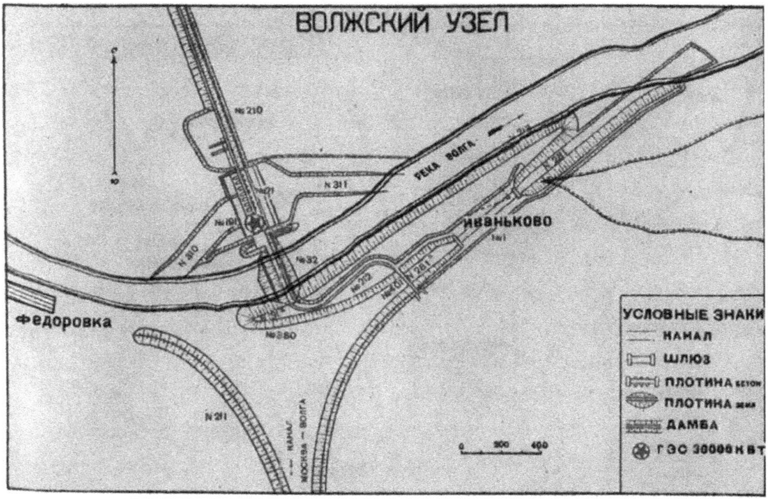

Figure 1.3 The engineering plan for the Volga Junction.

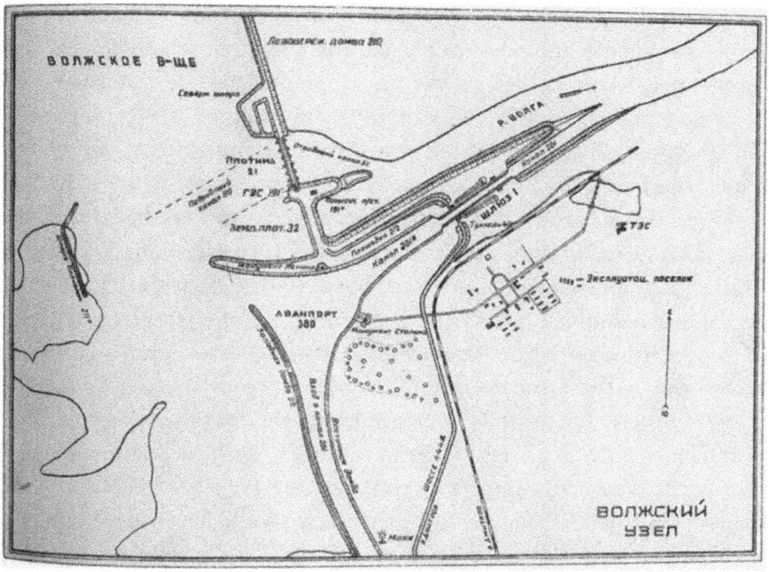

Figure 1.4 Plan for the construction of the Volga Junction; north is up and south is down.[79]

On 23 June 1936 workers detonated 28 explosions that destroyed the coffer dams separating the Volga channel from the dam, and water first flowed through the new river channel. As a witness noted, "Now we will blow up the coffer dam and the river water will flow between the dam's embankments, says the head of the region Shaposhnikov. Now the Volga will flow through a new path that was demarcated for it by the Bolsheviks."[80] In January 1937 the first parts for the bases of the turbines (all parts of which were constructed in the USSR) were installed at the dam's power station. In March 1937 the *avant-port* on the canal's right bank, as well as the first safety gates along the canal route were completed. On 23 March 1937 the portal shields at the Ivan'kovo Dam were lowered. This stopped the Volga River for 3 minutes and tested the shields' ability to manage the pressure exerted by the river current. This pause likewise ensured that the level of the river downstream would not fall dramatically. It did not, and the filling of the constructed areas commenced. By 27 March the *avant-port* was filling with water. At 9:30 a.m. one of the dam's shields was lowered by 75 cm from its previous position, which meant that the *avant-port* would begin filling more quickly. As an orchestra played, the last carts, whose horses were often up to their bellies in water, exited the floor of the *avant-port*, at which point the water began to visibly demarcate its outline.[81] By 29 March, Volga water had reached the first closed safety gates, after which the Ivan'kovo Reservoir started filling to create the Moscow Sea.

When construction was finally completed, workers had built the Ivan'kovo Dam, whose concrete segment is 216 meters long, 29 meters high and 20 meters wide, buttressed by an earthen dam on the left bank and an earthen dike on the right bank, bringing the total length of the dam to 350 meters. The dam serves as a bridge over the Volga River, across which the Dmitrov Highway passes. From its foundation the dam's 29-meter height includes eight upper and four lower portals. Two portal cranes, the first such cranes in the USSR with such large capacity, size, and structural complexity, traverse the length of the dam and operate the shields through which the water passes. The overall capacity of the hydro-electric station is 82.2 MW, while it typically generates 89 million kWh of electricity. In late 1941, with German forces approaching, the dam and hydro-electric station's equipment were disassembled and removed for safekeeping; they were reinstalled in May 1942 and the structures have been in operation ever since. The resulting reservoir – the Moscow Sea – has a surface area of 327 km^2 with a perimeter of 320 km; it is 120 km long and approximately 4 km wide, with a maximum depth of 23 meters and an average depth of 15 meters. The Moscow Sea's total water volume is 1.12 million cubic meters.

In constructing the dam, canal workers removed 750 million cubic meters of earth and laid thousands of cubic meters of concrete. Integral to this work was the labor of Dmitlag inmate Galina Taraskaya and her brigade, who consistently set labor records. From the opening of the cement plant at the Volga Junction on 1 May 1935 until 31 October 1935, Galina and her 340-member team laid 360,000 cubic meters of concrete, a feat for which the team received accolades and Galina herself received an early release, having served roughly two years of her four-year sentence. Upon her early release Galina opted not to return to her native Ukraine, but instead remained at the Moscow Canal construction site, where she continued to set records with her team. Unfortunately, this decision ultimately claimed her life when she was rearrested in 1937 as part of the alleged "Firin Affair," but not before she had contributed mightily to the effort to build the Ivan'kovo Dam and associated structures.[82]

Figures 1.5 and 1.6 show the Volga Junction shortly after its completion and as it looks today. The completed junction is also depicted on a tiled disc that graces one of the outside colums of the Northern River Station (see Plate 1). As the lower half of the image illustrates, the Volga, now coralled by a long earthen dam on its left bank, moves through the shield-protected gates of the Ivan'kovo Dam, its flow regulated by the portal cranes that move the shields depending on the needs of the hydro-electric plant. The river's original channel is visible between the Ivan'kovo Dam and the earthen dike that directs the water's flow between the monuments to Lenin and Stalin (the small figures on either side of the approach to the lock) toward Lock 1 at the far left of the image. An additional earthen dam ushers the Volga further along a channel that directs part of the flow (upward in this image) along the canal toward Moscow. When approaching the Volga Junction from downstream (from the left in this image) the Volga's original channel literally dead-ends at the Ivan'kovo Dam.

Figure 1.5 An aerial view looking downstream toward the first lock of the Moscow Canal taken shortly after the waterway's completion that features the *avant-port* and monument to Stalin (on the right side).[83]

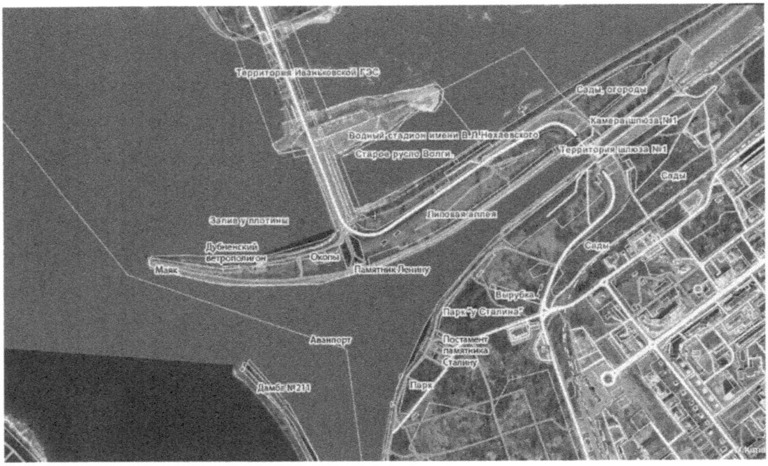

Figure 1.6 A contemporary view of the Volga Junction.[84]

This new, markedly altered landscape not only changed the flow of the Volga River, but also altered the lives of thousands of people who called this region their home. The rechanneling of the Volga embodied the ability of the Stalinist state to literally transform the course of nature, and in so doing make its mark on the landscape. The excavation of the foundation pits for the dam and Lock 1, the erection of the coffer dams and the permanent earthen dams and dikes, the building of the dam/hydro-electric station and the first lock, with towers at both ends – all these structures and projects permitted Stalinism in thought and deed to command space under ground, above ground, and under water, as well as the water itself. In so doing, it marked the landscape as Soviet and claimed as its own all the spaces that it shaped. The actual and metaphorical production of power at the hydro-electric station, coupled with the imposing structures, underscored how a landscape could be reshaped into an emblem of Stalinist ideology. More importantly, Soviet power's ability to control the iconic Volga River signaled the triumph of Soviet over Russian culture and the shift from Russian to Soviet spaces. Like similar forced labor projects before and after, at the Moscow Canal Soviet power in its Stalinist manifestation paid little heed to the people involved, be they Dmitlag inmates or the populations of soon-to-be-submerged villages and towns.

The Russian Atlantis

The process of building the Volga Junction required creation and desecration, innovation and repudiation, liquidation and ideologizing. The reconfiguration of space at the Volga Junction wrought intense and irreparable destruction on the landscape, especially through the relocation of several villages and the complete watery inundation of old Russian towns, foremost among them the county seat of Korcheva. In the fullest literal and metaphorical sense, old Russia was drowned so that a new Soviet state could rise out of the water.

The villages and towns situated along the banks of the upper Volga had existed for centuries, and they sustained their existence by the riches the Volga provided. From fish stocks to potable water, from barge hauling to river transport, denizens of these areas viewed the Volga with reverence and respect. The waters that provided sustenance and livelihoods could just as easily wreak havoc, especially during the spring thaws that often flooded river settlements. In addition, farmlands and livestock formed the center of village life on land that had been in families for years and that had been farmed and inhabited for centuries. Generations of families lived and worked along the Volga's banks, creating personal histories and traditions that were inseparable from the river. When plans for the canal and its Volga Junction were formulated attention was paid not to these traditions and histories, but to the creation of new traditions and new histories. Two emblematic sites that faced inundation and relocation were the village of Ivan'kovo and the town of Korcheva, often referred to as the "Russian Atlantis."

The NKVD department within the Moscow-Volgostroi administration charged with relocating the population was established on 26 September 1933. Subsequently, the Volga Junction canal administration located their headquarters at the village of Ivan'kovo, where the first lock of the canal was to be built. Ivan'kovo was a typical Russian village replete with homesteads, gardens, and pasture for animals, and the recently established collective farm. On 17 April 1934 the first domicile was disassembled in Ivan'kovo as part of the plan to move the village and collective farm 4 km away from the construction site.[85] The disassembled houses were then transported on horse carts to the new location, where they would be reassembled for their inhabitants. As villager I. K. Fedotov recalled:

> How, you ask, did they take everything down? It's well-known that it is not easy from a well-established place. The top brass came, called everyone to the village soviet and they say: well now, you've lived here for a while, but now – it's enough! How can that be, I think to myself? I was born here, on this very street I played games with the boys, grew up, got married, raised a family, grew a beard, but now suddenly – to a new place! I won't be able to set foot there. Here, I think, in front of the window is a pussy willow. It has grown up with me; I'm used to it like it's my own brother. You glance out the window and you see it – the pussy willow ... and now suddenly no pussy willow. How can that be? Oh well, they took everything down. The canal soldiers did a good job putting up my cottage; they put it in a pleasant place. I thank them ... But the pussy willow, of course, perished. I still feel sorry about the pussy willow.[86]

These recollections by the villager Fedotov go to the heart of the spatial displacement that occurred during the construction of the Volga Junction. Moving a village was not just a matter of dis- and reassembling cottages and outbuildings. In deconstructing this village, like others, a way of life was being dismantled and, more importantly, the tight connection between a place and its inhabitants was reduced to a memory. While the water that would subsequently flow over the village would wash away and submerge the former site of Ivan'kovo, its inhabitants' memories would continue, thanks in no small part to the eponymous names of the dam and reservoir. Notably, no sources mention whether or not the village's graveyard was moved to the new site or submerged under the Volga Junction. Still, connection to the place, as represented in Fedotov's mind by the pussy willow, persists and haunts. The displacement also provided some comfort – Fedotov's homestead is pleasant – yet the longing remains. Indeed the space the pussy willow occupied still exists in Fedotov's memory, even if a new landscape has been created.

Related to this, of course, is the notion that transferring the inhabitants of Ivan'kovo to a new location physically encouraged and reinforced their sense of self and their place as Soviet citizens. The initiative to displace and relocate carries with it the understanding that the "old" must be destroyed in an effort to create the "new."

This action emphasizes the power of the authorities (the top brass, in Fedotov's words) to literally and figuratively wash away the past in order to create the future. While the new settlement was renamed New Ivan'kovo, it failed to preserve the true connection to the land that the old village had instilled in its inhabitants. By 15 May 1934 the relocation of "old" Ivan'kovo to New Ivan'kovo was complete. When workers finished laying the concrete for the Ivan'kovo Dam in July 1936, near the old site of the Ivan'kovo village, they had managed to excavate over 3 million cubic meters of earth and lay 250,000 cubic meters of cement.[87] The aged, natural wooden structures of the Russian past had been replaced with the manufactured concrete of the Soviet future.

Ivan'kovo was not the only village moved. An October 1935 decree stated that 4740 households had to be moved in order to clear away any structures from the future site of the Ivan'kovo Reservoir. Any territory that was less than 124 meters above the level of the Baltic Sea would be flooded, thereby requiring the demolition, submersion, or removal of any buildings within that area. To accomplish this task the authorities created three districts to manage the moves. In the Kimri region 382 homesteads needed to be moved, in Zavidovsky 239, and in Konakovo, where the town of Korcheva was located, 1719 households required resettlement.[88] Indeed more than any other town, the remnants of Korcheva still haunt the shores of the Moscow Sea, and its loss stresses the price paid for Soviet progress. Korcheva is a space that can never be reconstituted.

The ancient town of Korcheva dates back to the eighth or ninth century, when it served as a trading post on the Volga for merchants traveling from Novgorod, Tver', and elsewhere up and down the river.[89] Korcheva's status as a town and county seat dates to the time of Catherine the Great, who officially established it in 1781. Its population grew to over 3000 by the mid-ninteenth century, as did its surface area, although the town never became densely populated; its inhabitants numbered 2353 in 1923. Merchants, peasants, white-collar workers, and craftsmen in local porcelain factories constituted most of the population. A quintessential Russian Orthodox cathedral, Resurrection Cathedral (Voskresensky sobor) and The Church of the Transfiguration (Preobrazhenskaya tserkov'), adorned the town's skyline, with the Kazan Church also located in the town. A variety of stone and wooden buildings were present, including stores, schools, a regional hospital, regional library, hotels, eateries, and a cemetery – everything a small, provincial Russian town needed to sustain life.

In order to clear the area for the eventual presence of the reservoir, wooden homes were relocated, as were their residents, mostly to the neighboring town of Konakovo, site of the Konakovo (previously Kuznetsov) ceramic factory. Stone structures, including the cathedral and two churches, were blown up. Forested areas within the town were cleared as well in preparation for the arrival of the water. After the Moscow Sea reached its appropriate level, it covered almost two-thirds of the territory that had been Korcheva; however, project designers slightly miscalculated the level to which the proposed reservoir would reach, which meant that not all of Korcheva disappeared beneath the reservoir. A full one-third of the town remained above water, thereby suggesting that Korcheva's full evacuation and destruction might have been unnecessary. This fact was little consolation to Korcheva's citizens, who had already been moved to various other locations and whose physical connection to the space had been lost. As Bulanov notes:

> On the bottom of the reservoir there remained the foundations of houses, the town cemetery, a livestock burial ground, bottom lands, 327,000 hectares of flatlands and forests. The water forever covered the squares and boulevards where for centuries lived generations of citizens of the town of Korcheva.[90]

Figure 1.7 and Plate 2 show how Korcheva looked before and after flooding. As an unattributed verse expresses it:

> When one fine day the Moscow Sea rose
> Some were joyful, some were aggrieved.
> Thus the Bolshevik again proved to the world
> That he is unbending, stubborn and great.
> The water hurried toward the ruined houses
> Along the fields, the graves, the gardens and the meadows.[91]

This verse captures the tension between the past and the future, the old and the new, the land and the water, that the Moscow Canal project engendered and revealed. These lines demonstrate how the space is contested, while submitting ultimately to Soviet power, by juxtaposing the emotions of joy and grief; power – the "unbending" Bolshevik and the ruined houses; and nature – the water and hardscapes that comprised the town. These conflicts, ranging from internal personal strife to external physical destruction, reveal how connected the landscape, the waterscape, and human interaction are with them.

Korcheva, a place to which its former residents traveled by boat to visit and mourn for years after it was submerged and which amateur ethnographers and historians still visit,[92] illustrates Tvedt's water-system approach. The natural properties of the water intersect with its metaphorical meanings, as registered through human intervention in the natural environment. The end product realizes the subjugation not only of one space by another (water over land), but one kind of power by another (Soviet authority over Russian history), and one system over another (Stalinism over traditional Russian life). Hence, the construction of the Volga Junction in general and the creation of the Moscow Sea through the rerouting of the Volga River, even more than the trope of Moscow as the Port of Five Seas, capture the spatial dynamics at work in the Moscow Canal project. Ideology, natural forces, human labor, and place coalesced to produce a new space that evoked elements of each. This is especially valid in view of the fact that Korcheva and Ivan'kovo were not the only inhabited areas to be relocated and reduced to waterscapes on the bottom of the canal. We need only remember the relocations that accompanied the excavation of the Khlebnikov segment of the canal, commonly referred to as the "big dig" (Bol'shaya vyiomka). More than 350 homesteads from various districts, as well as numerous collective farms, dachas, and garden plots could not escape the flooding. The relocations related to the Khlebnikov project required an expenditure of 1,483,000 rubles in 1934.[93] The demise of Korcheva remains especially poignant, in no small part because of its long history, but also because of the sense of loss that arises whenever those interested in local history, or any viewer who happens upon them, looks at old photographs of Korcheva. The vitality and sense of place resonates in the views of the riverbank, the religious sites, the tree-lined streets and paths, and the sturdy stone buildings that comprised the heart of Korcheva. Yet a deep sense of loss also is evoked by the abandoned structures, overgrown plots, and mostly submerged islands that once pulsed with the life of a traditional Russian river town.

Figure 1.7 Korcheva as it was situated on the Volga River for all of its existence. The Church of the Transfiguration on the left and the Resurrection Cathedral on the right appear as the center and left red circles in Plate 2.[94]

Some would argue that the loss of towns and villages is the price a society pays for progress. Certainly, water projects often exact a high price for the sake of progress because of the force of the water itself and the power required to harness it for human use. The Panama and Suez Canals, as well as the Hoover and Three Gorges Dam, all illustrate the cost of controlling nature in the service of the state. Some land, some homes, some historical sites lose out to the push for a better future. This commonality makes the Moscow Canal story resonate across time and space and among different cultures. Yet the Moscow Canal project moves beyond similar undertakings in one significant way: the use of forced labor as official economic policy and ideology to achieve that which had hitherto been unachievable. This component – the deployment of the Gulag, in itself a particularly Soviet space – to manage and accomplish mass construction projects, which reshaped both real and imagined space, provides further evidence as to how the Moscow Canal built Stalinism.

The dual characteristics of water as life-affirming and life-taking, as well as the intentional program to replace or even vanquish the old with the new, both gain deeper significance within the context of Dmitlag and its inmate canal builders. Just as water reshaped the geography of the canal site, so too did it reshape the attitudes of many Dmitlag inmates, who were the most important and significant actors in the creation of these newly demarcated Stalinist spaces. The water brought these prison laborers both life and death; it created new imagined spaces and places of memory within those who survived the experience. The water flowed through the Moscow Canal, and the Dmitlag inmates likewise flowed through the Gulag system, whose contradictions are the subject of the next chapter.

CHAPTER 2

HOW THE GULAG BUILT THE MOSCOW CANAL

We dug a channel,
We defeated the Volga,
A mighty dam
Holds back the river.
We have changed the flow
Of the ancient Volga!

Drink Volga water
Our capital Moscow!
The waters of the Volga flow calmly,
The lighthouses are in place.
Steamships sail
Along Stalin's canal![1]

The most vivid images of the construction of the Moscow–Volga Canal come to life in the documentary film *Moscow–Volga. Film-documents about the Greatest Structure of the Stalinist Epoch. 1933–1937*.[2] The film, directed by Rafail Gikov and released in 1937, chronicles the construction of the waterway from the first surveys conducted by civil engineers to its triumphant opening. Along the way the viewer is treated to scenes of the construction process, the quotidian routine of its builders, and the exultant spectators greeting the first ships to travel its waters. The narrator does not directly mention the Dmitlag camp,[3] but most of the film illustrates just that space: inmates (with implausibly happy faces) arriving at the work site in cattle cars; NKVD officers (although not identified as such) calling roll by asking inmates for identification and the criminal article under which they were sentenced; work sites populated with little mechanization and much physical labor performed to the accompaniment of brass bands; and work brigades called to action by a bugler and marching to the work site led by musicians.

Throughout the film the narrator calls the inmates "an army" and the construction process a "battle" that they are waging against nature. This is not surprising given that the forced laborers who built both the Belomor and Moscow–Volga Canals were referred to as "canal soldiers," a sobriquet coined by Lazar' Kogan at Belomor.[4] As the film's action proceeds rousing music plays in the background. In fact, this musical accompaniment is a song written specifically for the film and in honor of the Moscow–Volga Canal. Titled *Listen, Volga!* the song was composed by G. Gamburg with lyrics by Sergei Alymov, the same person who was instrumental in organizing cultural activities at the Belomor Camp.[5] The march-like tempo of the song accompanies the narration and visual images throughout the film, thus providing an energetic and steady beat, as if mirroring in sound the tempo of the work on the waterway. Yet the toe-tapping music belies the harsh reality of the camp, which an observant viewer can detect. For example, while the narrator joyously notes that this "army is well-armed" with excavators and other forms of mechanization, the images on the screen show canal workers hauling dirt in wheelbarrows and horse carts, digging with shovels and pickaxes, and driving metal rods into solid rock with sledge hammers. Inmate workers perch precariously on steep inclines, while others scale all manner of scaffolding on various construction sites. While authentic, slogans such as "Not a minute of idleness!" and "We won't leave the work site until construction is finished!" fail to adequately convey the long days and nights of back-breaking labor that inmate workers endured. In fact, some of the most potent scenes in the film were shot at night on brightly lit construction sites. Even scenes of construction carried out in obviously freezing weather, while accompanied by the musical score, suggest a reality much different from that which the film tries to depict for its propagandistic purposes (and such purposes it certainly had, or it would not have been made).

It is these contradictions between hard physical labor and upbeat music, purported mechanization and pickaxes and wheelbarrows, dancing inmates and guarded gates, that capture the world of Dmitlag, a place simultaneously creative and confined, brutal and life-affirming (for some). As Steve Barnes has cogently argued, the Gulag and its attendant camps promised either death or redemption depending on an inmate's crimes, attitude, work regime, and predilections.[6] Dmitlag was no different, for it brought death, illness, and psychological trauma to many, and skilled trades and hopes for a brighter future to some. Like so much of the Gulag, one's fate often depended less on ability and talent (which could ultimately be liabilities) and much more on the vagaries of circumstance or association.

With this in mind, the ensuing discussion explores two topics that focus on the physical and artistic spaces that Dmitlag created. This examination of Dmitlag is by no means exhaustive nor does it presume to be; a whole volume could be devoted just to the organization and operation of the camp.[7] However, any treatment of the Moscow–Volga Canal project must include a discussion of the camp and its instrumental role in creating Stalinist space. This is significant because the Moscow Canal and its attendant structures exemplify the transformation of a Russian landscape into a singularly Stalinist and, by extension, Soviet landscape saturated with signs that claim, as Groys suggests, that the territory is "ours" and not "theirs."[8] On the most basic visual level, the Moscow Canal demonstrates Stalinist ideology in action: The Dmitlag prisoners changed the landscape by altering, destroying, and reconfiguring great swaths of land; any geographical peculiarities were erased or changed according to the Marxist notion that man could conquer nature, and Stalinism's contention that it could control everything it touched, including nature itself. The space that came to be known as the Moscow Canal exemplified Soviet control not only over nature, but over human beings as well, as witnessed in Dmitlag.

Just as the Dmitlag inmates were reshaping the space, so too was the space shaping them.[9] On the most basic level the landscape, and the labor needed to transform it, were the death of many prisoners. For other inmates, the experience building the Moscow Canal served as the pivotal point in their lives, for it provided them with a useful skill and a source of pride in their achievement. Still others were victimized by a landscape (and a system) that left them physically and psychologically injured.

Figure 2.1 Dmitlag NKVD SSSR sign near Yakhroma.[10]

Yet each outcome demonstrates the symbiosis that occurred as workers and landscape interacted with and often destroyed each other.

DMITLAG[11]

The Dmitlag, short for Dmitrov Corrective-Labor Camp, was the largest camp in the Gulag system, given the massive nature of the project undertaken (Figure 2.1). In its heyday the camp housed over 198,000 inmates, a figure which did not include "free workers" – those who worked at the site of their own volition – and NKVD personnel.[12] Likewise, Dmitlag, as a satellite in the Gulag universe, conformed to the "landscape of terror" that defined the camps. In fact, the Moscow Canal project, like similar undertakings in the camp world, functioned as a microcosm of the larger issues and tensions at play in Stalinist society. The site provides a cinematic "close-up," as it were, of the Stalinist enterprise, with its social tensions, shortages, ideological battles, work brigades, shock work, and myriad other common problems that existed in parallel outside Dmitlag. As a result, it reflects the landscape of terror as an inseparable segment of Soviet space, and of which the Moscow Canal is one integral part. The uneasy co-existence of camp and non-camp space illustrates how Stalinist totalitarianism contained contradictions and conflicts, elements that stress not uniformity in totalitarian space, but rather, as Groys suggests, "a total struggle of all oppositions against each other, a struggle that simultaneously unites these oppositions by making them part of a single world event."[13] The result is a dialectical union of Stalinist space that superficially seems a cohesive whole, but simultaneously reveals tumult under the surface, which constantly redefines the space.

One of the most significant aspects of Dmitlag is that it was the only Gulag labor camp to operate within the Moscow city limits. Barkovsky was able to locate 69 sub-camps (*lagpunkty*) along the canal route, including those near the Tushino construction site, as well as near the site of the Pererva dam in southern Moscow and below Lock 10 on the right bank of the Moscow River near Kolomenskoe.[14] The various Dmitlag sub-camps were organized according to the divisions of the work sites set up along the canal route. In an order dated 8 June 1932, construction chief Kogan outlined 14 sectors that would comprise the Dmitlag camp and cover the length of the canal.[15] These sectors stretched from the north at the future confluence of the Volga River with the Moscow Canal to the south in the area of Pererva on the Moscow River, which was considered the far southern outskirts of the city at that time. Locks 7–11 were to be located at the edge of the city limits, as were various bridges and both the Karamyshev and Pererva dams. At the city's then northern edge the Khimki reservoir and Northern River Station and Port would be constructed. This exception to the general rule of locating camps far from attractive urban centers or in far-flung locations rich in natural resources such as nickel, gold, uranium and timber was surely permitted due to the importance of the Moscow Canal to the city. This was perhaps one reason why an NKVD directive from 29 April 1935 ordered that no prisoners convicted under Article 58 of the Criminal Code of the USSR were to be sent to Dmitlag. The categories included convictions for treason, espionage, terrorism, sabotage, membership in anti-Soviet political parties, counter-revolutionary activities and other related political crimes, as well as prisoners convicted of any crime who were native Muscovites or residents of Moscow or the Moscow region.[16] Presumably, since construction on the Moscow Canal commenced in 1932, political prisoners and convicted Moscow residents were already deployed to the Moscow Canal project and remained there for the duration of their sentences.

The first official pronouncement regarding the construction of the Moscow–Volga Canal occurred in 1931. Party functionary and mastermind behind the reconstruction of Moscow, Lazar' M. Kaganovich, writes in his memoirs that the Moscow–Volga Canal was the "blood brother of the Metro."[17] In his discussion of the Moscow Canal, Kaganovich traces the history of the decision to proceed with the canal's construction, and laces his narrative with details of the planning stages. Not surprisingly, Kaganovich reveals nothing about the loss of life, dire construction conditions, or NKVD management of the project. Rather, he focuses on those elements of the project that illustrate the force and energy of Soviet construction methods in general, and in particular the wise planning of the Party elite, especially the Moscow leadership.

In Kaganovich's account, the issue of slaking the growing thirst of the expanding capital was the "most pressing question" facing Moscow at that time.[18] According to him the Politburo entertained the idea of building a canal to connect Moscow with the Volga as early as 1931, and invited engineer Avdeev to present his plan. While Avdeev's plan ultimately was not accepted, it fostered discussion and re-examination of the possibilities of building a canal powered by a mechanical system, rather than relying on natural currents and rivers to bring water to the capital. Three options – Staritskii, Shoshin, and Dmitrov – were proposed for the route of the future Moscow–Volga Canal; after considerable deliberation, the Dmitrov option was chosen since it promised a relatively easier topographical path: Rivers such as the Klyazma, Khimki, Iksha and others would be co-opted into the waterway's system, but the proposed canal route would have to traverse a 6-km long ascent that required building a series of locks that operated like a staircase to traverse this elevation. In addition, the Dmitrov route produced a shorter waterway that saved both the time and distance required to reach important destinations such as Leningrad and Gorky. The shorter Dmitrov route was also more cost-effective because the expenditures for it were significantly less than the other two options.[19]

Kaganovich asserts that the construction plan ultimately accepted was based on engineering and science,[20] and neglects to mention that the proposed completion date for the waterway repeatedly changed. While Kaganovich cites data indicating that Gulag inmates were vital to the construction effort and were trained to be qualified workers able to return to the labor force outside the Gulag, he fails to mention that the management of the project under the auspices of the NKVD was vital to the canal's completion. Instead he emphasizes the efforts of the Communist Party in realizing this goal. As he notes, "The leadership of the MK and Mossovet, including, of course, me personally, often went to the construction site, saw to specific questions about the pace of the canal's construction, gave orders and, truth be told, simultaneously applied pressure so that the work pace enabled the completion of the project."[21] Clearly, Kaganovich saw no reason for humility in describing his participation in the project.

The official acceptance of Kaganovich's proposal to the Communist Party Central Committee in June 1931 set in motion the planning and implementation of the Moscow–Volga Canal project. Construction was slated to begin in 1932 and was assigned to a newly commissioned entity, "Moskanalstroi," which was responsible for overseeing all facets of construction. It is noteworthy that the OGPU/NKVD was not initially charged with construction. Rather, Moskanalstroi fell under the jurisdiction of the Presidium of the Moscow City Executive Committee, which initially supervised the project and made personnel appointments.[22] It was likely the lack of swift action on the part of then Moskanalstroi leader P. Ia. Bovin, an employee of the Ministry of Water, which prompted the resolution of 26 May 1932 to name Kogan the new head of the Moscow–Volga project.[23] Kogan, who at the time was serving jointly as the head of the Gulag and of the Belomor Canal project, was released from his duties as the Gulag chief to manage both canal projects. In his place, Matvei Berman was appointed the head of the Gulag, a position from which he would be removed and purged in 1937.

Responsibility for construction of the waterway then shifted from the Moscow City Government and Ministry of Water to the official security agencies, first the OGPU and then the NKVD, thereby permitting the marshaling of resources and manpower to construct the waterway. OGPU Order No. 1005 "Concerning the Appointment of the Management Team for the Construction of the Volga-Moscow Canal," dated 31 October 1932, officially charged the OGPU/NKVD with the oversight of the project.[24] Ultimately, this shift also helped solidify the cadre of NKVD officers who would supervise the project. After various personnel changes from 1931 to 1933, by the end of 1933 the roster of Moscow–Volga supervisors was finalized and remained the same until April 1937: L.I. Kogan, Head of Moscow Canal Construction; S. Ia. Zhuk, Chief Engineer; S. G. Firin, head of Dmitlag.[25] These three men bore the responsibility for seeing that the Moscow–Volga Canal was built. Also during this period, the official title of the project changed from "Moskanalstroi" to "Stroitel'stvo kanala Moskva-Volga," abbreviated as "Moskva–Volgostroi" according to Construction Order No. 50 dated 13 April 1933.[26] Subsequently, all official waterway documents, stamps, and publications would bear this official title.

The completion of the waterway was initially scheduled for November 1934.[27] The date of completion was later moved to 1936. As Decree No. 2640 "On the Volga–Moscow Canal" of the Council of Peoples Commissars of the USSR stated:

> 1. The channel for the canal and its principal structures are approved. 2. In view of the increased size of the Volga–Moscow Canal and the structures on it, and also in view of the significant increase in connection with the volume of work [it is decreed] that the timeline for the completion of construction will be extended to the end of 1935, with the canal beginning operation with the start of the 1936 navigation [season].[28]

As this document suggests and as reality bore out, Soviet officials consistently under-estimated the time needed to build such a large and complicated system of structures. While weather certainly played a role in delaying construction, it is also likely that the number of workers needed to complete the task was not accurately calculated. This, coupled with idlers among the workers and attempted escapes, hindered efforts to complete the project within the time frame stipulated in this order. Having finally understood this, Nikolai Ezhov, who had replaced Genrikh Yagoda as the head of the NKVD in September 1936, issued an order to the effect that the principal work on the Moscow Canal was to be completed between 20 May and 20 June 1937 and that most of Dmitlag was to be liquidated by 20 June.[29] Those Dmitlag inmates who still had time to serve would be sent to other camps, while those who earned an early release would be free to leave the camp. After 20 June, "for the remainder of the work only those inmates convicted of petty crimes for short sentences should be allowed to stay" on the work site.[30] The dates for the completion and official opening of the Moscow Canal were finalized in a decree dated 9 April 1937 that stated that the waterway would be able to accept steamships by 1 May, with the waterway fully completed by 1 July in order to officially open on 15 July 1937.[31]

With the original construction plans set, Yagoda issued an order that created the Dmitlag camp, which would house the bulk of the work force for the Moscow–Volga Canal project. OGPU Order No. 889/s, dated 14 September 1932, "Concerning the Organization of the Dmitrov ITL OGPU" reads with a simplicity that belies what this order actually meant for the thousands of inmates who would soon populate its ranks: "1. To form on the territory of the Moscow Region the Dmitrov Corrective-Labor camp of the OGPU with its administration to be located in the city of Dmitrov. 2. The personnel department of the OGPU will carry out the staffing of the Dmitrov camp of the OGPU. Signed Vice-Chairman of the OGPU, G. Yagoda."[32] With this action, both inmates and materials would begin being sent to work sites along the canal route in order to launch the arduous task of constructing the waterway and its attendant structures.

Before Semyon Firin was appointed to the post in September 1933, the first head of Dmitlag, A. E. Sorokin, issued an order on 9 October 1932 that outlined the daily routine for camp inmates. Their schedule was as follows:

> Wake up at 5:30 a.m.; Breakfast from 5:45 to 6:30; transfer to the work site from 6:30 to 7; work day from 7–17:00; dinner from 17 to 19:00; from 19–22:00 time spent for work in the Cultural-Education Center; from 22:05 bed time.[33]

Ten-hour work days regardless of the weather demanded much of the Dmitlag prisoners and, as Maslov points out, the schedule was often not followed: the work day ultimately depended on the amount of work completed vis-à-vis the plan for that day. As with life outside the camp, life inside the camp was regulated by a raft of bureaucratic orders that addressed every detail of labor and life, coupled with minutely detailed plans based on which all production would be measured and implemented. Plans and dictates failed to account for weather, illness, and accidents, but the quotas needed to be met regardless of such interruptions. This also meant that daily inmate rations were calculated based on a worker's productivity. If a laborer over-fulfilled his/her plan then s/he would receive coupons to purchase additional rations or cigarettes in the camp canteen.[34] Such a scenario was depicted in the film *Moscow–Volga* (at point 20:23 in the film). Those fulfilling 90 percent of their work quota received 400 grams of bread, while those not fulfilling even that percentage received 300 grams.[35] As these data suggest, a cruel logic guided the camp leaders, not only in Dmitlag but throughout the Gulag system. They wanted maximum labor output from the prisoners and rewarded those who acted accordingly. Yet if workers failed to meet the norm, they were punished with reduced rations. The less food a prisoner received, the less able that person was to fulfill the norm, thereby creating a vicious circle from which it was hard to extract oneself. The physical labor was exhausting, especially for anyone not equipped to handle ten-hour work days or longer, moving earth, digging ditches, or building scaffolding. As time wore on, the stamina of many workers

Figure 2.2 Inmate laborers and the ubiquitous Moscow–Volga Canal wheelbarrows designed on site.

faltered, resulting in illness, malingering, attempted escapes, and even death. The photographs of inmate laborers that Maslov also includes in his book testify to the difficulty of the working conditions and the often primitive tools used to dig this enormous canal (similar to the images in Figures 2.2 and 2.3).[36]

Even in Dmitlag's early days, when it had barely begun to function, the issue of escapes was raised. Yagoda's order of 25 October 1932 speaks directly to this problem and puts Dmitlag personnel on notice to be vigilant in preventing escapes and catching escapees. According to the order:

> The construction of the Moscow–Volga Canal has been entrusted to the OGPU and we are now carrying out the organization of the Dmitrov camp of the OGPU. The special conditions of the work of the OGPU Dmitrov camp (several tens of thousands of prisoners working in close proximity to Moscow) poses especially acute questions of an agent-operational nature and demands from all OGPU agencies of the Moscow region and the RKM

Figure 2.3 Construction of the control towers at the lower gates of Lock 8 and the assembly of the lock gates.[37]

> {worker-peasant militias} every kind of assistance to the Dmitrov camp. Before the authorized representatives of the Moscow Region OGPU {PP OGPU MO} and the GULAG OGPU I have put forth this task – to prevent all escapes from the Dmitrov camp.[38]

That Yagoda was already instituting measures to combat escapes in late 1932, when Dmitlag still had not been completely populated and the work was still in its early stages, suggests that the potential for escape was indeed significant. The size of the work site, spread over 130 km and intersecting Dubna, Dmitrov and Moscow, explains the perceived ease with which escapes could be organized. The entire work site could not be cordoned off given the kind of labor involved. Moreover, the Moscow–Savelov rail line and the Dmitrov highway both ran parallel to and within the waterway's construction channel, thereby providing additional opportunities for escape.[39] Thus far it has been impossible to determine the exact number of escapees from Dmitlag.

Escapes were not the only problems that the Dmitlag leadership encountered from their workforce. Malingering ranked high on the list of problems that plagued the work tempo. Posters and wall newspapers exhorted inmates to be productive and not feign illness in order to avoid work. Honor boards were posted in each sector bearing the names of highly productive individuals, along with those who failed to fulfil their work quotas. Agitation brigades traveled throughout the camp and staged performances that tried to inspire the work force and denigrate loafing on the job. As Dan Healey has observed, "Such, in the eyes of the early Gulag authorities, was the face of the malingerer as {a} politically unconscious, childlike petty criminal: elemental, willful, but because he came from the ranks of the proletariat, ultimately, redeemable."[40] Idling on the job, however, came at a price. "At the Moscow–Volga Canal, fakers of illness in May 1933 got two to five months' confinement to the punishment cell for their misdeeds, and a 1935 investigation at the same camp complex penalized several men who apparently colluded to injure themselves, with threats of transfers to harsher regimes, revocation of remission earned for high productivity, and other penalties."[41] Both camp authorities and prisoners were held accountable for their loafing, a two-pronged attack to address the problem.[42] We should not assume, however, that idling and other criminal activities were singularly a Gulag phenomenon; idlers outside the camp presented a problem for

Soviet managers and factory foremen; human nature did not change simply because one was in or out of the Gulag. As Oleg Khlevniuk asserts, "The vast Gulag contributed significantly to the increase of crime across the Soviet Union: for example, to 'recidivism' among those who had been previously sentenced to long stretches for petty crimes committed in the context of hardship and privation."[43] Thus the interaction between Gulag and non-Gulag space, as it existed at the Moscow Canal construction site, represented part of a larger phenomenon that occurred wherever camp sites were located, due to certain "gray zones" where the Gulag and non-Gulag worlds overlapped.[44]

As the population of Dmitlag increased, so too did the pace of work. As of 1 January 1933 the Dmitlag population was 10,400 inmates, and it reached its peak in 1935–6 during the most intense construction phase, ranging from 195,648 on 1 April 1935 to 192,034 on 1 April 1936.[45] Within this period the inmate population peaked at 198,000. If we tabulate the camp population for each of the time periods that Kokurin and Morukov delineate, then the total population of inmate laborers over the life of Dmitlag was 2,654,698.[46] Barkovsky, however, believed that such a high total was inaccurate, even when he was given data that potentially supported such a high figure: "I received information in 2002 from A. I. Malin regarding the total population of Dmitlag, which in his words reached 800,000 inmates, [but] this seems improbable."[47] Recall, however, that many inmate laborers served a large part if not all of their sentences on the Moscow Canal construction site, given the timeframe for its completion. This means that there existed a consistent base inmate population that increased or decreased depending on construction needs.[48] Even if this total seems high, it still points up the amount of manpower that the construction of the Moscow Canal necessitated. The sheer magnitude of the construction projects was astounding.

The totals for inmate laborers did not include voluntary workers, who numbered in the hundreds and included drivers, doctors (250), geologists, engineers, accountants (400), cashiers (275), typists (175), economists (325), telephone operators (175), laboratory workers (350–400), waitresses (150), and others.[49] The infusion of voluntary workers, along with the location of the canal work sites made it possible for prisoners to interact with the local population and with the free employees. According to Barkovsky, collective farms near the construction site were ordered to provide food to the camp. The flow of foodstuffs into the camp was relatively constant, to the point that one cart driver reported that "My horse could never rest."[50] Those same carts would bring out the corpses of those who had died on the construction site. While the official death toll for the Moscow–Volga Canal project stands at 22,842 (based on official records at GARF), it is impossible to know just how many inmates actually did perish.[51] As Bulanov and others contend, the official death toll likely does not account for those who died as the result of prolonged illnesses or while escaping, or even those who perished on the job and whose deaths went unnoticed or untallied. Indeed the death toll vis-à-vis the total inmate population at Dmitlag comes in at a stunning 0.008 percent, a figure that seems impossibly low given the dangerous work and harsh weather in which the prisoners labored. In fact, according to Golfo Alexopoulos, "the Stalinist forced labor camp system routinely dispatched its weakest and dying population beyond the limits of the zone."[52] She argues that the quest to keep reported mortality rates low resulted in the systematic release of those prisoners whom camp authorities considered no longer fit for work. Having been exploited to the fullest, these prisoners were discarded like trash.[53] It is safe to assume that Dmitlag embraced the same practices, thereby keeping the official mortality rate artificially low. In addition, a huge cache of Dmitlag records was destroyed as the Germans advanced on Moscow in 1941, so even extant archival records are likely inaccurate, thereby further clouding the accuracy of the reported death rate.[54]

Nonetheless, inmates did die on the work site and many of their graves are reputed to be along the Moscow Canal. When a house was being built not far from the canal's channel in the hamlet of Dedenevo, excavators were digging to erect the foundation for a garage. In the process skulls were dug up that did not belong to a nearby cemetery, and locals believe that this was a burial ground for Dmitlag inmates.[55] As Barkovsky notes, "At practically every junction on the canal where large-scale work was undertaken, piles of skeletons are periodically found that immediately are distinguishable from old, abandoned cemeteries. For example, such piles of human skeletons were discovered in the 1970s on the construction site of Infectious Disease Hospital No. 1 at 63 Volokolamsk Highway and at the second tunnel by Lock 8 on the side where the MPS hospital stands."[56] In preparation for the commemoration of the Moscow Canal's 80th anniversary in 2017, efforts are underway under the auspices of the Moscow branch of the Memorial organization, along with the compilers of the Moskva-Volga.ru website, to determine where these graves might be and to conceive of a way to mark them. This would be some small redress of the egregious practice during the waterway's construction of dumping bodies into unmarked mass graves and them depriving them of the respect of a proper burial. Kokurin and Morukov paraphrase a Dmitlag order from 3 July 1934 that spoke to the issue of unsanitary and careless burial practices:

> The cemeteries have not been dug or fenced off. Burials are undertaken carelessly, especially in winter. It is ordered that . . . in those sectors located close to civilian population centers, local cemeteries are to be used, and self-standing cemeteries are to be opened only in extreme situations with the approval of the head of the sanitary section and the civilian organizations for sanitation.[57]

The interaction between the Gulag and civilian authorities, as well as the movement from Gulag to civilian territory speaks to the porous nature of the Dmitlag boundaries. This liminal area between true Gulag and true civilian spaces serves as a place of negotiation and interaction that arose at other camps as well.[58]

Labor had its reward for some of the supervisors and prisoners who built the Moscow Canal (Figure 2.4). As with the Belomor Canal project, awards were given to those whose efforts were perceived as exemplary. Commendations included the Order of Lenin, the highest award one could receive. Figures in this list of 42 awardees include the architects Fidman and Rukhliadev as well as the Deputy Chief of the Gulag I. I. Pliner. Matvei Berman, Sergei Zhuk, and Lazar' Kogan, who had previously received the Order of Lenin, also received the Order of the Red Star, along with 25 other recipients, among whom were NKVD support staff and commanders of various sectors on the construction site. No canal laborers received either of the two highest awards, which went mainly to members of the NKVD staff and personnel in supervisory positions. The 208 recipients of the Order of the Red Banner of Labor included doctors, engineers, and heads of the many offices that comprised the administrative bureaucracy of the

Figure 2.4 A construction site, the images of which are reminiscent of a Shchelokov painting (see Chapter Three).[59]

project. The 129 Badge of Honor winners included other support staff, such as secretaries, mechanics, camp guards, and excavator operators, but no clearly identified canal soldiers. An excavator operator or camp guard could have come from the ranks of Dmitlag inmates, but the honor roll fails to note whether this was the case for any of the awardees.[60]

All of the official awards celebrated the work and the achievements of the administrative staff and the project leadership. 55,000 Dmitlag inmates received a different and likely more prized reward: early release from the camp (Figure 2.5). Other inmates, who had served out their prison terms but voluntarily remained on the Moscow–Volga construction site, would have their criminal records expunged, especially if they were stellar workers. Finally, shock workers who had earned a release from the camp were awarded certificates that documented their exemplary work on the project, as well as transportation tickets and monetary awards ranging from 100–500 rubles.[61]

The horrible working conditions and treacherous tasks do not present a complete picture of Dmitlag, for in the midst of the human suffering and degradation there arose an active cultural life that for a select few

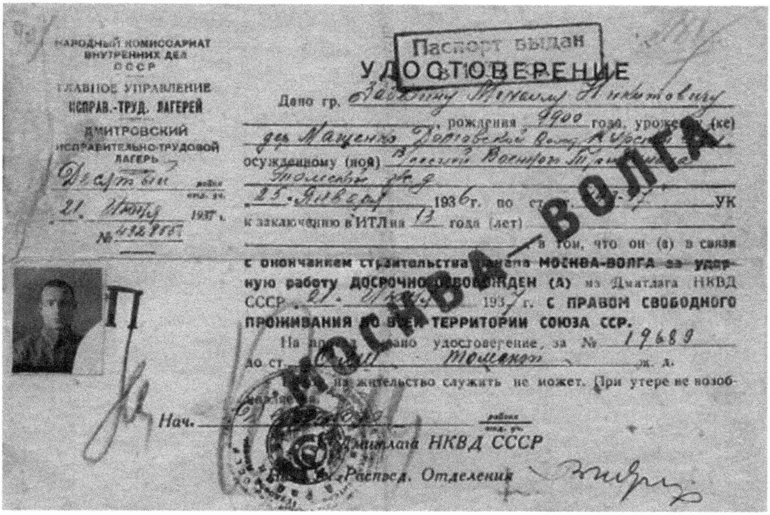
НАРОДНЫЙ КОМИССАРИАТ ВНУТРЕННИХ ДЕЛ СССР
ГЛАВНОЕ УПРАВЛЕНИЕ ИСПРАВ.-ТРУД. ЛАГЕРЕЙ
ДМИТРОВСКИЙ ИСПРАВИТЕЛЬНО-ТРУДОВОЙ ЛАГЕРЬ

21. Июня 1937 г.
№ 432955

Паспорт выдан

УДОСТОВЕРЕНИЕ

Дано гр. Зайцеву Михаилу Никитовичу, рождения 1900 года, уроженцу (ке) дер. Мащенко ... осужденному (ной) ... 25 Января 1936 г. по ст. ... УК к заключению в ИТЛ на 13 года (лет) ... в том, что он (а) в связи с окончанием строительства канала МОСКВА-ВОЛГА за ударную работу ДОСРОЧНО ОСВОБОЖДЕН (А) из Дмитлага НКВД СССР 21. Июня 1937 г. С ПРАВОМ СВОБОДНОГО ПРОЖИВАНИЯ ПО ВСЕЙ ТЕРРИТОРИИ СОЮЗА ССР.

На проезд выдано удостоверение, за № 19689 до ст. ... ж. д.

... на жительство служить не может. При утере не возобновляется.

Нач. ... Дмитлага НКВД СССР

... Распред. Отделения

МОСКВА–ВОЛГА

Figure 2.5 An official ID card issued to a Dmitlag inmate who received an early release because of his shock work on the Moscow–Volga Canal. The stamp at the top notes that the former inmate's passport has been given to him; he now has "the right to live anywhere in the territory of the USSR."[62]

mitigated the dark side of life in the camp. This cultural programming permitted some prisoners to create for themselves an identity beyond that of forced laborer and to develop artistic skills that might have otherwise been dormant or gone unrecognized. Other talented individuals who were trained as writers, artists, musicians, and architects likewise found both the opportunity to pursue their craft and to escape the brutally hard labor on the construction site. Such programming fell under the rubric of an initiative called *perekovka*, or re-forging, the name suggesting a belief that it was possible to remake social miscreants into productive Soviet citizens. Re-forging applied only to criminal inmates, since the authorities considered political prisoners to be beyond redemption. Re-forging occurred as the result of hard labor, as well as the skill an inmate might acquire on the job site. The idea of re-forging was reinforced by cultural activities that sought to increase the level of literacy among the criminal inmate population and to inculcate in them the values every good Soviet citizen should possess: patriotism, a solid work ethic, honesty, integrity, and faith in the cause.

These cultural products included newspapers, illustrated magazines, literary series, posters, musical compositions, all manner of art work, and theatrical performances. The theme of becoming a new Soviet citizen united all these products and underpinned the re-forging initiative.[63]

Re-forging would not have occurred, however, had it not been for Semyon Firin, who devised the initiative at the Belomor Camp that supplied the work force for construction of the Belomor Canal.[64] Firin, an NKVD officer who later assumed the leadership position at Dmitlag, believed that inmate participation in cultural events supplemented the re-forging that was supposedly happening on the work site. First at Belomor and then at Dmitlag, Firin gathered around him a group of writers and artists that comprised both free workers and Dmitlag inmates. This collaboration enabled talented members of both groups to practice their craft amid the drudgery and hardships of the Moscow Canal work site.

Firin was a career officer in the secret police, first in the OGPU and then the NKVD. In the early 1920s he served as an intelligence officer for the Soviet government in various European countries and then returned to the USSR, where he continued to advance his career until his arrest in April 1937 and subsequent execution. Yet his complex personality revealed both cruel and solicitous sides that seem incongruous given his career choice. As the official Moscow–Volga website currently characterizes him:

> Semyon Firin was a very complex and multi-faceted man. It is impossible to forget and forgive him for the deaths of thousands of prisoners who were killed during the construction of the White Sea Canal and the Moscow–Volga Canal on his direct orders, or from hunger, cold, disease, and overwork in the camps he controlled. But we must not forget his unwitting (or unpremeditated) attempt to rescue talented people under the umbrella of numerous KVOs (cultural-educational centers).[65] Of course work in a KVO differed markedly from working directly on the construction site – the staff, the inmates were often unescorted by guards and could live in rented apartments, and some even had their families come to them. And of course, Firin pursued not the "salvation" of these people, but rather used their intelligence with maximum efficiency for propaganda purposes within Dmitlag.[66]

Those whose talents he cultivated included the artist Gleb Kuhn, the writers Lidia Mogilianskaya, Mikhail Brilev and Nikolai Zhigul'sky (all executed in 1937), who actively participated in Dmitlag publications, including the 3–5-day per week camp newspaper *Perekovka/Re-Forging* (Figure 2.6), the literary journal *Na shturm trassy/Storming the Work Site* (Figure 2.7), and *Biblioteka Perekovki/The Library of Re-Forging*, three of the approximately 15 publications produced at Dmitlag. All of the publications featured editorial boards consisting of the chief NVKD officers at Dmitlag: Semyon Firin, Sergei Zhuk, and Lazar' Kogan. The composition of the editorial boards shifted depending on the publication and the theme; sometimes the editorial group included engineers, for example A. I. Fidman, who was an engineer and free worker, or artists such as Gleb Kuhn, a Dmitlag inmate.[67]

The legacy of their work remains in extant copies of all three publications and in artwork that Gleb Kuhn supplied for posters and print materials. Each of these publications deserves attention, but perhaps the most interesting of the three is the *Biblioteka Perekovki/Library of Re-forging* because of the diversity it displays in terms of genre and authorship. In fact, *The Library of Re-forging* encapsulates the many

первого мая встретим в чистом лагере!

ПЕРЕКОВКА

Москва-Волга

20 апреля 1935 г.

№ 28 (210)

ТРЕТИЙ ГОД ИЗДАНИЯ

ОМИССИЯ ПО ЛЬГОТАМ ЗАКАНЧИВАЕТ СВОЮ РАБОТУ

ТТЕСТАЦИИ ПРИНЯЛИ АКТИВНОЕ УЧАСТИЕ ВСЕ ЛАГЕРНИКИ ПЕРЕРВЫ

льник Гулаг'а т. Берман посетил Перерву

В ПОХОД ЗА ЧИСТЫЙ ЛАГЕРЬ

ДИМ ПО ЗАСЛУГАМ

НАВСТРЕЧУ ПРАЗДНИКУ

УЧАСТОК ОХОРАШИВАЕТСЯ

Figure 2.6 A section of the front page of an issue of the Dmitlag newspaper *Perekovka*.

Figure 2.7 The illustrated cover of the Dmitlag journal *Na shturm trassy*.

nationalities and experiences of inmates at Dmitlag and provides a rich cross-section not only of Firin's initiative to inculcate Soviet values through culture, but also of the wide swath of the Soviet population that found itself incarcerated at Dmitlag.

Creating Cultural Space in Dmitlag

Among the fascinating cultural artifacts produced in conjunction with the construction of the Moscow–Volga Canal is the KVO–NKVD-published *Library of Re-forging* (*Biblioteka Perekovki*, hereafter *BP*), a series of paperback pamphlets authored almost exclusively by Dmitlag camp inmates working on the canal. Extant copies of the series are housed in the library of GARF, the Memorial Library, and in the Russian State Library. While the collections are incomplete, they represent the largest known holdings of these extremely rare documents. In fact, at a recent auction 19 *BP* booklets were sold for 800,000 rubles (40,000 rubles per booklet), although the collection bore a preliminary auction estimate of 80,000–85,000 rubles.[68] As an official NKVD publication, this collection naturally glorifies the construction of the canal. What is surprising is that, despite its officially sanctioned status, *BP* also documents and valorizes the opinions and voices of the inmate-authors and thus provides an outlet for their self-expression.[69] As such, the collection provides the opportunity to analyze how some residents of Dmitlag exercised their artistic talents and to investigate which artistic genres they chose to portray their personal experiences on the Moscow–Volga project: short stories, poetry, biography, music, and the visual arts. These unique documents offer exceptional evidence of the regime's attempts to remake "socially dangerous elements" into new Soviet citizens, and inmates' efforts to manipulate the system as a way to take hold of a modicum of personal choice in a situation otherwise generally devoid of it.

An assessment of the *BP* series brings us face to face with traditionally ignored or understudied issues in the critical discourse on the Gulag. The current understanding of the Gulag experience relies primarily on memoirs and accounts written by political prisoners. *BP* authors, however, typically represented the criminal underclass, so their narratives expand and, to some extent, contradict the picture that the political eyewitnesses have left us. These "criminal" narratives may thus vie for dominance with the established dissident accounts of the Gulag as the only legitimate "histories" of that event, and stake out for the criminal prisoners a creative space that has heretofore been ignored.

The definition of "criminal inmates" requires explication since the rubric subsumed two categories of prisoners: the first category consisted of those who were considered "socially harmful elements" (*sotsvredelementy*) and were labeled as either petty or hardened criminals who had participated in genuinely criminal activities – theft, rape, and murder. This category also included those who were deemed marginal members of society – prostitutes, the homeless, recidivists and hooligans – whose presence, especially in urban areas, was regarded as damaging to the new Soviet society. Many of these prisoners were the so-called 35ers (*tridtsatipiatniki*). The issue of the 35ers deserves particular attention since the composition of this group evolved in parallel with the changing political situation in the USSR in the 1930s. N. Ryzhkova notes that the term 35ers "was how those who had been convicted and were serving a term under Article 35 of the Criminal Code were called. This Article called for 'removal from the RSFSR or from a particular area ... in conjunction with corrective labor.' It was applied, as a rule, to professional criminals and those closely connected to the criminal world. In other words, 35ers were those who had been convicted of criminal acts."[70] In his article from *Storming the Work Site* about the *Musical Library of Re-Forging* (*Muzikal'naia Biblioteka Perekovki*) the Soviet composer Dmitry Borisovich Kabalevsky stated that "The series of songs are written by the authors – canal-soldiers, the majority of whom were 35ers."[71] Hence the 35ers received their name from their conviction under Article 35 of the Criminal Code of the RSFSR (revised in 1934), which outlines the punishment for "socially harmful elements." According to Article 35, whether or not a defendant was considered socially dangerous, and more importantly what constituted socially dangerous behavior, were determinations left to the discretion of the judge, which speaks to the power of a judge or a troika (three-person judicial tribunal) to decide the fate of thousands of accused defendants.[72]

Western sources expand and modify this argument based on time periods: criminals sentenced according to Article 35 prior to 1932 tended to be "a narrowly defined cohort of recidivist or 'professional' criminals."[73] After 1932 officials began a more concerted effort to round up "dangerous elements," especially in urban areas, most likely following the guidelines set forth in Article 35. The cohorts of arrestees included vagrants, swindlers, beggars and prostitutes, as well as "professional" criminals.[74] By 1937, however, the mandate to rid the population of "socially harmful elements" accelerated, in part because of the fear among the highest echelons of Soviet power – namely Yezhov and Vyshinsky – that such people could threaten the very existence of Soviet power. As David Shearer notes, "Vyshinsky ordered a letter be sent to Yezhov declaring his support for renewing the campaigns against 'these 35-ers' (tridtsatipiatniki) [No italics in the original.]. This was an odd epithet, and very likely a reference to the original operational order against socially dangerous elements, number 00192, from May 1935."[75] Arguably, however, the epithet could just as easily hark back to the name given those prisoners sentenced under Article 35.

Significant to the discussion of the *BP* series is the fact that many of its authors *were* 35-ers.[76] As surprising at this may seem in retrospect, it was their "socially harmful" designation that marked these inmates as the prime targets for re-forging. These "socially harmful elements" were considered the best candidates for re-forging into "socially acceptable" individuals. Since debates over the Gulag sometimes adopt an approach that focuses solely on the fates and experiences of political prisoners, it is important to remember that, in their quest to promote re-forging, camp authorities sought out those prisoners who were the least politically sophisticated. Such prisoners were frequently illiterate and they were potentially the most ideologically malleable and motivated to improve their lot based on the benefits that the rhetoric of re-forging promised. The Cultural Education Departments were charged with combatting illiteracy in order to give these prisoners the ability not only to read, but also to write. While the ability to read does not necessarily lead to a career as a writer, literacy was the first step in the process of *creating* new writers in the camp who would document their experiences through their stories, poems, essays, and articles. The editors of Dmitlag publications would work with professional writers who were free employees at the camp to coach and mentor these budding authors.

The second category included prisoners who were convicted of seemingly minor criminal offenses – stealing grain or bread during a famine, for example – yet were sentenced under Article 58 and were therefore considered counterrevolutionaries.[77] Insofar as it is possible to identify the authors in the *BP* and to excavate their biographies, the majority of them seem to have been 35ers, complemented by a few non-inmate free employees who chose to join the construction effort and some political prisoners sentenced under Article 58 (Figure 2.8).

Within this context, the veracity, authorship, and creative originality of the *BP* raise the question of whether an NKVD-sponsored cultural

Figure 2.8 The poster reads: "Thirty-fivers! Become drivers – this is the path to a Soviet life!"[78]

project can withstand close scrutiny regarding the quality and artistry of each pamphlet. Were the series' authors and their presumed readers re-forged, as the dominant rhetorical phrase of the Moscow–Volga Canal suggested? Or does the issue of re-forging fade in prominence against the backdrop of inmate cultural production in general?

Before proceeding to answer these questions, it is useful to review the details, scant though they might be, concerning the series itself. T. Valentinov, in his article "The Pages of Life & Struggle" in the September 1936 issue of *Storming the Work Site*, took special pride in the series' productivity: "Who among us, the creative staff of Dmitlag, would have thought twenty months ago that in less than two years the *Biblioteka Perekovki* would have 50 books?"[79] Publication seems to have commenced in late 1934 and continued through 1936, the period of the most intense labor on the canal. The GARF holdings contain 17 of the purported 50 or so published issues. The circulation of each issue ranged from 10,000 for the first two to 3,200 for some releases to 1,000 for later issues.

Forthcoming issues, along with other camp publications, were initially advertised in the camp literary journal *Storming the Work Site*, typically on the inside back cover. According to the announcements, the booklets were released three times per month at a cost of 15 kopecks each, although it is questionable whether Dmitlag inmates would be willing to spend their hard-earned special wages on the *BP*.[80] As one advertisement for the *Biblioteka Perekovki* noted, "The stories and verses of canal-soldier authors are published in the library, as well as methodological and popular-scientific sketches."[81] Another issue of *Storming the Work Site* from February 1935 informs readers that the first two issues of the series had already appeared: Issue 1, authored by the head of Dmitlag Semyon Firin and entitled *The Moscow–Volga Canal*,[82] and issue 2, penned by the leader of the Maksim Gorky-Volzhsky agitational brigade Nikolai Zhigul'sky and entitled *Life is Being Constructed*. This announcement also promised forthcoming issues, one authored by V. Barabanov entitled *The Camp in 1935* and another, *Stories* by a certain Loginov. While Barabanov's booklet is pictured in an article about the *BP* in *Storming the Work Site*, there is no evidence that Loginov's work was published, unless it is one of the missing numbers in the series.[83]

The booklets themselves are all soft-bound and include illustrated covers that often symbolize their content. The covers were designed and executed by artists of the Dmitlag artists' studio, some of whom were free employees of the NKVD. Others, such as Konstantin Sobolevsky, were political prisoners.[84] The booklets typically run 50 pages or less, and each opens with a title page that features the author's name, the title of the work, and the notation "A Publication of the Cultural-Educational Sector of Dmitlag of the NKVD," followed by the date. The booklet's inside front cover bears the admonition: "Not for distribution beyond the camp." Introductions penned either by the authors themselves or by compilers of multi-author collections open most issues, while every booklet concludes with a table of contents and publication information that includes both the print run and the fact that the publications were produced by the typographical services of Dmitlag.

Of the 17 issues found in GARF, ten are the work of single authors, while the remaining seven were produced by multiple authors. The series was designed for consumption within and for Dmitlag. Because there never was any question of these works being circulated beyond the confines of the camp, why was so much effort generated to highlight inmate literary work? The answer is twofold: first, the *BP* was a propaganda tool that strove to inculcate in its presumed readers – the canal-soldiers of Dmitlag – the sense that their re-education was possible as long as they applied themselves to the task at hand, whether they were operating an excavator, shoveling out the "big dig" for the reservoir in Khlebnikovo, or performing any number of jobs integral to the construction of the Moscow–Volga Canal. Each item in the series ignores the facts that the labor in question was forced and could be lethal. Rather, the works emphasize that change is possible and desirable. As presented in these booklets, re-forging was a goal to be achieved, not just a process to be experienced.

BP also provided a forum in which inmates at Dmitlag, who might otherwise be silent, were afforded a modest opportunity to let their voices be heard. Their visual, literary, and musical production created a space of expression for those willing to accept the rules according to which they needed to function. The rhetoric we encounter in many of the *BP* works is evocative of the same tropes found in official pronouncements outside the camp; educators in the KVOs and camp administrators routinely heard and read these pronouncements in the Soviet press and official statements broadcast to the entire Soviet population. These slogans, themes, and phrasings were routinely proffered and repeated by the agitation brigades that performed in each of the canal's 14 sectors and in the Cultural Education branch for each. As a result the individual works of *BP* produce a mixed impression, depending on how faithfully an author adhered to official rhetoric or how subtly s/he deviated from the norm.

In Issue 27, *Canal Army Posters*, for example, the more than 20 artists who produced propaganda posters adhered to the operative political rhetoric and artistic sensibilities of the time. Slogans and captions such as "A Stakhanovite Experience for Everyone," "New Times/New People," "Stop! Have you given 150 percent today?," or "35-ers! Be drivers – this is the path to a Soviet life!" generally conform in style, tone, and substance to the kinds of agitprop posters found outside the camp (Figure 2.8). The obvious difference, however, is that the messages are targeted at Dmitlag inmates and the construction context in which they were laboring. Likewise, because many Dmitlag prisoners were illiterate or semi-literate these visual images were more accessible and efficient in reinforcing the camp administration's goals and concerns. Especially evocative is the image of 35-ers literally driving themselves into a different physical space beyond the confines of Dmitlag – a new Soviet life through their work.[85]

The posters also reflected broader themes that prevailed in Soviet society as a whole: the important and equal role that women were supposed to play in the Soviet Union, the contributions of various nationalities (other than Russians) to the construction of the USSR, and the battle with social ills such as alcoholism and loitering on the job. Posters in the collection depict women serving as drivers, national minorities exhorting their countrymen – in languages other than Russian – to work honestly and assiduously, and numerical figures touting the (over) fulfillment of the plan and work quotas. One poster maps out the route of the Moscow–Volga Canal and duplicates on paper that which was actually being inscribed into the landscape. Comic representation also figured into the mix with a series of posters entitled "A Window on Re-Forging" that illustrated the correct and incorrect way to be re-forged, thereby underscoring appropriate social comportment.

Artistically, the posters depict healthy, strong workers, often against realistic backdrops of construction sites. Some posters are more schematic, with charts and editorial comments included in the space of the poster. Bold lettering draws attention to the message, and light/dark shading is used to produce a three-dimensional effect. It is difficult to detect the original colors of the posters based on their reproduction in this *BP* issue. Typically, workers depicted on the posters cast their gaze outward, off the two-dimensional plane of the poster, as if gazing into the future. The artists who drew the posters were free workers in the Dmitlag artists' studio or were culled from the ranks of political and criminal prisoners. While other issues in the *BP* collection contain drawings and photographs, Issue 27 is the only booklet dedicated completely to visual art.

Yet creating visual artistic space was not the only goal of the *Biblioteka Perekovki.* The *BP* offered an opportunity to hone one's writing skills by composing documentary accounts of the exploits of model workers or the legitimately remarkable construction achievements that occurred during the waterway's construction. Issue 14, *The Conquered River Sestra: Episodes from the History of the Collectives and Construction of the Sestra River Sector of the MVC*; issue 20, *A Night on the "Big Dig"* (Figure 2.9); and issue 34, *The Stakhanovite Excavator. Stories from the Participants of the Two All-Union Records of Excavator No. 30* recount particularly noteworthy feats of construction on the Moscow Canal.

Figure 2.9 The cover of the *Biblioteka Perekovki* issue No. 20 *Night on the Big Dig.*

Each issue is written in clear, prosaic language in a tone reminiscent of widely circulated newspaper articles from the Soviet press that touted industrial achievements or engineering feats, or characterized the USSR's industrialization efforts as a battle against all manner of forces. In the case of the Moscow Canal, as with the Belomor Canal, one of the chief enemies of the construction project was nature itself. Thus the title *The Conquered River Sestra* deploys the metaphor of capturing in battle or taking prisoner the River Sestra through the use of the past passive participle from the archaic verb *polonit'*. *A Night on the "Big Dig"* evokes a sense of mystery as to what will occur during a night on this massive excavation, emphasizing that work on the canal never stopped even in the darkness. The single adjective deep (*glubokii*) would be instantly recognizable to the denizens of Dmitlag since that was the common epithet ascribed to this location on the waterway. Of course, *The Stakhanovite Excavator* immediately revealed the topic of its narrative and called to mind every image connected with being a Stakhanovite, i.e. a worker who routinely over-fulfilled work norms and exemplified the ideal Soviet worker. These issues include photographs that provide visual proof of the ability of the canal-soldiers to imprison the River Sestra by constructing the channel of the canal *over* the river, which then flowed in a perpendicular direction *under* the canal; to document the work carried out throughout the night on the "big dig"; and to celebrate the excavator itself and its operator.

In fairness to the Dmitlag inmates featured in these narratives, the engineering and construction feats were indeed remarkable, especially when we consider the conditions under which the canal soldiers were laboring and the equipment with which they had to work: the bulk of the early construction work on the Moscow Canal was carried out with wheelbarrows, shovels, horse-drawn carts, and pickaxes. While there were a few excavators (some imported from the US) on site in 1934, only in 1935 did the type of excavator that graces the cover of *The Stakhanovite Excavator* appear on work sites. The featured excavator, produced domestically in the city of Kovrov – a great source of pride given its domestic pedigree – was used most notably in Khlebnikovo, and it is the topic of the narratives in *A Night on the "Big Dig."* Not until summer 1936 did a critical mass of excavators – around 200 – significantly improve the movement of large quantities of earth. These documentary booklets, more journalistic than belles-lettristic in tone, not only provided readers with positive accounts of the construction achievements on the Moscow Canal, but also afforded their authors the opportunity to create some of the few eyewitness accounts that we have of these moments on the building site. As such, they permit more voices of Dmitlag's inmates to be heard, even so long after the events occurred. The creation of this metaphorical and literary space through which Dmitlag writers created the landscape of the Moscow–Volga project on the page highlights a unique aspect of camp life in the 1930s – the notion that cultural production, like labor, serves to re-shape attitudes and behaviors. Just as outside the camp Soviet citizens received countless messages through newspapers, films, and literary works informing them how to be model citizens, Dmitlag inmates received a similar message, thereby creating a liminal space where events within and outside the camp met. Outside the Gulag, citizens heard songs that enjoined them to take pride in the advances the Soviet Union was making, and this trend was paralleled in Dmitlag.

A less construction-centric and more propagandistic tone characterizes issue 36, *Music of the Work Site*, which presumably was conceived of as the first of two collections of musical compositions written about and for the construction of the Moscow–Volga Canal.[86] While those unfamiliar with the history of the Gulag might find it strange that music and forced labor co-existed, we need only remember photographs from the Moscow and Belomor Canal sites that showed inmate musicians performing on the floor of a lock under construction while other forced laborers carried on with their tasks (Figure 2.10).

We see this also in frames from the *Moscow–Volga* film, in which laborers march to the work site in step with a brass band. The use of music as a tool for regulating the rhythm of work on the canal echoed the staged musical productions and songs that agitation brigades performed along the Moscow Canal construction site. Issue 36 (Figure 2.11) is one compendium of compositions produced in the companion *BP* project – *The Musical Library of Re-forging (MBP)* – of a two-volume set. As Aleksandra Orlova notes:

> Two volumes of songs with the title *Re-forging. Music of the Work Site*, edited by D. D. Shostakovich (!) and stamped with the warning that this publication was forbidden to be widely distributed, were housed in the library of my late husband

Figure 2.10 A brass band on the construction site of a lock. Musical accompaniments on the work site were used supposedly to increase the tempo of the work as if in harmony with the music.[87]

> G. P. Orlov. One of the authors of *Re-forging* gifted G. P. Orlov these collections.[88]

Of course, most startling is Orlova's assertion that the two volumes of *Music of the Work Site*, of which Issue 36 is one, were edited by Dmitry Shostakovich. No record of Shostakovich's participation in this project has been found, but this does not necessarily mean that he did not participate. Indeed, if Shostakovich served as an editor, then his contribution to *The Musical Library of Re-forging* would bestow upon it a certain gravitas and legitimacy that the Dmitlag bosses could only have welcomed.

The existence of this parallel program is confirmed by the composer Kabalevsky in his aforementioned article in *Storming the Work Site* and in an article that appeared in the journal *Neva* in 2003 by N. Ryzhkova entitled "Music from the Gulag: The Musical Library of 'Re-Forging'."[89] Neither Kabalevsky nor Ryzhkova allude to Shostakovich's purported editorship of this series. In regard to *Music of the Work Site* Ryzhkova writes:

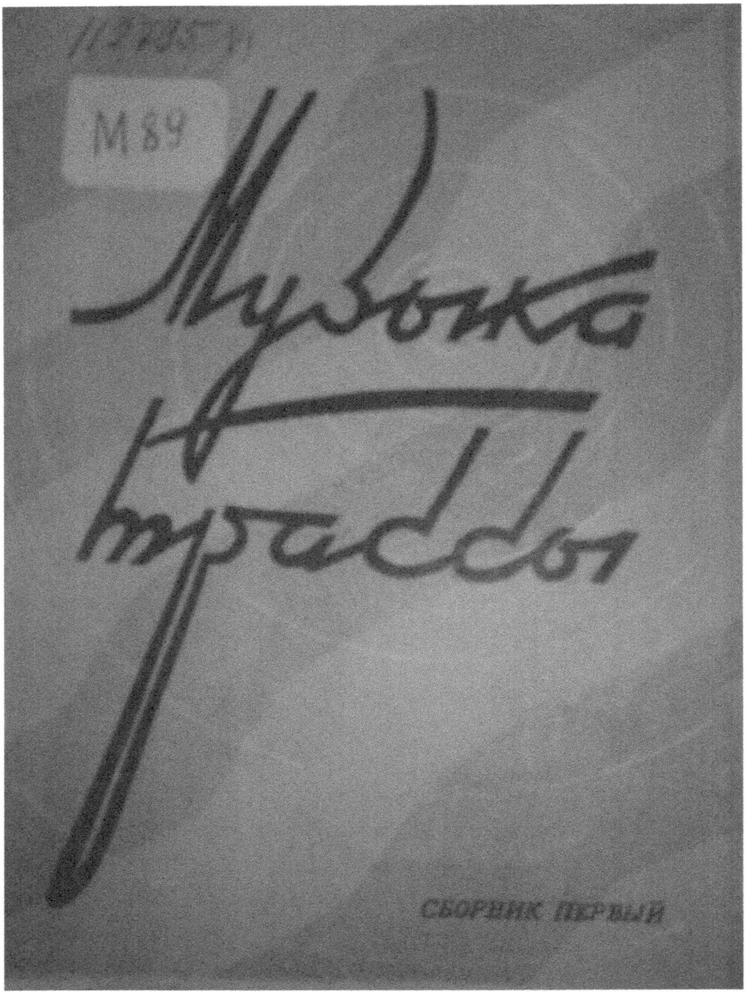

Figure 2.11 Cover of the booklet *Music of the Work Site*, Collection 1.

A pile of thin booklets with musical notes is in front of me. These are the words and music for songs published by Muzgizom in 1936 – small, pocket-sized format, coarse, yellowish paper. At first glance they are nothing special – a typical publication of songs from that time of which there were many . . . In a word just musical notes. Nothing special except for one thing: On the cover

> next to Muzgizom, one other organization is noted, the one that produced [the booklets]: the cultural-educational section of Dmitlag, NKVD USSR. And the title of the entire series of booklets with musical notes is *The Library of Re-forging*.[90]

Ryzhkova does not disclose how she discovered this collection, although she notes that it is available in the archives. She proceeds to recap a brief history of the construction of the Moscow–Volga Canal and discusses the compositions from both musical and historical viewpoints. Ryzhkova's argument casts the compositions of the *MBP* in a sympathetic light, and she offers detailed readings of some of the songs that she groups thematically as songs of "labor (*trudovye*)," lyrical works that to a large degree reflect the true feelings of the canal soldiers,[91] and "songs of dreams." They are about the completion of the canal, about the time when ships would sail along it and Moscow would become the port of five seas.[92] Ryzhkova's comments reveal that she understands how creating music "on command" (*po zakazu*) requires much from those who participated in this aspect of re-forging. As she concludes, "In the lists of those who were executed, published in the *Martirolog* there are no names of the authors of the songs of re-forging. Apparently they earned the right to survive because of their creative work."[93] We know, however, that this typically was not the case because no amount of creativity could save someone if that person was considered an enemy of the state; just because their names were not published in the *Martirolog* does not mean they did not perish. Rather, the details of their possible deaths remain a mystery.

In his article, Kabalevsky examines the musical value of the compositions, which include songs and instrumental music for the balalaika, piano and small orchestral ensembles. As he notes:

> The series *The Musical Library of Re-Forging* is an excellent example of the level of musical activity in the camp. With the exception of M. Chernyak and A. Rozanov, all the authors not only had no special musical training, but the majority also could not do musical notation themselves. Among them there had to be many who never thought about creative work. However, *The Musical Library of Re-Forging* is interesting not only from the standpoint of showing how many talented people there were among the camp

> inmates. Many compositions in this series are complete and interesting works that often approach the level of professional art.[94]

The composer's comments highlight three important points regarding the compositions in the *MBP* series. First, the professional composers Rozanov (an esteemed musicologist incarcerated at Dmitlag) and Chernyak (who was a music "inspector" for the KVO)[95] composed music for the series and likely supervised the composition of other pieces, especially given that some of the inmate composers could not notate the music themselves. Perhaps this was one of Chernyak's responsibilities as a KVO music inspector: to ensure that whatever music was produced was playable, sing-able, and truly musical. This offers proof that the process of re-forging was tightly controlled and managed. Second, veteran Dmitlag poets such as Kalent'ev, Zhigul'sky, Mogilianskaya, and other canal-soldiers supplied the lyrics to the songs. This suggests that there was a collaborative enterprise between composers and lyricists that likely also provided an organizing principle for the work and helped ensure the compatibility of the music with the lyrics – as in other musical collaborations, the creative process was not conducted in isolation. Third, Kabalevsky implies that without the opportunity the *MBP* provided, the latent talent of certain inmates would have gone undetected and undeveloped. His comments suggest that the cultivation of inmates' musical talent was expected to acculturate and reform these "socially harmful elements."

A survey of the compositions in *Music of the Work Site* reveals that most of them had already appeared on the pages of *Storming the Work Site* as individual submissions, included as examples within articles devoted to music on the canal or as entries in a music contest for canal soldiers, or else had been published as separate issues in the *MBP*. Chernyak, who wrote the introduction for *Music of the Work Site*, likely collected these individual pieces from the *MBP* and combined many of them into this one work that was slated to be the first of two collections. The instrumental pieces and songs fall into two tidy categories based on their titles and content: construction themes and lyrical tributes to nature or personal fate (Figure 2.12).

Within the first category we find compositions such as: *March of the Concrete Workers, Thirty-fivers, Stakhanovite March, March of the Navvies,*[96]

Figure 2.12 The song "My Canal," lyrics by N. Zhigul'sky and music by A. Rozanov.[97]

Victorious Canal March, and *To the Builder.* The march genre, typified by regulated tempos to which inmates could stride in step, enthusiastic or solemn melodies, and energizing rhythms, suits the constituency for whom it was written: the Dmitlag inmates were canal soldiers waging a battle against nature and themselves to build the Moscow–Volga Canal, and they were marched to and from their construction sites in orderly formations. Those to whom the marches are dedicated likewise figure prominently in rhetoric about the canal. Concrete workers, vital to the production of one of the most important construction materials on the project, merit their own composition, as do Stakhanovites, and diggers, without whom production on the building site would likely cease. Listeners typically associate marches with military victories and parades, so it is not surprising that there should be a march dedicated to victory in the construction of the Moscow Canal, the ultimate prize in the battle against nature and "socially harmful elements." In the larger context military metaphors permeated the rhetoric used to describe Soviet construction, collectivization and de-kulakization. "War" was being waged on "fronts" against internal and external enemies, so the widespread deployment of the march genre in these Dmitlag musical compositions dovetails completely with the slogans outside the camp. Here too the 35-ers figure prominently as the group most likely to be re-forged. Like the other celebrated heroes of labor – concrete workers, diggers, Stakhanovites (groups to which they might also belong) – the 35-ers claimed pride of place within the Dmitlag hierarchy.

Songs about nature and lyrical contemplation carry equal importance within *Music of the Work Site*. *Encounter with a Canal Soldierette*, a piece without lyrics, suggests that romance with a political twist was possible within the confines of Dmitlag. Other instrumental songs, *Melody for the Balalaika* and *Melody for the Bayan* (the second composed by 35-er V. Sarancha), rely on familiar folk instruments to create a mood and to situate the music within a tradition likely familiar to and preferred by many inmates. *Spring*, *Evening* and *Fall*, all with lyrics authored by V. Kalent'ev, simultaneously evoke the beauty of the seasons interspersed with references to the Moscow Canal and its place within the poet's world. For example, in *Spring* Kalent'ev conveys a sense of optimism prompted by the emergence of spring, which might seem incongruous with his surroundings, given the harshness, death and hunger that constituted camp life for most prisoners. As he writes:

Once again spring, invigorating and teasing,
Encircles my noggin and splashes about in my chest.
I will traverse the earth from end to end,
My whole great life is before me.

This great life is in the full swing of stormy construction,
And it seethes in a cauldron of hot days
In the remote steppes, in the factories and plants
Of my great, wise homeland.

Today the sun rises brighter for me than for all the rest,
And my crazy heart is crowded in my chest,
All because I am needed for something,
And my whole great life is before me.[98]

The references to factories and construction sites optimistically root the words in the reality of Soviet life inside and outside the Gulag. Likewise, the cyclical ebullience of spring and the fresh start it promises, metaphorically and in reality, imbue the lyrics with a sense of hope that is emphasized by the line "My whole big life is before me." The lyrics reveal a personalized message woven into the fabric of praise for the Motherland (*Rodina*) and the writer's sense that he is needed (*goden*). This combination works because Kalent'ev de-emphasizes many of the rhetorical structures common in the press and on posters. Instead, he chooses to personalize his feelings while situating them in the larger context of the life of the country: his life, like his country, is big and destined for great achievements in the future. Indeed, here is a voice that we would never expect to hear from Dmitlag, yet it echoes clearly, if subtly, in the lyrics.

BP afforded those canal soldiers willing, chosen, or forced to participate in it an opportunity to express themselves with voices, be they musical, visual, or journalistic, and in ways that hard labor could not and did not. Perhaps this opportunity is nowhere more evident than in the issues of *BP* devoted to poetry and prose. The authors of these booklets represented the diversity of the camp population, which meant that they also represented the diversity of the USSR. The women and national minorities who contributed to the series gave voice to groups that were encouraged or coerced to build the new Soviet state. The following discussion highlights a few of these works to illustrate how some Dmitlag inhabitants gained their voices.[99]

Two issues within the *BP* collection, numbers 4 and 5 from 1935, feature the work of national minorities. The title of issue 4, printed in Latin letters, is *Kanal askari* (*Canal soldier* in the Uzbek/Tatar/Kazakh languages), with the Russian subtitle *A Collection of Stories of National Minority Prisoners* (Figure 2.13), while Issue 5 is titled *Records: Poetry of National Minority Prisoners*. Of the seven selections featured in issue 4, the lone sketch (*ocherk*) was written in Uzbek, two stories (*rasskazy*) were written in Kazakh, and four stories were written in Tatar. All were translated for this issue into Russian by an unknown translator, thereby formalizing the dominant language in the USSR, Russian. It is possible to assume that the Uzbek, Tatar, and Kazakh authors of issues 4 and 5 knew Russian to some extent, but having their works translated into Russian might have limited the accessibility of the booklets to non-native Russian speakers, especially those who feature in these stories. Each narrative relates the tale of an ethnic Uzbek, Kazakh, or Tatar who

Figure 2.13 Cover of Issue 4 of the *Biblioteka Perekovki*, *Kanal askari*. Note the cotton bolls that signify the production of Central Asian cotton.

negotiates life on the Moscow Canal site or who regales his listeners with a tale of bygone days. All the stories share the common theme of the national minority prisoner's ability to accommodate the peculiarities of his national character to the new world of Soviet power, as embodied in the Moscow Canal project.

Tea Room on the Istra, for example, relates how a tea room (commonplace in Central Asia) was established on the Istra construction site to the delight of the Uzbek workers stationed there. *Battal's Mother*, whose narrative structure resembles that of a fairy tale, reveals how the lazy ne'er-do-well Battal is reshaped into a productive member of his brigade, because of the scolding and encouragement of his mother, who carries a level of authority of which canal supervisors can only dream. She is the quintessential Soviet "Hero-Mother" who contributes to the growth of the USSR through the birth and upbringing of her children. As the narrator says, "This is the story of the ne'er-do-well Battal and his mother, about that same Battal who now considers it beneath him to give less than 105 percent."[100] In *The End of the Hunt* the main character, the Kazakh Rashid, feels more comfortable around horses than around people. Throughout the story the narrator downplays Rashid's seemingly anti-social behavior by complimenting his keen horse sense.

The story *Abdullah's Heels* explores the theme of the Golden Rule: Abdullah informs on the narrator, who supposedly stole rice, only to find himself in the same camp with the narrator. The story concludes with the narrator revealing that Abdullah won a "shock worker's pin," to which he adds, without any apparent hint of irony: "Honest to gosh, I'm happy for him!"[101]

Issue 5, *Records: Poetry of National Minority Prisoners*, features poems translated into Russian from Uzbek, Bashkir, Tatar, and Kazakh. The title page for each author is embellished with an illustration that visually links folk motifs from the author's homeland to an image depicting labor on the waterway. Like the prose works, the poems assembled here share certain themes that resonate throughout the *BP*. Titles such as *Records*, *We Are Canal Soldiers*, *We Are Building Life*, and *The Old and the New* describe labor achievements, the significance of the Moscow–Volga Canal to the USSR, and the pride of accomplishment shared among national minority inmates. Lines such as "My verses – cubes of earth – / are creating the greatness of the Canal" typify the tone and language of the poems. Structurally, most of the poems contain rhymed stanzas with standard meters. A few, however, defy that canon and use repetition, of a select word or phrase, in visually and rhythmically non-standard stanzas. For example, in the poem *People and Concrete*, each stanza is constructed as follows:

> Life is changing the geography of the country:
> By the stagnant waters, on the quagmire of the swamps
> Fruit is ripening.[102]

Each stanza begins with a variation of the first line: something changes the geography of the country, be it life, people, iron, or cement. This verse speaks to the creation of a new space that will provide abundance while overcoming stagnation and swamps, allusions to life before Soviet power. Perhaps the poem that best captures the style and summarizes the tone of the booklet is *We are Canal Soldiers*:

> We are the shock troops of the canal.
> We are canal soldiers,
> We are the creators and children of the Canal.
> We are canal soldiers.

We arrived from the East
And we won't leave for the East,
Without finishing our project.
We are canal soldiers.

I'm an Uzbek, you're a Georgian,
And our neighbor is an Armenian,
We are canal soldiers.
And the canal is ours alone.[103]

As this last stanza emphasizes, the inmate workforce on the Moscow–Volga was multi-national and (if we are to believe the author's words) proud of that fact. This notion was mirrored in official rhetoric outside the Gulag, which called for the friendship of nations. Just as the world outside the camps was being Sovietized, so too was the world within them.

Not to be outdone by national minorities, female Dmitlag inmates also contributed to the literary production in the *BP*. A few issues, such as numbers 9 and 10, both published in 1935, provided women with the opportunity to showcase their talent. Issue 9, entitled *Two Canals: Poems*, is the work of the poet Lidia Mogilianskaya, who published prodigiously in most of the major Dmitlag publications and also contributed the issue *Female Inmate-Stakhanovites* (Figure 2.14). According to her biographical card in the NKVD catalogue at GARF, Mogilianskaya, an ethnic Ukrainian, was sentenced to the Gulag in 1929 under Article 58–8, II for a term of ten years. At some point she was transferred to the Belomor Camp, where she served until her release in June 1933. According to her official file, at Belomor she worked as a typist, but before that had labored in an excavation brigade. Upon her release, she became an "inspector" of the KVO at Dmitlag, where she began her employment in October 1934.[104] She held this position until she was arrested in May 1937. Given her active profile in the literary life of Dmitlag under the tutelage of Semyon Firin, she was arrested as part of the purported terrorist "Firin group" and executed in June 1937.[105]

Mogilianskaya's biography is important here because, unlike many of the other *BP* authors, she was not a 35-er, but rather had originally been convicted under Article 58 as a "counterrevolutionary." As such she was not among the groups considered most re-forgeable, yet her literary

Figure 2.14 Cover of one of Lidia Mogilianskaya's contributions to the *Biblioteka Perekovki*, *Female Inmate-Stakhanovites*, Issue ?, 1936.

production suggests that she took advantage of the opportunities provided to her when she was granted an early release from her sentence. She had also worked with Firin on the Belomor Canal (from which she was granted an early release thanks to her labor), so her transfer to the Moscow Canal project was a logical continuation of her activities.

Her contribution *Two Canals: Poems* comprises three sections. The first contains poems written in honor of the Belomor Canal; the second features poems devoted to the Moscow Canal; and the third includes poems written in Ukrainian about the canal projects.[106] Mogilianskaya's poetry focuses on the themes we would expect: the construction feats of the two canals, the heroism of the laborers on the canals, and lyric poems that link the four seasons with the tempo of construction. Stylistically the poems range from the *Belomor Sonnets*, each of which is dedicated to a well-known site on the Belomor Canal, to poems structured in four-line stanzas with regular meter and end rhyme. Some poems are single stanzas with 10–15 lines; others mix stanza length and rhyme scheme. Her poems often refer to friends and colleagues (one is dedicated to the Moscow Canal's chief artist Gleb Kuhn). She thus situates her oeuvre in a personal, self-referential framework, as these closing lines from the poem to Gleb Kuhn, entitled *To the Artist*, illustrate:

> And this is why we talk about him
> In a language understandable to all,
> I – in the assonance of obedient rhythms,
> You – in the contrast of black and white dots.[107]

That Mogilianskaya managed to secure a position at Dmitlag reveals her facility in taking advantage of a situation, as well as her relationship with Firin. Yet to dismiss her work because of that neglects the fact that she was able to create a literary and quotidian space for herself and to give a woman's voice to the Moscow Canal project. She perceived herself not as a victim, but rather as a contributor to the modernization of the Soviet Union. She created a personalized poetic and physical space that provided employment as an ex-prisoner, but she did so at the expense of the many inmates at Dmitlag who were neither privileged nor able to enjoy a less exhausting and demeaning existence in the camp. Unlike the camp inmates, Mogilianskaya lived in an apartment in Dmitrov proper, a situation that afforded her privacy and normalcy in an environment marked by extreme hardship and a lack of personal space.

In addition to Mogilianskaya, other women embraced the call to write, and their work is found in issue 10, *Canal Soldierette* (Figure 2.15).[108] In this collection ten authors contributed prose stories and poems that cover a diverse range of topics, from the requisite construction themes

Figure 2.15 Cover of Issue 10 in the *Biblioteka Perekovki*, *Kanal Soldierette.*

(reminiscences of Belomorstroi, concrete, the canal, cars, drivers, building a new life through labor, and so on) to more personal themes such as poems about friends, lovers and children. Perhaps one of the most poignant pieces in this collection is the poem by Polya Chetverikova, entitled *Little Son* and translated from the Roma language into Russian:

My little son is growing up
On the canal day and night,
He will be an honest worker.

He will be like all of you people – a person,
He'll never steal,
He'll forget the nomadic life.

It's not for nothing we are digging the canal –
We'll build a kolkhoz for the gypsies,
We'll make a hero out of my son.[109]

Presumably the poet is raising her son while working on the Moscow–Volga Canal, and likely has been imprisoned because of her nationality. The language is simple and comprehensible, the message is direct and the sub-text clear: the concern of the mother for the success of her son remains regardless of the circumstances in which he will be formed. Likewise, there is the implicit message of control: after a collective farm is built for the gypsies, they will be contained and no longer free to pursue a nomadic lifestyle. Important to the author is not so much the method, but the result, which seems to provoke pride and relief in the worried mother. Yet this pride is questionable given the fate that awaits the Roma, who are no longer free to be itinerant travelers valuing and exercising freedom of movement. The cover of this collection projects the most positive and optimistic message: a woman in close-up, a red head scarf covering her hair brushed back by the wind, is driving a truck, a symbol of the mechanized future and of her ability to occupy a responsible position on the construction site. She looks straight ahead with clear, bright, wide-open eyes. Her face shows a confident smile, and the viewer gets the impression that this woman is driving optimistically straight off the page, into the future beyond Dmitlag and into Soviet society, thereby creating a new space that defines what the future should be.

The theme of the future appears throughout the poetry and prose in the other seven issues of *Biblioteka Perekovki*. Authors whose work frequently appeared in *Storming the Work Site*, such as Zhigul'sky, Brilev, and Kalent'ev, contributed booklets to the series, while lesser known writers such as Puzirev and Mol'kov contributed poetry collections as well. Stylistically, each author exhibits his own sensibility and thematic emphasis, although it is possible to generalize that each writer devoted a good portion of his composition to the themes of labor on the canal, a new life, the importance of the Moscow Canal as a historical event, and the re-forging that he witnessed in Dmitlag. Less dominant, but no less present, are poems that specifically speak to personal dreams, feelings, and experiences, the kind of topics that we might not expect to find in the *BP*. These are often the most interesting works, creating for their authors a personal space and an identity on which camp life could not impinge.

In his booklet, *Spring*, Anatoly Mol'kov (Figure 2.16) divides his compositions into four thematic rubrics: *My Building Site*, *Spring*, *Poems About a Girl*, and *Dmitrov*. The most fascinating part of the collection is the series of poems about a young woman, never named, but clearly someone to whom Mol'kov devotes a great deal of thought. For example, the first poem of the series of five is untitled and begins with the lines:

Figure 2.16 Portrait of author Anatoly Mol'kov, Dmitlag inmate and poet. From the opening pages of his *Biblioteka Perekovki* contribution *Spring*, Issue 24.

It is indeed a milk cap mushroom, large and good-looking,
The fog having spread along the grass,
Dawn with a diamond ray has burned off
The sleepy twilight on the bushes.[110]

As the poem unfolds, the poet reveals that he is dreaming of his beloved, who is far away, and only the realness of the dream sustains him as he completes his work quota for the day. In *White Verses about a Black Girl* (a wordplay on the Russian term for blank verse, "white verses" (*belye stikhi*)), Mol'kov revisits the absence of a beloved woman, who again seems real only in a dream.[111] The dream descriptions are filled with reminiscences of how his beloved looks, walks, and dresses. Yet remembering his beloved does not weaken the poet, but rather strengthens his resolve to survive and work. As he writes:

And it becomes easier for me because of that,
And I notice that my mind becomes fresh,

That my muscles are hard and strong,
I want to live, work, and sing.[112]

Mol'kov's *Unsent Letter* attempts to mitigate the distance between the lovers through recollections of their morning meetings. The poet visualizes his sweetheart attending classes and intently absorbing lectures on voyages of the past. Indeed, these descriptions of historical sea voyages metaphorically join the poet and his beloved, for as she learns to "sail" through history, he builds the canal on which she can in reality sail to Moscow. Mol'kov closes the poem with the following stanzas:

You are far away. Laid down between us
Along the emerald forested plains are
Miles of humming dark blue rails,
Miles of humming telegraph lines.

Only my heart beats joyfully:
We both are joined by the same task.
You've buried your head in your studies,
In the pages of wise, heavy books.

And the guys and I, just like the banner,
Having belted out a happy, energetic song,
Are digging, preparing the way for the steamship,
That will bring you to Moscow.[113]

Yet this is an unsent letter, so the feelings the poem conveys remain known only to the poet, which means the distance between the two lovers remains despite the author's hopes to the contrary. Through the poem the author has been able to traverse space and time, but only on the page.

Feelings of separation and yearning imbue the poem *To My Beloved*. Mol'kov deploys a variety of images from nature to create the scene in which the lovers were last together, from the mossy smell of mushrooms to the blue hills. He urges his beloved to remember him whenever she looks at these landscapes. He imagines seeing her eyebrows and scarf before his eyes. The separation, however, is not all for naught, since the poet notes that:

In the warm blue sky
Spring makes one giddy with jasmine dust,
And I will arrive as a different, good,
Useful, new person.

And double joy furtively
Shines from the depths of your eyes.
In my good country it is sweet
To bloom, work and love.[114]

Although Mol'kov manages to acknowledge the greatness of a country where he can work and fall in love, two rather quotidian activities, the predominant image in these stanzas is the beauty surrounding the couple, which is even more meaningful because the author will return to her a changed, better man. There are no direct references to labor or the camp. What is important to the poet is rather the reaction of his beloved to his return. These highly personal emotions and images are startling considering Mol'kov's actual surroundings, and emphasize his ability to create for himself a highly personal space in the midst of a labor camp that afforded little, if any, privacy or time for quiet contemplation.

Mol'kov's final poem in this series, *To a Woman*, concludes this section on a note of optimism and shared success. Throughout the poem, the woman to whom it is addressed is praised for her ability to attain any profession she chooses due to her own skills. The sub-text here is that because she lives in the Soviet Union she is able to achieve whatever she desires because the system permits her to. She is lauded for her adaptability and resourcefulness. Indeed, she is able to overcome any obstacle, even her separation from her beloved, for as the last stanza reveals:

And you with a happy jolly look
Swim in the blue.
And you walk next to me
A woman. A human being.[115]

The use of the informal personal pronoun *ty* throughout all the poems, the rich, vivid descriptions of shared places, and the dreams of future meetings combine to produce verses that are highly personal and lyrical and devoid of many propagandistic rhetorical phrases. When the poet alludes either to his work on the canal or his incarceration, he does so in a nuanced way that a careless reader could miss. These poems emphasize the personal over the collective. As such they reveal a voice that maintains hope in spite of uncertainty, love in spite of pain.

As this discussion makes clear, the obvious function of *Biblioteka Perekovki* was to generate propaganda demonstrating that the stated goals of re-forging were being achieved at Dmitlag, if not at other sites within the Gulag. Dmitlag, however, was special because its director, Semyon Firin, propelled re-forging into the public eye as a way to call attention to his own initiative and enthusiasm. If this was a system of reeducating and re-forging "socially harmful elements" into solid Soviet citizens, then culture in the form of music, the visual arts and literature were part and parcel of this program. In Firin's system it could not be otherwise, especially because this veneer of culture created an illusion that masked and ignored the difficult and life-threatening work inherent in the forced labor project to build the Moscow Canal.

When we examine the circulation data for *Biblioteka Perekovki* we see that the numbers are minuscule in relation to the number of inmates at any given time at Dmitlag. Recall that Dmitlag was the largest camp in the Gulag system. Publication runs of 3,200, 3,700 or even 10,000 would never begin to put the booklets in the hands of every prisoner. It is safe to assume that not every canal soldier would want a copy or even be literate enough to read it (in spite of the camp's literacy programs). So at whom were these publications targeted?

We may posit three populations for which the *Biblioteka Perekovki* served a purpose. Of course, Firin himself would benefit from their publication because he could provide tangible proof that re-forging was a viable system through which camp enlightenment could be organized. He need only pull out a recent issue to show how education in the KVO was proceeding apace. The series offered concrete proof that Dmitlag was actively engaged in reshaping illiterate, unskilled criminals into literate, skilled Soviet citizens. No matter the level of literacy or skill; the point was general appearances, not statistical details.

To aid Firin in this task the Cultural Education Sections were likely recipients of copies of *Biblioteka Perekovki*. The booklets served two important educational functions: 1) they exemplified what was possible if prisoners gave themselves over to being re-forged, and 2) the booklets could be used as reading primers because of the straightforward language and seemingly uncomplicated themes and structure of many of the works. To this end, issues of *Biblioteka Perekovki* would be useful additions to the Cultural Educational Sections to assist in the actual literacy efforts at each camp sector along the canal construction site. However, as Fedorov notes, "In Dmitlag [there were] courses to liquidate illiteracy and schools for the semi-literate. However, the courses succeeded in grabbing only around 10 percent of the 'zeks.' So, in the fourth quarter of 1933 in Dmitlag's educational institutions 13,500 people were enrolled, but when school finished, there were all of 80 prisoners."[116] To say that literacy efforts at this point in canal construction were less than successful is a generous understatement. Nonetheless, these figures from late 1933, while compelling, do not necessarily represent the situation in 1935–6 when *BP* was in its heyday. The success and nature of literacy campaigns in the camp remains a tantalizing topic for further investigation. In any case, the readership among prisoners for *Biblioteka Perekovki* remained limited.

The third possible cohort for whom these publications were intended would be the upper echelons of the Soviet dignitaries who visited the Moscow–Volga Canal construction site. These visits were not unusual; Stalin and his subordinates made three visits to the waterway's construction sites prior to its completion. What better way to promote the use of forced labor for large-scale construction projects than through the use of booklets in which the latent talents of the Dmitlag population were displayed? Each of these uses emphasizes the propaganda function that supported the *BP*. It would be a mistake to contend that there were no other consequences and results of this initiative.

Arguably, *Biblioteka Perekovki* was detrimental to inmate health and well-being because the booklets constructed identities for Dmitlag and its inhabitants that were accurate only for a select few. For every prisoner who was fortunate enough to serve the KVO and write or draw during his/her incarceration, there were tens of thousands who hauled wheelbarrows, operated excavators, and dug tons of gravel, sand, and dirt with shovels, pickaxes and their own strength as their only tools. Dmitlag was, after all, a forced labor camp charged with the enormous task of building a canal that would bring Volga water to the capital of Soviet power. Yet to assume that only a negative function can be ascribed to the *BP* enterprise would be to ignore the cadre of individuals, the Dmitlag inmates, who produced this series. While for some an assignment as a writer or artist did not guarantee survival, others may have benefitted from their work on this project.[117] As examples of the former, the prolific artist Gleb Kuhn and the oft-published writers Mikhail Brilev and Nikolai N. Zhigul'sky perished in 1937 in spite of the quantity and quality of their work for various Dmitlag publications. On the other hand, the former inmate Veniamin P. Kalent'ev stayed on at Dmitlag after canal construction was completed. He served in the Finno-Soviet war, where he sustained a concussion, and then studied at the Gorky Institute of Literature in Moscow, after which he enjoyed a successful career as a poet. Unlike his colleagues Brilev, Zhigul'sky, Mogilianskaya, and Sobolevsky, he managed to survive the Gulag in spite of the potential for ruin that it engendered.

It is also true that, despite the heavy hand of the NKVD in the project, moments of talent emerge. The booklets are uneven in quality, and it is impossible to determine how frequently the professional writers on staff intervened to edit the texts or how much the professional composers rewrote musical scores. Moreover, some of the booklets were indeed authored by Dmitlag staff writers. But the fact that there are well-crafted poems, original music, and witty posters in the booklets authored by non-professional inmate writers demonstrates, yet again, that even when art is produced on command, it remains possible to display one's talent and create cultural products, albeit of varying quality.[118] Even more important is the fact that we still have access to the words and thoughts of a group of prisoners who heretofore have been mostly silent about their experience in the Gulag. Is their experience atypical? Yes. Does that disqualify it as a legitimate basis for investigation and explication? Absolutely not. The Soviet Union was a conglomeration of various ethnicities, political interests, cultures, and attitudes, and the Gulag was an institution that, as Steve Barnes has cogently argued, seeped into, overlapped with, reflected, and affected Soviet society as a whole. If we are to integrate the multiple voices that comprised the USSR into our understanding of its history and legacy, then we must also explore the existence of those voices in the Gulag. To ignore them would be to forfeit a chance to add to its history.

Finally, the processes and artistic production that the *Biblioteka Perekovki* series illustrates stand not as an exception, but as the rule for the variety of print materials that Dmitlag produced. In particular, the journal *Storming the Work Site* and the main camp newspaper *Re-Forging* resulted from the use of professional and non-professional inmate writers and artists to craft publications that highlighted events, successes, and problems in Dmitlag, and also celebrated the artistic, literary, and construction achievements of its denizens. Of course, these publications presented a picture of Dmitlag that failed to reflect the true nature of life in the camp. They functioned to exhort and inform everyone in the Dmitlag world, as well as to link the camp to events occurring outside of it. No wonder then that a lavishly illustrated issue of *Storming the Work Site* dedicated to the centenary of Pushkin's death appeared in 1937 in parallel with the Pushkin celebrations staged in the non-Gulag world. Reports on achievements outside Dmitlag in the spheres of polar exploration and industrialization, as well as important speeches by Stalin and other leaders, likewise were celebrated in the newspaper *Perekovka* (*Re-Forging*), among other publications. Technical achievements that were realized on the Moscow Canal project found expression in the pages of *Moskva–Volgostroi*. Inmate writers, be they criminal or political prisoners, functioned as the common denominator among all these publications. As such they afford an expanded view of life in Dmitlag, a view that brings into sharp relief the good and the bad of camp life during the construction of the Moscow Canal.

Water and Power Revisited

Dmitlag existed as one of the harshest and largest Gulag camps within the system. Its inmates produced a huge waterway with a plethora of unique structures that advertised and applauded the Stalinist system at every lock and along every kilometer of the waterway. The 151 million cubic meters of earth that inmates moved with the help of only of some 150 excavators, 160 steam engines, 225 rail cars, 300 tractors, and 2,000 automobiles required an intensity of labor that seems unimaginable. But build it they did, and the testament to this labor exists to this day, fully operational and vital to the continued sustainability of the Moscow metropolis.

On a broader scale, as Volga water flowed through the Moscow Canal after its construction, so too did a sizeable contingent of forced laborers flow through Dmitlag. For them the water that so strongly emblematized this project served to kill some of them, invigorate others, and move all of them along a time–space continuum drawn by the canal's construction. No other participants in the Moscow Canal project were closer to the water than the inmate laborers who created the spaces into which it would flow. As the instruments through which Stalinist spatial politics were realized, the prisoners, much more than the free workers or NKVD supervisors, created a landscape that simultaneously celebrated their achievements, while thoroughly, indeed insidiously, hiding their suffering. It is as if the water of the Moscow Canal drowned not only history, as realized in the flooding of Korcheva, Ivan'kovo and other villages, but also submerged the terror inherent in Dmitlag. The metaphorical dualities of water, as a source of both life and death, refreshment and subjugation, power and weakness, obtained in the physical labor of camp inmates and in the canal channel, dams, locks, and associated structures that they built. In the most literal sense, Dmitlag inmates built a power structure that visibly, ideologically, and symbolically invoked the power of the USSR, under the guidance of Stalin, and in typical Stalinist fashion at the expense of those for whom it was created. For many prisoners, they were building the structure that ultimately killed them.

Beyond this is the realization that Dmitlag typified a truly Stalinist space and landscape that emerged as the direct products of the ideology and economic needs of the burgeoning Soviet Union. As Karl Schloegel notes, "The Soviet space [was] held together by large-scale projects that remade nature according to scientific and political ideas of utility."[119] This philosophy guided not only the construction of the Moscow Canal, but also the establishment of Dmitlag, for without the creation of the figurative, ideological, and physical camp space, there would be no Moscow Canal. The landscape would not have been altered, nor would there exist, "Lines [that] are drawn that mark projected canals and highways, pipelines and railroads. Rivers [were] redirected and seas connected, deserts ... irrigated and swamplands reclaimed."[120] Both Dmitlag and the Moscow Canal duplicated the collision of the Gulag and non-Gulag worlds (as had previously happened at Belomor) and provided a blueprint for subsequent projects within and outside the Gulag. As Bettina Greiner argues, "the Gulag was the most extreme variant of captivity in a continuum of incarcerated geographies within the Soviet Union as a whole."[121] These "incarcerated geographies" subsumed life not only in the Gulag, but in the non-Gulag world as well given the ever-tightening limits on movement, livelihoods, personal space, and relationships imposed during Stalinism.[122] The glue that made the discrete parts of this continuum adhere was control: of life, death, nature, and culture.

Surprising, perhaps, was the level of cultural activity that took place in Dmitlag not only as a function of the need to produce propaganda, but also to afford the opportunity for inmate talent to be displayed and lauded. The link between re-forging and artistic production might seem tenuous, but it was sustained in Dmitlag's rich and vital print culture, a culture that prospered due to Semyon Firin. Arguably, no other camp after Dmitlag enjoyed this relatively rich cultural life. While the percentage of those who engaged in these cultural activities was small compared to the overall work force, the fact of their existence and the promotion of their efforts to stake out a creative space for criminal prisoners remains one of the most significant aspects of the Moscow Canal project. However, their work would not circulate beyond the confines of Dmitlag for many years, so it fell to other artists – sculptors, painters, and prominent Soviet writers – to create a metaphorical and literary space that documented and celebrated the construction of the Moscow–Volga Canal. As the following chapter reveals, these attempts also failed to reach a large audience, but the scope and themes of their work nonetheless bear witness to the ways in which Stalinist space in all its manifestations was created largely through the perceived harnessing of water to the service of the state.

CHAPTER 3

CREATING METAPHORICAL AND IDEOLOGICAL SPACE: CULTURAL PRODUCTION AND THE MOSCOW CANAL

> The various coverings – dark labradorite, grey granite, white stones, bronze, cast iron, iron, the memorial plaques with the names of the canal's heroes – all this turns a seemingly conventional transportation structure into a true work of art.[1]

> Our canal is an authentic monument of human creativity {and} human culture.[2]

While the previous discussion of the *Library of Re-forging* illustrates how inmates of the Dmitlag camp created cultural artifacts that documented and lauded the Moscow Canal project, the picture of cultural reactions to the project is incomplete without an assessment of other cultural products that likewise sought to depict and celebrate the construction of the canal. Of particular interest are the sculptures placed along the canal between Locks 2 and 3, paintings by artists within and outside Dmitlag, many contemporaneously with the construction, and two draft volumes that sought to document the history of the project and thereby created a metaphorical space in which the Moscow Canal is situated. The tactile sculptures that rise gracefully above the canal and embellish an otherwise unremarkable shoreline; the paintings whose canvases outline a defined two-dimensional space that injects elements of painterly beauty into a prison camp milieu; the two unpublished manuscripts whose words, images, and authors capture and describe the highlights of canal construction – each of these cultural products creates two kinds of space: the imagined, abstract space in the mind of the viewer or reader and the physical space that each object occupies. These cultural artifacts produce metaphorical, imagined space just as potent and laden with meaning as the physical space that the Moscow Canal occupies: with each new reading, the imagined space of the canal supplies a counterpoint to the other spatial considerations that the Moscow Canal engenders.[3]

The issue of aesthetics is, in general, critical to our apprehension of the spatial ramifications of the Moscow–Volga Canal. The canal project supervisors and designers intentionally included aesthetic elements to provide both examples of visually pleasing works and models for inculcating Soviet aesthetic values in the canal builders and canal visitors. In particular, a segment of the Moscow Canal between Dubna and Dmitrov reinforces the idea that spatial configurations, features, and figures – how the space is decorated and monumentalized – not only define those spaces, but also convey the ideology behind them. This very calculated approach imbues a physical environment with the ideology of those who design and finance it. This practice, common to all designed spaces, is reflected in the case of the Moscow Canal through the objects placed along the canal route. All of these were meant to enlighten and educate the viewing public as to the standards of Soviet aesthetics and the proper Stalinist conception of the world as it was in the process of becoming through the implementation of Socialist Realism in all artistic production.

Sculpture[4]

Sculptures are a ubiquitous art form along the Moscow Canal. Figures of inmate laborers decorate the lower gates of Lock 1, while figures of NKVD personnel stand guard atop the towers at Lock 2. The towers at Lock 6 feature rows of the waterway's technical and engineering personnel facing each other across the lock chamber, while muscular workers are fixed in granite at the catchment area of the Pestov dam. The light-footed statue entitled "The Waterway" graces a bluff near Lock 5 and likewise welcomes visitors to the Northern River Station at Khimki.

These statues feature a young woman with arms raised and balancing a sailing ship above her head. All of these figures imitate the style and presentation of classical sculptures, while using the art form to capture the strength, beauty, and power of people integral to the construction of the Moscow Canal.[5]

Consider, for example, the stretch of the canal between Locks 2 and 3 in the Orevsky district, where viewers on the water or from the banks encounter a series of white sculptures designed to impress and inspire.[6] These sculptures, four in all with two on each bank, face each other across the canal from the site of a set of emergency gates.[7] Approximately 4 meters tall, these granite figures rise over the waterway on their solid pedestals and greet passing tourists with faces etched in stone for eternity. Sited on gently sloping banks, two sculptures are titled "Sport," while two others portray a female aviator and a peasant woman. Extant photos from the 1930s show neatly manicured lawns and large pristine white urns filled with flowering plants.[8] Each sculpture represents one tenet of the totalizing ideology that Stalinism strove to realize: a way of life and a system of aesthetic appreciation. These figures were sculpted in bright white granite that sets them off against the green background created by the summer landscape along the canal. Those viewing these sculptures from the waterway would rarely see them in the dead of winter. Rather, the cruise season, which reaches its peak in the summer, witnesses the abundant foliage that serves as a backdrop for the statues.

As if rising out of the ground on their firm square pedestals, the statues evoke strength, vertical movement, and permanence. The plasticity of each captures its subject mid-motion, frozen in time. One sculpture depicts an aviator, that quintessential Stalinist hero, who gazes pensively into the distance, perhaps contemplating her next flight into glory. That the pilot commemorated in this sculpture is a woman highlights not only the Soviet promotion of women as equal standard-bearers in the fight for aviation supremacy, but also the purported equality of Soviet men and women. This image was especially important in the 1930s given the aviation feats that Soviet pilots, most notably Chkalov, as well as Marina Raskova, Polina Osipenko and Valentina Grizodubova, were accomplishing, presumably because of Soviet power and technology.[9] Aviators in particular were a source of communal pride, for they represented not only the ability of Soviet citizens to command technology and use it for their ends, but also the movement of the USSR into the forefront of twentieth-century technology.[10] Moreover, aviation offered yet another mode through which space, in this instance the air, could be appropriated and controlled. Indeed, as was the case with water, Soviet power remained undaunted in its quest to control that which cannot be contained or mastered, in this case air.

Similarly, an image of three athletes, two women with a man between them, poised in mid-leap, arms straining skyward, highlights the drive for physical fitness and strength that filled Soviet media of the time. The statue situated on the canal's west bank captures these athletes in the seconds after they have served a volleyball across the canal at their opponents directly opposite them. This image, conveying not only athleticism, but also (likely unintended) sexual tension, evokes a sense of the energy of youth.[11] Sport, like aviation, was considered the sign of a well-developed, strong society whose members physically embodied action, power, and agility, images distinctly contradicting the stereotypical peasants of Imperial Russia with their thick build, clumsy movements, and lethargic pace. The slim, extended arms of the athletes capture not only the physical embodiment of movement, but also incarnate the oft-repeated Soviet slogan, borrowed from the Olympic motto "Citius, Altius, Fortius,"[12] "higher, faster, stronger." Attired in athletic outfits, the trio exudes the vigor of youth, a trope that coincided with the notion that the USSR was a young state being built by Soviet youth whose ideological profiles were formed after the Revolution. These typical Soviet youths served as behavioral and physical models for the viewers sailing past them.

A twin sculpture directly across from this on the canal's eastern shore captures three volleyball players all striving to hit the ball served from the opposite bank (Figure 3.1). Here, too, a muscular, athletic man is paired with two similarly fit women, who all simultaneously stretch skyward to hit the ball. The figures' finely sculpted bodies, replete with rippling muscles, clearly defined breasts, and strong legs are planted on the sculpture's pedestal. Significant here is that these athletes are standing on one leg, perfectly balanced, with their other legs extended behind them. This pose couples movement with stability, while affirming the strength with which these athletes compete. Unlike its partner, this sculpture places the two women next to each other, with one of them in the middle, higher than her companion figures. The male

Figure 3.1 Sculpture of athletes on the banks of the Moscow Canal.

figure assumes a bent or crouching position, as if overwhelmed by the power and aggressiveness of the female athletes. This image intimates a sexual subtext in which women are equal competitors with men, while maintaining their femininity, shapeliness, and sexuality. This statue offers a relatively more sexualized image than other statues of the period, as well as the companion statue of a peasant woman: the male figure is shirtless and the women's nipples are visible through their shirts. Indeed the male figure looks as if he is raising his right hand to defend himself from the aggressive play of his female counterparts, although in actuality he is stretching to make the hit.

A fourth statue depicts a peasant/worker woman, rooted to her pedestal on sturdy, broad legs that imply power, stability, and solidity, who faces northward, away from Moscow and toward Dubna and the canal's confluence with the Volga River (Figure 3.2). In another rebuff to

Figure 3.2 Sculpture of a worker/peasant woman.

pre-revolutionary stereotypes she looks outward, not inward, suggesting vision and progressiveness; she gazes toward the future. This woman, serious and contemplative, exudes surety, calm, and purposefulness. Her modest clothing – a shirt and skirt with a scarf tied around her head to hold back her hair – presents her as Every Woman, the female archetype on which the new Soviet society would be built. Her muscular arms celebrate the latent power her figure reflects, while her pose, with left hand perched on her hip and right arm hanging casually at her side, conveys readiness coupled with determination and superiority. She stands not only prepared to work, with her sleeves rolled up to her elbows, but ready to share her opinion as well. She embodies that which makes a Soviet woman strong: a sturdy body, mind, and will.[13]

No specific authorship has been ascribed to these sculptures. Consequently, it is most likely that they are the work of Gulag artisans. Presumably these craftsmen followed the designs of a master sculptor who conceived of the images and who obtained official approval for the model. Those same forced laborers would have then placed the sculptures along the waterway between Locks 2 and 3, just as they did other sculptures that adorn some of the lock towers elsewhere on the canal.

For all the symbolism and aesthetic value these sculptures carried in the late 1930s, they also have value to posterity and to the contemporary understanding of the Moscow Canal in two ways. First, as relics of the Stalinist past, these sculptures provide a window into the interweaving of art and industry, technological progress and aesthetic values that were inextricably linked in the Stalinist program. The statues' resemblance to Greek and Roman sculpture with their classical material, features, and poses, further enhanced by decorative urns placed near them, emphasizes the Stalinist tendency to look to the distant past for models of art, beauty, and permanence to construct aesthetic models for the future. According to a report on Lazar' Kaganovich's perception of how the canal should look:

> Right then Com.[rade] Kaganovich posed the question about the synthesis of art – about the use of "monumental" sculptures, [and] paintings on the canal. Com. Kaganovich also talked about the use of classical art of the past, for example, the experience of ancient Rome, in order to create the hydro-technical structures.[14]

This practice provided physical and artistic links with the ancient empires that infused their quotidian structures with idealized grace and beauty. As Andrei Sinyavsky has so cogently argued, the socialist realist canon sought as its model not the abstract work of the avant-garde, but rather the concomitant aesthetic practices of the ninteenth-century realists, coupled with the monumentality and timelessness of classical art and architecture.[15] These sculptures form a carefully designed landscape, all the elements of which create for the viewer a sense of grace, vitality, and movement. The concrete stairs adjacent to the sculptures invite visitors onto the bank to interact with the statues and to view them up close. Likewise, the accessibility of the water, in tandem with the placement of the sculptures in a pristine natural setting, link the viewer with nature to reinforce the notion that Soviet power has been able not only to harness the power of water through the construction of the canal, but also to unite art and nature. It is no accident that this sculptural ensemble is further adorned with a small neo-classical building with pale walls, white trim, and steps leading down to the water's surface. In its 1930s incarnation, this location probably served as a disembarkation point for travelers along the canal, or was at least intended to. Now it remains a relic of past grandeur.

In addition, these sculptures contributed to the seemingly mythical qualities of the "Stalinist body." As Soviet citizens were admonished to become "new" men and women, whose ideological, sociological, and psychological make-up was transformed through the advancement of Soviet power, they were similarly exhorted to maintain physically fit bodies that became the living space of Soviet ideology. Physical fitness, strength and endurance all figured into the composite image of the new Soviet wo/man. This was complemented by the notion of "socialist competition" that gained prominence in the 1930s. During the construction of the Belomor Canal and other projects, collective action, be it in artistic production, canal building, kolkhoz farming, or indeed any activity, provided the energy, motivation, and manpower to accomplish a task. However, by the mid-1930s this collective sensibility had given way to an emphasis on individual achievement and personal bests.[16] Even if a collective worked together to achieve a goal, as did the labor brigades on the Moscow Canal, individuals were still singled out for their over-fulfillment of a plan, zealous industriousness, and tireless striving for excellence. Each of the sculptures along the Moscow Canal embodied these contours and reinforced the importance not only of a strong body, but also of competition both with oneself and with others. The physical structures strove to inculcate these values into those who viewed them.

As Toby Clark argues, "One of the features of representations of the new man is a collapsing of conventional notions of time and history. In the transformation of aviators and champion workers into mythic heroes of the past and the future, present-day reality tends to disappear."[17] This breakdown of time constraints resonates as well in the Moscow Canal sculptures: because they are frozen in time and space, they reflect neither the present, nor the reality of the past during the construction of the Moscow Canal: the physically grueling manual labor of prison camp inmates whose emaciated and underfed bodies hardly lived up to the Stalinist ideal. Sport served as an integral element in the making of the new Soviet wo/man, as the pair of sculptures of the athletes suggest. And Dmitlag inmates did partake in some organized sports activities, typically soccer. Yet an unbridgeable gap existed between the idealized bodies depicted in the sculptures and the actual bodies of Dmitlag prisoners. That gap was plastered over by the sculptures on the banks of the Moscow Canal, a landscape that also served as the graveyard for many Dmitlag inmates.

This disguised reality is now visible, however, when we contemplate the contemporary condition of this ensemble. The sculptures bear the signs of wear, with a broken appendage on one and cracked plinths on the others. Some of the whiteness of the stone has become dingy and gray. The steps leading down to the water are cracked and eroded, while the decorative urns are devoid of any flora. Cars that now line the upper banks bring swimmers to the canal, a practice that harks back to one of the waterway's original purposes: to provide recreational opportunities for Soviet citizens. These days, however, in the strictest sense, these drivers and swimmers are trespassing on federal land and legally should not be swimming in the canal. Stone portholes that lined both sides of the canal at the sculptural ensemble during its glory days now lack the electric lights that once illuminated them. Many are devoid even of the opaque glass covers and resemble gaping eye sockets without eyeballs. These holes are overgrown with weeds in the summer. The lack of financial support necessary for the restoration of these features reflects a general tendency not only to underfund the canal, but to demur from restoring that which memorializes a contentious past, a past with which Russian society has yet to come to terms.

Painting

Painting is physically and metaphorically the space of art. To convey meaning, it depends on time – both the context that produced the work and the moment when it is viewed – and space, both of the canvas itself and the space depicted (However, comprehension of a visual image in space is supposedly instantaneous, in contrast to a written work, which has to be read over time to be understood.) The paintings commemorating the Moscow Canal are no different. These artistic depictions produced during and after the canal's construction render idealized, often brightly colored images that situate their subjects along the continuum of the canal's history. Conspicuously absent are dark, forbidding scenes and truthful depictions of construction sites and camp life, a sin of omission not without precedent. We need only look at the many photographs and paintings from which Soviet leaders were removed after their falls from grace, such as the Dmitri Nalbandyan painting of Stalin's visit to the Belomor Canal. Accompanying Stalin on this trip was the OGPU chief Genrikh Yagoda, whose arrest in 1937, at the time Nalbandyan was finishing the painting, prompted Yagoda's removal from the canvas. Or a photograph of Uzbek Party leaders from which the famed photographer Alexander Rodchenko blacked out the faces of Babaev, Yenukhidze, and Kodzhaev.[18]

Instead, artistic representations of the canal are typically bathed in bright colors or gentle, reassuring pastels. If workers are included, they often are faceless, while construction equipment is reproduced in great detail. The intentional anonymity of the workers emphasizes the fact that the forced laborers building the canal were not valued as individuals, but rather as part of the labor force united behind a common goal – to build the canal. Because the laborers were Gulag inmates and, as such, non-citizens, they were not worth making identifiable to viewers. Similarly, the system demanded that those artists who were members of the Dmitlag art studio use their talent to serve the cause and to expiate their guilt. Their talent was exploited for the sake of the project, and because of what they were painting these artists would presumably be remade into model Soviet citizens, even if no such re-forging was appropriate given that they were political prisoners who were deemed unable to be re-forged.

The construction of the Moscow Canal was conceived not only as a building project, but also as a cultural event. Thus it makes sense that painting was included as one of the arts through which this monumental effort was celebrated and documented. This approach was consistent with the dominant philosophy in Stalinism that art, no matter what form or genre, was to be used for the purposes of the state. Painting's role in this system was to create spatial images that captured a moment in time and recreated the space each time the painting was viewed. The canvases were designed to appeal to and inspire viewers by convincing them that they were accessible to anyone; no special skill was required to "read" the paintings. Each was crafted according to the general principles of the socialist realist aesthetic, central to which was the notion that the visual arts should depict Soviet socialist construction not as it actually was, but as it should be or was in the process of becoming. These canvases dedicated to scenes from the Moscow Canal thus ignored the gritty Gulag realia of the space to imagine an ideal view of the structure, the colorful present and bright future that it had purportedly created and promoted.

The paintings immediately grab the viewer's attention, some due to the skill of the execution, and all due to the varying techniques and individualized color schemes displayed. Whether it is a watercolor or an oil painting, each canvas washes the scene in rich oranges and reds, bright azure blues, warm browns, and verdant greens. The paintings are housed in both unlikely and likely places. The bulk of the paintings discussed here constitute part of the collection of the Dmitrov Kremlin Museum-Preserve, not surprisingly given Dmitrov's prominent role in the construction of the canal. E. G. Satel"s painting (120 cm x 200 cm, oil on canvas, 195?) hangs in Hall 21, floor 24 of the Museum of Earth Sciences at Moscow State University. It depicts the canal's embankment beyond Lock 2 in the distance. Other works are held in private collections or hang in other Russian museums, and the locations of many of these paintings are often impossible to determine. Most recently a number of these paintings have been located in the Saratov Art Museum.[19] A few have come up for auction within the last ten years at various art auction houses in Moscow, perhaps snapped up by collectors eager to own a piece of Stalinist history.

Each canvas freezes an idealized moment in time during or after construction. One of the most common images is the third lock near Yakhroma with its Columbus caravels with billowing sails atop the northern lock towers. Similarly, the domestically produced Kovrovets excavators figure prominently in some of the paintings as a symbol of technological progress, Soviet ingenuity, and the dynamism of construction.

Most significantly, these paintings expand the space that the canal inhabits. As Henri Lefebvre notes, "A picture, as a painted surface, privileges one dimension, orienting itself towards the viewer and grouping its subjects, inanimate or living, according to the same logic. It is a sort of face and a sort of façade."[20] While the canvases confine the images within the borders of their frames, the psychological space created by the paintings extends infinitely. According to Lefebvre, "A painting turns in the direction of anyone approaching it – that is, in the direction of the public. A portrait looks out before, while and after it is looked at. A canvas, or a painted wall, has a countenance, one which actively invites scrutiny."[21] Each time a painting is examined, the viewer steps into the space of the work and creates a space of memory, as well as an idealized space that does not exist, save for her interaction with the canvas. Indeed, these works have created a further dimension of space that captures an image of the canal at a particular moment and continually recreates that moment each time the canvas is viewed.

It should be noted that the following treatment of these paintings will focus less on their painterly qualities and the general quality of the artwork than on the spaces they demarcate and illustrate. The pivotal questions here are: what kinds of space do these paintings create and how do they interact with the places that are the foci of the visual depictions? As Matthew Cullerne Bown notes:

> Socialist realist painting adhered nominally to an empirical reality – a single moment in time, a single unified space – but it strove to apply the multi-temporal principle in the construction of pictorial space and narrative. In essence, the metaphor of time was created through the illusion of space: passage through time towards the bright future was signified by passage through vast pictorial space.[22]

This time/space juxtaposition is both appropriate and visible in all the Moscow Canal paintings, even those that depict construction sites. As Bown continues:

> Broadly speaking, the move during the 1930s away from a new-classical, frieze-like, shallow space towards deep baroque perspectives may be understood as reflecting a growing realisation among artists that space was a metaphor for time and that the eye – be it that of a protagonist in a painting or the viewer of a painting – that beheld vast spaces was also conquering the road to paradise. Vast light airy spaces evoked even greater expanses, thus standing for something like the Communist utopia itself.[23]

It is here that we find the creation of a space that was truly Soviet and designed to inculcate the value and worth of the presumed bright future specifically as a consequence of the construction of the Moscow Canal and its attendant philosophy of re-forging prisoners into new Soviet citizens. Like the sculptures, these paintings conveyed social etiquette and aesthetic values to the viewer.

When something is committed to canvas, it is deemed significant enough to preserve for posterity. The paintings that depict scenes of the Moscow Canal do so in such a way that none of the violence of construction or terror of the labor camp intrudes on the picture. Rather, scenes that capture construction vignettes render them as calm and organized. If workers are included in the frame, they are indistinct and secondary to the overall portrayal of the setting. Canvases that capture a landscape after the canal has been open for navigation highlight tourism and quotidian activities rather than construction: couples strolling along the canal's banks, a cruise ship plying its waters or canal employees monitoring navigation. Like other art forms, the paintings instruct and guide viewers as to how to see, interpret, and apprehend their subjects in order to prescribe how the spatial entity on the canvas should be perceived.

That some of the Moscow Canal paintings were produced after the canal opened testifies to the enduring importance of the structure as a landmark and a symbol of Soviet power. Of the 13 paintings that I have been able to locate and identify, half were produced after the canal opened, roughly from 1938–59. This high Stalinist period seems to have been receptive to the artistic depiction of a forced labor project, especially since this project was located not only in the Moscow region, but in the city itself. The canal was cast as a work of art that deserved to be captured on canvas for posterity. Not surprisingly, these works depict the canal as a source of beauty that fulfills practical functions, from transporting tourists to supplying Moscow with potable water. Despite their obvious importance, it is difficult to trace the provenance of all the paintings. Of the 13 works examined, five were painted by S. I. Shchelokov (1897–1973), four by F. A. Modorov (1890–1976), two by E. V. Egorov (1901–42), one by G. E. Satel' (1917–2012) and one by A. Berezkin (dates unknown). Of these artists, only Shchelokov served a term in the Dmitlag camp. Egorov, Modorov and Satel' were critically accepted, and indeed Satel' was a decorated and officially sanctioned artist: Satel', winning a third-place Stalin Prize in 1951 for his painting "In the Vocational School." Little if any biographical information is available for A. Berezkin.[24]

To put these artists in context, all of them were trained in art institutes immediately prior to and after the 1917 October Revolution, and regardless of their backgrounds each one subscribed in varying degrees to the socialist realist doctrine of art. All of them except Satel' were born before the Revolution and came of age as it was unfolding. For example, the oldest, Fedor Aleksandrovich Modorov, was born in Mstera in 1890 and died in Moscow in 1976. Modorov, from a family of icon painters, attended art school in Moscow, Kazan, and Petrograd. In 1918 he famously helped restore the deeply revered icon "The Vladimir Mother of God" under the direction of the master artist Grabar. He built on this experience, coupled with his background and diverse training, to become an astute practitioner of Socialist Realism. As one biographer notes, "All this did not prevent Modorov from becoming a fiery revolutionary and one of the founders of Socialist Realism in art. He [drew] Soviet leaders and [produced] paintings of the new reality, meetings, and congresses."[25] Subsequently Modorov frequently exhibited in major venues in the USSR, and from 1948–62 served as the Director of the V. I. Surikov Moscow State Institute of Art, a further testament to his place within the official Soviet art establishment. Modorov's works can be found in major art museums, among them the Tretyakov Gallery and the Russian Museum, and his paintings have come up for auction at various art auction houses in Moscow.[26] He was a corresponding member of the

USSR Academy of Art, a People's Artist of the RSFSR, and an honorary artist of the Belorussian SSR.

Unlike the other artists discussed here, Sergei Ivanovich Shchelokov was an inmate in the Dmitlag Camp. Born in 1897 in the Saratov region, Shchelokov was convicted under Article 58 for "counter-revolutionary agitation" and sentenced to ten years in a labor camp. He served the first part of his term in the camp for the Belomor Canal project, and completed it on the Moscow–Volga project in Dmitlag. While there, Shchelokov was one of the artists assigned to the Central Artists Studio under the direction of famous caricaturist M. M. Cheremnykh. As part of his responsibilities Shchelokov participated in a camp-wide art exhibit, along with other Dmitlag artists including Gleb Kuhn and Konstantin Sobolevsky. After he completed his term, Shchelokov remained in Dmitrov, where he lived until his death in 1973. While living in Dmitrov, Shchelokov studied with the artist Nikolai Ivanovich Varentsov, who instructed small groups of young artists at his studio. Shchelokov was a member of the Union of Artists.[27] A sizeable collection of his work can be found at the Atkarsk Regional Studies Museum in the city of Atkarsk in the Saratov province. This museum, which is a branch of the Saratov Province Regional Studies Museum, houses three oil paintings, ten graphic designs and three etudes that Shchelokov produced primarily in the late 1960s and early 1970s. Shchelokov was a native son of the Saratov region and it is thus no surprise that the museum includes some of his work in its collection.[28]

Like Shchelokov, Evgeny Vasilievich Egorov was from Saratov, where he was born in 1901. Critics consider him to be a major figure and exponent of the Saratov School of painting, and during his short career he was celebrated for his talent as an artist who "with equal success pursued both contemporary and historical themes, studied production methods [and] was a master of figurative composition, portraiture, landscapes and still lifes in graphic art as well as in decorative easel paintings."[29] Egorov exhibited his works throughout the 1920s. He lived in Saratov until 1934, when he moved to Moscow and joined the Moscow Organization of Soviet Artists (MOSA). The available sources do not make clear what prompted this move, although it is possible to conjecture that Egorov's admission to the MOSA signaled official acceptance of his work. According to Grigorenko, Egorov traveled to the canal construction site each summer in order to capture scenes from the project on canvas.

When his wife went to Dmitrov to work, Egorov joined her and became the official city artist of Dmitrov, a position that conferred on him responsibility for organizing festivities to celebrate the opening of the Moscow–Volga Canal. In honor of this event he produced the work "The Opening of the Canal," which he gifted to the city of Dmitrov and which hung for a time in the city's train station.[30] Egorov's other works that feature the Moscow Canal include "The Moscow–Volga Canal" (1937), "The Yakhroma Lock" (1939), and "A Holiday on the Canal" (1940).[31] When World War II broke out Egorov and his family were evacuated to Saratov, where he died in 1942 of tuberculosis. His works remain in the collections of major Russian museums, including the Tretyakov Gallery, the Pushkin Museum, and others.

The youngest of this group of painters, Georgy Eduardovich Satel' was born in Moscow in 1917 into the family of the Russified Frenchman Eduard Satel', a mechanical engineer. In the 1930s he began his studies at the Moscow Institute of Architecture and in 1938 enrolled at the V. I. Surikov Moscow State Art Institute, where he later completed his studies. Satel' began to exhibit his works in 1947. Satel', whose works decidedly conform to the socialist realist canon, focused his paintings on cityscapes, especially those of Moscow, as well as still lifes, landscapes, and depictions of industry and famous Soviet leaders. He won a Stalin prize in 1951 for his painting "In the Vocational School," and from 1959–61 he taught at the V. I. Lenin Moscow State Pedagogical Institute. Satel' died in Moscow in 2012. Currently his works are featured on a number of art auction sites, illustrating his place as a popular mainstream Soviet artist.[32]

As the biographies of these artists attest, their paintings illustrate two main themes: the canal under construction, featuring work sites, laborers and landscapes; and the canal after construction, most often featuring depictions of Lock 3 at Yakhroma, as well as various vessels sailing along the waterway. Within both thematic categories, the landscape into which the canal is inscribed figures prominently, as do renderings of the canal itself. Less important are the canal builders, canal workers, or tourists who populate some, but not all of the paintings.

Consider Georgy Eduardovich Satel''s landscape, "The Moscow Canal" (oil on canvas, 120 × 200 cm), which features the canal, one of its locks, and the surrounding countryside. Satel' illustrates the canal panorama in vivid, saturated colors (Plate 3). The light is clear, bright, and welcoming; the sky is pale blue. The puffy fair-weather clouds float effortlessly across the landscape. The sky occupies one-third of the canvas, and the dappled sunlight thus makes the upper third of the canvas appear pleasant and non-threatening. Although the work was not dated, it entered the collection of the MGU Museum of Earth Sciences when it opened in 1955, which means that the work was presumably produced between 1937 and 1954. As an artist firmly committed to the artistic dictates of Socialist Realism, Satel' chose to capture one of the signature Stalinist construction projects on canvas. Satel''s other works include "Stalin's Funeral" (1953), "Samorskaya Steelworkers" (1957), and "Pouring Steel" (1957), among others, all of which feature the main subjects of socialist realist painting: workers, industry, collective farmers, and bustling cityscapes.

Yet the style of the Moscow Canal canvas differs slightly from other canvases precisely because of the rich colors Satel' used to capture the image, especially when we consider that the natural elements of the painting, such as the trees, water, clouds, and grass, are treated impressionistically. The contours are not defined and the edges are blurred, whereas the man-made elements are rendered in sharp relief that makes them clearly identifiable and distinctly defined within the landscape. As Bown argues, the use of vivid colors and impressionist brushwork gained currency as the 1930s progressed. As he notes:

> As the decade progressed Soviet painting on the whole got brighter. High-key color is one of the features that distinguishes many works of the 1930s from those of earlier years ... This was partly owing to abandonment of the puritanical values of the period of "class struggle"; but it would also appear that the increased interest in sunshine was lightening and brightening the Soviet palette, as it had done that of the impressionists and post-impressionists.[33]

The bridge, pumping station, and lock are rendered with technical precision and accuracy, as are the ships sailing through the canal and the truck on its banks. The greater detail devoted to these man-made objects implies their relative importance over the natural environment. Hence the canvas graphically manifests the inevitable success of the Soviet project. The smoke from a train traversing the distant bridge is visible, thereby adding to the sense of movement in the painting. That forward motion, tracking from the left of the canvas to the right (or right to left in the direction of Moscow), is underscored by a steaming tug boat pulling two barges while another ship navigates the lock. The four lock towers form the compositional center that draws the spectator's eye farther along the canal. Indeed, the sunlight in the painting highlights and brightens the canal lock towers and reinforces their centrality to the landscape. The nearby trees that border the lock towers frame them and highlight the architectural elements of the towers, emphasizing that these man-made elements are the focus of the painting. Aside from the sky, the most substantial element of the painting is the water as it flows through the lock and as part of it is channeled into the pumping station. The water, cast in lavenders, grays, and muted greens, conveys the movement of the vessels through the ripples on its surface, as well as its own constant motion.

Given the architectural significance of the lock towers along the Moscow Canal, it is not surprising that the structures figure prominently in Modorov's and Egorov's work. In particular, Lock 3 at Yakhroma, famous for the replicas of the Columbus caravel, the Santa Maria, that adorn the northern two lock towers, is a favorite topic. Likewise, Modorov's "Lock 5" (1937, no dimensions provided), as well as his "'Tushino Lock' Canal Moskva-Volga" (1937, oil on canvas, 66 cm × 102 cm) make the space of the lock the primary focus of the painting. Modorov even captures the construction of the lock in his work "The Yakhroma Lock Before 1937" (oil on canvas, no dimensions provided). Each depiction of the locks, regardless of the artist, focuses on two key elements: the structures and the water.

Consider Modorov's painting that depicts Lock 3, "The Moscow–Volga Canal. Yakhroma" (1937, oil on canvas, no dimensions provided) where, like Satel' and in spite of his resolute Socialist Realist practices, he employs the same "impressionistic" technique in portraying the natural vs. man-made elements on the site (Plate 4). The background landscape, as well as the sky and water, are rendered in vibrant colors with brushstrokes that become clear only when the viewer moves back from the painting. Edges of landscape features are smudged and blend into each other. The figures in the painting serve as intermediaries between the natural and built environment. As with other artists of this period, Modorov's work reveals an interest in and application of impressionist techniques that, while officially criticized as the 1930s drew to a close, nonetheless remained an integral element of Soviet painting. As Bown argues:

> In essence, all the positive qualities discerned by painters in impressionism – the interest in plein-air effects, the bright colour, the freedom of mark – could be blended into an academic language to the extent that they did not militate against the solid and detailed rendering of form and construction of a narrative.[34]

The artist renders the three men standing on the banks of the canal with the same bright, sharp colors – lush blues and greens – and the same technique as in Satel"s work, yet their outlines are sharper, more focused, and more identifiable, from their distinct outfits (a worker and two guards) to their faces. It seems as if a fourth person has been painted out of the scene, given the shapeless blue form next to guard standing behind the painting's other two chief protagonists. However, the figures closest to and actually on the water are again formless, and could very well be prisoners who are meant to blend into the nature-scape in which they appear.

In contrast to these illustrations are the buildings at the lock. The use of light, in this case the bright white/beige tones of the buildings, draws in the viewer's eye. They become the focus of the painting, and as such reinforce the importance of the built structure as a tactile embodiment of the ideology. The canal structures command the view, although the people depicted on the canvas face away from the lock and cast their gaze downstream toward an unidentified object. The direction in which the individuals on the bank of the canal are facing mirrors the direction that the Columbus caravels face, for they look away from Moscow and northward toward the Volga River and, consequently, the world beyond Moscow and the canal. It is as if they are gazing toward the future since the water, by virtue of its constant motion, flows toward the next point along the canal route, thereby conquering both time and space.

Similarly, Egorov's depictions of Lock 3 command attention because of the vertical motion and upward thrust they capture. The lock towers, again the central feature in the paintings, pierce the sky and literally tower over the landscape, the water, and the people visible in the scene. In both "The Yakhroma Lock" (1938–9, oil on canvas, no dimensions provided) (Plate 5) and "The Moscow–Volga Canal near the Volga" (no date, oil on canvas, no dimensions provided), the position of the lock towers on the canvas directs the viewer's apprehension of the painting (Figure 3.3). Whereas in "The Yakhroma Lock" the lock towers are positioned right of center, in "The Moscow–Volga Canal near the Volga" they are situated left of center. In both paintings, the artist's vantage point is from behind the Columbus caravels: we see them from the back, while the steamships navigating the lock indicate motion away from them. In "The Yakhroma Lock" the ship is sailing toward Moscow with its prow resolutely pointed in the direction of the capital. The northern gate of the lock, visible above the water level, firmly prevents the vessel and its passengers from backward motion and seemingly forces them forward as they make their way through the lock. Spectators on the banks, again drawn with little attention to detail or sharpness of image, wave the steamer onward as it sails toward Moscow. The image captures both time passing, as the ship progresses in its voyage, and time standing still: the spectators on the shoreline are fixed in place as they

Figure 3.3 E.V. Egorov. "The Moscow Canal near the Volga."

wave to the passing ship. While the countryside is visible beyond the lock in both paintings, as are the pastel blue sky and puffy white clouds, the focus remains on the light beige lock towers, with the steely gray ornamental ships atop them and the white steamship moving along the lavender-toned, blue-gray water in the canal.

In "The Moscow–Volga Canal near the Volga" the steamship ventures to the great beyond after traversing the lock. The title is something of a misnomer, because this painting also depicts Lock 3 and its Columbus caravels, a location some 32 kilometers from the Volga River. The waterway opens ahead of it, underscoring the movement of the ship through time and space. The ship leaves the spectators on the shore behind; they are static, as are their parked cars, and it is the wake that the ship produces on the water that emphasizes it as the object in motion. The gray clouds and pastel-tinged sky, perhaps signaling an oncoming storm, do little to diminish the motion, while the bend in the canal directs the viewer's attention forward, just as the ship moves on. The protagonists in the painting, those invisible passengers in the steam ship, sail on toward the future, perhaps not the distant future, but a future nonetheless. These paintings resonate with the romanticism of travel, the sense of hope that often accompanies a journey, especially if that journey is on a pleasure craft. That the passengers sail along and above the likely graves of some of those who built the canal fails to figure at all in the composition. The paintings celebrate the beauty of the Moscow Canal to further aggrandize its construction and emphasize the important place it holds within Soviet life and culture. These canvases depict, literally and figuratively, the way to Communism that socialist construction projects were ostensibly building.

The builders of the canal, however, figure much less prominently in pictorial images, particularly because of their status as Gulag inmates. Nevertheless, they are visible in the work of S. I. Shchelokov who devoted his canvases to depictions of various construction sites along the canal route. This, too, is not surprising given that Shchelokov himself was a Dmitlag prisoner who was officially assigned the task of visually documenting construction as it was occurring. In each of the five paintings, in oil and in watercolor, on canvas and wood, the viewer is invited into a construction vignette where the building work itself serves as the focus of the scene. The identifiable titles of three paintings further emphasize the subject matter: "The Construction of the Moscow Canal,"

"Work on the Canal," and "Work on the Moscow–Volga Canal" each highlight a defined moment in construction, along with two other untitled paintings (I have been unable to locate official titles) that depict the building of the gates of a lock and workers framing the concrete molds for lock towers.

Both form and content differentiate Shchelokov's work from that of the other painters discussed. Each of Shchelokov's paintings includes canal workers, often operating some sort of rudimentary equipment, from wheelbarrows and horse-drawn carts to excavators, or engaged in various forms of manual labor. Their faces are never clearly drawn, nor are they shown in close-up. The viewer sees them either in the distance or at close range, always with indistinguishable faces but easily recognizable labor camp garb: padded jackets, caps or hats with ear flaps, oversized work gloves, and the ubiquitous felt boots. Two of the oil paintings, "Work on the Canal" and "Work on the Moscow–Volga Canal," capture winter scenes full of billowing snow drifts and snow-laden roofs. The other three paintings document scenes in milder weather as conveyed through blue skies, puffy clouds and green fields in the distance. These are not the illustrations of a romantic trip on a steamship down the canal, but rather the nuts-and-bolts labor, often intense and life-threatening, that went into producing the canal.

One of Shchelokov's untitled works (no date, materials or dimensions provided) (Figure 3.4), features the construction of the massive gates in a lock. Pride of place in the painting is given to the unfinished gates. They occupy the majority of the canvas, with the workers situated in the lower third of the painting. Either carrying boards or operating some sort of apparatus, they labor on the site. Lumber is strewn on the floor of the lock, while workers install steel panels on the gates. The painting evokes neither movement nor action, but rather freezes the frame to isolate the building of this particular object. The gates are painted in a dark brown that, against the pale background of the lock's cement walls, makes those elements the focal point of the painting and a counterpoint to the smallness of the workers on the site. This scene presents a wealth of meaning. These seemingly insignificant workers are capable of erecting huge structures that dwarf the builders, yet are the products of their hands. The importance of the scene is the structure itself, not the individual builders who work there. This is socialist construction captured at the moment of its birth, yet the fact that the gates are open

Figure 3.4 S. I. Shchelokov. "Untitled".

suggests a message of hope and the proverbial bright future. The gates open toward the workers and as such they offer access to a vanishing-point perspective that alludes not only to what lies further along the canal, but also to what lies beyond the canal for those building it. The pastel shades of the sky coupled with the bright colors of the lock chamber visually suggest a bright future beyond the gates of the lock.

Like his fellow artists, Shchelokov similarly uses a pastel blue sky adorned with puffy white clouds to frame other construction sites along the canal. The sky and the pastel landscape beneath it occupy half of the canvas in the painting "Construction of the Moscow–Volga Canal" (no date, materials or dimensions provided) (Figure 3.5). The viewer's attention is attracted to the scaffolding and poured cement structures that dominate the rest of the scene. The canal construction site occupies the space both in terms of structure and color. The white of the large poured concrete foundation (likely for a lock tower or gate mechanism) spreads horizontally to comprise the lower half of the scene, coupled with the brown and beige hues of the landscape into which it is inserted. The scaffolding extends vertically, seeming to pierce the sky as it

Figure 3.5 S. I. Shchelokov. "Construction of the Moscow–Volga Canal."

demarcates where the future fixed structure will be. The whiteness of the cement contrasts with the browns of the ubiquitous wood that is applied as scaffolding, stairs, roadways, ramps, and houses. Anything that is temporary is rendered in wood, while anything permanent is set in concrete.[35] While the construction process is finite, the structure it produces conveys the promise that it will last forever. If the viewer did not know that the project was staffed predominantly by prisoners, the painting would do nothing to disabuse her of this notion, for the depiction of faceless workers in neutral garb reveals nothing about the identities of the builders, only their presence on the site, and their function as cogs in the larger machine of canal construction.

This same color scheme – blue sky, white clouds, soft sand-colored soil, and various shades of brown structures and landscape – captures the scene of the construction of two lock towers in another unnamed painting (no date, materials or dimensions provided) (Plate 6). The work brings the viewer face to face with the primitive construction tools, as workers haul dirt away from the site in the ever-present wheelbarrows, while harnessed horses wait nearby to pull wagons bearing the construction debris brought in the wheelbarrows. The scene foregrounds a construction innovation that aided efficiency all along the canal route: wooden troughs through which water, cement, and various other materials could be pumped into or out of the site. The painting captures the needed synthesis of stasis and motion, thereby implying the desired constant state of achieving the completion of the project. While the gray material in the trough suggests this is concrete being poured, there are few other clues to suggest any other mechanization on the site. Instead, work is carried out through the physical labor of the inmates and the transport power provided by horses. No excavators, train cars, trucks, or other mechanized objects are in sight. The lock's foundation pit, carved out by hand, dominates the space, thereby emphasizing the most important element – the construction itself rather than those who are constructing it.

Lest there be any suspicion, however, that canal builders enjoyed uniformly good weather for their exhausting manual labor, Shchelokov captures construction scenes in the winter as well. Snow is draped over the eaves of buildings and covers the ground. Insofar as it is possible to determine, workers appear to be dressed in padded jackets and hats with the requisite ear flaps. In the oil painting "Work on the Canal" (1937, oil on canvas, no dimensions provided), the artist focuses on a construction crane, an essential yet rare commodity on the site (Plate 7). The crane dwarfs the faceless workers around it and is free of any snow cover. The placement of the crane in the center of the painting draws the viewer's eye to it, a perspective that is further emphasized by its location in a depression framed on two sides by piles of earth. The extended arm of the crane, depicted in light browns, creates the sensation of height and prominence in the scene. The pale smoke billowing from its smokestack denotes that work is being carried out, even if the figures and the crane itself are static in the landscape. The snow remains the only element that suggests cold, since the human figures in the painting fail to provide any clues as to the temperature. The gray sky is a few shades darker than the snow and creates a sense that it is pressing down on the scene, in contrast to the uplifting blue sky featured in other canvases.

Many of the elements that Shchelokov used in "Work on the Canal" recur in the gouache on paper "Work on the Moscow–Volga Canal" (1937, no dimensions provided) (Figure 3.6). Here too the viewer encounters a snow-covered landscape with a pale blue sky that covers almost half of the scene. The abundance of snow and wood reappears to

Figure 3.6 S. I. Shchelokov. "Work on the Moscow–Volga Canal."

create a construction scene that, perhaps unwittingly, reinforces historical accounts of the canal's construction: the intensive, often back-breaking, manual labor assisted by faithful horses pulling carts to and from the building site. In this painting Shchelokov captures not the finished product of construction, but rather the process of reshaping a relatively nondescript landscape into an emblem of Soviet power and Stalinist ideology. The canal workers are again minimized and faceless, scattered around the work site, with a lone excavator in the distance providing the only mechanized assistance in digging a potentially enormous foundation pit. Nature in this scene is neither abundant nor beautiful. Rather, meaning is being dug into the landscape with each shovel of dirt removed from the site. This process symbolizes the removal and repurposing of the "old," in this case the earth that is replaced with the "new," the waterway and its attendant structures. The painting records the spatial displacement that occurred all along the canal's building site, an act of simultaneous destruction and creation. Shchelokov's canvas captures a moment early in the canal's construction and conveys in soft colors and muted tones a rather sanitized and

Plate 1 A decorative ceramic plate featuring the Volga Junction. The plate is mounted on the façade of the Northern River Station.

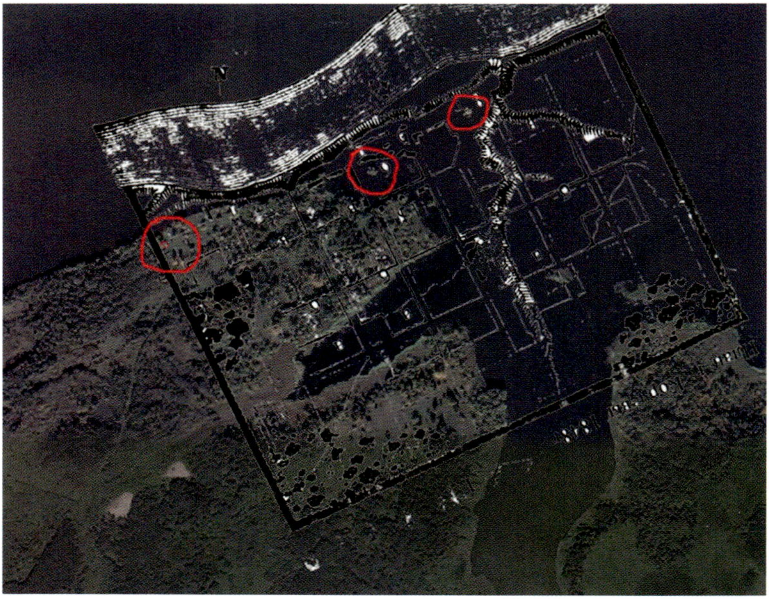

Plate 2 An approximate overlay of the town map of Korcheva and the old channel of the Volga River onto the current configuration of the Moscow Sea. The red circle on the far left denotes the last building standing in Korcheva – the former home of a merchant – while the center circle marks the spot of the Resurrection Cathedral and the right circle marks the former location of the Church of the Transfiguration that are now small islands in the Moscow Sea. They had previously stood high on the banks of the Volga.

Plate 3 G. E. Satel'. "The Moscow Canal."

Plate 4 F. A. Modorov. "The Moscow–Volga Canal. Yakhroma."

Plate 5 E. V. Egorov. "The Yakhroma Lock."

Plate 6 S. I. Shchelokov. Untitled.

Plate 7 S. I. Shchelokov. "Work on the Canal."

Plate 8 Moscow–Volga Canal shock worker pin for sale on eBay.

romanticized view of what we know to have been an excruciatingly difficult and exhausting task: excavating a large pit in which the canal's channel and structures would eventually be placed. Moreover, the scene conveys to the viewer that the construction and the inscription of meaning into the landscape were unceasing, because neither weather nor lack of mechanized implements could halt the building of the canal.

The view of construction that Shchelokov presents in this painting is cleansed and softened by his technique and color palette, illustrating a theme that unites all of the painted depictions of the Moscow Canal discussed here: the impetus for these canvases was to document a certain kind of construction and a certain outcome, one that cast the entire project and its subsequent exploitation in terms of ideology, power, and the control of perception. As Nick Baron argues, "Whereas Mendeleev and the centrographers strove to establish a dialogue between society and nature, Stalinism sought by force of political will to vanquish the landscape and overwhelm space, to recreate both nature and society according to its own ideological vision."[36] All these artistic works capture an idealized vision of a Gulag-supervised, forced labor project that dovetails perfectly with the dominant artistic ideology of the time: per the Socialist Realist canon, even with deviations into the painterly techniques of the Impressionists, the works shaped perception, rather than reflecting reality.

Furthermore, it would have been unacceptable to cast the prisoners working on the project in any other light save for their depiction as small cogs in a larger system, the importance of which overshadowed any individual accomplishments. Although there were in fact many individual accomplishments, the painted canvas was not the place to celebrate these. Instead, because of the totalizing space of the paintings and their ability to capture both a moment and place in time, presented in a manner accessible to any viewer (presumably one need not be highly literate in order to understand a Socialist Realist painting), these Moscow Canal paintings manage to create beauty that paints over the suffering and destruction in the midst of construction.

While these paintings vary thematically, they are united by the mandate to celebrate the Moscow Canal and to document its construction in a positive light in a way that was consonant with the desired attitude toward the project at that time. As Nick Baron notes:

> In the 1920s Soviet post-revolutionary thinking assigned primacy to objective space, the real, lived space of experience and abstract mathematical space, in accordance with Marxist-Leninist materialist doctrine. Through social science and artistic experimentation, Soviet culture strove to understand the innate constitution of space, identify its dynamics and triangulate its expanse, better to remodel it and redirect its energies toward the socialist reconstruction of humanities and nature.[37]

This philosophy likewise guided Soviet culture in the 1930s, as these canvases demonstrate. Such images go to the very heart of the Socialist Realist ethos, for they depicted not what was, but what should be: paintings in which the canal was bathed in soft light, pastel colors, or rich hues that celebrated not only the beauty of the landscape, but more importantly the structure that had been placed into it. While these paintings re-create the physical spaces they depict with each viewing, so, too, do they create a new imagined space within the viewer that is then subject to further scrutiny. Indeed, the changed landscape with its attendant man-made structures, such as steamships, lock towers, and wooden barracks, promoted the idea that they enhanced and improved the physical environment. Just as the sculptures conquered space through the upward motion they implied, so, too, did the paintings stake a claim in the space of the imagination of the viewer.

In this larger imagined space physical structures were intended to be more important than the people building them, as well as more imposing and significant than the natural world into which they were inscribed. The vertical, horizontal, and diagonal occupation of the physical space by man-made structures as displayed in the paintings asserts both the dominance of those structures and the domination of the ideology that made them possible. However, the natural environment in which those structures were situated also commands attention, as does the water that features in many of the paintings. The nature-scape and water suggest a permanence that weathered the imposition of the massive canal on them. Note, too, that everything included in the paintings refers back to water, either in the buildings erected to control it or its motion as rendered in oils and watercolors. The constancy of the flowing water and the pictures themselves parallel each other, given that viewers of the canvases bring a fresh reading of them each time they are scrutinized, just as Lefebvre posited.[38] Ultimately, the paintings move beyond the sculptures in staking out even more territory for the Moscow Canal. This space expands still further in literary depictions of it.

Literature

Having examined representative samples of the sculptures and paintings produced to shape perceptions of the Moscow Canal, our attention now turns to literary works that likewise created textual and metaphorical space that, no less than other art works, attempted to formulate an idealized picture of the Moscow Canal. This attempt strove to displace an actual landscape and replace it with a liminal space situated between that which existed on the page and in the reader's mind and the space which the canal actually occupied, while simultaneously ignoring other equally real but more ideologically fraught space, namely that of the Gulag. That neither of these volumes was published attests to the highly charged ideological space that surrounded them, most notably because of the proposed dates of publication: *Moscow–Volga Canal* in 1937 and *The Handcrafted River* in 1938, the years in which the Great Purges reached their zenith and during which some of those featured in these manuscripts were summarily executed for purported crimes against the State. Indeed as the *History of the Construction of the Stalin White Sea–Baltic Canal* volume attests, the removal of public figures from the national scene prompted the purge of photographs, paintings, and literary works in which they appeared as author, subject, or both.[39] While the earlier Belomor volume was pulled from public circulation, destroyed, or hidden deep within personal libraries in 1937, the publication of these volumes was prevented for the same reasons. Yet this reaction to the events poses a fascinating question that the following discussion attempts to answer: what impact does a manuscript that is never published and remains hidden in an archive have? That is, does preventing the publication of a potentially controversial tome neutralize the space in which it exists? Is there a void that remains, as in the many doctored photographs of the era in which enemies of the state and Stalin were expunged, or does the space mapped out by the literary work continue to occupy that space, even without readers? The old problem of the tree falling in an unpeopled forest applies here as well, for if a book is never read, does it cease to be a book and relinquish the literary space it might have created?

For almost 70 years a noteworthy book remained buried among the materials catalogued in the Library of the State Archive of the Russian Federation (GARF). Covered in a soft yellow binding, this volume boasts original watercolors and ink drawings commissioned from some of the era's most talented illustrators, who were also Dmitlag prisoners: Vasily Elkin, Gleb Kuhn, and Konstantin Sobolevsky, among others.[40] Technical illustrations, photographs, maps, and charts grace its pages, as does a frontispiece with a portrait of the man for whom such works ostensibly were created. A reader might wonder why this book has remained in such pristine condition: no smudges, torn pages, inked out names, or defaced portraits. The large, highly stylized letters that were supposed to begin the first word of each chapter are strangely absent. And it is this last clue that provides the key to solving the mystery, for this volume, the *Moscow–Volga Canal*, was never published. Indeed this single extant copy, a *maquette* or "dummy" copy in printing parlance, languished in obscurity from its creation in 1937 until Gulag scholar and GARF archivist, the late Alexander Kokurin, rediscovered it in 2004.

Similarly, the archives house the manuscript of another volume written to laud the achievement of the construction of the Moscow Canal. This manuscript, *The Handcrafted River* (*Rukodel'naia reka*), was likely due to be published in 1938, a date surmised from "permission to reprint" letters submitted to the volume's editor by the authors of articles.[41] *The Handcrafted River* was supposed to be produced under the auspices of the publishing house "The History of Plants and Factories,"[42] the very same entity responsible for publishing *The History of the Construction of the Stalin White Sea–Baltic Canal* that appeared in early 1934.[43] However, unlike its unpublished companion volume *Moscow–Volga Canal* and the Belomor *History of Construction*, both original narratives, *The Handcrafted River* was conceived as a collection of previously published newspaper articles that had appeared during and immediately after the construction of the Moscow Canal. Its roster of authors included not only well-known writers such as Vsevolod Ivanov and Viktor Shklovsky, but also technical and political figures such as Chief Moscow Canal engineer Sergei Zhuk and Gulag head Matvei Berman (who would not have lived to see the publication of this volume had it appeared in 1938, since he was executed in 1937). Presumably the book was conceived as a compendium of the best articles about the Moscow Canal in order to make them accessible in a single volume. Yet like *Moscow–Volga Canal* it remains in manuscript form in the State Archive of the Russian Federation.

Moscow–Volga Canal

The *Moscow–Volga Canal* narrates the construction of its namesake. Yet this work, the creation of multiple authors, never fulfilled its promise as the authoritative account of the construction of the canal that, upon its completion in 1937, was feted as the most significant engineering marvel of the USSR and the masterpiece of Dmitlag, the largest forced labor camp in the Gulag system. The vagaries of fate, in this instance the year 1937, sealed the destiny of the *Moscow–Volga Canal* (in Russian *Kanal Moskva-Volga*, hereafter *KMV*). Many of its contributors perished just as the text was supposed to be published, a circumstance that ensured its future as a forgotten account of a construction project, whose history was best ignored from then until now.

Unlike *The History of the Construction of the Stalin White Sea–Baltic Canal* produced to commemorate the construction of the Belomor Canal, the *KMV* text stands neither as the product of a writer's brigade nor as an experiment in literary montage. Nor does it overtly declare itself a "history." In contrast to its predecessor this narrative systematically explains, often in highly technical terms, how the Moscow–Volga Canal was built, which engineering innovations the project engendered, and how the construction process affected those who built it. While the narrative moves somewhat chronologically within each chapter, the overriding sense is not that of a historical account. Rather, the unifying idea that resonates in each chapter remains how the Moscow Canal transformed the landscape and created a space evocative of Soviet ideology and creativity. The themes of large-scale industrialization, Soviet innovation and engineering, and the hard work of exemplary individuals who worked as a team are writ large in the volume. Missing, however, is the name of the publishing house destined to produce the work, as well as the names of the editors who compiled the entries and organized the material. Indeed, no archival materials reveal this information.

The highly charged rhetoric of re-forging that saturated the pages of the Belomor volume is also lacking, replaced with a narrative tone that is at once triumphant and measured. Arguably the text's tone and thematic emphasis reflect the time in which it was produced: not only were the purges in progress, but the drive for and the rhetoric of re-forging had seemingly disappeared from public discourse, replaced by the new paradigm of the Soviet man, the Stakhanovite.[44] This shift from communal achievement to individual glory was woven into the fabric of *KMV*. In *Moscow–Volga Canal*, it is Lazar' Kaganovich who leads the cadres of individual heroes. Their ranks included the engineers and architects who fashioned the canal, as well as a select group of Dmitlag inmates whose literary output celebrated its construction.

The text's structure reflects this new emphasis. Spanning 350 pages over seven chapters, this account explicates the significant moments in the Moscow–Volga Canal's construction. A map of the canal's route is the first page the reader encounters, followed by the title page, devoid of any editorial or publisher information, with the next page featuring a full-page portrait of Stalin without any attribution to the artist who drew it. The preface, entitled "The Greatest Structure of the Stalinist Epoch" embeds the ensuing narrative within the history of Stalinist construction projects and argues for the Moscow–Volga Canal's primacy in this history. As the preface author A.V. Kosarev notes, "Our canal serves the objectives of the development of the socialist economy and culture by multiplying the waterways of the country and turning the red capital into the port of five seas."[45] Aleksandr Vasilievich Kosarev, who had led the Young Communist Organization, or Komsomol, was appointed to the Central Committee of the Communist Party in 1929, only to be arrested and executed in 1938.[46] Hence the list of those associated with this volume who fell victim to the very system they sought to praise begins with the very first named contributor.

The ensuing seven chapters contextualize their authors' experiences within the framework of the "greatest Stalinist structure." Chapters One and Seven frame the narrative of the intervening five chapters. Chapter One, "The Great Stalinist Highway," highlights the efforts, speeches, and guidance of Lazar' Kaganovich. This chapter includes excerpts from three of Kaganovich's speeches, as well as two complete edicts from the Communist Party's Central Committee and the Party's Moscow City Committee. These edicts include a *Resolution* that Kaganovich proposed in 1931 to unite Moscow River with the Volga, thereby supplying Moscow with a stable source of potable water; two speeches that Kaganovich delivered in 1931 and 1934 about the construction of the Moscow–Volga Canal; Stalin and Molotov's Decree of 1 September 1935 "On the Construction of the Moscow–Volga Canal," and the 1935 Decree of the joint plena of the Moscow Regional and Moscow City Committees of the Communist Party to provide whatever assistance was warranted to aid the construction of the canal.

The prioritizing of the Kaganovich materials as the rightful introduction to the volume underscores that the construction of the Moscow–Volga Canal was undertaken within the larger context of the reconstruction of Moscow. Arguably, it was the single most important element of that reconstruction, given the need for a sustainable supply of potable water to ensure and protect Moscow's growth as the first Soviet metropolis. Likewise, the official tone of the documents situates the event and its subsequent narrative not within the context of the Gulag, but within the context of state-sponsored construction projects to modernize the USSR, another illustration of Toby Clark's argument that perceived history trumps actual reality.[47] Missing, however, are those edicts produced at the completion of the canal that announce its opening, as well as the awards presented to its supervisors and engineers and the early releases awarded to worthy Dmitlag inmates. We can only guess why these decrees and resolutions were not included in this volume. The arrests of Semyon Firin and those associated with him no doubt precluded any official pronouncement that applauded his efforts, for how could he be simultaneously a state enemy and a praiseworthy NKVD officer?

Chapter Seven provides the closing bookend for the volume and returns to the epic proportions that the construction of the Moscow–Volga Canal reached. I. Fridliand, the chief architect of Moscow-Volgostroi, authored this chapter, entitled "Monument of the Epoch." In it he discusses the architectural achievements – lock towers, pump stations, dams – situated on the Moscow Canal, all the physical elements that create a spatial totality intended not only as an architectural monument of that moment, but also as a testimonial for the ages.[48]

Chapters Two through Four focus exclusively on the engineering achievements of the canal. Chapter Two, "The Project and the Work Site" includes four texts that detail how the canal's final route was chosen. Discussions of the three possible canal routes, as well as the intensive geological and geographical surveying work that comprised the pre-construction activities serve as the foci for two contributions to Chapter Two: "Three Options" and "The Search for the Route," each authored by a canal engineer, respectively A. Fidman and M. Muraviev. The director of the erstwhile Moscow-Volgostroi Museum, F. Ernst contributed a history of Dmitrov, the center of the Moscow–Volga project.[49] Ernst highlights how Dmitrov had long been considered a focal point for the construction of any waterway that would connect the Volga River with Moscow, from pre-Petrine times to the 1930s. N. Beliansky's essay, "The Moscow Taiga," describes the terrain that the canal route had to penetrate in order to connect Moscow with the Volga. Chapter Two defines the spatial parameters, both physical and imagined, into which the Moscow Canal was carved. As such it presents the landscape as a wilderness that must be tamed, as well as an environment that confounded prior attempts to organize it. That is, until the assumption of Soviet power in general and Stalinist ideology in particular, through which the industrialization of nature was both process and goal. Chapter Two segues cleanly into Chapter Three and its discussion of how the canal's builders managed to overcome nature.

A cadre of engineers, including the project's chief engineer Sergei Zhuk, authored Chapter Three, "The Conquest of Nature." Here the theme of overcoming and taming nature (in the spirit of Marx and the Belomor Canal project, where Zhuk was also the chief engineer) supports each entry and emphasizes the ability of Soviet engineering to dominate nature in ways that were hitherto impossible. A conquest of nature implies a reconfiguring of the space that it occupies such that natural processes and landscapes are altered in the service of progress. In this case, each contribution to Chapter Three locates the "conquest of nature" in processes devised on the canal construction site to remove, transfer, solidify, or otherwise alter the natural configuration of the land which would be dug out to create the canal. As a result the ensuing discussion in the chapter focuses on built spaces such as pumping stations and lock control rooms with their attendant technological achievements, and on the materials, such as concrete, deployed in this conquest. In addition, the essay "Water Works for the Bolsheviks" discusses how nature is turned on itself as a highly effective means of earth moving. The chapter concludes with a piece penned by Professor E. Skorniakov, director of the central research group for the construction of the Moscow–Volga Canal. "From the History of Two Canals" does not, as one might expect from the title, compare the construction of the Moscow Canal with its sister canal to the north, the Belomor Canal. Belomor, famously dismissed by Stalin as "shallow and narrow," neither carried the cachet that foreign waterways possessed, nor provided the USSR with the required real and imagined spaces as did the Moscow Canal. Moreover, the Moscow Canal linked Moscow with the rest of the world and figured heavily in the remaking of Moscow as the iconic Soviet capital. Any comparison with Belomor would detract from the achievement that was the Moscow–Volga Canal.

Instead, Skorniakov places the construction of the Moscow Canal in context with the history and construction of the Suez and Panama Canals for, as he argues, "The Moscow–Volga Canal is one of the greatest canals on earth. Only two canals – the Suez and Panama that have always been the source of pride of the hydro-technology of capitalist countries – can be compared with it based on the scope of work."[50] Skorniakov asserts that this comparison proves quite instructive in that Soviet power has been able to achieve that which took many years, if not centuries, in the capitalist system. As he notes:

> The history of the development of the Suez Canal is counted in centuries. They labored on the Panama Canal for 35 years. The greatest river canal in the world – the Moscow–Volga – was completed in record time: work was started in 1932, and the entire project was put into use in 1937.[51]

By pursuing this comparison, Skorniakov delineates the space occupied by the construction of the Moscow Canal in the spectrum of world history and world-wide canal construction. His account attempts to legitimize the rapidity with which the longer and more complicated Moscow Canal was built by ascribing it to the ingenuity and perspicacity of Soviet engineering, not to the intensive, back-breaking manual labor of the Dmitlag inmates. This provides a vivid demonstration of the change in ideology in the short period between 1934 and 1937, wherein the re-forging of social enemies was subordinated to the intellectual and ideological prowess of the Stalinist system. Unlike the Belomor *History of Construction*, which celebrated the remaking of purported social miscreants into honorable, skilled Soviet citizens, *KMV* emphasizes the work of skilled professionals in service to the state.

Chapter Four, "The Engineers," highlights the achievements of individual engineers and their skill at putting theory into practice. Significantly, this chapter includes the contribution of yet another L. Kaganovich (*not* the Moscow Party boss),[52] the person in charge of the division of equipment installation, entitled "The Canal was Built by the Whole Country." This is accompanied by two accounts of Stalin's visits to construction sites along the canal route: a visit in 1934 to the "Big Dig" near Khlebnikovo and an excursion to the Perervo lock in southern Moscow.

These accounts of Stalin's visits to construction sites at Perervo and the "Big Dig" bring up issues crucial to our understanding of the period. For example, Stalin is rhetorically cast as the engineer of society, technology, and human souls and the reconstruction of Moscow. He is put on par with the engineers who possess the real expertise to complete the project. As G. Afanasiev notes in his entry in *KMV*, "I answered the questions [posed by Stalin] and was increasingly surprised by how precisely and deeply the head of the Party and leader of our socialist homeland knew all the details and fine points of the excavation work."[53] Afanasiev, a captain in the NKVD and head of the Khlebnikovo region, not unexpectedly lavishes praise on Stalin, without whom the "Big Dig" would have been impossible:

> I am sure that our subsequent victories, the conquest of the Mossovet banner, the completion of the "Big Dig" eight months ahead of schedule – all this was the result of comrade Stalin's visit ... Instead of the formless chaos of the hills and valleys the calm ribbon of the canal stretched along the deep, even channel; but comrade Stalin's visit forever remained in the memory of all the participants in the glorious battle for the "Big Dig."[54]

Because Stalin assumes the mantle of the great, all-capable leader, he manages to inhabit the space of engineers in spite of his complete lack of expertise; he conquers engineering just as the professional engineers have conquered nature. This equation in turn elevates the importance of engineering to Soviet society and its ability to industrialize nature in pursuit of its higher goals. Stalin's ubiquitous portrait, which was to grace the first page of the *KMV* volume, as with so many other publications, provided the necessary imprimatur for the narrative and claimed the literary space therein as Stalinist space.

Similarly, by dubbing his contribution "the whole country built the canal," the technical specialist Kaganovich hyperbolically implies that every Soviet citizen contributed to building the Moscow Canal, and indeed helped reconstruct not only Moscow but Soviet society as well. As the builders of this new space, the Stalinist Soviet state, each member has a stake in it. Kaganovich's rhetorical claim that the whole country built the canal is clever: by including all of society as construction workers, he skillfully elides any mention of those who actually constructed the canal, namely the inmates of the Dmitlag camp. In similar fashion, *KMV* manages to avoid any treatment of the human cost of the project by limiting the discussion of the presumed re-forging of canal workers to the single, albeit hefty, Chapter Five.

Chapter Five, "Rebirth," features presumably inspirational stories mostly of the re-education of common criminals as skilled laborers and new Soviet citizens as a consequence of their experience on the MVC, with a few essays by political prisoners included for good measure. The essays are interlaced with illustrations produced by Dmitlag inmate artists, such as Gleb Kuhn and Vasily Elkin, as well as with posters designed to exhort the canal workers to achieve maximum productivity while reshaping their lives: "Not a single canal soldier will fail to compete. To the Completion of the Canal Ahead of Time!" or "Canal soldier! Heated labor melts away your sentence."[55] Inmate poets and prose writers produced these accounts, some of which were autobiographical, while others narrated particularly important moments during the canal's construction.[56] Only one essay openly refers to re-forging (*perekovka*) per se, "The Path of *Perekovka*," authored by the director of the cultural-educational sector, I. Lipsky. The director catalogues the various re-forging success stories because it fell under the purview of the cultural-educational sector to inculcate in prisoners the values of Soviet society. Another account, "The Continuation of One Life," links the Moscow–Volga volume to the Belomor history through the autobiography of Abram Roitenburg, the hero of Zoshchenko's contribution to the *History of Construction*, "The Story of One Life."[57] In *KMV* essayist Grigory Sorokin supplies the latest chapter in Roitenburg's journey through the Gulag, thereby illustrating for readers how Roitenburg's re-forging from criminal raw material into the labor-hardened metal of a new Soviet man was accomplished on both the Belomor and Moscow–Volga construction sites.

Significantly, Chapter Five is the longest chapter in the *KMV*, coming in at just under 100 pages. The chapter is generously interspersed with artwork, posters, and photographs of the canal construction site at various stages and in various places. Inmate poetry likewise graces the narrative. Yet the abundance of this material vis-à-vis the other chapters in the volume, as well as the inclusion of inmate authors who figured prominently in both the *Library of Re-forging* series and the journal *Storming the Worksite*, suggests that the volume's editor(s) intentionally created a space in which these voices could be heard. That these ideologically acceptable inmates, who include authors well-known within Dmitlag such as Nikolai Zhigul'sky, Mikhail Brilev, Lidia Mogilianskaya, and Valery Kalent'ev, occupy narrative space within the volume testifies to the enduring relevance of re-forging, even late in the 1930s; however, the inclusion of Lidia Mogilianskaya, lends further credence to one possible reason why this volume was never published. The compromised ideological integrity, arrests, and execution of Firin and his so-called "Firin Group," to which Mogilianskaya and Brilev purportedly belonged, torpedoed the political acceptability of the *KMV*.[58]

Finally, Chapter Six, "A Night on the Site," concludes the main segment of the narrative. This anonymous piece, subtitled "A Correspondent's Notes about One Night on the Construction Site," details life at various sites along the canal on a typical December night. A stunning watercolor of a lock illuminated against the night sky (between pp. 318 and 319) adorns the chapter, as do architectural drawings of lock towers and pumping stations. The text narrates the lives of Dmitlag bosses, engineers, and inmate laborers at this particular moment in time, and implies that the reader can extrapolate this single night into the standard scene at any point along the canal route. The chapter includes a breakfast and lunch menu for MVC Stakhanovites: "Breakfast for Stakhanovites: 1) Barley kasha with sauce. 2) Mashed peas. Dinner for Stakhanovites: 1) Meat soup with barley. 2) Pork with mashed potatoes. 3) Sweet roll with 65 percent flour. 4) Sweet tea."[59] In comparison to the rations typically allotted to average Dmitlag inmates, these offerings are positively spectacular, as indicated particularly by the meat on the menu. Likewise, the narrative describes leisure activities that include conjugal visits for Dmitlag inmates. Engineering innovations wrought through the ingenuity and audacity of the canal builders and engineers figure prominently during this particular night. The anonymous author regales the reader with the architectural details of a pumping station, the ingenuity behind the propeller pumps, and the labor-saving devices created on-site in the camp. Camp bosses play leading roles in shaping the lives of the inmates and managing construction, while Stakhanovite laborers demonstrate what it means to over-fulfill the production plan. In this regard the chapter blends examples of individual achievement and singular re-forgings with exemplary illustrations of collective effort, thereby uniting the two models of Soviet labor that dominated the 1930s. Oddly, although this is the penultimate chapter of the volume, it reads as if it is the concluding chapter, given that the anonymous author weaves the narrative strands previously developed in the preceding chapters into whole cloth, as it were, thereby seemingly drawing the text to a logical close.

Yet Chapter Seven, chief architect I. Fridliand's treatise on canal architecture,[60] moves this conclusion from the mundane to the sublime by asserting that the Moscow Canal undeniably serves as a monument of the epoch. Fridliand argues that the clean architectural lines of the structures erected along the Moscow Canal act as a counterpoint to the seeming medieval chaos of Old Moscow with its winding streets and ring roads. These new structures impart not only societal and ideological values, but also visual models for the new Soviet city that Moscow was in the process of becoming. While Fridliand compares the Moscow Canal with "capitalist" canals, such as the Panama, Suez, and Kiel, his most illustrative comparison comes when he links the construction of the Moscow Canal to the Moscow Metro, a concurrent project that likewise claimed new space and Sovietized it: whereas the Moscow Canal conquered vertical and horizontal space while inscribing itself into the landscape, the Moscow Metro claimed space underground by literally and figuratively forcing Soviet space into the earth. According to Fridliand, "Both the metro and the canal combined remarkable technology with new architecture to create works of art."[61] Fridliand goes on to comment:

> But there is a difference between the architecture of the metro and the architecture of the canal. The metropolitan is located underground and deprived of natural light. It is as if the metropolitan is self-contained . . . The canal is inextricably linked to the surrounding space – to the forests, roads, plains and urban landscapes. The canal's architecture fills out this landscape, enriches it and merges with it.[62]

At least rhetorically, the canal project has tamed nature in service to the Soviet state, just as it was intended.

Fridliand repeatedly asserts that the monumentality of the canal, as realized through the waterway itself and the structures constructed on and along it, makes it the grandest of structures and worthy of the labor and innovation that went into producing it and the praise garnered by the finished product. Indeed, Fridliand takes the reader on a virtual tour of the canal and highlights the architectural uniqueness of each lock, as well as the waterway's bridges and dams. In so doing, Fridliand intensifies and expands the reader's perception of the space through rich details and descriptions. Fridliand's virtual cruise from the junction where the Volga River meets the Moscow Canal, to the Northern River Port at Khimki, to the confluence of the canal with the Moscow River and its path to the Southern River Port in fact traces the actual space that the canal inhabits. He situates this journey spatially through his highly descriptive observations about each major architectural element, while further locating those elements in the larger whole of Soviet architecture and the reconstruction of Moscow. From this perspective, it is entirely appropriate that Fridliand's chapter concludes the *KMV* volume. The chapter simultaneously concludes an imagined excursion through the canal while focusing on the actual built environment. This approach subsumes all the preceding essays in the volume: the chapters leading up to Fridliand's discuss specific elements, from location, to materials, to free and inmate laborers that were unified to build the structure as a totalizing space. Fridliand locates his narrative within and beyond those constituent parts to create a textual version of the waterway that is fixed in space and time, yet also creates an imagined time/space continuum as visualized by the *KMV*'s readers, had there been any.

Spatially and literally Fridliand offers the last word on the canal. He concludes by stating that:

> The Moscow–Volga Canal is part of the grandiose plan of all time for the reconstruction of the city. The canal will raise the embankments of the abundant Moscow River, [and] will give denizens of the capital plenty of water, light, and greenery. The canal will enrich the capital with parks, gardens, stadiums; it will open magnificent vistas and will be the example of the marvelous confluence of technology, art, and nature. The canal, like the metro, and like everything else that is being created in our wonderful country, epitomizes the wonderful concern of Stalin for every member of our happy fatherland.[63]

Significantly he discusses the canal and Stalin's reputed concern for his citizens in resolutely spatial terms. Not only does the space of the canal itself provide benefits to Moscow, but it also creates new spaces that further enrich and territorialize the city. Stalin's concern is rendered through constructed spaces like the metro and the canal, and also through spaces that take shape as a consequence of these intentionally built landscapes. That Gulag labor built this environment ultimately becomes a minor point within the ever-growing space that Stalinist power creates and dominates.

This analysis of the *KMV* maquette offers a preliminary reading of a text that is vital to our apprehension of the literary space created to celebrate the waterway. The question posed at the beginning of this analysis, as to whether a book that has not been published nonetheless makes an impact, must be answered in the affirmative. Although it has never been published, the *KMV* occupies an important and necessary place within the space of literary production about the canal. The very existence of this work preserves original artwork that might have otherwise been lost. In so doing, it also reveals the identities of Dmitlag artists, thereby extending their agency through both space and time. This text also captures a moment in time on the cusp of the Great Terror and supplies further evidence of its sweep and vengeance, given the many *KMV* authors who perished in it. The rhetorical space that the narrative outlines substantiates the premise on which the present study rests: the creation of a Stalinist space relied not only on the construction of a visible physical structure and its surrounding landscape, but also on literary and figurative spaces that complemented and reinforced the built environment. Like the *KMV* text, *The Handcrafted River* also created a narrative space for the Moscow Canal, with a different approach but with the same outcome: it too was never published.

The Handcrafted River

The second manuscript, entitled *The Handcrafted River: The Moscow–Volga Canal* (*Rukodel'naia reka. Kanal Moskva-Volga*), roughly parallels the Belomor volume but not the *KMV*. Like the Belomor *History of Construction* this account was intended for publication in the *History of Factories and Plants* series.[64] The multiple authors of the narrative similarly included leading Soviet writers such as Viktor Shklovsky, Vsevolod Ivanov, and Aleksandr Avdeenko, all of whom also contributed to the Belomor volume. In addition, in *The Handcrafted River* Gulag Chief Matvei Berman authored an entry, as did the People's Commissar for Water Transport N. Pakhomov and the chief engineer of the Moscow–Volga project Sergei Zhuk. The authorial collective also included Maxim Gorky, whose name headed the contributor list and whose emotional speech at a rally of canal soldiers at Dmitlag provided a modicum of credibility and authority, similar to Gorky's imprimatur on the Belomor volume.[65]

Unlike the Belomor or *KMV* volumes, *The Handcrafted River* exists not as an original documentary literary work, but rather as a collection of previously published news stories and sketches that had appeared in major Soviet periodicals during and immediately after the construction of the Moscow Canal. The work's title likely was taken from an eponymous 29 April 1937 *Pravda* article by D. Zaslavsky that was to be included in the collection. The title of this book is significant for its allusion to the most characteristic element of the canal's construction: the immense manual labor supplied mostly by wheelbarrows and shovels wielded by labor camp inmates who often built the waterway with their bare hands. Taken in its most literal meaning, this title stresses that the canal was built by hand, indeed by many hands.

Furthermore, the title suggests the deeper meaning ascribed to this adjective. Typically *handmade* (*rukodel'nyi*), a conversational form, is applied to knitting, weaving, crocheting, or any form of needlework. These articles are usually produced by women who are accomplished mistresses of their craft. The adjective unites the notion of handmade with hand-crafted, thereby contributing an additional layer of meaning that extends the metaphor. In the case of the Moscow Canal, not only was it made by hand, but it was also hand-crafted, i.e. crafted by those who often were or became master craftsmen and thus produced an authentic work. More telling, of course, is the fact that the waterway is called a handmade *river*, an entity normally produced in nature, by nature and, as some would argue, by the hand of God. In supplying this title for the book the editor chose a richly metaphorical epithet that further promoted the notion that only as a consequence of Stalinist construction projects, bolstered by his namesake ideology, could a natural feature of the landscape, a visible and palpable inscription into that landscape, be achieved. The implication was that Soviet power was able not only to change nature, but to create and even re-create it. Yet the irony of the sobriquet that a major construction project was built by hand, with minimal mechanization, could not have been lost on readers, given the supposed apex of Soviet industrialization occurring in the 1930s as well as news reports filled with the metaphors of industrial development. To publicly applaud "handiwork" seemed to fly in the face of the accepted rhetoric of industrialization.

As the archival materials reveal, contributors received letters from a certain comrade Rudoi (no initials or forename provided), an official with the "History of Factories and Plants" publishing house, in which he requested their permission to reprint their articles in this volume.[66] The archival file also discloses that the design of the proposed volume was to include before and after maps of the canal route, portraits of Stalin, Molotov,[67] Kaganovich, and other important figures, photographs of various stages of canal construction, and pictures of the so-called "best people" that the project produced. Likely the list of "best people" would include the most skilled engineers and the most thoroughly re-forged Dmitlag inmates, as well as some of their NKVD bosses.

The aforementioned reprints of news stories comprised the majority of entries. In addition, official government edicts and resolutions, as well as an article and letter by Maxim Gorky, would round out the book's contents. These include Kaganovich's 15 June 1931 Resolution concerning the Moscow Canal project and its role in Moscow's reconstruction (also found in *KMV*);[68] a decree signed by Molotov and Stalin dated 4 July 1937 that announced the official completion of the Moscow–Volga Canal; a decree dated 17 June 1937 awarding the Order of Lenin to NKVD chief Nikolai Ezhov; and the 15 July 1937 decree signed by Kalinin,[69] Molotov, and Gorkin[70] that outlines the awards and prizes given to some of the canal builders.[71] Based on the manuscript, it is unclear for whom this volume was intended. Given the scope of the articles and the inclusion of maps and official resolutions, presumably the editor posited a wide readership because of the accessibility of the reprinted articles and the laudatory tone that imbued them. The original publication date for each entry has been crossed out, and a few of the authors' names have been removed. One page of the archival file clarifies the surnames of workers, engineers, and NKVD supervisors that a reader would encounter in the text (l. 195), further suggesting that the book would appeal to a broad audience.[72] Minor editorial changes sparsely dot the manuscript. In a final twist, two entries that also were set to appear in *KMV* were reproduced verbatim in *The Handcrafted River*: the contributions from Chief Engineer Zhuk and from Professor E. Skorbiakov. Why these two narratives are included in both manuscripts remains unclear. Likewise, no evidence explains who derailed the book's publication, especially since censors and editors had already vetted all the materials for publication when they originally appeared in various newspapers such as *Pravda, Izvestiia, Trud, Literaturnaia Gazeta*, and others. It still is possible to conjecture why this book did not see the light of day given, for example, the presence of soon-to-be-purged Matvei Berman as well as the mention of numerous figures involved in the Moscow Canal construction such as the ubiquitous Semyon Firin who suffered the same fate as Berman.

In all, 40–5 items were potentially set for inclusion in *The Handcrafted River*; however, there are two Tables of Contents for the book. The first of these lists the submissions chronologically and displays check marks next to 40 presumably approved entries. The 15 June 1936 article from *Pravda* by Zheleznov and A. Khvat is unchecked,[73] and selections by I. V. Yavitz (an article in *Trud* dated 8 September 1936), D. Zaslavsky (a *Pravda* article from 4 May 1937), and A. Avdeenko (a *Pravda* article from 7 July 1937) are crossed out.[74] The second Table of Contents lists 45 entries, of which five are crossed out, bringing the total to 40 reprints. While there are a few discrepancies between the two Tables of Contents in terms of which materials were included and excluded, the bulk of the content remains the same. While the second Table of Contents does not follow chronological order, it reflects the actual order of the reprints in the assembled manuscript; the reprints are grouped thematically. The informal thematic groupings seem to be as follows:

(1) Early work on the Moscow Canal and its comparison with other canals;
(2) technological advances and laborer industriousness;
(3) specific work sites and the overcoming of nature;
(4) the results;
(5) the engineers and laborers;
(6) the achievement of the canal and its significance; and
(7) resolutions and awards to mark the canal's completion.

These rough categories disrupt the chronology of the articles' original publication dates, but present a more logical progression of ideas organizing the materials.

As the editor T. Kovenev[75] states in the plan for the book, "From 385 articles and sketches dedicated to the construction of the Volga–Moscow Canal, I have chosen the selected materials above. The sketches and articles have been chosen and organized in such a way that the collection generally will present a coherent picture of this greatest structure."[76] Kovenev continues:

> Of course it is impossible to consider this volume a complete sequential history of the canal's construction. Here only particular states of construction are highlighted and a sufficiently complete explanation of its significance [is presented]. Many of these articles and sketches appear to have been subjected to editing ... This work must be done in concert with the authors or with their agreement.[77]

This wording suggests that Kovenev's explanation was intended to justify publishing the volume, especially since he supplies the anticipated length of the finished product and reinforces the necessity of collaboration between the contributors, the editor, and the publishing house.[78]

The ordering of the selections notwithstanding, all of them address three main themes: 1) The achievement of the construction project thanks largely to the vision of Stalin; 2) The ability of Soviet power to overcome any natural obstacle in its quest to deploy nature in the service of the Stalinist state; and 3) The ingenuity and fortitude of the engineers, NKVD bosses, and Dmitlag laborers in completing the project. In contradistinction to the *KMV*, *The Handcrafted River* omits selections authored by the Dmitlag inmates. Rather, the featured articles retell the stories of some criminal re-forgings as told to the authors by those who have been re-forged through their labor. Hence established writers and journalists assume the telling of the tale.

While these themes unify the material, the most salient unifying factor remains the attempt of each submission, regardless of its topic, to claim rhetorical space that reveals how the Moscow Canal project indeed created Soviet and Stalinist space. To achieve this unstated, though no less significant, goal the contributors to *The Handcrafted River* take the expected approach, frequently reiterating Stalin's vision and leadership in making this Tsarist dream a Soviet reality. We see titles such as "The Pride of Stalin's Second Five-Year Plan," repeated references to Stalin in several articles, descriptions of Stalin's visit to the canal work site, and oft-repeated phrases such as:

> In the first place and the most important reason for our success is that the Central Committee of the Bolshevik Party, the Council of Peoples Commissars of the USSR, and especially personally comrade Stalin demonstrated exceptional concern and attention, and offered help and support to the construction collective ... Stalin's concern inspired us and we worked with maximum enthusiasm and energy.[79]

Stalin's presence is woven into the narrative in both obvious and subtle ways so that the "history" being revealed rests on the ideological foundation that Stalin supposedly built.

Repeatedly throughout the collection nature is cast as the enemy of Soviet power, to which it submits when the canal is completed. Natural spaces and the built environment that replaces them feature prominently in each article. Some articles note the landscape into which the waterway is carved, while others applaud the victory over nature. In his contribution, "The Newborn River," B. Agapov notes that "The water flowed! At first as mankind's idea, and now in reality. Man has created a river. And nature has accepted it as an inevitability because we are more powerful than nature."[80] Note that Agapov's title reaffirms the life-giving quality of water in that the "river" has been born, while imbuing the waterway with a trait shared by all animals: birth. The author gives agency to nature by noting that it has "accepted" the created waterway, an act impossible for an abstraction such as "nature" to perform. In this short statement Agapov manages to accentuate the ability of Soviet power to overcome nature by using the natural element of water, albeit imbued with human/animal traits, to turn against itself. This "new birth" signals a new beginning.

Similarly, titles such as "The New Geography of the Country," "Earth," "The Volga Arrives in Moscow," "Volga Water Goes to the Capital," and "The Intelligent River" emphasize the spatial dimension central to this coordinated set of articles. Each title reveals human intervention in a natural space such that the very contours of the landscape emerge from the new technology, the plan, and the work accomplished on the project. These pieces likewise narrate how the canal should be rendered on a map: trees, hills, bogs, marshes, and forests are the landscape features that stood in the way of construction only to be vanquished or marshaled into the effort to build the canal. Manual labor and the mastering of water to achieve this task coalesce to emphasize that the metaphorical landscape that the articles have constructed has materialized to reshape the country's geography.

In an effort to create this new geography, the implication is that socialist construction also was charged with creating art. As Eksler argues in his article "The Face of the Canal," itself another attempt to imbue the canal with human qualities:

> The construction of socialism is creation. In it knowledge and labor are not divorced from inspiration, from the poetic implementation of reality. The Volga–Moscow Canal was an artistic representation before it became a project on paper. It remained an artistic representation, absorbing into itself all the magnetism of the battle for the happiness and culture of the nation.[81]

Not only does *The Handcrafted River* illuminate significant moments in the construction of the Moscow Canal, thereby locating it in both time and space, it also claims additional space in casting the construction project as an artistic endeavor. This blends the metaphorical space created in the reading of the text with the artistic space that engendered it, coupled with the imagined space of greatness, power, and superiority that underpinned rhetoric about the waterway. Of course, this volume is laden with propagandistic tropes that are quick to praise the enterprise and ignore its negative effects. With hindsight we can see, however, that this contradiction does not detract from the impression the volume gives and the inspiration, no matter how ideologically colored it might be, behind this literary project.

In fact, as Katerina Clark argues in *Moscow, the Fourth Rome*, this combination of "joy and terror" points to a trend in literary texts of the late 1930s to create what, borrowing from Harsha Ram's words, she terms the "Imperial Sublime." As she notes:

> It could be said that the appropriation of sublime imagery by the Soviet rhetoric of the late 1930s was a move to make Soviet "reality" adequate to the terror. These extreme times demanded a Stalin and a nature (reality) of hypostasized, awe-inspiring dimensions.[82]

This understanding applies to *KMV* and *The Handcrafted River* because of the rhetorical landscape of power relations and the physical space those power relations created through the Moscow–Volga Canal. In reality, both terror and joy infused the canal project, while in the texts the enthusiastic attitudes of those involved purposely overshadowed any hint of terror. Clark also notes that "Stalinist culture of the late 1930s to a marked degree favored settings well away from the cities, in untamed nature."[83] This trope of untamed nature was tightly woven into the fabric of both the Moscow Canal project and the volumes written about it. The notion that underpinned both of these texts, as well as the sculptures and paintings, emphasized the reshaping of nature, that is the landscape into which the Moscow Canal was inscribed, and the taming of it through architectural features and sheer force of will as realized through the labor of Dmitlag inmates.

Whereas Clark stresses the counterpoint of arctic landscapes and other locations on the Soviet periphery as the means through which literary characters "realize themselves in sublime nature, far from urban centers,"[84] in these Moscow Canal narratives, the sublime is realized in the physical existence of the canal and through those who built it, from inmate laborers to engineers to architects. Clark argues that "The sublime provides a counterpoint to the bureaucratic world, compensating for its grayness."[85] Certainly this is the case not only in the canal texts, but in the paintings and sculptures discussed above. Moreover, as she notes, "The sublime in Stalinist culture functioned to naturalize and enhance power relations, and to transpose action from an urban, bureaucratic world with its obvious restrictions and constraining conventions to a dramatic periphery, thereby minimizing the presence of the banal world of apartments and offices."[86] Clark further posits that "the new sense of the periphery was largely conveyed in terms not of construction sites but of a grandiose natural landscape."[87] The Moscow Canal captures this sense of the periphery through the natural landscape into which it was placed and through the space of the construction site. The waterway likewise emblematizes the sense of center because of the construction of Moscow as the focal point of Soviet power and the "Port of Five Seas." The "ribbon of water" ties together the periphery and the center into a single Stalinist whole that embodies physically and metaphorically the "imperial sublime," especially as narrated in these two unpublished texts.

As regards the Moscow Canal, its physical periphery reached only as far as Dubna to the north and included Moscow itself, the socialist metropolis. Yet this periphery might just as well have been in the Far North or East given that the territory the waterway's construction site covered was part of the Gulag, a constellation of prisons, camps, and settlements that operated on the periphery of the country, but most definitely was fixed within the social periphery of Soviet society. In contradistinction to the literary hero who embodies this "imperial sublime" and who "goes to Moscow on a mission from his far-flung village or work site . . . meets some high official . . . and returns to his community recharged and ready to pull off its state-assigned task,"[88] canal workers, if they were lucky, would return to their homes having pulled off the state-assigned task, having perhaps met a high official on the work site, and would be ready to blend into life somewhere on the periphery. If they were "recharged" at all it was likely the result of the skill and literacy they acquired while working on the canal. For the free laborers, engineers, and architects on the canal project, they arguably left the waterway's work site inspired by the colossal structure they had designed and created.

Despite the care and effort that went into them, both *KMV* and *The Handcrafted River* remain unpublished, relegated to the shelves of an archive, which prompts the question as to whether any officially sanctioned text was issued to document and applaud the achievement of the Moscow Canal. Indeed such a text exists, and its contents reveal why it was *the* permissible text.

The Moscow–Volga Canal 1932–7

How was it that *The Moscow–Volga Canal 1932–7* (or *KMV: 32–7*)[89] saw the light of day when its companion volumes did not? This question is easy to answer if we examine its contents and authorship. Published in 1940 by the State Publishing House of Construction Literature, this volume bore the imprimatur of the NKVD on its title page, along with the admonition that "The transfer or resale {of this volume} is not permitted." Instead of a single identified author or authors' collective, the "author" of this text was the "NKVD-USSR: Office of Technical Reports Concerning the Construction of the Moscow–Volga Canal." Unlike the volumes discussed above, this book was not only officially sanctioned by the NKVD, but was its own in-house publication. Significant too is the stamp on the title page that reads: "Use of the primary data, as well as the designs, plans, and photographs in other publications without the consent of the NKVD Office of TechReports is forbidden." As page 1 reveals, both the contents and distribution of this book were tightly controlled, even to the point of its limited 3000 copy run.

Moscow–Volga Canal 1932–7 is the first volume in the series of "Red Books," so named because of the crimson covers with which ten of the 11 volumes are bound. The decision to publish this series was made in a 1939 decree that outlined the contents for each volume. Sixteen volumes were projected in the series, but only 11 were published. The outbreak of World War II interrupted publication and only one volume appeared after the war in 1945, *Moscow–Volga Canal 1932–7. Ancillary Materials* (*Vospomogatel'nye materialy*); its cover is beige rather than bright crimson. The other ten volumes appeared 1940–1 and covered a wide range of topics, including: transport structures in and on the canal (such as locks, emergency gates and ports); bridges and highways; water supply lines and sanitation; assembly work during the project; research projects, and other topics. Igor Kuvyrkov of the Moskva-volga.ru site notes:

> I call the multi-volume set of technical reports "Red books" that were released based on the results of the engineering and scientific

> work on the construction site of the Moscow–Volga Canal. Canal old-timers talk about them with deep respect and even in hushed tones. For them these publications are like *The Bible* is for Christians.[90]

As Kuvyrkov also explains, the volumes vary in tone and quality, ranging from dry, technical treatises to highly readable, informative works that would appeal to a diverse audience beyond those interested in the technical aspects of the waterway's construction.[91] As it turns out, the first volume under discussion here, published in 1940, is one of those readable works.

KMV: 32–7 is not without its rhetorical and decorative flourishes. As the book opens, the reader encounters an illustration of a commemorative Moscow–Volga Canal pin, along with the familiar exhortation "Workers of the world unite!" A color map of the Moscow–Volga Canal graces its frontispiece, with the requisite red color designating Moscow and pastel blue marking the canal and its attendant water features. Excerpts from the 4 July 1937 decree signed by Molotov and Stalin, which announced the completion of the canal, feature prominently on page 3. After a brief introduction,[92] the reader discovers the obligatory portrait of Stalin that marks the true beginning of the narrative. Neither on the title page, nor in the Table of Contents, does one find the names of the specific authors of each chapter. Rather, the Introduction is signed by the Editorial Board, whose members are noted on page 2 and include the main engineer of the Moscow Canal project, Sergei Zhuk.

Over the course of the 316 pages it becomes clear that the *KMV: 32–7* will feature neither literary texts nor original artwork. Instead, explicit discussions of the engineering feats achieved during the construction of the canal are included, as are detailed data concerning all elements of the project, from the amount of earth moved to the dimensions of each lock chamber; from the layout of dams and dikes to the specifics of the turbines. This text devotes itself to those topics that generally escape any tinge of politics or dangerous personalities by describing in neutral language the intricacies of the Moscow Canal. Numerous photographs, maps, drawings, and construction designs accompany the narrative in order to illustrate more clearly the topics under discussion. The editors divided the work into six sections, each of which features multiple chapters. Each section focuses on one major element of the construction process: Section I: The National Economic Premises of the Construction of the Moscow–Volga Canal; Section II: The Natural Conditions of the Canal's Path; III: The First Attempts and Options for Uniting Moscow with the Volga; IV: The Realized Canal Project; V: The Organization and Pace of Construction; VI: Preparation for the Development and Initial Operation of the Canal. As each section heading attests, the narrative delves into the engineering, expertise, and labor required to realize the project, coupled with the wise and firm guidance of the government in the person of Stalin.

The only nod to any cultural products related to the project is a chapter entitled "The Canal's Architecture."[93] Although not attributed to a specific author, much of the narrative reads very much like A. I. Mikhailov's paperback booklet *The Architecture of the Moscow–Volga Canal*, which was published in 1939. Certain phrases in fact paraphrase segments of Mikhailov's narrative, while others repeat the general ideas Mikhailov expressed, as well as those found in the larger, hardback volume *The Architecture of the Moscow–Volga Canal* that also appeared in 1939.[94] This richly and generously illustrated book contains a chapter that Mikhailov wrote, along with other chapters written by famous Soviet architects and professors of architecture. The same tone emanates from the pages of all three discussions of the canal's architecture. However, in *KMV: 32–7* the scant 12 pages that describe and applaud the architectural achievements on the waterway feature a condensed version of the need for and function of architecture in this project.

The required castigation of capitalist countries opens "The Canal's Architecture" and is juxtaposed with the more just cause of the Stalinist state: "It is a different story here, where in general any capital construction project is first and foremost directed at the benefit of the workers and in the end follows the maximum possible satisfaction of the material and cultural-aesthetic demands of a citizen-creator and participant in communist society."[95] The chapter then details some of the more striking elements of the canal's architecture, such as the sculptures discussed previously, as well as lock towers and the Northern River Station at Khimki. This narrative is couched in the sentiment that, "Together with the Palace of Soviets, these structures will serve as artistic monuments of socialist culture of the great epoch of Stalinism."[96] It would have been odd to exclude a discussion of the canal's architecture even in this NKVD-sponsored volume that ostensibly deals with engineering issues, because of the importance placed on the architectural elements that graced the canal. The monumental nature not only of the waterway itself, but also the architectural triumphs achieved on it, were worthy of the praise bestowed upon them (As we will see in Chapter Four, the issue of monumentality is writ large over the Moscow Canal project.)

On a different note, the three Moscow Canal volumes (*KMV*, *The Handcrafted River* and *KMV: 32–7*) intersect in a chapter entitled "The Whole Country Built the Canal" in *KMV: 32–7*. This chapter, which concludes the section entitled "The Organization and Pace of Construction," parallels two similar sections of the two unpublished Moscow Canal tomes. In *KMV*, a chapter with the same title was authored by L. Kaganovich, *not* the Party official in charge of the reconstruction of Moscow, but rather the head of the Supply Sector for Installation Work. In *The Handcrafted River* S. Figner's article, which originally appeared in *Komsomol'skaya Pravda*, was to be included with the title "The Working Hands of the Whole Country." Each narrative details how small and large industrial enterprises from across the USSR contributed to the building of the Moscow Canal. While Figner's one-page version is the most concise, it nonetheless manages to name a number of cities and republics whose industries supplied parts and materials for the project. As the article concludes, "Large and small enterprises – they all bear the title of producers of the greatest hydro-technical structure."[97]

In *KMV* the "other" Kaganovich provides a year-by-year account of the entire country's increasingly prominent role in the waterway's construction. With each year more Soviet industries were enjoined to assist through the production of heavy equipment, machinery, and raw materials, including larch boards from the Urals and Eastern Siberia and red granite from Volynia. Similarly, Kaganovich emphasizes that the Moscow Canal project served as the impetus for creating homegrown Soviet solutions to issues such as building adequately large portal cranes for the Ivan'kovo Dam or sufficient earth-moving equipment or turbines that would be up to the task of creating energy or operating the pumping stations. As the narrative progresses it reveals stronger and broader cooperation, competition, and ingenuity. Kaganovich reaches the same conclusion as Figner:

> The south and north, the east and west of the immense Soviet Union sent their products to the Moscow–Volga construction site. Hundreds of industrial firms – from the titans of heavy industry to small factories, tens of thousands of people there produced the most diverse kinds of equipment for the canal – from gigantic booster transformers to doorknobs. The construction of the canal turned into a nationwide job. Under the leadership of the Party the whole country built the canal.[98]

In contrast, the authorship of the chapter in *KMV: 32–7*, "The Whole Country Built the Canal," is never explicitly stated.[99] Like the two narratives discussed above, this chapter in *KMV: 32–7* focuses on the technical and industrial achievements of the Moscow Canal. There is the required delineation of all the industries and locations that contributed raw materials, finished goods, and know-how to the waterway. The narrative also describes how technical challenges were overcome through the ingenuity and dogged determination of workers from across the USSR. However, this chapter differs from those discussed above in key ways: the *KMV: 32–7* narrative features several passages quoted directly from *Pravda*, although the publication information is not provided. In addition, direct quotations with footnoted references from *The History of the All-Union Communist Party* published in 1938 also appear in the narrative. This is no accident.

Unlike its companion volumes, *KMV: 32–7*'s "The Whole Country Built the Canal" offers generous praise for the Party and its leaders, foremost among them Stalin. References to Party cadres or the lack thereof appear frequently. The narrative implies that without these cadres the waterway would have never been built. We see statements such as:

> This was a serious danger, arising as a consequence of the fact that the growth of cadres able to harness technology had not succeeded and lagged far behind the growth of technology ... [Workers] did not understand that technology is dead without people who have technical expertise. They didn't understand that technology can achieve the highest productivity only when there are skilled specialists. The question of cadres that possess technical know-how thus gained paramount importance.[100]

That there were insufficient cadres on the canal construction site meant that "The Moscow Party committee came to [its] aid . . . At the beginning of 1935 groups of Party, Komsomol and trade-union workers were sent to the construction site and played a large role in rallying the collective of the canal construction workers."[101] Similar rhetoric recurs in the chapter, thus intimately connecting the successful construction of the Moscow Canal with the Party and its cadres: "All together at the construction site there were more than 3,000 engineers and 3,150 technicians and master craftsman, of whom a significant part were Communists and Komsomol members."[102]

No references discuss the more than 200,000 Dmitlag prisoners who built the canal. Neither are specific engineers or particular NKVD officers mentioned by name, largely because most of said officers had been liquidated in 1937–8. The only outright reference to the NKVD is in connection with the purported sabotage of the canal project, including the damning phrase "enemies of the people":

> However, enemies of the people wanted to put their hand to this wonderful structure of the second five-year plan. On the construction site more than a few hangers-on of the Trotsky–Zinoviev and Bukharin–Rykov gangs, spies and saboteurs, malefactors tried to undermine the canal's construction and turn history back to capitalism with the return of workers being oppressed by landowners and the bourgeoisie.[103]

Thanks only to "the sharp eye of the Soviet intelligence service, [and] the vigilance of the organs of the NKVD were the dastardly activities of spies and saboteurs and the exposed hirelings of capitalism destroyed in time."[104] Significantly, none of the extant sources on the construction of the Moscow Canal, aside from this chapter in *KMV: 32–7*, discuss any sort of sabotage or espionage in connection with the project. This is not surprising, given the overall tone of *KMV: 32–7* and its omniscient narration. The penultimate paragraph of *KMV: 32–7*'s "The Whole Country Built the Canal" states that "The completed canal is one of the most striking pieces of evidence of Stalin's concern for the common man, and provides workers both now and in the future with material prosperity and a cultured way of life."[105]

"The Whole Country Built the Canal" thus adds a new spatial dimension to the Moscow Canal enterprise. Labor across space creates another way of imagining the geography of the country, because supply lines from around the USSR trace pathways that converge at the Moscow Canal and, by extension, in Moscow. The metaphorical labor flow, coupled with the tactile flow of finished goods and raw materials, forge the connection between the country and its capital, between the leader and his people. This imagined landscape implies the strength of Soviet power to marshal its forces in pursuit of building "the greatest structure of the Stalinist epoch," while trying to convince every citizen that s/he will benefit from and has participated in its construction. Labor and socialist construction become new ways of identifying the territory as Soviet, as conceived by Stalinist ideology and practice. These spatial markers likewise provide the channels along which the Stalinist way of life transports itself to every corner of the USSR. The success of this process varies and can be debated, but it epitomizes the rhetorical and metaphorical space that the Moscow Canal created and concretizes the significance of the *Moscow–Volga Canal 1932–7*.

Prior to the release of *KMV: 32–7* in 1940 no officially sanctioned text had been published to document and glorify the completion of the Moscow–Volga Canal in 1937. This situation contrasts with the publication of *The History of the Construction of the Stalin White Sea–Baltic Canal*, which was written in record time: the Belomor Canal opened in August 1933 and its attendant volume appeared in January 1934 in time for the 17th Communist Party Congress. That no similar work about the Moscow Canal existed, a more significant undertaking on many levels, left an empty "space" in the growing library of books dedicated to Stalinist achievements. How could it be that lesser projects occupied these spaces, while no substantial work about the Moscow Canal existed? The answer of course centers on timing. The Moscow Canal was completed just as those most invested in its construction, such as Semyon Firin, Matvei Berman, and others were arrested and charged as "enemies of the people." These were precisely the presumed "saboteurs and malefactors" who were weeded out by the sharp-eyed NKVD (their own organization) as noted in *KMV: 32–7*.

Showing once again that timing is indeed everything, *KMV: 32–7* was published, while *Moscow–Volga Canal* and *The Handcrafted River* never saw the light of day, because of their anticipated publication dates in 1937 at the height of the Great Terror and because many of those connected with, celebrated in, or responsible for these volumes found themselves the victims of the very system they sought to applaud in these texts. Just as *The History of the Construction of the Stalin White Sea–Baltic Canal* was pulled from library shelves, hidden away in private apartments, and destroyed wholesale because of its connection to purged state enemies, so too were *Moscow–Volga Canal* and *The Handcrafted River* relegated to obscurity for the same reason. Yet how could a project as celebrated and visible as the Moscow Canal not capture any narrative space aside from the ephemera of newspaper and journal articles?

To rectify this situation, the NKVD produced *KMV: 32–7* to occupy this empty space and to create a metaphorical and literary space into which the Moscow Canal project could be placed. Rather than celebrate the art and artistry of the waterway, *KMV: 32–7* instead focused on technology, innovation and Party-mindedness, pertinent but somewhat neutral topics in an era fraught with suspicion and perceived treachery. The growing cult of Stalin precipitated this necessary shift in the Moscow Canal narrative from personal testimony and specific authorship to omniscient narration and authorial responsibility shared by an editorial collective that included perhaps the most lauded Soviet hydro-technical engineer, Sergei Zhuk, who managed to escape the Purges. The structure and content of *KMV: 32–7*, with its emphasis on the general facts of the waterway's construction and subsequent exploitation as a water and transport resource, permitted a retelling of the story from the perspective of the Party and, most importantly, Stalin's leadership. Like so many other publications of the time, the opening lines of *KMV: 32–7* set the tone of the entire volume: "The brilliant idea of the fundamental Bolshevik solution to the age-old problem of uniting Moscow with the main waterway of the Soviet Union – the Volga – belongs to the great Stalin."[106] As subsequent paragraphs detail, the Communist Party's Central Committee, under Stalin's leadership, finally settled the problem of Moscow's water supply through the construction of the Moscow Canal. Just as with its oft-compared twin project, the Moscow Metro, Stalin's wisdom and foresight reputedly created the space in which these projects could be realized:

> Comrade Stalin proposed building the metropolitan simultaneously with the development of the tram and bus

> systems, thereby guaranteeing the mass and swift transport of passengers. And here the idea of comrade Stalin naturally turned out to be correct, fundamentally solving the problem completely. The Moscow–Volga Canal, like the metropolitan, is the most striking expression of Stalin's concern for the common man. Only the Party of the Bolsheviks, only Soviet power is capable of putting to the service of workers the inexhaustible natural wealth and resources of our boundless homeland with such scope and daring unprecedented in history.[107]

In using these formulaic and excessively laudatory expressions concerning the audacity and wisdom of Stalin and the Party, which were repeated endlessly and considered de rigueur for any official publication, *KMV: 32–7* secured for itself a physical, metaphorical, and rhetorical space that permitted an official account of the construction of the Moscow–Volga Canal that was simultaneously officially acceptable and selectively true.

Bridging Physical and Metaphorical Space

The idea of the Moscow–Volga Canal was made real not only through the construction of the waterway, but through the cultural products created to capture and interpret the space it physically occupied. The sculptures, paintings and narratives each presented a spatial representation of the canal that simultaneously supported Stalinist ideology, and also created for viewers and readers a metaphorical space in which their apprehension of the waterway was conditioned by how it was represented. Whereas the sculptures positioned along the waterway impressed viewers with their physicality and dynamism, the paintings often conveyed a calm, pastel scene that belied the forced labor and harsh conditions in which the canal was constructed. Similarly, the unpublished manuscripts for *Moscow–Volga Canal* and *The Handcrafted River* depicted a project imbued with cultural creativity coupled with engineering genius and astounding construction feats. Yet these versions of the canal's construction failed to find their readership because of the time and place in which they were produced. Only after the peak of the Great Terror had passed was it possible on the third try to produce an acceptable written account of the Moscow–Volga Canal's creation: this narrative was designed not so much to celebrate the achievement of the canal, but of the system that was able to produce it. How else to account for the paucity of description of the canal as a cultural space (save for the lone chapter on the canal's architecture), contrasted with the abundance of technical information, photographs and diagrams that in a sense raised the manipulation of technology in the service of man to an art form? Detailed diagrams, illustrations, and numerous photographs graced *KMV: 32–7* in a celebration of technical achievement and ideological stamina.

The sculptures, as the most visible cultural product, and the paintings managed to romanticize not only viewer perception of the canal, but the waterway itself. The written accounts evolved from a wholly author-driven creative enterprise as conceived in *Moscow–Volga Canal* to the less dangerous reassembly of previously published material in *The Handcrafted River*. The difficulty with these texts, however, resided in the fact that their authors were identified and celebrated by virtue of their inclusion in these volumes. This creates a highly problematic situation when some of those very same authors or the people about whom they were writing are forcibly removed from the scene. Their physical absence leaves an empty space, but their texts remain fixed in place. The only way to deny these narratives the rhetorical space they sought to occupy was to not publish them at all and instead replace them with a book that would satisfy ideological conditions while appropriating the rhetorical space that needed to be filled by a history of the Moscow–Volga Canal.

All of these cultural products had at their core the goal of creating spaces in which cultural norms and behaviors would be situated and celebrated. The sculptures, paintings and written narratives, while dedicated to capturing the essence of the Moscow–Volga Canal, also emphasized the canal and its construction as a metaphor for the whole USSR. While the space of the waterway was delineated by its channel from the Volga to Moscow, the everyman quality of the sculptures (they depict the ideal Soviet man and woman), the inviting and approachable paintings, especially of those cruising along the canal in steamships, and the contention advanced in all three written narratives that the entire USSR built the Moscow Canal, invoke the metaphor that the Moscow Canal *is* the Soviet Union and vice versa. The metaphorical and rhetorical spaces discussed in this chapter reveal how image and word managed to defy physical space by making it seem as if the Moscow Canal reached every corner of the USSR, while all of the USSR could enjoy it at least vicariously if not in reality. As *KMV: 32–7* relates, "Millions of workers not only from Moscow, but from the country's other industrial centers, as well as kolkhoz farmers, Soviet and foreign tourists rushed to the canal for a first-hand look at this marvelous structure of the second Stalin five-year plan."[108]

More important, these cultural products, just like the trope "Moscow – Port of Five Seas," underscored Moscow's position as the red star at the center of the Soviet universe and whose light covered every hectare of the USSR. This also meant that Moscow's most important resident, Stalin, was not only the center of Soviet power, but that his power extended throughout the entire territory of the Soviet Union. It is no wonder that the penultimate paragraph in *KMV: 32–7* concludes:

> At the present time the three principal problems put to the construction of the Moscow–Volga: supplying the capital with water, linking it with the Volga, and raising the water level of the Moscow River, have finally been solved. Thanks to the Moscow–Volga Canal Soviet workers have received one of the greatest world-class structures that satisfies their everyday, cultural, and aesthetic needs.[109]

A photograph of the steamship *Joseph Stalin* in front of the Kremlin is inserted within this paragraph to further reinforce the spatial importance of the Volga flowing to the Kremlin walls, thereby keeping the *Joseph Stalin* afloat on the page, in the river, and in real life, while also once more inserting Stalin into the text. *KMV: 32–7* concludes with a quotation from a 1935 Decree that further outlined the construction of the Moscow–Volga Canal:

> The construction of the Moscow–Volga Canal, [and] of the Moscow Metro, like other grandiose structures of our country, is the greatest investment in the structure of socialism. Only our country, having overcome its technical and economic backwardness, having built the foundation of socialism, can create such majestic structures directed at the betterment of the life and daily routine of the people.[110]

It is no accident that this rhetoric resorted to spatial images in order to convey the importance and perceived grandiosity of the Moscow Canal.

Not forgotten of course is the importance and function of water in and to all these cultural products. As we have seen, Tvedt posits that water, in addition to its function as a natural resource and its susceptibility to human intervention, also is constructed by culture: "The special character of water makes it a unique medium for cultural constructions and metaphorical traditions."[111] The two-fold construction of the Moscow Canal as a multi-purpose waterway and as a cultural event that demanded interpretation and celebration attests to the power of water in its most elemental form and to the metaphorical possibilities it offers. The very same conceptions of water that applied to Dmitlag obtain in the cultural products as well: they illustrate and celebrate the life-giving qualities of the element; they offer the medium through which the Stalinist impulse to control water is concretized; they supply the inspiration for art works and engineering projects, in their own way a form of art; and they reinforce the timelessness of water as a flowing natural resource and time/space continuum along which life and culture can be constructed. Taken as a whole these considerations reveal the monumentality of water as a resource, as a vital element in a social environment, and as the inspiration for cultural projects. As Tvedt's approach reminds us, without water the Moscow Canal project would never have achieved its status as a unique and grandiose structure.

This atmosphere of monumentality and grandiosity was realized on the waterway in the form of the canal's architecture. Coupled with that monumentality is the companion notion of memorialization, two spatial concepts that were inscribed in the Moscow Canal then and remain there now. How monumentality and memorials coalesce, as well as contribute to and conflict with each other, society, and ideology, is the focus of the next chapter.

CHAPTER 4

MONUMENTS, MONUMENTALITY, AND MEMORY: FORGETTING AND REMEMBERING

> Physical geography, the realm of the real and material, and spatial science, with its abstract yet no less objective gravitational centres and force fields, were overwhelmed by symbolic space, the idealist landscape of metaphor and imagination.[1]

On a dark night in the early 1960s Joseph Stalin was beheaded on the southern bank of the Moscow Canal, while Vladimir Lenin looked on from his vantage point on the north shore of the confluence of the canal and the Volga River. While the 37-meter high monument to Lenin still stands, all that remains of the companion Stalin monument is the pedestal on which it stood. To this day barges, cruise ships, and all manner of pleasure craft traverse this segment of the canal unaware that they are sailing over Stalin's head lodged on the bottom of the canal bed. This gruesome image is not lost on the contemporary scholars who study the Moscow Canal. Nor should it be in an analysis of the spatial dynamics and relationships that obtain on the waterway. The physical and metaphorical destruction of Stalin serves as an apt metaphor for a discussion of monuments and monumentality, memory and memorial space constructed and encountered along the Moscow Canal. The two granite monuments to Lenin and Stalin, the distinct architecture of each canal lock, and the Northern River Station on the Khimki

Reservoir share the space with a steel-beamed cross and granite headstone, a Russian Orthodox chapel, and Dmitrov buildings and street names all redolent of elements of the canal project. These juxtaposed images reveal the temporal contrast between Stalinist era/ Soviet and post-Soviet monuments. These contrasting spaces likewise illustrate the contradictions inherent in any detailed discussion of monuments and memorials situated along the Moscow Canal. This has to do with the very nature of monuments and memorials themselves, and viewer perception of them.

The impulse to design the built environment of the Moscow Canal according to seemingly classical architectural principles and aesthetics underscores the intention to create not only a monumental waterway, but also a deftly woven architectural monument to Stalinism. Each physical feature deployed along the canal was intended to encapsulate Stalinist ideology through its size, design, and artistry. Large statues, high lock towers, and emblematic buildings were designed to impress and amaze, and offer proof that the system that constructed them, even though reliant on forced labor, was both legitimate and powerful. These spaces were imbued with grandeur and solidity that virtually screamed monumentality through their size, shape and location. That the Moscow Canal led directly to Moscow, the ultimate monument to Soviet power, was no accident, for the first socialist capital, the potential "fourth Rome" demanded, indeed deserved, a waterway equal to the city's status and power. Just as the Moscow Metro would enchant and impress visitors underground, so too would the Moscow Canal, not only on the ground but above it as well.

In constructing this monumental waterway, the Stalinist system in spite of itself created fertile ground for planting and nurturing the memory of and memorials to those who suffered and died in the quest to build that which had not been built before in the USSR. Granted, this memorial space developed in the post-Soviet era long after the canal had been completed. But material concerning the canal's construction has only been more freely available within the last 10–15 years, which makes it no surprise that memorial space is a later addition overlaid onto the canal's monumental space. This memorial overlay thereby makes the waterway's monumental spaces even more highly contested, illustrating how monumental and memorial spaces often overlap, subsume, or co-exist with each other.

This chapter will explore monumental and memorial space in order to examine how they reflect or detract from Stalinism, and how their spatial configurations embody the ideology and motivations behind them. Indeed, the monumental and memorial structures along the Moscow Canal serve as a spatial synecdoche for the systems that created them and into which ideology, symbolism and rhetoric have been inscribed. Thus, the discussion of monuments and monumentality will focus on the statues of Lenin and Stalin at the beginning of the Moscow Canal by Lock 1, on Locks 5 and 8, and on the Northern River Station at Khimki. This chapter's route from the Lenin and Stalin statues to the Northern River Station parallels a physical journey along the Moscow Canal. The imposing figures created a sense of the monumental in terms of their physical size and the leaders they represent. When a passenger disembarks in Moscow or sets off on a cruise, she generally does so from the Northern River Station, a building purposely constructed in the shape of ship so as to underscore the importance of water and waterways even before passengers board a vessel. Finally, no discussion of the canal's architecture would be complete without an examination of some of the locks on the canal, each of which was designed by a prominent architect and intended to be a distinct structure with its own architectural theme and façade.

Because the memorial spaces have been constructed in post-Soviet space, they are, by virtue of the memories they seek to preserve and engender, fewer in number, less grandiose, and less visible. This lack of visibility, however, should not detract from their importance within a discussion of the structural heritage of the Moscow Canal, because they attempt to fill the space that the waterway's 1930s structures cannot: spaces of remembrance not just for those victimized by the system on the Moscow Canal project, but also as part of the larger space of the Gulag. This is also why the city of Dmitrov itself, the Moscow Canal Museum, and various individuals belong in a discussion of the memorial space on the Moscow Canal. Their construction of it signals a broadening of the spatial parameters and significance of the waterway.

Before beginning the discussion proper, a note about terminology and precedents is in order. The idea to build monumental public structures certainly did not belong only to the Soviets in the 1930s. We need only look at the massive federal buildings constructed in Washington, DC during this period, as well as the numerous Works Projects Administration (WPA) structures scattered throughout the US in order to see the monumental nature of many of them.[2] The period 1931–6 also witnessed the construction of the Hoover Dam, certainly a path-breaking construction achievement in terms of size and design.[3] New York's skyscrapers similarly contributed to this impulse to build big and build artistically. As Katerina Clark argues, "This dichotomy in the typical monumental building should not be seen as specifically Stalinist, since it was a trend in America and Europe at this time."[4] As will become apparent in the following discussion, and as Clark details, ornamentation or *dekorativnost'* became an essential element of monumental structures. The design of building façades assumed more significance within the Stalinist system not merely as imitations of structures elsewhere, but as political statements that offered tangible and tactile proof of the efficacy of the system that produced them. As Clark states, "In a society that was drunk on codified representation, the outsides or façades of its buildings – their face to the outside world, that which is maximally read – was critical, a reason why authoritative spokesmen did not want those blank 'faces' that were so typical of the international style of architecture."[5]

This "mask" as Clark terms it functioned as the face of the regime on its buildings and became a principle element of Socialist Realist architecture. According to Clark, "The ornamentation or 'mask' that Stalinist architects put on their buildings was not to be individual or 'arbitrary,' ... but integrated into a coherent system. No decorative detail, not even the slightest curlicue, could be considered random or politically neutral. The function of the new buildings was both aesthetic and 'discursive'."[6] Certainly the locks, pumping stations, the Northern River Station and other structures along the Moscow Canal adhered to this principle. They joined the practical with the artistic in just such extreme detail. "Thus in socialist realist architecture, buildings functioned both as practical spaces – office blocks or apartment buildings with modern conveniences – *and* as proleptic rhetorical devices."[7]

The monumental architecture and sculpture on the Moscow Canal dovetail perfectly with this turn toward uniting politics with aesthetics in the practice of architecture. Indeed, the architecture of the Moscow Canal exemplifies the shift to Socialist Realism in its reliance on Renaissance and classical Greco-Roman architecture as models.

> Socialist realism was not just about heroes building power stations or even about the wisdom of Party decrees. Aesthetic value and political value were closely linked ... In architecture, those in authority, in seeking to define what Socialist Realism might mean for that field, generally invoked classical precedents.[8]

These "classical precedents" permitted the buildings to be read not as imitations of their forbears, but as "texts" in and of themselves. The buildings simultaneously had to convey simplicity and power, ideology and functionality, beauty and concision:

> Buildings were to "say a great deal" both powerfully and convincingly ... When in the 1930s prominent Soviet architects declared recognized principles of classical architecture central to a "socialist realist" architecture, they did not merely mean that a particular inventory of stylistic features was to be adopted. As they called for such alleged qualities of their preferred architectural styles ... these "qualities" were themselves markers of an ideological and epistemological stance.[9]

The qualities of "serenity" and "unity" were realized in the architecture of the Moscow Canal, thereby creating the "face" of Moscow for those traveling the waterway.

As regards terminology, the following discussion will examine the interplay between monumentality, monuments, and memorials.[10] For our purposes, this study considers a monument to be any material object that celebrates an achievement of the state for the purposes of promoting and making real its ideology in the most tactile way, through structures and sculptures. Memorials represent silent testimony to the memory of those lost, either through a state-sponsored project or through the personal loss of beloved or cherished individuals. Monuments convey a public, civic-minded sense of the achievements they represent; memorials convey a sense of personal loss and remembrance, the memory of those who are no more. Monuments, even when dedicated to a specific person, mark large-scale achievements, while memorials call on viewers to remember individuals who might have contributed to that achievement. We see here an element of the public versus private, although a memorial can be the most public space, thus calling to mind a broadly civic responsibility to remember. Memorials prompt remembering, while monuments often do not. Ultimately, both monuments and memorials are fraught with politics, sometimes obvious and sometimes not. It is this interplay of public and private, political and personal, grandiose and humble that informs our examination of the monumental and memorial spaces that inhabit the Moscow Canal and its attendant structures.

Of Monuments and Monumentality

> Classical simplicity, harmony and grace combined with the inventive fertility of modern times, are what the architects sought to achieve when designing the various structures of the canal.[11]

Monuments and monumentalism on the Moscow Canal take shape in the sculptures, locks, and Northern River Port, as well as the dams and other architectural features on the waterway. Yet the structures that make the biggest statement are those through which all travelers on the Moscow Canal pass. Even if a vessel sailing from the north immediately enters the canal without navigating its first lock, that vessel cannot miss the large sculpture of Lenin that still stands on the northern bank of the waterway. Until the early 1960s it was impossible not to see the large Stalin sculpture as well. Likewise, passengers and vessels traversing the waterway must pass through its locks in order to reach their destination, a destination that often turned out to be the Northern River Station, whose spire was visible from a good distance. These were and are the landmarks according to which locals and travelers alike mark the space of the Moscow Canal and the various points along it. These structures commandeered the spaces in which they were situated, spaces that previously contained bogs, marshes, fields, granite, and villages. How impressive it must have been for travelers in the 1930s to see their leaders Stalin and Lenin towering over the waterway and visible for kilometers, or to pass through a lock bearing its own granite sculptures and unique architecture, or to finally arrive in Moscow at the Northern River Station with its ruby red Kremlin star shining brightly atop its tall spire. The intention to amaze and impress motivated every aspect of the design of these structures. Their designs made statements about the system that produced them and its ability to create markedly Soviet space imbued with all the glory and spectacle absent from the Gulag camps and the Soviet periphery.

The Lenin and Stalin Monuments

> In the Lenin and Stalin monuments, in the numerous sculptures and bas-reliefs in the canal's architectural ensemble the image of the beloved leaders of the Soviet people and leading figures of our Motherland is organically included.[12]

The idea of building large sculptural monuments to great Soviet leaders was not a novel concept. Statues of Lenin proliferated throughout the Soviet Union after his death, while those of Stalin appeared later, but were not as ubiquitous. No one could unseat the "father" of the USSR, the man who brought the Bolsheviks to power, who engineered the October Revolution and created the Soviet Union, the author of Marxist-Leninist ideology. Yet Stalin, as Lenin's purportedly hand-picked successor, claimed equal space with Lenin in the Moscow Canal monuments: they were the same height – 25 meters (not counting their pedestals), of the same materials – gray granite, produced by the same sculptor – Sergei Merkurov and posed in similar ways, with one leg forward as if to step off the plinth, shoulders squared, and eyes gazing into the future. The sculptures served as companions to each other, dominating space vertically and horizontally, as well as metaphorically, given that they surveyed each other and their domains from their high vantage points (Figures 4.1 and 4.2).

While this description might seem overly dramatic, it is important to bear in mind that Stalin viewed himself as Lenin's heir, and likely presumed himself to be even greater than Lenin as the result of his efforts to reconstruct and re-inscribe Soviet space as truly Stalinist space. Granted, it was impossible to construct Stalinist space without the literal and symbolic foundation that Lenin built. But in reconstructing Moscow, claiming far-flung territories through the Gulag, and building city- and industry-scapes that physically embodied the ideology, Stalin surpassed his presumed mentor. In fact when the Vladimir I. Lenin Volga–Don Canal was completed in 1952, only a sculpture of Stalin was

Figure 4.1 The Lenin monument as it appears today.

erected by the waterway's first lock. Standing 24 meters high, with a total height of 54 meters including its plinth, the sculpture surveyed shipping on the canal until it was removed in 1969(!). Its plinth remained empty until a sculpture of Lenin, measuring 57 meters (statue 27 meters, plinth 30 meters) was erected on the site, where it stands to this day as the tallest monument to Lenin in Russia.[13] As with the

Figure 4.2 The monument to Stalin as it looked upon completion in 1937.

Moscow Canal, Lenin turned out to be the only man left standing. Nonetheless, the spatial initiatives that the Stalinist system produced proclaimed its power and reach loudly and boldly, to wit the "twin" Lenin and Stalin sculptures at the mouth of the Moscow Canal, the most consequential construction project of the second five-year plan.

The idea for the sculptures reportedly did not originate with Stalin. Indeed, as the sculptor Merkurov noted, the inspiration for these grandiose images stretched back to ancient Egypt and Athens. As he notes, "In the epoch of the blossoming of artistic culture, monumental sculpture always played a leading role."[14] To Merkurov the installation of these two sculptures dovetailed perfectly with the prevailing ideology:

> The depth and universal character of the ideological content of these images of the leaders of the socialist revolution provide the best foundation for these monumental works. The construction of the Moscow–Volga Canal is inseparably connected with the names Lenin and Stalin. The peoples of the Soviet Union are indebted to Lenin and Stalin for their happy lives, their wise leadership that made possible the realization of these grandiose undertakings about which people only dreamed in the past.[15]

The sculptures make imagined space real through their size and verisimilitude. When lit with large floodlights, the sculptures undoubtedly produced a sense of power and might that awed onlookers and reinforced the rhetoric of the time. Of course Merkurov, as an officially sanctioned sculptor, especially for such a large project on the site of a Gulag camp, was obliged to create his narrative about the design and implementation of the monuments in an acceptable way. He needed to weave into his narrative the strands of history, thereby linking both the monuments and their temporal milieu with the great empires of the past, most notably ancient Egypt. His position also necessitated the inclusion of quotations from Marx, as well as abundant praise not only for the leaders, but for the country and lifestyle they had created. To do otherwise, especially in 1939, would have been treacherous.

Merkurov's observations explicate the connection between ideology and space, between the metaphorical and the built environment. Just as the Lenin and Stalin monuments reached high into the sky as tactile manifestations of Stalinist power and might, so too did Merkurov's words create the rhetorical space of monumentalism. Even the process of creating and installing the monuments assumed epic proportions, given that the official order for their construction was issued in February 1937 and the project was completed by 1 August 1937, thanks completely, we can be sure, to the labor of Dmitlag inmates who worked around the clock to ensure that the project would be finished on time. Upon completion the monuments were described thusly:

> Vladimir Ilyich Lenin is depicted at the moment he is delivering a fiery speech. Vladimir Ilyich's figure, embodying the powerful energy of the leader, is directed forward; his left hand is bent in a decisive gesture and his head is raised in an inspiring call to battle. Iosif Vissarionovich Stalin is depicted brashly walking forward with a firm, sure step. His right hand is in its usual position laid on the side of his mess jacket; the left is clasping the scroll of the Constitution. The calm expression of his face conveys the greatness and steely will of the leader of the laboring masses.[16]

While the impulse might be to dismiss these rhetorical flourishes and oft-repeated tropes that were commonly used to describe Lenin and Stalin, to do so would be to ignore the movement implied by these static figures. The presumption that the leaders are poised to walk off their pedestals increases the space they have conquered with their physical presence. Their figures, caught at the moment of impending motion, underscore their ability to command and conquer space, be it physical, ideological, imagined, or metaphorical. The physical power of the monuments conveys stability and longevity, if not of the men they immortalize, then of their deeds and words, a meaningful statement in an era of terror and looming warfare that slowly enveloped the second half of the 1930s. These monuments fomented a sense of righteous action in the face of enemies, be they domestic or foreign, real or imagined. This sense created a space of power that, coupled with the Moscow Canal itself, promoted the idea that Soviet society had already achieved great things and was poised to achieve even more, because of the forward-looking leaders depicted in these monuments. The brutal irony, of course, was that inscribing these monuments into the landscape, no matter how powerful the ideas implied in them, fell to the inmates of Dmitlag and their superiors, many of whom would soon face execution or further incarceration in spite of their labor for their leaders.

Within this context it turns out that the idea for the construction of these monuments originated with the head of the NKVD, Genrikh Yagoda, after a visit to the construction site at the future canal's Volga Junction in 1935.[17] On 8 February 1937 Order No. 57 was issued to begin work on the monuments and their site. On 12 February 1937 inmate laborers along with free workers began excavating the foundation pit for the Stalin monument. They dug a pit 11 meters deep for the foundation, and a similar pit for the Lenin monument, into each of which were poured 6,000 cubic meters of reinforced concrete.[18] Only the most qualified and trustworthy laborers and technicians among the inmates and free workers were deployed on the job. Simultaneously with the construction of the foundations, workers also shaped the enormous granite blocks that would form the pedestals and figures of the monuments. Scaffolding 30 meters high was constructed in order for the monuments to take shape.[19] The most important and potentially life-threatening job was attaching the leaders' heads to the bodies of the monuments. Lenin's head was 3.4 meters tall and weighed 20 tons, while Stalin's head, although only 3.2 meters tall, weighed 21 tons, perhaps suggesting the enhanced brain power of the current leader?[20] Those working on the project waited with nervous anticipation to see if the apparatus designed (and produced in Dmitlag) to lift the heads to their joining points would work. Previous attempts to deploy the apparatus failed when a large boulder used in place of a head fell to the ground before reaching the appropriate height. When this mishap was reported to Matvei Berman, head of the project and the Gulag, he was reported to have said, "If the head falls, yours will go flying too!"[21] Actually, heads did go flying, but not as the result of a mishap on the monument construction site. Rather, in May 1937 there was a rash of arrests for "anti-Soviet conspiracies in the agencies of the NKVD and for terrorist activity." Those arrested included the construction supervisor both for the Volga Junction and the monuments, S. M. Bykhovsky, as well as the chief Moscow Canal architect I. S. Fridliand, who happened to be Yagoda's son-in-law.[22]

With Berman's threat in mind, on 24 June 1937 workers attached Stalin's head very quickly, in 48 minutes.[23] Lenin's head was attached on 25 June 1937 just as efficiently and successfully. Subsequent work on the site included finishing the pedestals, removing the scaffolding and construction materials, and completing the landscaping around the monuments. The monuments were completed on 1 August, the scaffolding was removed on 10 August, and the statues were officially dedicated on 18 August 1937, more than two weeks after the canal's official opening.[24] Sixty powerful spotlights were trained on the monuments in order to illuminate them at night, thereby making them into highly visible beacons of Soviet power and Stalinist ideology. However, Stalin's light shone for only 25 years, until in 1962, as part of the USSR's second wave of de-Stalinization efforts as first outlined at the 20th Party Congress in 1956, the Stalin monument was pulled down. Stalin was removed from the Lenin Mausoleum on Red Square in the same year. Workers attached a cable to Stalin's head to pull down the monument, but the labor of the Dmitlag inmates and free workers was of such high quality that the figure could not be pulled down. Instead it was blown up, with the exploded pieces of the sculpture cast into the Moscow Canal where they rest to this day[25] (Figure 4.3).

The remaining Lenin sculpture not only reminds us of the history of the era in which it was constructed, but also serves as a monument to its

Figure 4.3 The base of the Stalin monument as it looks today.

builders, those purported "socially harmful elements" and enemies of the state whose craftsmanship, skill, and assiduousness produced a figure that still commands the space in which it is situated. While the trees in the surrounding park have grown and cover part of the Lenin monument when viewed from certain angles, the towering landmark still inspires a sense of respect, if not for the person it represents, then for those who built it. In fact, the Dubna memorial to the builders of the Moscow Canal, dedicated in 2013, stands a short distance from Lenin.[26] Although not as tall or imposing, it too creates a space of remembering amid the monumental structures of the Ivan'kovo Dam, Moscow Sea, and Lenin monument.

The Architecture of the Locks

Locks serve a vital function on any canal and many rivers that have been dammed to produce a stable water supply, electrical power, or both, as well as sustaining sufficiently deep channels to permit heavy ships and barges to ply their waters. Locks enable vessels to navigate changes in elevation along their routes; they regulate the flow of traffic on a waterway in order to maintain smooth operations. Locks can be simple or complicated, but remain vital to water transport systems everywhere. As was recently noted in an article about locks and dams on the Ohio River:

> A towboat and its barges need at least nine feet of water to stay afloat. To guarantee the depth ... The United States Army Corps of Engineers built dams. The dams make pools. Each pool is like a step, climbing from sea level to the Appalachians, say or St. Paul. To get from one step to another, boats use water elevators, called locks, that raise anything that floats from one pool to another.[27]

The process sounds deceptively simple, but locks require exact calculations and masterful engineering to operate in conditions that constantly stress the materials from which they are constructed. Water pressure, accidental collisions between watercraft and the walls of the lock, well-maintained machinery to open, raise or lower the lock gates, all exert themselves on the lock chamber and its control towers. Given the demands on the locks it would be reasonable to expect that their construction and architectural features by necessity would be simple, practical and functional.

This was not the case with the 11 locks of the Moscow Canal. Architects designed each lock to be a unique structure with embellishments such as statues and decorative ornamentation. The lock towers were constructed so as to rise high above the lock chambers and the watercraft in them, thereby creating an imposing presence as vessels entered and departed the lock. Of course, the locks preserved their practicality and functionality, but these elements were clothed in a mantle of granite walls, columns, arches, and balconies that moved the locks from the realm of necessity of navigation to monumental works of architecture. As one of the posters produced in Dmitlag proclaimed, "Through their architecture, the monumental structures of the canal must correspond to the high-level technology of the structures themselves."[28]

Each lock on the Moscow Canal deserves its own narrative, but this discussion will focus on four of the 11 locks: Locks 5 and 6 situated in the valley of the Iksha River and Locks 7 and 8, the waterway's only two-chamber locks, which form a connected, visually striking channel within the Moscow city limits. These locks typify the construction and style of all the locks and stand at the highest points on the canal (Lock 5 is 154 meters above sea level and Lock 6 is 162 meters above sea level) before descending to Moscow to the south or the Volga River to the north. When journeying from the Volga to Moscow, Lock 6 is the last one before the Moscow Canal traverses a series of reservoirs: Iksha, Uchinskoe, Klyazma, and Khimki. Lock 7 channels the waters of the Khimki Reservoir back into sharp parallel banks that continue to Lock 8 and drops the level of the waterway approximately 20 meters to continue on its way to Lock 8. All the locks, including those under discussion, display elements of classical architecture. The lines of the buildings tend to be sharp, with details such as arched windows, balconies or open porticos enhancing the overall impression of the buildings while softening some of their sharp edges.

Every lock on the Moscow Canal was designed by a different architect, including some of the most famous practitioners of the day: Lock 1, I. K. Beldovsky; Lock 2, V. M. Lisitsyn; Lock 3, V. Ia. Movchan; Lock 4, A. L. Pasternak (brother of the writer Boris Pasternak); Lock 5, D. B. Savitsky; Lock 6, G. I. Vegman; Locks 7 & 8, V. F. Krinsky; Lock 9,

A. M. Rykhliadev (also the architect of the Northern River Station); Locks 10 & 11, I. K. Beldovsky. In general Locks 1 through 8 are the most ornate since the majority of passenger traffic passed through them; they were designed to create the impression of beauty, power, and stateliness. Locks 5 and 6 are no exception to this practice, for they provide viewers with classical architectural styles set off by distinctive ornamentation.

Locks 5 and 6 comprise the Iksha Junction of the canal. In his design and implementation, architect D. B. Savitsky chose to modify the typical rectangular shape chosen for other lock towers by including curves in the structures. The upper lock gates were designed as a pair of oblong structures running parallel to the waterway. Each end features a small wrought iron balcony, while the top level is marked by open porticos that wrap themselves around each tower. These rounded edges soften the buildings' façades and give the impression of ease of movement through the lock, as if the semi-circular ends of the structures permit the water to flow smoothly past. Gracing the bank of the canal before the upper lock gates is a granite sculpture entitled "Waterway" by Yu. A. Kuhn. The female figure holds aloft a sailing ship. She is clad in simple attire, with the curvaceous outline of her figure visible. Her arms raised to hold the sailboat create a triangle above her head that is capped by the top of the sail. Her pose implies upward motion and physical strength, while her gaze looks out on the canal as it approaches the fifth lock. The sculpture's figure, coupled with the design of the upper lock towers, imparts a sense of power through grace; that which is beautiful is also strong. In the words of architect Krinsky, "This young woman, lifting the model of the yacht up high, symbolizes the idea of the canal as a waterway created by people for people; here the triumphant victory won by our young socialist motherland is expressed."[29]

In designing the lower lock towers at Lock 5 Savitsky preserved the motif of rounded edges by situating open, round, columned rotundas atop each structure (see Figure 4.4). Arched windows adorn each end, and are joined on the same level by small columned balconies that look out on the waterway. The mechanisms for opening and closing the gates occupy the bottom halves of the structures. While these lower gate towers have sharper edges, the curved windows and rotundas soften the effect and create a sense of unity with the upper gates. These same rounded elements reappear in the adjacent pumping stations where

Figure 4.4 Upper lock towers of Lock 5.

the top level is adorned with elongated, rounded windows and each pump is denoted by large windowed half-circles that provide a view inside the working of the mechanisms. The carry-over of the architectural theme to the pumping stations is not surprising given that the architects were charged with designing the whole constellation of buildings at a given lock site, including the lock towers, pumping station (if present), safety gate housing, and any other attendant structures. Krinsky suggests that Savitsky's design "without losing the specifications features of a hydro-technical structure, connects well with the water and the landscape. The architecture crowned the landscape, gave it a face; the landscape acquired the character of a park."[30] Throughout his analysis of Lock 5 Krinsky stresses that the architectural ensemble is consonant with its natural surroundings, thereby accentuating both.

In contrast to Lock 5, G. G. Vegman's plan for the control towers of the upper gates of Lock 6 reminds viewers of an ancient Greco-Roman temple with its tall, graceful columns seemingly supporting the structures' roofs. As Krinsky notes, "The architecture of this junction, like all the others, uses classical principles, but has its own distinct, individual characteristics: here the influence of ancient Greece is felt, and at the same time the desire for laconicism of contemporary forms is clearly expressed."[31] False façades create the upper levels of the towers, which display four sculptures on each side (Figure 4.5). These figures stand tall over the upper gates and strike

Figure 4.5 Upper tower at Lock 6.

various poses that capture them as if in motion with an arm raised, a leg poised to take a step, a hand gesturing toward the distance. The verticality of the columns, coupled with the statues above, invokes a sense of height and grace, as if the structure extends upward without limit. The lower gates seem far less grand, but still preserve the sense of upward movement. It is as if they are encased in columns that fall flush with the building and underscore the structures' rectangular form. The "quiet rhythm of the vertical and horizontal divisions, the laconic combination of smooth walls with large apertures – all this creates an industrial façade,"[32] which shapes the Lock 6 pumping stations, the same features that obtain in the lower gates of the lock.

The most fascinating features of the lower gates were the frescoes depicting scenes from the canal's construction. The artist L.A. Bruni produced the frescoes, which were intended to be visible from aboard steamships that passed through that part of Lock 6. The volume *The Architecture of the Moscow–Volga Canal* features a photograph of part of the frescoes (p. 142) that decorated the outer ends of the façades of the lower gate towers. In them we see Dmitlag inmates at work presumably on Lock 6: they are pushing wheelbarrows, operating cranes, and working on scaffolding. However, as one commentator notes, "The figures of the frescoes are ambitious and proportional; they successfully enliven the flatness of the walls. However, there is one significant shortcoming: the middle tower support visually severs the general composition of the frescoes, and in the future it should be eliminated."[33] Rather than the middle tower support, it was the frescoes that were eliminated. They were subsequently painted over (it is unclear exactly when this occurred; they were not there when Valentin Barkovsky was working at the lock in 1960), and ultimately were replaced by construction tiles such that they are now no longer visible.[34] Given that the frescoes depicted Dmitlag inmates using the ubiquitous wheelbarrows, it is not surprising that they were painted over. Barkovsky concludes that the problem with the frescoes likely stemmed from their illustration of how the canal administration "used wheelbarrows and prisoner-diggers rather than massive excavators and jolly excavator operators" to build the waterway, an image that was deemed inappropriate to display to those sailing along the canal.[35] By tiling over the Bruni frescoes, the monumental was changed to inscribe forgetting instead of remembering onto these lock towers. This action sanitized a graphic depiction of labor on the Moscow

Canal, thus neutralizing the space. Viewer perception of the space shifts from observing a meaning-infused wall to a blank one that unceremoniously hides a reference to the waterway's Gulag past. In effect, an image of the Stalinist past has been replaced by a devalorized wall that carries neither meaning nor memory, which suggests that it was far better to hide the past than to confront it.

Locks 7 and 8 avoid any such controversy due to their classical styles and calm façades. As the two locks most visible within the Moscow city limits, this configuration, which includes a tunnel under the canal and a railroad bridge over the waterway, produces the impression of a cohesive, harmonious group of structures that inscribe a rigid straight line from the Khimki Reservoir to the Moscow River. The waterway tour website map at infoflot.ru quotes a section from the book commemorating the Moscow Canal's 50th anniversary in 1987 to describe this segment of the waterway:

> The locks on the southern slope of the channel, numbers 7 and 8, are each twice as long [as the other locks] and have three pairs of towers. Located on the relatively short section of the southern slope of the canal from the Khimki Reservoir to the Moscow River, these locks have benefitted from a comprehensive architectural design (architect V. F. Krinsky). Twelve towers architecturally designed according to general classical motifs form an avenue that embellishes the waterway. The use of classical forms in multicolumned towers crowned with architraves and cornices that copy the proportions of the towers themselves stemmed from a desire to give the appropriate design to these structures located within the capital. The achievement of this goal is also facilitated by the use of valuable types of stone on the walls of the towers: pink and gray granite, polished black labradorite, green diorite, and white marble. On the sides of the porticos that complete the towers decorative elements are arranged in the form of cast iron anchors with chains.[36]

This passage captures the unity of design that marks this stretch of the Moscow Canal.

A viewer standing on a footbridge at the lower gates of Lock 7 can look up and down the waterway, upward at the two-chamber Lock 7 and downward at the first chamber of Lock 8 in the distance (Figures 4.6 and 4.7). Between them stretches a straight channel that seems graceful in its simplicity. Part of the shoreline between these two locks offers a path that is widely used by area residents as they stroll along the canal. Commuters on the Volokolamsk Highway that runs through the tunnel under the canal can often observe cargo ships sailing by as if riding on air; from below viewers cannot see the water level, but only the straight line of the waterway's bank. The combination of marble, granite, labradorite, and diorite make these locks the most colorful on the Moscow Canal, even if the colors seem a bit faded. When the waterway was built this section of Moscow had not been fully developed, so no tall apartment buildings or vegetation obscured the view of the channel. The lock towers rose high above the landscape into which they were inscribed and claimed pride of place because of their architecture and size. Now modern high-rises stand not far from the canal, offering their residents an outstanding view of the waterway, a view that passengers on the trains to and from Tver' also enjoy as they traverse the railway bridge that crosses the canal

Figure 4.6 Second lock chamber at Lock 7 looking northward.

Figure 4.7 The canal channel looking southward toward the upper gates of Lock 8 in the distance.

downstream from Lock 8. These modern high-rises tower over the locks and make them seem much smaller than they are in reality.

The true genius of this segment of the Moscow Canal resides in the comingling of five forms of transportation at one nexus: water, rail, and automobile transport joined with pedestrian traffic and linked to air travel. The Volokolamsk Highway, both then and now, leads to the Tushino Air Field, formerly used as a major Moscow airport and currently used for air shows and private planes. The tunnel under the canal features the sculpture of a young pilot, whose aviator's scarf blows in the wind and who holds an airplane in her hands in tribute to Tushino. The joining of these various transport systems was crafted to symbolize the foresight and planning of the Soviet system that, if the rhetoric is to be believed, designed its urban centers in service to the working class. As Krinsky notes in his discussion of Locks 7 and 8:

> All the territory along the locks and the approaches to them has been planted with greenery, landings have been created, paths constructed; in a few years all the greenery will have grown, and

> the territory bordering the locks will turn into a cultural park in which the capital's workers will find repose.[37]

Not only did the Moscow Canal bring water to the capital, it also provided restful spaces for its workers and readily available, modern transportation that would fulfill the needs of the growing metropolis. Of course, Krinsky could not have foreseen the explosion of development along the waterway that would cause multi-story apartment complexes to rise high above the canal and seemingly overtake Locks 7 and 8.

The current landscape along this stretch of the Moscow Canal, illustrating the overlay of new Russian space on Stalinist Soviet space, does not diminish the monumentality of the project in terms of its size and the architectural styles that helped achieve it. Given how the landscape looks today it is difficult to imagine what the area must have looked like shortly after the canal's completion when the waterway was the main feature in the landscape. Yet it is safe to assume that between Locks 7 and 8 the waterway was a truly impressive site due to the towering lock structures with their nautical ornamentation, the opportunity to stand on the canal's shoreline and take it all in, and the impression that ships on the waterway were floating on air as they passed over the Volokolamsk Highway. What today might seem commonplace was at the time of its construction, and many years after, a tribute to the skill and artistry of the architects and builders who erected these structures that continue to stand the test of time. This is the monument and these are the monumental spaces that continue to impress viewers. Proof of this is the crowds that gather on the aforementioned pedway over the channel at Lock 7 to observe the operation of the locks. Children and adults marvel at the machinery and the energy of the water, which suggests that the Moscow Canal still has the power to amaze despite all the changes in its context.

The Northern River Station[38]

> One of the main virtues of the compositional solution of the Khimki station is the successful combination of monumentality and lightness.[39]

Indeed, anyone approaching the Northern River Station from the Khimki reservoir appreciates this description: the Northern River Station is at once large and airy, as if ready to sail away (Figure 4.8). The architects A. M. Rukhliadev and V. F. Krinsky designed the structure in the shape of a ship, with portholes, "decks," and a mast. As Mikhailov noted, "From afar the station, especially in the evening when it is illuminated, reminds one of a gigantic steamship with a tall mast in the center."[40] The building stands parallel to the Khimki reservoir; it is 150 meters long and 75 meters high and occupies its space with a commanding presence when viewed either from land or from the water. The star that caps the moveable spire was brought to the station from the Kremlin's Spassky Tower, thereby anointing the river station as a structure representative of and belonging to Soviet power. Emblazoned on the star is a hammer and sickle encrusted with precious gems from the Ural Mountains.[41] The architects designed the spire with the intention that it would be raised in the spring at the commencement of navigation on the waterway and lowered in the fall when navigation was

Figure 4.8 The Northern River Station as viewed from the Khimki Reservoir.

suspended; however, this practice was never systematically employed, and the spire has been raised and lowered only a few times since its completion in 1937. The spire's tower also features sculptural embellishments on each corner. "They depict famous people of our Motherland: a Red Army soldier in an overcoat thrown open, a Red Sailor, a collective farm girl, and a northern hunter."[42]

The Northern River Station's entrance from the Leningrad Highway through its adjacent park impresses a visitor with the grandeur of the design and ornamentation. A sculpture at the entrance to the park pairs with an identical sculpture that stands on the banks of the approach to Lock 5: a young woman stands with feet firmly planted and hoists aloft a sailboat perched on rolling waves. With this nautical motif established, a visitor then approaches the Northern River Station itself through an entrance with three arches that Mikhailov describes as a "monumental portal." The façades that shape the arches are adorned with 12 majolica discs that depict emblems of Soviet power – ships, airplanes, notable construction projects (including one of the Moscow Canal's first lock), and geographical landmarks such as rivers and lakes. This design is copied on the reservoir side of the building with the addition of a large stairway that leads from quayside up to the portal and 12 more majolica discs. As Mikhailov notes, "Each portal is designed in the shape of three large arches covered with green diorite."[43] This comprises the first "deck" of the building. As Mikhailov continues, "The second tier is decorated with arcades, the third with colonnades, and the fourth with corbels."[44] In addition, "The first-floor gallery (from the Leningrad Highway side) is framed by 150 four-sided columns of white Tarusa stone. The arches of the second-floor gallery rest on smaller round columns. A wide granite stairway links the station with the quay."[45] These design features imbue the structure with airiness and lightness; the "ship" of the Northern River Station expands the space that the Moscow Canal occupies by making it seem as if this structure is not firmly planted on the land, but rather is floating on water.

The nautical theme and atmosphere are further enhanced by the wings on both sides of the structure that purposely face north and south.

> At the ends of the sides of the building in enclosed semi-circles are two fountains featuring sculptures. The northern-facing fountain is designed on the theme of mastering the Arctic: its pedestal

> features a group of polar bears and above the fountain {fly} bronze images of loons and wild geese (sculptor Kordashev). The south wing is decorated with a fountain with bronze dolphins (sculptor Efimov).[46]

Or as one of the building's architects, A. M. Rukhliadev, described it, "The south wing of the station transports the viewer from the harsh Arctic to the sultry Crimea and Black Sea."[47] The restaurant continued the sea motif:

> The main room of the restaurant is separated by artificial marble the color of green malachite; in the cartouches of the dome one can see depictions of the cruiser Aurora that participated in the October battles of 1917, the ice breaker Krasin, the sailboat Comrade, and a caravel as the general emblem of sailing. In the center of the ceiling we see a depiction of flying gulls, and on the walls the locks of the Moscow–Volga canal are depicted. The waiting room's ceiling is painted with flowers.[48]

The final interior flourishes include a 220-square meter vestibule. "Four powerful columns form it, the tops of which are adorned with hammers and sickles surrounded by sheaves of wheat. The coffered ceiling is painted with images of water transport; on the walls the seals of the union republics of the USSR are depicted."[49] At the time of its construction a sculpture of Stalin likewise stood in the center of the vestibule, a feature that disappeared presumably in the late 1950s.

These descriptions of the inner and outer architectural details and flourishes of the Northern River Station reveal the attention to detail and the ideological underpinnings of the project. Aerial views of the Northern River Station best reveal its shape as a large vessel. In describing the station architects repeatedly refer to its "organicity" or the "organic connection" it promotes between the Moscow Canal and Soviet citizens, between man and nature, between state and citizen, and among different artistic genres. The central unifying element here remains the space of the Northern River Station and the interplay of its constructed space with the waterway and the people for whom it was intended to serve. In describing the Northern River Station's utility, Rukhliadev asserts that "These moments ... speak to the fact that the station is designed not only to fulfill its purely utilitarian function, but also in service to the multi-faceted demands of its visitors, among them the demand to interact with nature ... In this service to the multi-faceted demands of the citizens of our Motherland resides the main feature of socialist architecture."[50] While Rukhliadev's assertion regarding citizens' interaction rings somewhat hollow given how much of the natural landscape had been destroyed in the construction of the Moscow Canal, its core significance nonetheless highlights the relationship between the space and its users. Like all the other architectural projects along the Moscow Canal, the Northern River Station was intended not only as a transit point between land and sea, but also as the gateway to Moscow for visitors to the capital, and as the embarkation point from which Moscow would symbolically reach the rest of the world (at least via waterways). The "entrance" to the capital via the canal needed to amaze and inspire.[51] This intention demanded that all the architectural elements be infused with both nautical symbolism and state symbolism. In many ways, the Northern River Station encapsulated the entire Soviet Union in one architecturally harmonious building.

Within its constructed space the Northern River Station staked out the territory of the USSR from north to south by means of the fountains at each end of the building. From the Arctic to the Black Sea, just as Moscow would become the Port of Five Seas via the Moscow Canal and later the Volga–Don Canal, so too would the Northern River Station provide visitors with the sense that they had traversed that same distance along the length of the building. The emblems of the 11 Soviet Socialist Republics adorning the main vestibule linked Moscow with the rest of the country while potentially evoking in visitors the notion of traveling there. All 11 republics united under the Soviet banner identified Moscow as their capital; in the vestibule of the Northern River Station all the republics symbolically were under one roof, again emphasizing that Moscow's reach extended in all directions and to all the republics.

The spatial configuration of the Northern River Station likewise illustrated the importance of constructed spaces within the Stalinist enterprise. The placement of a sculpture of Stalin in the middle of the building's vestibule physically underscored that Stalin was the center of everything: supposedly all ideas emanated from him and all citizens gravitated to him. If Moscow was the political, economic, and cultural center of the Stalinist universe, then Stalin was its core. The spaciousness of the building itself similarly reflected the need to both create and control space. In this the Northern River Station succeeded in that it simultaneously created a unique built environment, from the dock to the Leningrad Highway, that made the ideology tangible.

In describing his structure, Rukhliadev maintains that spatial considerations and ideology formed the bedrock for the Northern River Station. The unity of these ideas obtains in the "synthesis of art – the commonweal of architecture, sculpture and painting – that were widely used in the station. The sculptural figures on the corners of the central tower, the fountain sculptures, the painting in the inner spaces had to organically blend with the architectural forms."[52] Rukhliadev argues that just this synthesis reveals both the ideology and the formation of a truly socialist architecture. Art and ideology intertwine to produce a utilitarian space infused with cultural elements that demonstrate the progressive nature of Soviet society, most notably because of the "genius" of Stalin. The genius of Stalin will not be debated here; instead this formulation points to the vital role that space played in constructing the Stalinist state. How spaces were conceived and constructed became an ideological enterprise, likely to the benefit of some architects and to the chagrin of others. In creating the monumental structure of the Northern River Station the architects, sculptors, and painters made power real, from the star laden with the ubiquitous hammer and sickle to the majolica discs that illustrated Soviet achievements, each element of the structure reinforced the Stalinist claim to space.

Space as a construct for state-building could not shed its aesthetic elements. These aesthetic elements resonated in the human element that the Northern River Station sought to address and exploit. In keeping with the notion that buildings, parks, waterways, and ostensibly all structures were constructed to benefit the working men and women, lavishly decorated and broad public spaces provided recreational areas intended to imply the vastness of Soviet physical space while counteracting the tight quarters of personal space in apartments, be they communal or single-family. With this in mind, Rukhliadev and Krinsky attempted to create the Northern River Station as a pleasing rest area in which to spend one's time enjoyably. As Rukhliadev argues:

> The principle of introducing rest and aesthetic enjoyment thus was conducted in all the interior spaces. It obtains, first of all, in

> the spaciousness [*prostornost'*] and spatiality [*prostranstvennost'*] of these rooms, in the abundance of color and air in them, and second of all with the design of the walls, ceilings and the very space itself of the rooms that made it pleasant to spend time in them.[53]

In creating this monument of Stalinist culture, the building's architects, like all the architects of structures along the Moscow Canal, sought to situate it within the tradition of classical architecture and deployed the descriptive nouns of spaciousness and spatiality to accurately characterize its interiors. In so doing they could argue that Soviet architecture laid a valid claim to the tradition by using its precepts and design elements to create a newer, better physical realization of classical techniques and ideas. Mikhailov notes that "In achieving this, the architect skillfully used the forms of classical architecture, in particular the architecture of the early Renaissance, the influence of which is visible in the treatment of individual elements of the tower and in the principle of its levels, and also in the use of the light arcades that surround the wings of the station."[54] As commentaries on all the architectural elements of the Moscow Canal attest, the desire to simultaneously link Soviet architecture with classical forms while re-interpreting those forms to reflect Socialist Realism worked to legitimize both the architects and their projects. As Mikhailov expresses this development:

> But the elements of Renaissance architecture were worked here into a new composition that is permeated by the aesthetics of our epoch, the aesthetics of Socialist Realism. The combination of monumentality with lightness, humanity, the embodiment of growth in the architectural forms, the display of socialist reality in figurative motifs, the bright, joyful character of the building – all this speaks to the new architectural style begotten by the epoch of socialism.[55]

Herein lies the key to the construction of monumental space on the Moscow Canal: by building structures seemingly comparable to classical architectural monuments the Moscow Canal architects in general, and the Northern River Station architects in particular, claimed space as heirs of the great architectural traditions (at least in their own view), thereby inserting themselves into the larger architectural history. Consequently their actions also implied that Stalin's Soviet Union likewise deserved a legitimate place in world history not only as the first socialist state, but also (rather than bourgeois architects) as the natural heir to and promoter of classical aesthetics and ideas, albeit in a socialist form.

In a broader perspective, the construction of the Northern River Station was woven into the narrative of the Stalinist conquest of water. In describing the architecture of the station, Rukhliadev notes that:

> The very position of the station in the system of the canal predetermined the character of its architecture as one of the most grand and monumental structures of the waterway's architectural ensemble. On the one hand the station is part of the canal system, and its architecture must give rise to an uplifting feeling and the joy that in our interpretation is linked to this wonderful creation of the Stalinist epoch; on the other hand, the station is the first stop on the way to Moscow with whose architecture it [the station] thereby must be organically linked.[56]

Rukhliadev's sensible reading of the demands of the project demonstrates both the importance of the Northern River Station to the Moscow–Volga Canal, and its vital role in creating the "new Moscow." If the Northern River Station is a visitor's first glimpse of Moscow, then it must impress and welcome her. The symbiotic relationship among architecture, sculpture and painting, coupled with the highest quality building materials and bright, spacious, airy interior and exterior spaces produced an impressive first experience for travelers to Moscow. The capital and its renovations warranted a river station that at first sight delighted and amazed viewers, whose experience only intensified after disembarking from their ships and entering the grand vestibule via the broad granite staircase. Each element of the station created a sense of grandeur consonant with the grandeur that Moscow itself was intended to invoke.

This sense of grandeur was especially prescient vis-à-vis the water that lapped at the Northern River Station's landing:

> The other characteristic of the station is its organic connection with the large surface of the water, with the broad vistas to the

> surrounding landscape. The station is located on the shore of the Khimki Reservoir, which is 5 kilometers long and up to 900 meters wide. The presence of such a large body of water next to the station predetermined not only a whole range of architectural functions, but gave the entire structure an additional use. When navigation ceases, the station turns into a sports stadium.[57]

Though sited on land, the Northern River Port functions as an extension of the reservoir on which it stands. The size of the Khimki Reservoir and its surface area demanded a companion structure that equaled it, if not in size, then at least in majesty. The linking of the Northern River Station with sport further enhances its stated function as a space for recreation, be it while sitting in the restaurant, strolling its balcony or in the adjacent park, or viewing water sports from a stadium built slightly downstream from it.[58] The Northern River Station owes its existence to the construction of the Moscow Canal. It helped the waterway realize its potential as a conduit for passenger vessels bringing visitors to the capital, while functioning as a worthy, majestic gateway to the city. As such it created a monumental space that joined the waterway's other architectural features to create a 128-kilometer long monument to Stalinism.

The value of the Northern River Station as an architectural monument and functioning river station, however, has steadily declined in the intervening years since its construction to the point that the building was closed and fenced off in 2010. Structural damage and lack of routine maintenance led to exposed steel struts, chipped granite, damaged statuary, and other signs of deterioration. At that time the structure was under the management of the Russian Federal Government. Subsequently management was transferred to the City of Moscow, which slowly began to proceed with plans to renovate the structure. In 2015 the city included the restoration and reinvigoration of the Northern River Station in its plans for the "Development of Moscow's transport system for 2012–6 and for the future until 2020." Reconstruction of the building was due to occur in 2015–6.[59] Work did not begin then, and only in late 2016 did the City of Moscow issue a call for bids to secure a contractor to develop plans to restore the Northern River Station.[60] Finally, in February 2017 the company Engineering Geology of Historical Places, Ltd (IGIT, Ltd.) won the contract to formulate a restoration plan, having worked on other historical places such as the monastery in New Jerusalem and the Ostankino Estate Museum.[61] The planning process is projected to take 11 months; project managers intend to study archival materials related to the structure and to assess the stability of its foundation. When restoration will finally occur has yet to be determined, but the fact that the Northern River Station is considered an architectural landmark worthy of it is already a positive step.

The Power of Landscape

Ideology did not singlehandedly create the monumental space of the Moscow Canal, for it would be meaningless without the architectural ensembles inscribed into it. In examining the significance of the architecture of the waterway within the development of Soviet architecture in general, Mikhailov stresses the importance of architectural elements and decoration in creating the sense of monumentality that pervades the waterway's structures. He notes, for example, that "The motif of the unbroken horizontal line, which emphasizes the scale of the building and gives the effect of monumentality, is used very well by the architect Savitsky in the gate house for Lock 5."[62] Similarly, he states that "monumentality is victorious because of the repetition on a smaller scale of motifs or elements already used on a larger scale. This repetition forces the viewer to compare analogous forms on a broad scale and to feel more powerfully the monumentality of the forms that are significantly larger."[63] He also contends that "the clarity and universality of the primary volume of the structures contributes greatly to the feeling of monumentality."[64] The architectural elements are inextricably linked with the creation of monumental space through a combination of significant and not-so-significant elements that works cohesively to produce a unified impression. Mikhailov's comments concerning monumentality apply not only to the architectural ensembles along the waterway, but to the Lenin and Stalin sculptures as well: their size coupled with smaller details such as their facial expressions, hand gestures, and clothing complement the impression of monumentality.

Equally important is the interaction between the architecture and the natural environment into which it is placed. Here again Mikhailov offers insightful comments as to how this interaction was perceived. "The canal's architectural structures, as a rule, provide a sharp contour powerfully and expressively drawn against the background of water and landscape. In this sharp contour, in the organization of the forms and in the vertical formation of the composition is embodied the activity of the structure, its dominance within the surrounding landscape."[65] As we have seen, the creation of Stalinist spaces relied on bending nature and the environment to its will. Water played a central role in this endeavor; in the case of the Moscow Canal's architecture, water served as the perfect foil for the built environment. In describing the Khimki railroad bridge (reputedly copied by bridge designers in Sydney, Australia) Mikhailov concludes that:

> The architecture, including nature, becomes the leading figure of the surrounding landscape. Against the background of it the structures themselves acquire greater poeticism and lyricism. In its turn, the landscape that includes the completed beautiful works of architecture immeasurably enhances its own expressiveness. Of course, the surface of the canal's water itself strengthens this impact even more. It is well known that against the backdrop of water structures acquire additional value. The combination of the water's surface with the design of the architectural monuments creates a series of new possibilities for [making an] impact through the use of harmonious combinations or contrasts.[66]

Not only does water serve as the natural force that Soviet power must tame, it also provides the artistic background against which the architecture plays to its best advantage. The landscape enables the structures to produce an even greater ideological and aesthetic impact that simultaneously exploits and complements its surroundings. This interaction with the landscape into which the Moscow Canal has been placed is not limited to water, but includes the soil and changing elevations that construction of the waterway had to overcome.[67]

The deployment of water as an architectural element parallels the function of water in the paintings discussed in Chapter Three. Just as water inspired the depiction of Moscow Canal landscapes in the paintings, so too did it inspire the waterway's architecture and its creation of an aesthetic and technical symbiosis between the water and the structures built to control it. Aside from the utilitarian function of the locks, dams, and Northern River Station to facilitate transportation, hydro-electric power, and drinking water, these structures also exploited the water as the literal and figurative mirror in which their aesthetic and cultural functions would be reflected. It should be remembered that the locks, dams, and station were designed primarily to be seen from the water and with the water. Water defined not only their design, but also the perception of that design, just as it did in the paintings of various scenes from the Moscow Canal. The timelessness and constant movement that water projects likewise provides the waterway's architecture with a degree of that same timelessness as the water continues to move through and up to this built environment.

The natural environment enhanced the reading of the structures along the Moscow Canal, and so did the "artificial-refurbished" landscapes that emerged on the waterway. While the natural features complemented the architecture, the creation of new spaces likewise intensified the apprehension and use of those spaces. Greenery, parks, walking paths, and flower beds ostensibly enhanced the banks of the canal, thereby creating aesthetically pleasing, useable space for relaxation and contemplation for those not on the water. Thus the space of the canal extended beyond the confines of the waterway itself to include any area adjacent to it. "Landscaped parks [and] lanes leading to the structures and monuments, large planted beds [and] flower beds are such artificial-refurbished landscapes (all these elements especially are deployed in the architecturally planned complex of Bol'shaya Volga, at the beginning of the canal, and in the Khimki River Station ensemble)."[68] Hence from the Volga to Moscow the built and natural spaces mingled to form a cohesive whole that presumably bespoke the power, majesty and wisdom of Stalinist ideology. It was then left for the creation of memorial space along and beyond the Moscow Canal to begin deconstructing this legacy.

(De)Constructing Memories and Memorial Space

The creation of commemorative and memorial spaces along the Moscow Canal evolved over time, revealing how different eras conceived of and remembered the waterway's history and construction. This evolution is not unexpected given the changes in the USSR and Russia that have occurred since 1937. As we have seen, the second wave of de-Stalinization resulted in the removal of the Stalin monument, while the hidden Bruni frescoes similarly testify to the notion that forgetting about the Moscow Canal project was just as important as remembering it. This process begins with the 10th anniversary of the waterway in 1947 and continues to the present as an ongoing quest to understand, remember, and memorialize the space in varying political environments.

Commemorations from 1947 to 1997

The Moscow Canal's 10th anniversary coincided with the 800th anniversary of the founding of Moscow. In honor of the city's long history the Moscow–Volga Canal was renamed simply the Moscow Canal, a change that further linked the metropolis to its now namesake canal. This renaming also emphasized the increased centrality of Moscow as the nation's core, especially coming two years after the defeat of the Nazis in World War II and the defense of Moscow from the invading army. Of particular interest in a discussion of the spatial dimensions of the Moscow Canal are the stamps produced in 1947 to commemorate the canal's 10th anniversary (Figure 4.9).

The complete set consists of six stamps, each 12 × 20 cm and in denominations from 30 kopecks to 1 ruble. Each stamp features what Evgeny Dobrenko terms "self-exhibiting landscapes, which are the principal subject of the stamp."[69] In this instance the self-exhibiting landscapes are: the control towers (with Columbus's caravels) of Lock 3 in Yakhroma, the Karamyshev Dam, the Yakhroma pumping station, the Northern River Station, a map of the canal with the Kremlin Spassky tower to its left, and Lock 8. This series coincided with the release of other postwar stamps, in particular a series of stamps to commemorate Moscow's 800th anniversary, which, as Dobrenko argues, augured the "canonization" of the spatial distinction between the center (Moscow) and the periphery (everywhere else), the representation of the stratification of space.[70]

Each stamp in this series presents a physical space framed and contained within the borders of the stamp. Taken as a whole, the six stamps chart the course of the Moscow Canal, both through the 60 kopeck stamp that bears the map of the entire waterway, and through the carefully selected points on the canal that take the viewer on a virtual voyage from Lock 3 in Yakhroma all the way to the Karamyshev Dam

Figure 4.9 Moscow Canal 10th anniversary commemorative stamps.

within the Moscow city limits. Important here is not the Volga River or its diversion to Moscow, but rather those images that point to Moscow's spatial and imagined centrality. Dobrenko notes that "As a means of propaganda and agitation, stamps are immeasurably more accessible than paintings. Thus they not only reflect but also form a certain spatial model of culture."[71] As such even a seemingly small item like a stamp can shape "habits of consciousness"[72] that incrementally and persuasively reshape a citizen's view of the space she inhabits so that a representational space becomes an actualized space to the viewer. "The fundamental contents of the Soviet stamp – the presentation of a topographical cultural mythology – allows us to see in it a true symbol of the new topography. Information about the country as contained in this token of postage payment is fully paid for: it is fast fixed in the Soviet mentality and sealed by history."[73]

While it is impossible to know how widely the Moscow Canal series stamps were used as official postage or limited to philatelic collections, extant ephemera suggest that some were likely used, given the postmarks that many bear.[74] This spatial message moved within and beyond the borders of the USSR, as did postcards depicting scenes from the Moscow–Volga Canal. Postcards with images of Locks 5 and 8, the Northern River Station and the Klyazma Reservoir were both posted and collected, thereby surviving as additional ephemera that keep the image of the Moscow Canal rooted in the present and continuing into the future. What gets lost, however, is the original intent of these items to create a new Soviet topography that promoted an idealized space to be internalized and transformed into a real space redolent of Soviet values and achievements. Instead, these items serve as mementos of another time and differently defined spaces that no longer carry the highly ideologized meanings with which they were initially imbued. Does this mean that the spaces and places these ephemera depict are now Russian spaces? It does only in the sense that the locks, dams, reservoirs, and attendant structures are physically located in Russia. The memory or interpretation that a given space evokes depends on the viewer such that the space can be rendered neutral or highly charged and contested.

The richly detailed images of the 1947 commemorative Moscow Canal stamps far surpassed the more quotidian matchbook covers that were produced to celebrate the waterway's 40th anniversary in 1977[75] (Figure 4.10). Yellow, blue, green, and white drawings outlined in black adorned the matchbox covers and depicted a dam, a lock, a pumping station, barrier gates, and the Columbus caravel (not perched on a lock tower, but sailing on a blue sea) with the titles of each illustration offering no more information that the generic name of the structure. Yet the images included highlight some of the Moscow Canal's key structures without which it could not operate. Here too we see the incipient emergence of the Columbus caravels as the waterway's signature image. In spite of the less lavish production standards, the impulse behind the matchbook covers, as well as behind a souvenir pin

Figure 4.10 40th anniversary commemorative matchbox covers.

that depicts the Santa Maria on the tower of Lock 3 or, in its most recent iteration, that features the Santa Maria in profile with the waterway's name underneath, is the same: to concretize and capture in a small space the totality of the Moscow Canal in order to celebrate and remember it.

That these ephemera are saved and collected ensures in some small measure that the waterway maintains a place in popular culture, if not in cultural consciousness, just as did the commemorative volumes that celebrated the Moscow Canal's 50th anniversary in 1987.[76] These two soft-bound publications honor the waterway with richly produced illustrations that capture the practical and recreational uses of the Moscow Canal. For example, the approximately 50-page, large format brochure entitled *The Moscow Canal* (*Kanal imeni Moskvy*) includes 51 photographs taken at various locations along the waterway. Starting with the monument to Lenin at Lock 1, the pictorial journey (with scant commentary) enables the reader to traverse time and space, especially due to the map included in the brochure's inside front cover and a photograph of a ship passing by the Kremlin on the inside back cover. Local attractions such as the World War II victory memorial outside Dmitrov, recreational facilities represented by sailboats on the reservoirs, and bikini-clad holiday-makers aboard steamships are interspersed with photographs of the canal's locks, ports, and pumping stations. By interweaving these images the brochure's unnamed author(s) create a spatial equivalency that places the recreational and practical functions of the Moscow Canal literally and figuratively in the same space.

Similarly, the soft-bound booklet *Moscow–Volga: The Moscow Canal* (*Moskva-Volga: Kanal imeni Moskvy*) was also published in 1987 as an official commemorative publication for the waterway's 50th anniversary.[77] Remarkably, the narrative opens with a discussion and photographs of the canal's construction 50 years before, which not surprisingly fails to mention the forced laborers that constructed it. They appear in photographs depicting construction methods used to build the waterway, but the narrative provides only a general history as to how the Moscow Canal came to be. Three more brief essays are interspersed with plentiful, excellently reproduced photographs that reveal diverse aspects of the Moscow Canal: the green spaces that border it and offer rest and recreation; winter scenes when the waterway is frozen and maintenance work is conducted; seascapes that feature ships, sailors, and boat pilots; and the waterway's architecture as evinced in its locks and the Northern River Station. The booklet's intent, given the profusion of photographs, is not so much to take the reader on a journey as it is to celebrate and glorify the spaces of the canal. As a result, both of these publications serve to celebrate rather than to memorialize the Moscow Canal, especially in its then-contemporary representation.

Dmitrov: Traces of the Gulag

Dmitrov and its environs, which housed the Dmitlag headquarters, provide memorial space on a number of levels. Alongside physical reminders of the Dmitlag camp stand recent structures that preserve and honor the memory of those who built the Moscow canal, as well as those who have worked and continue to work on the waterway. This intersection of past and present provides a pivot point around which the various reactions to and memories of the construction of the Moscow Canal turn.

Among the reasons why Dmitrov remains relevant to a discussion of memorial space is that the late *Dmitrov Herald* editor Nikolai Alekseevich Fedorov singlehandedly initiated efforts to uncover and document the history of the Moscow Canal, especially as it pertained to Dmitrov. The city's place as the Dmitlag headquarters serves as a dubious and remarkable distinction given the Gulag's legacy and Dmitrov's close proximity to Moscow. Through his path-breaking book *Did the Minister Have a Wheelbarrow?* and numerous articles in the *Dmitrov Herald* newspaper, Fedorov illuminated not only the history of the Moscow Canal's construction, but also revealed the biographies of many of those whose labor built it.[78] In addition, he documented the many landmarks in contemporary Dmitrov that still bear the signs of Dmitlag. To this end, in honor of the Moscow Canal's 70th anniversary, a map based on Fedorov's research was published in the *Dmitrov Herald*, indicating every location in the city and surrounding areas that had been part of Dmitlag.[79] The city plan highlights 69 sites that feature either structures that still exist or the spot where Dmitlag buildings used to stand but have since been torn down.

Fedorov also played an important role in helping the organization *Memorial* to determine which Dmitlag inmates were executed at the Butovo shooting range in the south of Moscow. Were it not for his untimely death in 2005, Fedorov would likely have continued the research on the Moscow Canal and Dmitlag that he began in 1989.[80] His work commenced at the time when archival materials became increasingly accessible. Under the rubrics "History and Truth" and later "The Canal and Fate," Fedorov published numerous articles in the *Dmitrov Herald* that examined the destinies of those repressed in Dmitlag during the Great Terror, as well as investigations concerning the construction of the Moscow Canal and the lives of many of its builders. It is not an exaggeration to say that Nikolai Fedorov opened the topics of Dmitlag and the Moscow Canal to a level of scrutiny that instigated subsequent scholarship and journalistic writings that continue to produce important findings.

The physical reminders of the Dmitlag camp within the city include the Saints Boris and Gleb Monastery that served as the headquarters for the camp administration, and whose grounds were confiscated for the camp's use[81] (Figure 4.11). To achieve this end, the OGPU disbanded the local ethnographic museum that had been at the Monastery and drove out the museum workers. The museum's director Kirill Alekseevich Soloviev and his associates were arrested in January 1933. At this time all the museum's holdings were unceremoniously dumped on the street, in an action that Fedorov characterized as "Let them know who the boss is now!"[82] This sacrilegious act certainly underscored the regime's disdain not only for the Orthodox Church but also for historically significant artifacts that celebrated pre-revolutionary Russia. These actions revealed the attitude that nothing, or at least any physical space that Stalinism had not created, was sacred. Hence a rather non-descript white building that stands adjacent to the monastery wall served as the headquarters for the Dmitlag administration, including a neon sign announcing that fact (see Figure 4.11).

In addition, street names including "Chekist (Secret Police) Street" and "Engineer Street," former housing for the canal's free laborers comprising two-story wooden structures that remain occupied, and the house built for Dmitlag supervisor Semyon Firin, are still found in Dmitrov (Figures 4.12 and 4.13).

The house built for the brilliant engineer and former member of the Russian Provisional Government Nikolai Vissarionovich Nekrasov, who was incarcerated in Dmitlag, stands to this day on Pushkin Street (formerly named Water Street) with a memorial plaque in Nekrasov's honor.[83] Standing and restored as well are two, two-story buildings that

Figure 4.11 A building at the perimeter of the Boris and Gleb Monastery that housed the Dmitlag administrative headquarters.

served as Moscow Canal administrative buildings. One now serves as the headquarters for fluorography, while the other houses a tuberculosis dispensary. Thus for anyone seeking traces of Dmitlag in Dmitrov, there exist a number of structures that continue to testify to the Gulag's presence in the city. Unfortunately, a number of other significant wooden structures in Dmitrov have been demolished. These include a pier on the waterway where passenger vessels would dock, a store, a summer movie theater, dining halls, barracks, former punishment cells and the "Finnish Village," a group of one-story barracks in the camp zone.[84] Fortunately, many traces of Dmitlag still linger and provide silent testimony to the city's Gulag past. However, precisely this silent testimony means that these spaces of memory are neither fully appreciated nor sacralized. If few people know of their existence, then their agency as memorials delivers less of an impact.

Not surprisingly, contemporary initiatives to create memorial spaces in Dmitrov that invoke the memory of the original canal builders and their sacrifice have renewed the sacredness of the monastery, and also created new sacred spaces that strive to honor and remember the tortured

Figure 4.12 Sign for Chekist Street in Dmitrov. The title Chekist was given to those who worked for the secret police; the organization originally bore the name Cheka.

history of the construction of the canal. This quest to reclaim memorial space along the Moscow Canal itself is best represented by the cross erected along the first experimental kilometer of the waterway in Dmitrov[85] (Figure 4.14). While the city sits on the eastern bank of the Moscow Canal, this cross constructed of two steel beams riveted together stands on the western bank. Although partly obscured by electrical and railway wires, the cross is visible to anyone entering or exiting the city on the main Moscow–Dubna highway or via the railroad. The cross is plainly seen by anyone who either swims in the waterway at Dmitrov or who sails to or from Moscow on any number of watercraft. Situated on a sloping hill, the cross is difficult to access since no direct route to it exists. Rather, anyone who wishes to leave a wreath there in memory of the canal builders must traverse a rutted dirt road through a grove of trees and then hike up the slope (there is no dedicated path) to reach the monument. The dates 1932–7 are etched in white into the slope. Upon arriving at the top of the slope, the visitor is towered over by the cross. Closer to eye level stands a granite tombstone with the following words:

Figure 4.13 Building constructed to house free workers on the Moscow Canal project. This building and others like it now house apartments for Dmitrov residents.

"To our fellow citizens who perished during the construction of the Moscow–Volga Canal (1932–7). The ashes of many of them are in the soil of Dmitrov." The inscription is signed and dated "The Citizens of Dmitrov, 1997" and coincides with the 60th anniversary of the completion of the Moscow Canal[86] (Figure 4.15). Until that time no dedicated space had been designated to memorialize those who perished constructing the canal, nor was there any public indication that the construction of the Moscow Canal was anything but a great achievement of Soviet power. That it was one of the signature projects of Stalin's second five-year plan, constructed through the use of forced labor and interwoven with the Stalinist terror, was ignored.

The choice of a granite headstone and steel cross were likely not accidental. Using granite affords the memorial headstone timelessness: the strength of the stone will succumb neither to the elements nor to time, thus carving out a space of eternal memory for those to whom it is dedicated. The placement of the cross behind the stone is meant to

Figure 4.14 The cross and memorial to the victims of Dmitlag on the west bank of the Moscow Canal at the first experimental kilometer.

resemble a burial plot in a cemetery. Moreover, the base of the cross features a mound of large stones that encircle the granite headstone as well. This configuration marks the space as sacred ground reminiscent of Golgotha. That the cross is made of steel beams weathered by the elements links the memorial to the canal's construction and the steel that was used to construct the lock gates, generators, turbines, bridges, and other structures. The granite headstone replicates the stone used throughout canal construction. Pairing the cross with the headstone likewise links the Dmitrov memorial to other Gulag memorials erected throughout Russia, and to the modest memorial erected in Dubna on 15 July 2013, the Moscow Canal's 76th anniversary. The Dubna memorial was created from one block of granite and one block of marble taken from the remains of the Stalin sculpture. The memorial bears a plaque that reads "To the builders of the Moscow–Volga Canal, 1932–7, to the heroes and victims – eternal memory." A replica of a Moscow–Volga Canal shock worker's pin graces the center of the inscription.[87]

From the Solovetsky Stone opposite the Lubyanka in Moscow to the Solovetsky cross anchored in a pile of stones at Butovo to the "Mask of Sorrows" sculpture in Magadan,[88] into which a stone cross has been inserted, the Dmitrov memorial continues the aesthetic tradition to claim memorial space through the use of these elements. In effect the materials used in the Dmitrov memorial are instantly recognizable as

Figure 4.15 The granite headstone with its inscription at the base of the steel cross in Dmitrov.

hallmarks of Gulag memorial space that is simultaneously encoded with religious motifs. As Zuzanna Bogomil has persuasively argued, the stone, the cross, and the mask have been used to concretize the memory of the Gulag, which has been increasingly dominated both by religious images and the support of the Russian Orthodox Church. As she notes, "Thus, the memory of the Gulag supported by the Russian Orthodox Church slowly dominates the social perception of the repressive past."[89]

Siting the memorial at the Moscow Canal's first experimental kilometer (marked on the waterway's banks by vertical red stripes every meter or so over the course of the kilometer) situates the remembrance of the project's victims at the place where it all began in Dmitrov. As the center of the Dmitlag universe, Dmitrov served as the physical and metaphorical symbol of the entire project. All directives, plans, and punishments emanated from there, as did any cultural, political, or social initiatives connected with the camp. Before it disappeared the original Moscow–Volga Canal museum was established in Dmitrov, and the canal project's leaders, Semyon Firin, head of the Dmitlag, and Lazar' Kogan, head of construction, lived in the city in sturdy houses constructed especially for them.[90] In short, Dmitrov encapsulated the entire Moscow–Volga Canal project, so it is not unexpected that the Dmitlag memorial would be erected there.

In addition, the Dmitrov Regional Public Library, as a result of the efforts of retired librarian Nina Lvovna Elovskaya, maintains a collection in its Dmitrov Ethnography room containing any print materials produced about the Moscow Canal. This collection includes historical accounts, recent newspaper articles, and contemporary works on the canal. These shelves also house the articles produced in conjunction with two conferences held in Dmitrov to commemorate the 65th and 70th anniversaries of the canal's completion. To mark the canal's 70th anniversary Elovskaya organized a small exhibit in the Dmitrov Library Ethnography room that showcased print materials dedicated to retelling the history of the construction of the Moscow–Volga Canal.

Elovskaya's efforts are not the only local initiatives organized to recount the canal's construction. Of great importance were the activities organized by Natalia Vasilievna Tabunova, a staff member at the Dmitrov Kremlin Museum-Preserve. The Museum houses a collection of paintings (discussed in Chapter Three) that depict the Moscow Canal during and after construction. To this end, the Museum organized and hosted two conferences dedicated to canal history. The first, which took place in 2002, brought together scholars and journalists whose interest in the waterway's history united them in a common cause. More significantly, the 70th anniversary of the Moscow Canal included a larger forum, again organized at and by the Museum to mark this notable date.

A final memorial event also placed Dmitrov in the space of Gulag remembrance. In the summer of 2007, to mark the 70th anniversary of the Great Terror, a slow-moving barge cut through the waters of the Moscow Canal. Its cargo held special significance for those who were victims of the Stalinist terror. Weighted down by the large memorial cross it carried, the barge likewise was pushed even deeper into the water by the burden of memory: the psychological space that the Moscow Canal and the terror of 1937 had created.

As the barge sliced through the waters of the Moscow Canal, it sliced through time as well, bringing personal tragedies and national horror back into consciousness, back to the present in an effort to remind Russian citizens of 2007 what tragedy had befallen the country in 1937. Symbolically, the barge journeyed from the first Gulag labor camp in Solovki to the sacred ground of the Butovo Shooting range, an execution site not only for Dmitlag inmates but for other victims of the Great Terror as well. This route traversed not only the Moscow Canal, but also its predecessor, the Belomor Canal. (Of course there is no other direct route to Moscow except through these canals, so to follow this route was both a matter of expediency and practicality and a way of inscribing meaning.)

As if to consecrate the channels of both the Belomor and Moscow Canals, then, the cross sailed over the burial grounds that these sites had become for many of their builders. This journey united symbolic, psychological, and physical space. It plowed through the constraints of time by forcing the present to confront and, perhaps, reconcile with the past. Indeed, it was as if this large cross and everything and everyone it symbolized was an instrument through which the sins of Stalinism could somehow be expiated. More significantly, as both Veronika Dorman and Zuzanna Bogomil assert, both Solovki and Butovo became known as "Russian Golgothas." As Bogomil states:

> Both Solovetsky crosses – the one on Sekirnaia Hill[91] and the one in Butovo – thus create a kind of axis that connects the Golgothas

> both on the level of their historical meaning (both places are marked by the presence of mass graves and linking them together suggests that the space between them is a "never-ending graveyard") as well as on the level of memorials which have a similar symbolism ... Both places are therefore connected ... geographically thanks to the Solovetsky crosses.[92]

Part of the "never-ending graveyard" that Bogomil notes is located along the banks of the Moscow Canal, and thereby creates both a spatial and temporal link between the two Golgothas.

As it journeyed from Solovki to Moscow the barge and its cargo docked in Dmitrov at the site of the former Dmitrov port. A Russian Orthodox service, in which religious and political leaders participated, was held to commemorate both the arrival of the cross and the victims it was meant to memorialize. It is no accident that the barge paused in Dmitrov; no other location along the Moscow Canal occupies as much memorial space devoted to Dmitlag as do this ancient Russian city and its environs. This event coincided with the opening of the Moscow Canal Museum in Dedenevo, as well as the laying of the foundation stone for the chapel that would ultimately be built on the canal's banks at the Museum site.[93] These concomitant events underscore what Dorman describes thusly:

> By charting a course from the Solovki to Butovo, members of the procession not only established a spatial link, but also suggested a chronology of the Gulag. The various places they passed are stations in both space and time as well as in the development of the camp system from experiment to extermination. In addition, the authors of the project sought to underline specific continuities by presenting profiles of those prisoners who followed the stations from the Calvary of the Solovki to the Butovo death fields.[94]

As Dorman suggests, the spaces traversed in this journey map not only the actual movement of the Solovetsky cross through the landscapes of terror and death whose victims the cross symbolizes, but they also map the symbolic space of terror, loss, and victimization. The construction of this symbolic space encompasses all the memorial spaces discussed above and highlights the unbreakable link between the space of experience and the space of memory.

The Moscow Canal's 70th Anniversary

Dmitrov's centrality as the primary memorialized space of Dmitlag in particular and the Moscow Canal in general has yet to be eclipsed. Nor should it be. However, memorial space committed to the prisoners who built the Moscow Canal has inevitably become bound up in remembrances of those who worked on the canal since its completion and never suffered the terror of the Gulag. These two competing narratives of memory were on display most strikingly during the many events staged in honor of the Moscow Canal's 70th Anniversary in 2007. The tension between the Gulag and non-Gulag worlds appeared especially in my efforts to obtain materials and information regarding the official Moscow Canal 70th Anniversary celebration held on 14 July 2007 (a Sunday), a day before the actual anniversary on 15 July. Attendance at the event was by invitation only, and only through dogged attempts to speak with knowledgeable Moscow Canal officials was I able to obtain some of these materials. This difficulty was especially frustrating given that I had participated in the 70th Anniversary conference in May 2007 in Dmitrov that included an excursion along the Moscow Canal, in which I was permitted to participate.

Part of the issue at that time stemmed from the official view that the Moscow Canal served as a waterway of strategic importance not only to Russia's capital, but also to the country's system of waterways in European Russia. As the canal's official website noted at that time (the page has since been deactivated), the canal is essential to defense as well as to sanitation: "To strengthen the security and anti-terrorist defenses – not for the arrival of dignitaries and commissions – but in order to avoid emergency situations and to prevent the obstruction of the operation of this especially important strategic object – this is our current task."[95] To this end the present Moscow Canal administration includes a "Department for the Protection of State Secrets."[96] As the lifeline of Moscow and in an age when terrorist threats strike practically everywhere, the FGBU-KiM is right to be concerned, although as an observer and participant this concern seemed somewhat misplaced at the time, since I had earlier interviewed the Moscow Canal's chief engineer.

Nevertheless, this strategic significance suggests why the canal's directorate was unwilling to speak with me during and after the 70th anniversary celebration of the canal's construction.[97] The notion of an American scholar probing not only the history of the Moscow Canal, but also its current condition and future use seemed to make the canal's directorate uncomfortable, perhaps understandably so. At least this was the explanation offered by Russian colleagues who marveled at the bureaucratic barriers that confronted me at every turn as I attempted to interview one of the canal's administrators, A. A. Sidorov, who was the Assistant Director for Economic Development in 2007. Instead, the newly hired public relations specialist L. V. Shvedova was entrusted with the task of answering my questions and providing me with the information I sought concerning the current operation of the canal.[98] Shvedova's hiring demonstrated both the newly re-discovered importance of the Moscow Canal and the desire of upper management to have a professional public relations specialist run interference. The canal suffered chronic underfunding following *perestroika*, which damaged its administrative hierarchy and its physical structure. Only recently have attempts been made to reconstruct, restore, and rehabilitate the canal itself and the unique historical and cultural space it inhabits.

Critical to this new direction was the celebration of the 70th anniversary of the opening of the Moscow Canal, an event that revealed the tensions that still exist vis-à-vis the very meaning of the canal itself: the continuing struggle between those who would rather ignore the past for the sake of the future and those who believe that forgetting the past will doom Russia to repeat it. This, then, is an account of how Russia feted the Moscow Canal and how that celebration attempted to reconcile these opposing tendencies.

In preparation for the 70th Anniversary, the Moscow Canal administration launched a website to promote the canal's activities and the jubilee celebration. The site's homepage http://www.fgbu-KiM.ru/ features a scene from the waterway as well as various useful links: About Us, Management, History, Employment, News, Contact Information, Corruption Prevention, and Services. Users can view archived news items as well as current articles about the canal. This initiative, instigated by then-Assistant Director Sidorov, brought the Moscow Canal into the twenty-first century.

The Moscow Canal administration building on the corner of Vodnikov Street and the Volokolamsk Highway also underwent a partial renovation. The entire first floor of the building, originally constructed by forced laborers from Dmitlag, was restored to its former grandeur. Marble floors, ambient lighting, and a pale azure ceiling reminiscent of the color of water all grace the main hallway. In addition, the first-floor auditorium, formerly used for official gatherings, has been transformed into a conference room equipped with the latest technology and comfortable furnishings. Even the security screeners no longer block the entrance, but rather sit in a redesigned, well-lit alcove in the main hallway. Turnstiles, operated by either the security team or employee identification badges, mark the boundary between the outside world and the canal's administrative territory. While limited finances derailed renovation of the entire building, its elegant first floor now presents a more polished, professional space to visitors and staff.

The Moscow Canal's actual anniversary fell on Monday, 15 July, but 14 July 2007 was chosen to mark the 70th anniversary of the FGBU-KiM. The waterway was feted with a celebratory concert and buffet supper at the Moscow International House of Music.[99] Admission was free but by invitation only. These elaborate invitations, adorned with "before" and "after" photographs of the waterway in 1937 and 2007, were designed especially for employees of the canal and important bureaucrats. The Minister of Transportation of the Russian Federation, Igor Levitin, was on hand to celebrate, as were members of the Moscow Canal administration, the Moscow City and Regional Administration and many canal employees with their families. Workers who had faithfully served the Moscow Canal received commendations for their service. Speeches were delivered, a variety of performers appeared and the audience joined in singing the Moscow Canal's official anthem, words and music helpfully provided in a program bearing the canal's signature symbol – the Columbus caravel[100] (Figure 4.16). Participants also received a souvenir pin noting the canal's name and "age" and embellished with the ubiquitous Columbus caravel. The pins were attached to postcards that sported a photograph of the canal. An emblem of *the USSR* (rather than Russia) was emblazoned on

Figure 4.16 Cover of the invitation to the official celebration of the Moscow Canal's 70th anniversary in 2007.

the lower right corner. A Canal employee, engineer-dispatcher E. P. Vasil'eva, even penned a new "anthem" entitled "The Romantics of the Azure Highways" in honor of the event.[101] This seemingly spontaneous individual initiative dovetailed nicely with the official tenor of the Moscow Canal's 70th jubilee.

The crowning piece of anniversary memorabilia, however, was a commemorative volume entitled *The Moscow Canal's 70th Anniversary* (*70 let Kanalu imeni Moskvy*). Loaded with lavish illustrations the 105-page book provides concise histories of each decade of the canal's existence and concludes with a brief discussion of the waterway and its constituent regions in the twenty-first century.[102] These celebratory albums were not sold commercially, but instead were presented to participants at the Jubilee event and to other official agencies, a practice reminiscent of the 17th Party Congress in 1934 when participants received a souvenir copy of *The History of the Construction of the Stalin White Sea–Baltic Canal*. Fortunately for those in attendance, no one was arrested after the Moscow Canal's celebration, in contrast to the 17th Party Congress after which 1106 of the 1996 delegates were arrested, and they and the Belomor volume condemned.[103]

This allusion to the 1934 Congress is by no means frivolous. The Moscow Canal's 70th Anniversary was marked not only by the august gathering at the House of Music, but also by an equally fitting, more sober group of officially sanctioned events that paid tribute to the darker side of the canal's anniversary, its Gulag past, and overlap with the Great Terror. This second set of events demonstrates the conflicting discourses that still compete for attention and legitimacy in contemporary Russia. Given the circumstances under which the Moscow Canal was opened, such complexity is not unexpected. This difficult past was marked in a more modest but no less compelling way in a series of events in May, July, and August 2007.

On 29 May 2007 under the auspices of the FGBU-KiM and the Dmitrov Kremlin Museum-Preserve,[104] a conference was held in honor of the Moscow Canal's 70th Anniversary. By holding the conference in Dmitrov, organizers recognized the importance of the city in the history of the Moscow Canal: Dmitrov, situated midway on the route, served as the geographical, political, and cultural focus for canal activity throughout its construction. The May 2007 conference, entitled "The Moscow–Volga Canal: Past and Present," featured presentations by a variety of scholars and canal specialists. In addition to the presenters, the audience included FGBU-KiM employees. Conference topics ranged from canal architecture to music; from the quality of the concrete used to build the waterway to the exploitation of state resources to address economic issues; from the environment to the Gulag. A total of 15 presentations were scheduled. Upon entering the conference venue participants encountered paintings of the Moscow Canal from the Dmitrov Kremlin's collection and viewed segments of the 1937 film about the project.

The subsequent planned cruise took conference attendees along the waterway from the third lock at Yakhroma to a point approximately 4 kilometers north of Dmitrov. A tight timeline had to be maintained in order to adhere to the transit schedule at Lock 3. Participants listened to a lecture delivered by the late GARF archivist Ivan Kokurin on NKVD officers and their victims who served at Dmitlag, observed a wreath being laid at the memorial to those who perished building the canal, and partook in a buffet during which the canal and its contemporary work force were toasted. Dmitrov Regional Administrator, Valery Gavrilov, and FGBU-KiM's Assistant Director, A.A. Sidorov, hosted the cruise.

This event produced mixed impressions. On the one hand, participants routinely referred to the Gulag and its central role in the construction of the Moscow Canal. There was a palpable sense of sorrowful remembrance among many conference-goers. On the other hand, several canal employees focused exclusively on the waterway's place in contemporary Russian society and chose to accentuate not its past, but its present and future.

Yet it was the theme of remembrance that triumphed on 5 July 2007 when the first stone was laid for the foundation of the Chapel of the New Martyrs and Confessors of Russia on the grounds of the Yakhroma District FGBU-KiM office in Dedenevo on the banks of the Moscow Canal. Officially the chapel is dedicated to the New Martyrs (*novomucheniki*), among whom undoubtedly were some Dmitlag camp inmates who died building the Moscow Canal.[105] The mayor of the dacha settlement "Turist," S. N. Tiagacheva, promoted the idea for the chapel with support from the Moscow Canal administration and the blessings of the Russian Orthodox Church.[106] Local dignitaries, Church officials, and canal employees participated in the event.[107] By June 2008 the chapel had been completed and was open for visitors (Figure 4.17). In fact, several people noted informally that people had talked of the chapel becoming a tourist stop for the cruise ships that routinely ply the waters of the canal on their way to and from Moscow. During the summer cruise season, ships pass the chapel, but it has not yet become a regular stop. For this reason, visitors to the chapel are few; it is not visible from the Moscow–Dubna highway, which means that anyone who wanted to visit the shrine on land would have to make a conscious effort to stop and seek it out behind the buildings that shield it from view.

A museum commemorating the Moscow Canal also opened at the Yakhroma District Headquarters on 5 July 2007 to modest fanfare. As a local paper noted, "As part of the celebration of the 70th anniversary of the Moscow Canal two events took place in the village of Dedenevo, each of which could be considered unique."[108] Although the event was low-key, the official delegation included the Moscow Canal's director at that time, A. A. Sokurenko, along with Dmitrov District Administrator Gavrilov, Serpukhov Bishop Roman of the Moscow Patriarchate, and Mayor Tiagacheva and her husband. The museum, which overlooks the memorial chapel on the banks of the canal, was a labor of love for

Figure 4.17 The Chapel of the New Martyrs on the bank of the Moscow Canal.[109]

Galina Ivanovna Yurchenko, an engineer at Yakhroma, who had worked tirelessly to collect artifacts, documents, photographs, and any information related to the construction of the Moscow Canal and to those who built it. Situated in a relatively spacious wing on the second floor of the building, the museum affords visitors the chance to immerse themselves in the history of the Moscow Canal from the earliest mention of the project in Petrine times to the present. Artifacts, including an exact replica of the wheelbarrows used on the canal construction site (with contemporary photographs displaying the wheelbarrows), a desk used by NKVD officers, numerous photographs, books, and interpretive texts provide a wealth of information.

Perceptive visitors to the museum will be struck by the subtle tension that the expositions create. The dark history of the construction of the canal is catalogued in a side room that is not immediately in view of visitors, while the main exhibition room is festooned with flags, banners, and all manner of artifacts celebrating the post-World War II life of the Moscow Canal and its work force. Were it not for the wheelbarrow and assorted tools on display to the left of the entrance, a visitor might not even realize that the Moscow Canal was forged from the labor and lives of Dmitlag prisoners. As one journalist noted, "The museum is open to visitors of all ages. One hopes that history teachers will bring their students here on excursions and tell them the whole story of a construction project that we, the older generation, did not know."[110] And, as described above, the third event to memorialize those who suffered in Dmitrov was the August 2007 voyage of the cross-laden barge on its journey from Solovki to Butovo. It was a fitting tribute that the barge passed the Moscow Canal Museum and foundation stone of the Chapel.

These seemingly minute details of the commemorative events connected with the Moscow Canal's 70th anniversary expose the complicated tug-of-war between official and unofficial discourses that seek to claim the MVC's physical and metaphorical space as their own. Like so many other relics from the Stalinist era, the Moscow Canal continues to prick the conscience of Russia by its mere presence. Although, as Alexander Etkind has argued, the majority of today's Russians know something about the Great Terror and the Gulag, many current FGBU-KiM employees, as well as the canal's administration, prefer to downplay that past in an effort to build for the future.[111] In spite of this attitude, in 2016 employees of the Moscow Canal visited the

Butovo Shooting Range to mark the official Day of Remembrance on 30 October for those who perished in the Great Terror. That year, as every year, they placed a wreath in honor of those canal builders who were executed at the site.[112]

This rare public display on the part of the FGBU-KiM administration, however, is counterbalanced by assorted private reactions to the Moscow Canal in its past, present, and intended future incarnations. It is often individuals, rather than official organizations, who have devoted themselves to the preservation of the memory of those who built the Moscow Canal, not only within its historical context, but also in its contemporary milieu, as a tangible reminder of both the positive and negative outcomes of Soviet power. These responses just as forcefully attempt to define the space the canal occupies as an historical, geographical, political and personal artifact whose past should be neither denied nor ignored. The struggle involving public and private reactions underscores how spatial relationships, between individuals and their government, between the landscape and its agents, between memory and reality, shape not only individual reactions to the space, but official policy initiatives that rely on and affect the space as well.[113] These dualities characterize continuing attempts to reshape, reinterpret, and reframe the Moscow Canal's highly contested space in order to reconcile it with the time in which it currently exists. This question of contested space suggests numerous interpretive dichotomies that merit further investigation. Particularly apparent in this regard is the tension between public and private historical space that the Moscow Canal's 70th Anniversary highlighted.

Contradictions between public and private historical space shape the question as to which elements of the canal's past are memorable and worthy. For example, the Moscow Canal's administration and its official pronouncements, coupled with the publication of the Moscow Canal's 70th Anniversary souvenir album, emphasized the waterway's importance as the main source of potable water for Moscow. Equally central to this position is the notion that the waterway must operate as a commercial enterprise that generates electricity, provides relatively cheap, if slow, cargo transport, and offers a unique recreational experience. Because the canal literally flows to the Kremlin, the spatial and political metaphors remain intact. Indeed, for the Luftwaffe in World War II the canal functioned as a roadmap to the center of Moscow.

Similarly, the canal's name underscores the symbiotic relationship that the Russian capital has with its namesake waterway, a bond that reinforces Moscow's dependence on the canal regardless of its past.

It would be unfair to insist that the FGBU-KiM administration routinely fails to acknowledge the canal's history: the organization's website features a link that discusses, albeit in generalities, how the Moscow Canal was constructed. Moreover, neither the Chapel nor the Canal Museum could have been erected had it not been for the support of canal administrators. It is equally clear that the chapel and museum projects would not have been realized had it not been for the personal initiatives of interested parties who individually pursued this spatial reclamation to ensure that the past and present co-exist, even if this co-existence proves troublesome.

Certainly these "private" initiatives to dedicate, describe, and preserve the historical space of the Moscow Canal reveal that personal reactions to a public space often convey the actual opinions held by citizens more accurately than official pronouncements. For example, the efforts of Galina I. Yurchenko to gather original canal artifacts, to reproduce an authentic Moskva-Volgostroi wheelbarrow, and to insist on the establishment of a Moscow Canal Museum illustrate how a private initiative can reclaim history in order to preserve and honor it (Figure 4.18). According to her colleagues, Galina Ivanovna struggled for years to make the museum a reality until the impending 70th anniversary, when FGBU-KiM officials realized the necessity of such an enterprise; they literally and figuratively gave the space onto which the history of the Moscow Canal could be re-inscribed.

Personal history can also parallel public history. The late hydro-electrical engineer Valentin Sergeevich Barkovsky, for example, marked the course of his personal history on a timeline of more than 40 years of employment at the canal. Barkovsky devoted his entire working life to the waterway. He received his apartment, his dacha in "Turist," and pension through his service to the Moscow Canal, and he could trace this journey along the hydro-electric stations that he helped maintain and upgrade along the waterway's route. Like his colleague Yurchenko, Barkovsky melded his personal history with the Moscow Canal's more public historical narrative to reclaim the canal's physical space as an historical one where public and private memory intersect. He did so most notably through his slim booklet entitled *Secrets of the*

Figure 4.18 Galina I. Yurchenko in front of the first large exhibit at the Moscow Canal Museum. The wheelbarrow is an exact replica of those used on the construction site, while the shovel and tools were found along the waterway.

Moscow–Volga Construction (*Tainy Moskva–Volgostroiia*), subtitled "A Collection of Stories about the History of the Construction of the Moscow Canal," published in 2007. He quietly collected pertinent documents, reports, publications and personal reminiscences, resulting in a personal archive on the Moscow Canal that fills ten file boxes. Due to his employment on the canal, Barkovsky had access to the official FGBU-KiM archive. This afforded him the chance to examine historical materials that heretofore have not been made widely available to researchers due to the potentially sensitive nature of the documents. In addition, because Barkovsky regularly traversed the canal on work assignments, he was able to talk not only to fellow Moscow Canal employees, but also to denizens of the areas around the waterway. The materials he gathered focused not on the technical aspects of the Moscow Canal, but on the history of its construction and existence up to World War II. As such, this booklet reads not as a scholarly monograph on the waterway, but rather as a series of vignettes that acquaint the reader with particularly poignant and instructive moments in the waterway's early history. As Barkovsky himself noted in a brief preface:

> The impetus for the creation of this small book was the wish of the author who, having worked at the Moscow Canal since 1960, wanted to raise the curtain of secrecy that had been created around the construction of the Moscow–Volga Canal ... On the occasion of the 70th anniversary of the Moscow Canal I succeeded in finishing the first part of a larger work on the Canal – about the time of its construction.[114]

The table of contents reveals that the majority of Barkovsky's narratives are devoted to revelations about the Dmitlag camp, the NKVD's supervision of the canal's construction, and the philosophy behind the waterway's architecture. Photographs of the canal's supervisory brigade Semyon Firin, Lazar' Kogan, and Sergei Zhuk,[115] of Dmitlag survivor Nikolai Kravchenko, and of the placement of Dmitlag settlements along the canal route, enhance Barkovsky's narrative. Barkovsky's choice to foreground the NKVD and camp experience on the waterway reveals a tension between official duty, responsibility, and personal conscience. Barkovsky was motivated both by his long years of faithful service to the Moscow Canal and his sense that the full history of it needs to be written to secure its builders a place in the collective history and consciousness of the nation. The metaphorical space that it creates covers precisely this intersection of the public with the private.

Consider, on the other hand, Galina Aleksandrovna Gerke, who worked for the Moscow Canal for 50 years and rose through the ranks to the politically important position of personnel director. Like Barkovsky, Gerke's entire working life was tied to the Moscow Canal, as was her personal life: she met her husband while working there and has it to thank for her apartment and current position as Director of the Moscow Canal Museum. For Gerke the historical space that merits reclamation is centered on the efforts and dedication of the post-World War II canal staff, especially the engineers and their subordinates, who devoted their careers to the maintenance and operation of the waterway. When Gerke speaks of the Moscow Canal's history, these are the people she remembers and reveres. The historical space of the waterway is realized not through the problematic days of its construction, but rather through the years of dedicated service rendered to it by cadres of specialists, particularly in the 1960s and 1970s. Perhaps the most striking evidence of Gerke's and Yurchenko's contrasting views are their photographs taken in the canal Museum: whereas Yurchenko chose to stand by the exposition of canal tools, including the aforementioned wheelbarrow, Gerke opted to pose next to the photographs of the canal directorate that she served (Figure 4.19).

The tension between the private and the public in response to the 70th Anniversary of the Moscow Canal remained unabated, and perhaps it was even exacerbated by the canal's jubilee. The Moscow Canal, a contested space since its inception, continues to provoke discussion and debate. The metaphorical, historical, cultural, and physical spaces discussed here afford a productive structure through which the history and the current life of the Moscow Canal can be interpreted.

The waterway's 75th anniversary in 2012 passed with little official fanfare, with none of the celebratory events staged to mark the canal's 70th anniversary. As of November 2017 the Moscow Canal administration had organized no large commemoration of the waterway's 80th anniversary. However, a new book about the canal was published with the financial support of FGBU-KiM. Only 500 copies of the book were published. Titled *The Moscow Canal at 80: A First-hand Account of the NKVD Dmitlag* [*Kanalu Moskva-Volga 80 let: pravda o Dmitlage NKVD iz {pervykh ruk*] was edited by members of the FGBU-KiM staff and the Moskva-volga.ru collective.[116] Efforts to mark the Moscow Canal's 80th anniversary instead fell to non-governmental organizations. The Memorial Society mounted an exhibition *Kanal imeni* that ran from 15 September to 19 October 2017, the purpose of which was to reexamine the legacy of the Moscow Canal.[117] On 31 October 2017 the Moskva-volga.ru group sponsored an event to honor the memory of the prisoners who built the last segment of the Moscow Canal near Kolomenskoe in southern Moscow.[118] Given that the waterway's anniversary year is essentially over, there is little chance that any other events will occur.

Figure 4.19 Galina A. Gerke in front of the portraits of the post-World War II leadership of the Moscow Canal.

Monumentality and Memory

Through the Moscow Canal project, Soviet/Stalinist power literally and figuratively etched itself into the landscape, most obviously through the Lenin and Stalin monuments. Both the achievements and the scars of these physical and psychological fissures are just as monumental, if not more so, as any other Stalinist architectural monuments, precisely because both the landscape and its shapers were forever altered. This notion of monument and monumentality appears throughout the history of the Soviet Union, but most ambitiously (and not unexpectedly) throughout the Stalinist era. As William Gass argues, a monument functions to "return an idea to consciousness" and to "focus the thoughts of a group upon a past person or event to get people *to remember together*."[119] In the case of the Moscow Canal the glorious revolutionary past and the promise of a bright future provided the focus of attention for the project as articulated in the Lenin monument. Gass further notes that this action thereby affirms the unity of the group and underscores that the monument has meaning.[120] Given the sheer size, scope, and history of the Moscow Canal it is appropriate to call it not only a monument, but monumental as well.

Gass's conclusions also apply to memorial space on the Moscow Canal. It is this desire to "return an idea to consciousness" that grounds the search for and creation of spaces of memory. The most important function of the memorial spaces connected with the Moscow Canal is in raising the consciousness of viewers or visitors of these places vis-à-vis the project's roots in the Gulag. In this regard the notions of memory, monument, and monumentality are inseparable, for they infuse each other with meaning. Memories of and memorials to the builders of the Moscow Canal remain feasible because of the continuing presence of the waterway. Just as literary works sought to create space on the page for the canal project and its builders, so too does memorial space, both visible and imagined, attempt to include those builders in any discussion of the Moscow Canal's place in contemporary Russia.

Of course, this massive structure not only speaks to the disturbing ability of the NKVD to force the production of large-scale structures; in addition, the very monumentalism of the Moscow Canal reflects in acutely physical terms how the Stalinist regime exploited large construction projects with their concomitant industrial metaphors to physically rhetoricize the ideology's success, foresight, and capacity to remold the Soviet Union (and by extension its inhabitants), psychologically, culturally, economically, politically, and physically into a country and populace worthy of the revolution that produced them. Arguably, the figure of Stalin still haunts the waterway through the empty pedestal that no longer supports his monument; he is still present even if submerged in the Moscow Canal's waters. This remolding became all the more striking when produced by the overlay of the Gulag on these spaces. Like the missing Stalin monument, the traces of the Gulag still haunt not only Dmitrov, but the entire canal route.

The magnitude of the Moscow Canal resonates not only in the history of its construction, but also in its very visible presence to anyone who arrives in Moscow from the north, to any tourist who takes a "Russian Waterways" tour or to any "new Russian" who builds, usually illegally, a palatial dacha along the waterway. As Galina Yurchenko noted, the waterway's shoreline, as well as the land at least 50–100 meters from the channel, belong to the Moscow Canal administration, but no one seems intent on enforcing any building restrictions. The enduring interaction of the space with its inhabitants and the changing parameters of this relationship further motivate the quest to understand what made this geographical feature Stalinist and to contemplate whether it has been re-inscribed as a Russian space.

The Moscow Canal achieves monumentality partly because of its enormity and partly because of its ability, as Gass aptly states, to "consume the clock in its effort to defy it."[121] While the original ideological legacy of the Moscow Canal has faded and its creation by Dmitlag inmates remains largely forgotten, its physical presence endures, thereby linking its past with its present. As such, the passage of time creates an ideological void that currently is being filled not with Stalinist rhetoric, but with a combination of infrequent genuinely pious remembrances of those who built the waterway and a blatant disregard for the past that espouses the seizure of as much valuable real estate along the Moscow Canal as possible.

Zuzanna Bogomil notes this tension between remembering and forgetting forced labor projects in her discussion of Gulag memorials: "as one of the memory researchers, Aleksander Etkind, points out diagnoses on [the] cold character of Russian memory are exaggerated (Etkind 2009) Sociological polls show that Russians remember the Soviet terror fairly well and are able to say what happened to their society and own family even fifty or seventy years ago."[122] As Etkind himself notes:

> far from demonstrating an outright denial or forgetting of the Soviet catastrophe, the vast majority of Russians are well aware of

> their country's recent history ... Sociological surveys reveal a complex picture of a people who retain a vivid memory of the Soviet terror but are divided in their interpretation of this memory. This interpretation inevitably depends upon the schemas, theories, narratives, and myths that people receive from their scholars, artists, and politicians.[123]

The exact way in which memories are interpreted looms large in the creation of memorial space along and in response to the Moscow Canal. We must also question just who remembers the Great Terror. If some citizens are too young to have direct memories of the period, then how can they remember an event that they did not experience? Perhaps a better way to conceptualize this attitude in Russian society would be to emphasize "not-forgetting" the Great Terror rather than remembering it. Memories emanate from experiences, while not-forgetting stems from the impulse to keep an event in personal or public consciousness. Related to this is the issue of who bears responsibility for deciding how to interpret memories and how those responsible shape or contextualize those memories based on their own perception of who and what should be remembered.

The entities responsible for the creation of these memories determine how those memories are conveyed and made palpable. This question retains additional significance when we consider the increasingly large role played by the Orthodox Church and religious motifs in this process. For example, the chapel on the banks of the Moscow Canal dedicated to the New Martyrs testifies to the memorialization of only some of those who suffered and died on the canal. As Bogomil suggests in her discussion of the Solovki Islands as a place of memory:

> On the one hand, the *lager'* [camp] history of this place can be generalized and can serve as a figure of broader meaning – it can serve as a warning for the future or deliver examples of heroism by means of the fate of the Solovki saints. On the other hand the Solovetski crosses which have been erected on the Islands constitute very concrete palpable signs of memory. That is why they are willingly used to mark places of Soviet repression in the Russian Federation.[124]

In the case of the Moscow Canal memorials, the symbol of the cross, as well as the physical presence of a consecrated Russian Orthodox chapel, inscribe any of the canal project's New Martyrs into Russian Orthodox history, an act that further legitimizes their suffering at the hands of Soviet repression. The category New Martyrs neglects any criminal elements and many political prisoners and instead focuses on those who perished at the hands of Stalinist oppressors because of their sustained faith.

In this sense the Orthodox Church assumes responsibility for constructing only some of the memory of the Moscow Canal project; its inclination to do to stems both from the Church's increasing power and influence in Russian society, as well as the abrogation of its duty by the State to officially create memorial spaces in honor of all those who suffered at the hands of the Gulag system. As Bogomil argues:

> the Orthodox interpretation may have an even stronger impact on the understanding of the repressive past. The Orthodox concept is easily visible in the cultural landscape and even if not all Russians are believers, the concept seems appealing also to other social groups. It does not renounce the whole glory of the past, proving rather that victims were important for the contemporary revival of the Church ... It also has a solid ally, the government ... This union of the Church and the state under the Solovetski cross at Butovo, was a historical event, because the latter one confirmed the duty to remember the victims of Soviet repression. However, this act of remembering confirmed something more than the need to remember. The state confirmed that not all victims of Soviet repression deserved to be remembered, but that there was a particular group, which society should remember – the Martyrs.[125]

Bogomil's assertion captures the difficulty in creating memorial space for the Moscow Canal or for other Gulag sites: if the state will not openly commemorate all the victims of Stalinism, then to whom does the responsibility for remembering fall?

Bogomil's explanation does not fully account for the Moscow Canal memorial spaces. While a cross figures prominently at the Dmitrov memorial, there is none in Dubna. Moreover, both memorials were erected with local government approval (it could not be otherwise) and in honor of everyone who participated in the construction of the Moscow Canal as a forced laborer, not just the New Martyrs. Arguably, the memorials in Dmitrov and Dubna are just as sacred as any religious consecrated space because of their intention to remember the dead and to honor their memory.

In discussing the intersection of religion, violence, memory, and place Roger Friedland and Richard D. Hecht note that:

> History is compressed in these {sacred} places. They are intensely located in the present, but the past impresses them and they bleed into the future. In the geographer's gaze, historical events may have taken place in multiple locations, but in the cultures of sacred place, those same historical moments all happened in that place.[126]

In terms of the Moscow Canal memorial spaces, they indeed concentrate the whole history of the construction and its attendant terror into the solid granite stones that denote each site. As Friedland and Hecht note, according to Pierre Nora, "places or emplacements are a substitute for memory. This means that history is not about the past. Memory is intensely present and not past."[127] This statement reveals a vital element vis-à-vis the places of memory on the Moscow Canal. The act of remembering unfolds in the present and recurs each time a memorial, architectural work, or monument is viewed or contemplated. Thus memory recurs anew each time these spaces are encountered. As Friedland and Hecht posit, "Memory is a facet of power ... It underscores that time is converted to space and space may be converted into time. Memory is a kind of alchemy that not only links time and space but also converts one into the other. This may be its most alluring power."[128]

The Moscow Canal monuments, architecture, and memorials, for all their civic, ideological or religious overtones, consolidate time and space into single palpable locations that simultaneously recall and remind us of a time and place that deserves to be remembered not only for the suffering it provoked, but also for the feats that were achieved and the agents who wrought these changes. These remembrances, coupled with the potent metaphor of ever-flowing water, operate on a space/time continuum that has no end; just as the water continues to flow through and past these spaces, so too do the re-inscriptions of those spaces continue. Certain memories or places might be washed away or softened by the constant movement of the water, but this constant movement permits fresh interpretations of these monumental and memorial spaces. The water itself assumes the mantle of monumentality and memorialization as a result of its enduring power and presence.

Seeing the monuments, architecture and memorial spaces on the Moscow Canal reminds us that, as Christopher Tilley has argued, "places, like persons, have biographies in as much as they are formed, used, and transformed in relation to practice . . . stories acquire part of their mythic value and historical relevance if they are rooted in the concrete details of locales in the landscape, acquiring material reference points that can be visited, seen and touched."[129] Until there is a more widespread official reckoning by the Russian government to celebrate the architectural achievements of the Moscow Canal architects and builders and to create a memorial space that adequately addresses the legacy and loss of Gulag construction projects such as the waterway, the current spaces of monumentality and memory, even the Lenin monument, suffice to reveal their biographies to anyone willing to "read" them.

CHAPTER 5

THE PRESENT AND FUTURE OF THE MOSCOW CANAL

The future of the Moscow Canal is indisputably linked to its past, as is the canal's present status. As long as the waterway exists, which will likely be for a very long time given its strategic importance to Moscow, the ties that bind it to the past will persist into the future as well. It is impossible to shake off the burden of the canal's difficult history, even if few people acknowledge that history. The water in the canal continues to flow and inhabit the spaces that it created, thereby suggesting a timelessness that is affected neither by defined historical time, nor by changes to the spaces around it, nor by the politics of a given era. Yet one key question for the canal's future is how its historical burden will be carried.

A consideration of the future of the Moscow Canal prompts pivotal questions that have ramifications far beyond its physical location. The issue of water resources figures prominently both locally and globally vis-à-vis the Moscow Canal. The effort to supply a steadily growing metropolis with potable water and electricity remains a problem defined by geography, i.e. by place and space. Will Moscow's continuing expansion face limits due to the (un)sustainability of the current water supply mechanism? If not, what measures can be taken to promote sustainability and at what expense? The city of Moscow survives because the Moscow Canal exists, a situation that mandates upkeep and restoration of its systems so that Volga water can continue to irrigate Moscow and quench its thirst. The canal is viewed as an object of strategic important by the Russian government not because it can carry men or materiel in defense of the capital or because it assures passage to five seas. Instead, the Moscow Canal's strategic value resides in its function as the main source of potable water to the nation's capital city, which also serves as the business, economic, diplomatic, political, and cultural center of the Russian universe. This factor alone assures a long future for the Moscow Canal.

Indeed the universality of the waterway's history illustrates similar issues beyond the borders of Russia, thereby tying its fate and functionality to the wider world.[1] For example, the town of Hasenkeyf, Turkey faces complete inundation when the Ilisu Dam on the Tigris River is completed. As an article notes, "The dam is more than 80 percent complete, but the part that will force ... thousands ... from their homes awaits: the filling of a reservoir that will cover much of the city."[2] As a scholar maintains, "It's going to ruin a historic city."[3] Like Korcheva before it, Hasenkeyf will become a watery grave for structures, streets, parks, and pastures, relinquishing its visible space to the liquid landscape that will overcome it. As in Korcheva, inhabitants stand to lose not only their livelihoods, but their centuries-old way of life as well. The physical space they inhabit will yield to an abstract space that resides in their memories, in old photographs, and in scholarly works devoted to the history and archaeology of the area. This "remembered" space will exist only as long as the memory of Hasenkeyf survives among its former inhabitants and only as long as those memories are passed down through the generations, as with Korcheva and Ivan'kovo.

In another parallel with the Moscow Canal project, the Turkish government is building a "new" Hasenkeyf to which residents of "old" Hasenkeyf will be relocated upon the completion of the Ilisu Dam. This mirrors the plight of the residents of Ivan'kovo who were relocated to "New Ivan'kovo" in order to relinquish the space for the construction of the Ivan'kovo Dam. The need to increase and enhance water supplies remains a process that has been and will continue to be fraught with conflict as water resources are further harnessed in service to a state, especially when a state ties its prestige and power to these large construction projects. Just as Stalin's vision propelled projects like the Moscow Canal, so too did Atatürk's plans for modern Turkey initiate construction of the Ilisu Dam. In fact, this project has been a source of political tension in the Middle East because of the destruction it will ultimately wreak not only on the Turkish landscape, but on the landscapes of neighboring countries, including Iraq: "Turkey's control of the headwaters of the Euphrates and Tigris, rivers that feed Syria and Iraq, has long been controversial in the Middle East, with critics saying decisions made by Turkey have led to water shortages in both other countries that have contributed to instability and wars."[4] Turkey is proceeding with the project although no set completion date has been given. To control the headwaters of the Euphrates and Tigris is to exercise political and spatial control over everyone downstream, as the history of the Moscow Canal so clearly illustrates.

Ephemera

It is the universality of a project such as the Moscow Canal that reinforces the necessity to understand its history and question its future, because the rationale for its construction and its ongoing importance resonate in a variety of locations. However, comparing the Moscow Canal with similar projects is valid only in its capacity as a water resource, since its history as a forced labor project sets it apart and, we hope, makes it unrepeatable. Yet this raises another question regarding the future of the Moscow Canal: how will memories about and of the canal as a prominent Gulag project and its forced laborers survive in the future? As the temporal distance grows between the canal's construction and the present, how will Dmitlag be remembered and memorialized? Or will it be remembered at all?

This question is especially pertinent in a country that arguably has failed to come to terms with its Stalinist past as a recent incident at the Gulag History Museum in Moscow has illustrated. An effigy of the writer Alexander Solzhenitsyn, himself a former Gulag inmate and one of its most potent chroniclers, was hung in protest outside the Museum's main entrance.[5] In an environment in which statements like, "[Solzhenitsyn is a] traitor who loved to mock truth and shamelessly lied about the Gulag," or that characterize the author as "that malicious anti-Soviet liar"[6] are uttered despite the abundance of archival proof to the contrary, what hope is there for truthfully and faithfully integrating the Moscow Canal episode and others like it into future historical narratives? Because the Moscow Canal inhabits so much physical space it cannot be ignored. Likewise, the memorials to its builders that exist in and around Dmitrov and Dubna keep these memories alive even if only in a modest way. These memorials, along with the Moscow Canal Museum in Yakhroma, preserve and promote the memory and history of the Moscow Canal project. Perhaps this is enough, although recent attempts elsewhere to destroy history and spaces of memory suggest that no structure or memorial space is safe.[7]

Other tangible reminders of the canal occupy both physical and metaphorical spaces that cannot be erased no matter how ephemeral they might seem. Into this category fall ephemera such as china, souvenir pins, and postcards – tactile objects that carry meaning in spite of the potential for their destruction or seeming unimportance. We need look no further than eBay to find a variety of realia that commemorate the Moscow Canal. Recent listings include a vintage china cup and saucer illustrated with art-deco images of the Moscow Canal and bearing the waterway's name. Advertised as "a unique vintage Russian Soviet Tea Pair" and produced as a work of "agitational porcelain" by the Dmitrov porcelain factory in Verbilki, the cup and saucer carry a $2500 price tag[8] (Figures 5.1 and 5.2). The tea pair's decoration features a map of the Moscow Canal (cutting across the space of the cup) with the Volga River and Moscow highlighted, as well as images of a lock, a ship, and other canal structures.

Likewise, for $899.99 a buyer can obtain an original Moscow–Volga Canal shock-worker pin (*znachok*) bestowed upon a Dmitlag inmate to reward labor beyond the stated norm.[9] Here too, the space of the Moscow Canal defines and dominates the image. As Plate 8 reveals, the canal's blue waters are plied by a steamship that has begun to traverse the waterway after navigating the dark blue ribbon of the Volga River that delineates the space of the pin through its slanted, horizontal path. The image of Moscow realized through the depiction of the Kremlin with the Spassky Tower, its crenellated walls, and an additional tower is emblazoned in red, thereby conveying the Kremlin's red brick and the metaphorical sense of Moscow as the "red" capital of the USSR and world-wide socialism. The pin captures movement through the image of the ship while also fixing the waterway in space and time on the artifact's surface. This item bears and re-creates a memory each time it is viewed.

Further scrolling through the listings yields postcards with photographs of the "water stadium" on the shores of the Khimki Reservoir, a reproduction of a photograph of Stalin on the banks of the canal, and the set of stamps produced in honor of its 10th anniversary in

Figure 5.1 Tea cup featuring the Moscow–Volga Canal.

1947, discussed in Chapter Four. Previous eBay listings included a souvenir pin produced in the 1960s, presumably to celebrate the waterway's 25th or 30th anniversary, a reproduction of the Elkin poster (seen on the cover of this book), and various books, such as the *Architecture of the Moscow–Volga Canal*. The existence of these items testifies to the fact that the memorabilia associated with the Moscow Canal still carries some currency as people, consciously or not, have preserved them and have found a small market to profit from these cultural artifacts.

Creating a Rhetorical Future for the Moscow Canal

As discussed in Chapter Four, the creation of memorial space along and on the Moscow Canal illustrates the tension where personal and private spaces intersect. By its nature, memorial space simultaneously

Figure 5.2 The Moscow–Volga Canal cup and saucer set.

remembers the past and hopes to relay it to the future, a potentially contentious proposition, depending on the era in which the remembrance takes place. Future readings of this space and its place in history are likely to be just as contentious. While this spatial tug-of-war will most likely be waged between the public space of the canal administration and the private space of those who continue to work to secure an accurate history of the Moscow Canal, physical space along the waterway promises to remain contentious as well.

Lest there be any lingering doubts about the waterway's significance, a scandal in 2010 surrounding the construction and demolition of houses in the village of Rechnik brings into even sharper focus not only the importance of the territory that borders the canal, but also those pieces of real estate that were deeded to canal workers years ago.[10] In recognition of service on the Moscow Canal, some workers were rewarded with dacha plots along the waterway and its reservoirs with waterfront views and in close proximity to the Moscow city limits. While the Soviet Union existed, those claiming these plots as their own faced no threat of development. In the post-1991 period, when private property was again permissible and new construction was allowed, this real estate undoubtedly brought its original owners a handsome profit. In 2010 few of the original owners remained and they faced growing bureaucratic and political pressure from Moscow authorities and wealthy buyers, who avidly pursued these prime properties. Likewise, recent buyers have also found themselves in the tenuous position of potentially losing their houses and their land because of issues with property titles, inheritance issues, and rights of eminent domain. This contemporary land struggle underscores that the legacy of the Moscow Canal lives on as a contested space fraught with ideology and memories that refuse to fade.

The negotiation between private and public space that the Moscow Canal engenders is not limited to those who worked for the Moscow Canal. In fact, various circumstances continue to contribute to this reclamation of Soviet space within the Russian context. The late Mikhail Ivanovich Bulanov's work typifies this kind of spatial re-appropriation. A science and ecology high school teacher by training, Bulanov began his research on the Moscow Canal for two compelling reasons: his personal fate was linked to its construction and he was a native of the city of Dubna at the entrance to the Moscow Canal. Bulanov grew up on the waterway and its landmarks in the Dubna area: the lighthouse, the Ivan'kovo Dam, the first Canal lock, and the enormous statue of Lenin that still towers over the canal's entrance. His father and uncle lived in the village of Ivan'kovo, the territory that was appropriated to the waterway and flooded in the process. The physical, social, cultural, and psychological space, including arable land and a village that had stood on the same spot for centuries, that was lost during the flooding of Ivan'kovo has been metaphorically regained through Bulanov's research efforts.

Bulanov's reclamation efforts were not limited to reconstructing lost space on the page. He was actively engaged in ongoing research about the Moscow Canal and hoped to facilitate not only the preservation of current canal structures, but also the creation of new ones intended to re-occupy the space of original buildings. Prominent in this plan was his desire to see the reconstruction of the waterway's *avant-port*, a floating passenger terminal. At the time of the Moscow Canal's opening, a floating ship was anchored to the shoreline at Bol'shaya Volga immediately before the first lock. Here passengers could disembark from and board the steamships that would ferry them up and down the waterway and along the Volga river. Rebuilding this structure would not only increase tourist traffic, which now consists of the occasional kayaker or curiosity-seeker, and support the local economy of Dubna and Bol'shaya Volga, but also expand accessibility to the site of the former Stalin monument and the extant Lenin monument.

For Bulanov this physical and metaphorical reclamation of seemingly lost space was to accomplish two important goals. First, the rebuilding of the *avant-port* would recapture a lost historical space that would link the past and present and create a useful feature on the canal to help secure its future as well. In addition, such a restoration would encourage a reexamination of the waterway's construction and would thereby achieve Bulanov's main goal: to reestablish this history in the consciousness of contemporary Russians, both the denizens of Dubna and the tourists who would visit this site. Bulanov even mused about the possibility of dredging up the remains of the Stalin monument lodged in the muck at the bottom of the channel. When queried as to whether this would ever happen, he replied that likely more time needed to pass in order to be able to mount such an effort without fallout from those who still remembered or lived through the Stalin era.[11] The question of salvaging Stalin from the bottom of the channel invites comparison to contemporary initiatives to dismantle monuments to Confederate personages in New Orleans, LA and around the state of Kentucky.[12] These efforts seek to remove from public view reminders of a painful history (the US Civil War and slavery), the effects of which are still being felt. However, these reconfigurations of contentious spaces raise new issues, as would the reclamation of Stalin's monument: does the removal or exhumation of historically important but emotionally charged remnants free the spaces they inhabited of their legacies? Or should these landmarks remain in place so that people never forget the terror and tragedy they embody, and to provoke further nuanced discussions of their relevance to contemporary life?

This dissonance between the safety of an undisturbed physical or mental space and the discomfort of disturbing those spaces illustrates one of the chief conundrums in predicting the metaphorical and rhetorical future of the Moscow Canal. The importance of reclaiming lost spaces, be they physical structures or mental images and remembrances, varies according to the contemporary situation in which these spaces are considered.[13] This is why efforts by younger armchair enthusiasts and professional scholars alike will affect the future consideration of the Moscow Canal. In this effort, the private and public spaces that the Moscow Canal has generated will need to co-exist, even if that co-existence remains only superficially cordial.

The desire to examine the Moscow Canal's past, thus contributing to its legacy, has motivated the production of news reports and documentary films and social media about the waterway. Even a cursory search on YouTube yields a variety of visual narratives that deconstruct and reconstruct the imagined and real space of the Moscow Canal. For example, a 2007 film produced for *The History Channel* as part of the *Lost Worlds* series examined Moscow as "Stalin's Super-city." The program, originally broadcast on 17 October 2007, features a segment on the construction of the Moscow Canal.[14] This program, broadcast nationwide in the US, reached an audience numbering in the millions, due in part to the popularity of *The History Channel* programming at that time. More importantly, the program presented how Stalin sought to spatially reconfigure Moscow through a variety of structures, including the Palace of Soviets (planned, but never built), the Moscow Canal, the Moscow Metro, and the famed House on the Embankment. Indeed, everything in the program focused on the plan to reconstruct Moscow so that the space it occupied and the places situated in it were evocative of the Stalinist ethos. Similarly, the television series *The Soviet Empire* included an episode on the canals built during the Stalinist era in general and the Moscow Canal in particular. The show, produced in 2007 (clearly in honor of the waterway's 70th anniversary), was broadcast on the *Rossiia* TV channel to a national audience in Russia.

More recently, other films, news reports, and television programs have brought the Moscow Canal to a wider viewership. In 2015 the main Russian television station Channel 1 broadcast a program in their *Legends* series entitled *Legends of the Moscow Canal*.[15] Viewers were taken on a cruise along the waterway during which the presenter discussed both its history and current condition as a shipping and tourist conduit. On 8 May 2013 on the Dubna television station, the TV host Viktor Kalitviansky dedicated a program to the Moscow Canal in his series

"Free View with Viktor Kalitviansky." The presenter, along with his two guests, discussed the significance of the canal in a program that also featured a segment providing a brief history of its construction. Finally, Moskva-volga.ru's Igor Kuvyrkov gave a lecture at the Moscow offices of Memorial in which he discussed his interest in and research about the Moscow Canal. His December 2015 lecture and the subsequent Q&A were recorded by Memorial as part of their initiative to invite speakers to present material about the Gulag and Gulag-related projects and to make those presentations available to a wider audience through the internet.

The authors of the site Moskva-volga.ru (who also sponsor a companion Facebook page)[16] are attempting to navigate between public and private spaces of memory and forgetting with their efforts to document and promote the history of the Moscow Canal.[17] As they note:

> Why was this site created? Our goal: To simply show and tell everything that we have found out about the Canal, both the good and the not-so-good. The authors are neither professional historians nor employees of the FGUP-Moscow Canal, nor employees of any organizations that have a professional relationship with the Moscow Canal. We simply were born on its banks and we live on different parts of its route. The canal came into our lives from childhood as a part of our world. We want to find out even more about the canal; we are trying to reveal the unknown pages of its difficult fate.[18]

To this end the authors continue to fill the site with facsimiles of original documents, photographs, and maps. The rubrics on the site include "Photographs," "News," "Publications," "Maps and Diagrams," and others. The authors consciously post diverse source materials that reflect the waterway's history since its inception and invite commentary from the site's visitors.

Moskva-volga.ru currently serves as the most extensive and exhaustive source of materials on the Moscow Canal. Books and newspaper and journal articles about the canal populate the site, as do numerous virtual photo albums that showcase views of the waterway before, during, and after its construction. Dmitlag publications and émigré publications and official documents can be accessed there. The site's authors provide some archival materials in addition to bibliographic information for archival files relevant to the Moscow Canal. This impressive collection benefits from constant updates that add new materials, including contemporary photographs of landscapes on and around the waterway. The authors have achieved what no other publication or organization has been able to thus far: to create an ever-expanding compendium of Moscow Canal materials that afford readers the opportunity to judge for themselves the moral, ethical, political, and cultural justification for and ramifications of its construction. Arguably, the authors of Moskva-volga.ru are, largely thanks to new technologies, preserving the Moscow Canal's history and legacy in ways that official entities either cannot or will not do.

Most recently, the authors have added numerous entries to the "Card Catalogue," an alphabetical listing of Dmitlag inmates (and some NKVD employees) who worked on the Moscow Canal.[19] This resource is currently 56 pages long and is emended every 3–5 days. While they have relied on published sources such as the Donskoy Monastery *Execution Notes* and the multi-volume *Butovo Shooting Range 1937–1938, Book of Memory*, they have also received materials from the personal collections of the families of former Dmitlag prisoners. As Igor Kuvyrkov notes, "Our card catalogue of those who worked on the Moscow–Volga canal continues to expand. There is unique information that is absent not only from the internet but in print materials as well. Why? Because relatives are providing it."[20] For these families the "Card Catalogue" offers a dedicated public location in cyberspace where their loved ones can be remembered and immortalized, which is especially poignant when there are no graves with physical remains for families to visit.

Remarkably, the site's creators contribute to it in their free time. This kind of activity typifies the most sustained and vigorous efforts to forge a legacy for the Moscow Canal. From interested professionals like the Dmitrov librarian Nina Elovskaya and the retired FGBU-KiM employees Valentin Barkovsky and Valentin Maslov to organizations such as Memorial and the Moskva-volga.ru website, the Moscow Canal's legacy is being crafted primarily through non-official channels and the efforts of a cohort of dedicated private citizens. They believe the waterway's past, especially in regard to its Gulag builders, is worth remembering and contributes to protecting its future.

This motivation bolstered the efforts of Memorial to organize an 80th anniversary remembrance for the Moscow Canal in July 2017.

Preparations commenced with a brainstorming session held in June 2016 to discuss possible activities, followed by a "Run along the Canal" in July 2016. Consequently, Memorial erected plaques of remembrance around Moscow to highlight places and people important to the waterway's construction and to refresh public memory about Dmitlag's existence near and within the Moscow city limits. Efforts have also been initiated to pursue the classification of the Moscow Canal as a UNESCO World Heritage site.[21] Were it to gain such classification, the waterway would enjoy a level of protection it currently does not have, and the FGBU-KiM administration, as an arm of the Russian Ministry of Transport, would then have to maintain the entire canal route on par with the standards for other UNESCO World Heritage sites. Finally, the Moskva-volga.ru team offers a permanent exhibit at the Dolgoprudnyi Ethnographic Museum on the northern outskirts of Moscow to showcase the artifacts they have collected.[22]

Two events were staged in Dmitrov to mark the Moscow Canal's 80th anniversary. On 23 April 2017 the Dmitrov Regional Public Library hosted "The Canal and its Fate: The Moscow Canal's 80th Anniversary." Nina Elovskaya moderated the afternoon's activities, which featured the screening of a film by R. B. Rostislavov about his father, who worked on the waterway, as well as an exhibit of Rostislavov senior's graphic artwork. S. V. Gaev, one of the members of the Moskva-volga.ru team, shared his collection of artifacts from the construction of the Moscow Canal and V. V. Rodionov discussed the activities of the Moskva-volga.ru collective.[23] Given that Dmitrov housed the headquarters of Dmitlag, it was fitting this event was organized and staged there.

In addition, on 12 May 2017 the Dmitrov Kremlin Museum-Preserve hosted a conference in honor of the Moscow Canal's 80th anniversary, just as it had in May 2007 for the waterway's 70th anniversary. This time, however, none of the participants were invited on an excursion to sail along the Moscow Canal, as they had been in 2007, nor did any of the canal's upper-level administrators attend the conference. Instead, the most high-ranking FGBU-KiM employee to participate was N. N. Ermakova, head of the Moscow Canal's Hydraulic Structure Services. The first part of the conference consisted of welcoming remarks not only from Ermakova, but also from Dmitrov Kremlin personnel, local ethnographers and the Administrator of the Dmitrov Municipal Region, V. V. Gavrilov. The conference's second half featured ten speakers who presented talks on a variety of subjects related to the Moscow Canal's history, such as "Dust in the Universe: The Fates of the Canal's Prisoner-Laborers," "Architectural Features of the Structures on the Moscow Canal," and "The Moscow–Volga Canal as a Line of Defense as Evaluated by the Enemy."[24] In comparison to the observance in Dmitrov of the 70th anniversary of the Moscow Canal in 2007, the 2017 event was more modest, with minimal participation on the part of FGBU-KiM personnel. In many ways Dmitrov, more than Moscow, has developed as the center of research on Dmitlag and the Moscow Canal. Starting with Nikolai Fedorov in the 1990s and continuing to the present under the auspices of the Dmitrov Kremlin Museum-Preserve and Dmitrov Regional Library in the persons of Natalia Tabunova (the organizer of the 2007 and 2017 conferences) and Nina Elovskaya, organizations and personnel continue to investigate the Moscow Canal's importance as a massive construction project whose legacy is fraught with contradiction, yet worthy of attention.

In conjunction with the Moscow Canal's actual anniversary on 15 July 2017 an exhibition opened at the Dubna Museum of Archaeology and Regional Studies dedicated to the waterway's history and construction. The exhibition ran from 15 July to 15 September 2017. It featured artifacts and displays, material from which has been culled from the private collection of Sergei Gaev of Moskva-volga. ru. The exhibition's official opening was held on 14 July and was attended by official dignitaries from the local government, the administration of the Volga Junction on the canal (including the junction's chief engineer), and a representative from the State Duma. Entitled "The Volga Flows to Moscow" the exhibition featured various displays that focused on the role of Dubna in the history of the Moscow Canal. According to newspaper reports, many of the visitors to the exhibition's opening brought their own photographs taken by and of their family members who worked on the waterway.[25] This exhibition would not have been possible without the support of the Moscow Canal's main administration. In addition, a few newspaper articles, radio spots, and television reports discussed the Moscow Canal's 80th Jubilee, but the coverage was limited.[26]

Insofar as it has been possible to determine, the Moscow Canal administration did not organize any formal activities as it had for the celebration of the waterway's 70th anniversary. This is not to say that the Moscow Canal administration completely refrains from shaping the waterway's legacy. By virtue of the fact that it operates and repairs the waterway, the administration ensures that the canal continues to operate. Of course, this on-going maintenance has likely been hindered by a recent financial fiasco within the FGBU-KiM administration that resulted in the "theft of 457.4 million rubles from the budgeted funds allocated for the development of a plan for the reconstruction of the Moscow Canal."[27] Subsequently, "The criminal case was sent to the prosecutor for confirmation of the indictment, and then will be transferred to the court for consideration on its merits."[28] In addition, on 30 October 2016, the official Russian "Day of Remembrance of Victims of Repression," a group of employees from the Moscow Canal visited the Butovo Shooting Range on the southern outskirts of Moscow in order to commemorate the 2,500 canal builders who were executed there.[29] There is clearly a sense of history that resonates with the FGBU-KiM administration, and perhaps this signals an intention to continue to weave the waterway's Gulag past with its non-Gulag future. Indeed, the topographic map of the Moscow Canal that was likely produced for the Soviet Exhibit at the 1937 Paris World Exposition now hangs in a place of honor in the main conference room of the waterway's headquarters on Vodnikov Street in Moscow. The official on-line site for the FGBU-KiM administration likewise features a rubric that briefly relates the history of the waterway's construction.[30]

Perhaps the most fascinating and unexpected addition to the legacy of the Moscow Canal is seen in a new literary mystical-fantasy series that has recently appeared in Russia. The series, entitled *The Moscow Canal*, currently contains two works. The eponymous first book, *The Moscow Canal*, appeared in 2015. The second book, *The Moscow Canal Labyrinth*, was published in 2016. The authorship remains unclear: depending on the information source, the author of both volumes is listed either as "Anonymous" or Roman Kanushkin. What is clear, however, is that fantasy fans in Russia have discovered and are reading this new series. While reviews of the two books are mixed, the fact that an author has chosen the Moscow Canal as the space in which to construct the narrative signals some recognition of the waterway's current relevance and history. As the promotional material for the first volume notes:

> The world has been consumed by fog and movement is possible only on the water. What is there in the fog: revived fears, ancient monsters or ancient gods? Those who know are silent. The canal connects Little Dubna, the capital Dmitrov and the sinister dark sluices with fading islands of civilization. From secret to secret, from lock to lock – to mystical Moscow, that presumably has also been covered by the mist.[31]

The action in both books occurs along and on the Moscow Canal in various structures and settings, with water playing a central narrative role.

The Moscow Canal is populated with a cast of characters that range from a mystical traveler to a young hero (Feodor) and heroine (Eva – perhaps a reference to Eve in the Garden of Eden?) who face a variety of challenges on their journey to and from Dubna, as well as in their own relationship. They are in love with each other, but must abandon each other for the greater good. Chapter titles include "Lock 1. The Gates are Open," "The Fear of the Canal," and "The Dark Locks," to name a few. Characters refer to locations on the canal, including the Sestra River, various locks between Dubna and the elevations at Locks 5 and 6, and the Komsomol Station, among others. The "dark locks" are said to be inhabited by ghosts who mysteriously open and close the lock gates for no discernible reason and at unpredictable times. The characters sense that there is potential danger in the seemingly haunted locks. The extant machinery at those locks and structures that locals run are dated (one piece of equipment bears the date 1984, perhaps as a nod to Orwell) and barely operational. Yet the machinery still functions, likely because of the "Ancient Builders" (presumably Dmitlag prisoners) discussed in Chapter Ten of the novel.

It will be interesting to see how the *Moscow Canal* series plays out: how many books will be written in the series, how the waterway will figure into subsequent narratives, and what image of the canal will be presented as those volumes appear. Central to this discussion remains the new imagined space that this series creates, infusing the legacy of the

Moscow Canal with a fresh perspective and perhaps more widespread curiosity about the waterway's actual, rather than fictionalized, history. Bringing the topic of the Moscow Canal to a wider audience will, if nothing else, raise awareness about the waterway, its past, and its future.

These are only some of the myriad materials featured on websites and in video format that examine the Moscow Canal both as a historical event and a contemporary feature of the landscape. These materials are not limited to documentary films or discussions of history and politics. In addition, various sites and video materials investigate the best fishing spots along the canal, as well as sights passengers will enjoy on a cruise along the waterway. All these sites and videos contribute to building the legacy of the Moscow Canal by disseminating all manner of information about the waterway. While it is possible to take issue with those materials that ignore the Moscow Canal's Gulag history, such an approach would pigeon-hole the waterway as a topic only for historians and activists. Instead, the fact that different approaches are taken to the Moscow Canal as a historical, political, cultural, and leisure space ensures that both the canal's future and its legacy are supported and enriched. Moreover, the diverse attempts to document the space of the Moscow Canal reveal its utility and importance as an identifiable landscape that continues to offer food for thought and spaces that demand further careful analysis.

Every discussion of the Moscow Canal must indeed, by the very nature of its location and size, refer to its spatial qualities. Such discussions bring new hope to those who wish to make sense of, if not peace with, its troubled past, a past with which Russian society still has not come to terms. However, as I complete this book, the Museum of Gulag History has announced that a "nationwide monument to the victims of political repression," a so-called "Wall of Sorrow," has been erected with the support of the museum in the person of its director Roman Romanov and Putin advisor Mikhail Fedotov. Sculptor Georgy Frangulian crafted the work.[32] Based on photographs of this monument, it features figures of suffering prisoners, a change from typical memorials among which "there are very few realistic sculptures that depict an actual prisoner in a moment of suffering."[33] The installation of this sculpture suggests a potentially positive change in how Russia is and will be processing the legacy of Stalinism, a development that might also affect the further development of memorial space along the Moscow Canal.

The Moscow Canal's roots in the Gulag and as a demonstrably Stalinist project underpin any reckoning of the waterway. As Simon Schama's work has shown, landscapes do bear memories, even if those landscapes have changed or evolved over the course of time. With memorials to Gulag camps far flung across Russia, and other contested sites such as Perm-36,[34] the Moscow Canal remains the most visible and accessible remnant of the Gulag. This condition alone makes the waterway an extremely valuable space that deserves both preservation and respect. This identifiable former Stalinist space, which now bears the marks of Russian space because of the yacht clubs, recreational green zones, and shoreline housing on its reservoirs, continues to reflect the cultural, political, and economic values of the society in which it is situated. The Moscow Canal likely will remain a contested space for years to come, but with this struggle comes the renewed hope that the disputes that the space produces will continue to remind those who view and use it of the countless men and women who built it as part of the Stalinist project. In particular, the Moscow Canal continues to memorialize those who lost their lives building it and to those whose lives were forever changed by it. If this obtains as the ultimate legacy of the Moscow Canal, then any secondary uses or readings of the space will not be in vain.

An Idea of Genius

"The brilliant idea of the fundamental Bolshevik solution to the age-old water management problem of Moscow by uniting it with the foundational waterway of the Union, the Volga, belongs to the great Stalin."[35] Thus begins the first paragraph of the "Red Book," *Kanal Moskva-Volga 1932–7*, and thus ends this study of the Moscow Canal and its centrality to the construction of Stalinism and Stalinist space. The themes traced throughout this study: from the importance of water as a vital natural resource, instrument of culture, and agent commandeered by Soviet power, to the recognition of the Gulag, its prisoners, and cultural projects as constructs in and constructors of Stalinist space; from the metaphorical and imagined spaces of sculpture, painting, and narrative prose to the built environment of locks, dams, and pumping stations; from the monuments and memorials to the presumed and true heroes of construction to contemporary explorations of the Moscow Canal project – all these ideas resonate in the pronouncement that the Moscow Canal had been the brilliant idea of Comrade Stalin. We know this to be untrue, for the idea to connect Moscow with the Volga dated to at least 300 years before Stalin. We know too that the engineering expertise necessary to drive the project was gained and perfected long before Stalin rose to power. And we know that rhetoric linking Stalin with all manner of brilliant ideas was a fixture of life during Stalinism. This is how physical space – landscapes, hardscapes, and nature-scapes, as well as imagined and figurative space – was constructed.

The geography of Stalinism emerges from a multi-valent process through which the physical act of building a new country required constructing rhetorical, ideological, and imagined spaces that often did not reflect reality, but created a space in which it could emerge. As Karl Schloegel astutely notes:

> From the outset it seemed that the new power had set itself the purpose of transforming the conglomerate of the old Russian Empire into a modern unified country that would operate on a uniform time – the future – and know neither vertical nor horizontal boundaries. This power appeared to possess the potency to remake the giant country as though it were a huge blank sheet on the drawing board, to model its relief as it saw fit – five-year plan after five-year plan, decade by decade.[36]

The image of the space of a blank sheet on a drawing board physically limited by the edges of the paper (but not by the ideas of the designer), in contrast with the notion that this "new power" recognized neither vertical nor horizontal boundaries, captures the essence of constructing Stalinist space. Space, like water, was considered a controllable commodity that with the proper application of planning and engineering could physically and visually convey the ideological underpinnings of the state. By the same token, the construction and control of space required an arsenal of "space creators" in the form of Gulag, artistic, monumental, and memorial space. This is why the building of the Moscow Canal was not just an engineering feat, but a cultural event as well. As James Scott argues, "A transformation of the physical world was not, however, the only item on the Bolshevik agenda.

It was a cultural revolution that they sought, the creation of a new person."[37] This cultural revolution has been well-documented. Scott also maintains that the notion of "high modernism,"[38] to which Soviet power subscribed, was not the hegemony of Soviet power alone given that states across the political spectrum from far left to far right followed these practices. So what, then, made the creation of Stalinist space different?

The simplest answer to this question is brute force, best actualized through the Gulag. Scott places Vladimir Lenin in the ranks of "high modernists," and in the case of the USSR we see "authoritarian high modernism." The reliance on brute force to achieve the state's goals goes back to Lenin, who:

> leaves no doubt that the application of state coercive power is the only way to build socialism. He openly avows the need for violence after the seizure of power: "The proletariat needs state power, the centralized organization of force, the organization of violence ... for the purpose of *guiding* the great mass of the population – the peasantry, the petite bourgeoisie, the semi-proletarians – in the work of organizing the Socialist economy."[39]

The urge to create an identifiable, ideology-saturated Stalinist space takes this admonition and pushes it to its farthest limits by creating the ultimate Stalinist state-within-a-state, the Gulag. Deploying Gulag labor to create the space of this new state naturally grows out of the twin desires to exert central control over the populace (cf. Bettina Greiner's assertion that "Almost all the state's citizens were subjected to this strict disciplinary regime that enslaved them in the name of ambitious modernization programs ... the Gulag was the most extreme variant of captivity in a continuum of incarcerated geographies with the Soviet Union as a whole")[40] and to saturate all physical space with the visual representations of Stalinist power, be it on the page, in the air, under the water, or behind barbed wire. As Scott says, "What strikes an outside observer of this revolution in culture and architecture is its emphasis on public form – on getting the visual and aesthetic dimensions of the new world straight."[41] These visual and aesthetic dimensions were realized through the cultural products from within and outside the Gulag.

The problem, of course, is that "getting the new world straight" required terror, bloodshed, violence, and often death. While we must remain indignant in the face of Stalinist terror and repression, we must also appreciate the great achievement that is the Moscow Canal: still functioning at 80 years old because of the thousands of men and women whose tenacity, knowledge, and will to live built this structure that still keeps Muscovites supplied with water, even if they do not realize the human sacrifices required to do that. Perhaps one day the faces of the canal's builders will grace a new monument that captures their suffering and recognizes their sacrifices. In the meantime, the Moscow Canal, especially through the constantly flowing water that refreshes and sustains it, stands as the best testament to those who built it.

Everything Flows[42]

This metaphor from Vasily Grossman's eponymous evocative novel appropriately concludes this study of the Moscow Canal and its contribution to the creation of Soviet-Stalinist space. The trope (like Grossman's novel) suggests that everything, from time to water, flows in a continual stream that carries with it meaning and memory. As the present study illustrates, the construction and reception of the Moscow Canal and all the space it occupies has evolved over time and will continue to do so along with the changing political, ideological, social, and cultural contexts in which it is embedded. This evolutionary process illustrates how spaces and places, just like cultural products and memory, are constantly reinterpreted within historical and contemporary frameworks. Landscapes change over time, so it makes sense that the reception of the Moscow Canal and its associated cultural products continues to be refashioned as more information emerges about its difficult past.

These alterations to landscapes and our perception of them are especially pertinent in Gulag spaces. The appropriate and necessary impulse to unearth these spaces in order to preserve the memories connected to them co-exists with the competing urge to keep these sites buried so as to not disturb the spirits of the past. No other spaces and places in the USSR were as Stalinist as Gulag spaces, which is why it is valuable to understand not only their historical dynamics, but also the actual landscapes in which they were situated. Just as the Kazakh Steppe affected and structured Karlag, or the forests and minerals of the far north conditioned the development of Vorkuta or Pechorlag, so too did the geography of the Moscow and Tver' regions structure the establishment and operation of Dmitlag. It could not be otherwise because these Gulag landscapes determined everything else in the camps, from housing to work quotas, from food rations to punishment cells, from labor productivity to death. It is difficult to imagine how differently the Gulag might have operated had it not been inscribed into these very landscapes. Consequently, the abstract, figurative, monumental, and memorial spaces that result from these Gulag landscapes broaden and deepen our understanding of this system, while also providing a more nuanced filter through which to further interrogate the culture and ideology that produced them. The fact that most studies of the Gulag include, consciously or not, a discussion of the locations of special settlements, camps, scientific institutes, or places of exile emphasizes the primary role of space and place, landscape and geography in comprehending this integral part of Stalinism.

That this "spatial turn" as an interpretive framework has increasingly been deployed to understand both Russian and Soviet history and cultural production (in the fullest sense of the word culture) suggests its utility and richness. The application of a cultural geography approach to a Gulag site, here the Moscow Canal, affords us the space in which to examine the multi-valent character of this structure as a network of interrelated engineering and cultural achievements; the interpretation of each constituent element cannot be divorced from the totality of the entire construction project. In this sense the present study both builds on and moves beyond Judy Pallot's groundbreaking work and site "Mapping the Gulag,"[43] and Dobrenko and Naiman's *The Landscape of Stalinism*, as well as other studies, to claim new territory in the quest to better understand Stalinism. As such, this study offers a more nuanced way to parse individual projects during Stalinism that testify to the paramount importance of space and place in every undertaking.

An assessment of the diverse spatial parameters of the Moscow Canal project neither condones nor softens the terror, injustice, and suffering that the waterway's construction inflicted on those who built it and those who stood in its way. (A massive waterway built mostly with primitive tools and back-breaking physical labor could not be treated otherwise.) Rather, this analysis has refashioned a space of remembrance and recognition of what the Moscow Canal project was and is. It is no accident that water comprises the main physical and metaphorical axis around which everything connected to the Moscow Canal turns. As both an elemental force and a life-giving element, water offers the ultimate test of man and machinery to control it. In the battle with nature Soviet power in its Stalinist incarnation believed in its ability to control every space and place it touched. Changing landscapes and reshaping geographical features were part and parcel of the ideology. Yet water also inspired technological, architectural, and cultural production in ways that continue to amaze. These inspired creations came at a high price, but their continued existence testifies as well to the power of the human spirit to fight and sometimes achieve victory over adversity. Thanks to the monumental and memorial space that the Moscow Canal created we can remember those who built this massive waterway, whose evolution continues. Indeed, everything flows in the Moscow Canal project, especially the water in it. Whither it flows remains to be seen.

NOTES

Introduction Surveying the Site: Historical Framework and Spatial Parameters

1. Karl Schloegel, *In Space We Read Time: On the History of Civilization and Geopolitics*, Gerrit Jackson (trans) (New York City, 2016), p. 417.
2. Henri Lefebvre, *The Production of Space*, Donald Nicholson-Smith (trans) (Oxford, UK & Cambridge, MA, 2000). This general idea supports Lefebvre's argument regarding the creation of absolute and abstract space as well metaphorical and physical space.
3. For further explication of this idea see Emma Widdis, "Viewed from Below: Subverting the Myths of the Soviet Landscape" in Birgit Beumers (ed.), *Russia on Reels: The Russian Idea in Post-Soviet Cinema* (London, 1999), p. 69.
4. Ibid., p. 66.
5. See Boris Groys, "The Art of Totality," in Evgeny Dobrenko & Eric Naiman (eds), *The Landscape of Stalinism: The Art and Ideology of Soviet Space* (Seattle, 2003), pp. 96–122. In particular, Groys notes that "The creation of any image, the erection of any building, the composition of any literary text could never be a neutral aesthetic act: it represent[s] either victory or defeat in the battle for symbolic occupation of space. Works of totalitarian art do not describe the world – they occupy the world. The aim of totalitarian art is to fill the largest possible territory with specific signs that are identifiable as 'our' signs, in contrast to 'their' signs, or the signs of the enemy power" p. 98.
6. As Lefebvre notes, "The illusion of a transparent, 'pure' and neutral space ... has permeated Western culture" p. 292. Soviet Stalinism clearly rejected this Western understanding of space in favor of the notion that all space is political and ideological. I am grateful to Mary Nicholas for bringing the Lefebvre quotation to my attention.

7. For an excellent analysis of the periphery vs. center dichotomy, as well as the rise of Moscow as the metaphorical Soviet center, see James Von Geldern, "The Centre and the Periphery: Cultural and Social Geography in the Mass Culture of the 1930s," in Stephen White (ed.), *New Directions in Soviet History* (Cambridge, UK, 1992), pp. 62–80. Here p. 68. This is also accessible online at https://works.bepress.com/james_von_geldern/5/. Accessed 9 May 2017.
8. The canal's name was changed in 1947 in honor of the 800th anniversary of Moscow's founding. It was originally called the "Moscow–Volga Canal."
9. Dmitlag is the acronym for the *Dmitrovskii lager'* or *Dmitrov Camp*. This Gulag installation was charged with constructing the Moscow Canal. Henceforth this camp will be referred to as Dmitlag.
10. Josephson argues that "brute force technology" produced an "industrialized" nature irrevocably changed through the construction of large hydro-projects such as dams and canals, deforestation schemes, highways, and mechanized fishing equipment. The urge to modernize came at a high price given the ecological damage that "industrialized" nature has wrought. Paul R. Josephson, *Industrialized Nature: Brute Force Technology and the Transformation of the Natural World* (Washington, DC, 2002).
11. Beginning in the early 1930s the NKVD (Narodnyi komissariat vnutrennikh del [The People's Commissariat of Internal Affairs], which later became the KGB in the Soviet era and the FSB since the fall of the USSR) was given responsibility for all Gulag construction projects. This meant that forced labor would be used to construct not only canals, but power stations, factories, and any structure that fell under its purview. In addition, the NKVD supervised forestry projects, coal, uranium, nickel and gold mining, agriculture, fur trapping and any other industry that required a large infusion of cheap labor. This included establishing camps in inhospitable places such as Norilsk, Vorkuta, Kolyma, and the open steppe of Kazakhstan in order to initiate these economic efforts. The literature on this is vast. Three useful sources are Michael Jacobson, *Origins of the Gulag* (Lexington, KY, 1993), Lynne Viola, *The Unknown Gulag: The Lost World of Stalin's Special Settlements* (Oxford, UK, 2007), and Paul R. Gregory and V.V. Lazarev (eds), *The Economics of Forced Labor* (Stanford, 2003). While Jacobson's is not the most recent treatment, he provides a detailed explanation of how the NKVD ultimately assumed control of these projects and merged with the OGPU (Joint State Political Directorate) in 1934.
12. The three major canals constructed in European Russia during the Stalinist era are the Belomor or Belomor–Baltiiksii canal, which originally bore the name of its initiator Stalin. The second canal is the topic of this study, the Moscow Canal. The third canal goes by its more popular title, the Volga-Don Canal, rather than its official title – Volga-Donskoi sudokhodnii kanal imeni Lenina (the Lenin Volga-Don Shipping Canal).

    The most detailed account of the NKVD's efforts to build these three canals is in A. I. Kokurin and Yu. N. Morukov, *Stalinskie stroiki Gulaga 1930–1953*.

(Moscow, 2005), pp. 9–166. This chapter provides informative chronologies for each canal and also includes previously secret and unpublished documents from the State Archives of the Russian Federation (GARF). Oleg Khlevniuk's *The History of the Gulag* (New Haven, 2004) also discusses the construction of these canals vis-à-vis their place in the Gulag. See especially pp. 111–19 and 338–9.

13. Because the Soviet Union had a planned economy it operated on a series of five-year plans that outlined the goals, achievements, and projects for each plan period. The Moscow Canal was one of the signature projects of the second five-year plan.
14. For a more complete discussion of the Belomor project see Cynthia A. Ruder, *Making History for Stalin: The Story of the Belomor Canal* (Gainesville, FL, 1998) as well as Julie Draskoczy, *Belomor: Criminality and Creativity in Stalin's Gulag* (Boston, 2014). Kokurin and Morukov also discuss the Belomor Canal in *Stalinskie stroiki Gulaga 1930–53*, pp. 30–59.
15. Serious scholarly studies devoted entirely to the Moscow Canal are scarce in Russian and non-existent in English. The most recent works about the history of the Moscow Canal are: Nikolai Fedorov, *Byla li tachka u ministra?* (Dmitrov, 1997); M. I. Bulanov, *Kanal Moskva-Volga: Khronika volzhskogo raiona gidrosooruzhenii* (Dubna, 2007); V. S. Barkovsky, *Tainy Moskva-volgostroia* (Moscow, 2007); and V. I. Maslov, *Kanal imeni Moskvy: Stroika veka. Sud'by liudei. K 75-letiiu otkrytiia kanala* (Moscow, 2012). See also Kokurin and Morukov's section on the Moscow Canal in *Stalinskie stroiki Gulaga 1930–53*, pp. 59–102. Works produced at the time of or shortly after the canal's construction were limited to children's books or technical treatises such as the NKVD SSSR, Biuro tekhnicheskogo otcheta o stroitel'stve Kanala Moskva-Volga's work *Kanal Moskva-Volga, 1932–7* (Moscow-Leningrad, 1940). Tourist brochures, anniversary booklets to mark landmark celebrations, newspaper articles and short memoirs round out the extant literature on the canal. For the current official representation of the Moscow Canal, see its website: Kanal im. Moskvy. http://www.fgbu-kim.ru/. Accessed 9 May 2017.
16. For the official figures on the inmate population and death rates see Kokurin and Morukov, *Stalinskie stroiki Gulaga 1930–53*, p. 77 and p. 523.
17. TsGAMO, f. 2589, op. 1, d. 86, l. 174.
18. TsGAMO, f. 2589, op. 1, d. 86, l. 172.
19. P(avel) I(vanovich) Lopatin, *Moskva-Volga* (Moscow and Leningrad, 1939), p. 72. Unless otherwise noted all translations from Russian are mine.
20. Engineers and supervisory personnel who presently work on the Moscow Canal echo this sentiment, although they admit that the amount and variety of cargo traffic has diminished over the years. Nonetheless, the importance of the canal as the main source of potable water and electrical power for metropolitan Moscow has not subsided. Personal interviews, Summer 2004, Winter 2007, Summer 2009.
21. Edith W. Clowes, *Russia on the Edge: Imagined Geographies and Post-Soviet Identity* (Ithaca and London, 2011), p. 3.

22. Here landscape means the natural environment, its physical contours, flora and fauna, while the term hardscape refers to the built environment – structures placed into a landscape.
23. See Evgeny Dobrenko, "The Art of Social Navigation: The Cultural Topography of the Stalinist Era," in Evgeny Dobrenko and Eric Naiman (eds), *The Landscape of Stalinism* (Seattle, 2003), pp. 163–200. In particular, note Dobrenko's discussion of stamps, pp. 163–79 and the book *Map of the Motherland*, pp. 189–99.
24. The different references to Moscow as the "Port of Three/Five Seas" will be discussed in Chapter One.
25. See Evgeny Dobrenko and Eric Naiman (eds), *The Landscape of Stalinism* (Seattle, 2003); Vladimir Paperny, *Architecture in the Age of Stalin: Culture Two*, John Hill and Roann Barris (trans) in collaboration with the author (Cambridge, UK, 2002); Vladimir Paperny, *Kul'tura dva* (Moscow, 1996); Emma Widdis, *Visions of a New Land: Soviet Film from the Revolution to the Second World War* (New Haven, 2003); Mark Bassin, Christopher Ely, and Melissa K. Stockdale (eds), *Space, Place, and Power in Modern Russia: Essays in the New Spatial History* (DeKalb, IL, 2010); Mark Bassin and Catriona Kelly (eds), *Soviet and Post-Soviet Identities* (Cambridge, UK, 2012). Mark Bassin in particular has contributed greatly to the "spatial turn" in the study of Russian, Soviet, and post-Soviet space. As a historical geographer Bassin has applied the theoretical work of cultural and historical geography to his investigation of Russian space, most formidably in his book *Imperial Visions: Nationalist Imagination and Geographical Expansion in the Russian Far East, 1840–1865* (Cambridge, UK, 2006). Indeed Bassin is the foremost expert in Russian/Soviet Historical Geography. Other scholars, notably Nick Baron, have likewise pursued a spatial approach in examining Soviet and post-Soviet space and history. See in particular N.P. Baron, *Soviet Karelia: Politics, Planning and Terror in Stalin's Russia, 1920–1939* (London, 2007); "Prostranstva utopii: geodeziia, kartografiia i visual'naia kul'tura v SSSR, 1918–1953" in Iu. A. Vedenin and O. A. Lavrenova (eds), *Geografiia iskusstva: sbornik statei*, Vypusk 5 Institut naslediia, 7–3, 2009; and *Vlast' i prostranstvo: Avtonomnaia Kareliia v sovetskom gosudarstve, 1920–1939* (Moscow, 2011).

    In addition, other scholarly works have addressed the issue of space in the former USSR and the Eastern Bloc. See David Crowley and Susan E. Reid (eds), *Socialist Spaces: Sites of Everyday Life in the Eastern Bloc* (Oxford, UK and New York, 2002); Jeremy Smith (ed.), *Beyond the Limits: The Concept of Space in Russian History and Culture* (Helsinki, 1999).
26. Katerina Clark, *Moscow, the Fourth Rome: Stalinism, Cosmopolitanism, and the Evolution of Soviet Culture, 1931–1941* (Cambridge, MA, 2011), here pp. 276 and 277. The chapters "Moscow, the Lettered City," "The Return of the Aesthetic," and "The Imperial Sublime" are of particular relevance to the Moscow Canal.
27. Gaston Bachelard, *The Poetics of Space*, Maria Jolas (trans) (Boston, 1994); Henri Lefebvre, *The Production of Space*, Donald Nicholson-Smith (trans)

(Oxford, UK and Cambridge, MA, 2000); and Simon Schama, *Landscape and Memory* (New York, 1995).

28. Yi-Fu Tuan, *Space and Place: The Perspective of Experience* (Minneapolis, 1977); Edward W. Soja, *Postmodern Geographies: The Reassertion of Space in Critical Social Theory* (London-New York, 2001); Don Mitchell, *Cultural Geography: A Critical Introduction* (Oxford, UK & Cambridge, MA, 2000); Denis Cosgrove and Stephen Daniels (eds), *The Iconography of Landscape* (Cambridge, UK, 2004).
29. I was able to acquire the manuscript of this work with the help of the Gulag survivor and founder of the Gulag Museum in Moscow, the late Anton Vladimirovich Antonov-Ovseenko. Upon visiting the museum in 2004, I was introduced to Antonov-Ovseenko, who proceeded to tell me about this fascinating literary text composed in honor of the construction of the Moscow Canal. Antonov-Ovseenko put me in touch with A. I. Kokurin at GARF, who then provided me with a photocopy of the manuscript. I owe a great debt to Mr. Antonov-Ovseenko for taking an interest in my research and generously sharing this information and contact with me. For more information about the Gulag Museum in Moscow see http://www.gmig.ru/. Accessed 17 May 2017. The site is available in both Russian and English.
30. See the bibliography for a complete list of archival sources.
31. This acronym stands for the Federal'noe gosudarstvennoe biudzhetnoe uchrezhdenie Kanal imeni Moskvy, or in English the Federal State Budget Institution the Moscow Canal.
32. *Stalinskie stroiki GULAGA, 1930–1953.*
33. See Dorothy Zeisler-Vralsted, *Rivers, Memory, and Nation-Building: A History of the Volga and Mississippi Rivers* (New York, 2015).
34. Karl Schloegel, *Moscow, 1937*. Rodney Livingstone (trans) (Cambridge, UK, 2012). See especially pp. 274–93. Schloegel's book is the only work to systematically examine how the year 1937 was witnessed, experienced, and endured in Moscow. His superb, far-reaching study covers not only cultural projects, but issues of space and place, as well as the biographies of those who managed to survive and those who perished during this critical period.

Chapter 1 Water as Power: Real and Imagined

1. Terje Tvedt, *Water and Society: Changing Perceptions of Societal and Historical Development* (London, 2016), p. 13. Tvedt defines the parameters of his approach on pp. 5–17, and then proceeds to apply it throughout the rest of his study.
2. I am indebted to one of the manuscript reviewers for this perceptive insight.
3. Simon Schama, *Landscape and Memory* (New York, 1995), pp. 260–1.
4. Ibid., p. 261.
5. Ibid.

6. Paul Josephson, *Industrialized Nature: Brute Force Technology and the Transformation of the Natural World* (Washington, DC, 2002), p. 4. See especially Josephson's chapter "Pyramids of Concrete," in which he discusses various Soviet water projects and the methods used to complete them.
7. Ibid., p. 28.
8. Ibid., p. 33.
9. As Paperny notes in his seminal work *Architecture in the Age of Stalin: Culture Two* "Culture Two is a model, a tool for the description and systematization of certain events that took place during 1932–54 ... The juxtaposition of Cultures One and Two is a convenient way to describe the events that transpired in the same space but at different times" (p. xxiii). See Vladimir Paperny, *Architecture in the Age of Stalin: Culture Two*, John Hill & Roann Barris (trans) in collaboration with the author (Cambridge, 2002). For the Russian original see Vladimir Paperny, *Kul'tura dva* (Moscow, 1996), pp. 18–19.
10. Vladimir Paperny, "Men, Women, and the Living Space," in William Craft Brumfield & Blair A. Ruble (eds), *Russian Housing in the Modern Age: Design & Social History* (Cambridge, 1993), pp. 149–70.
11. Terje Tvedt, *Water and Society: Changing Perceptions of Societal and Historical Development*, p. 7.
12. Ibid.
13. Ibid., p. 8.
14. Ibid., pp. 12–13.
15. Ibid., p. 13.
16. An abbreviated version of the ensuing discussion of Moscow as the port of five seas was previously published as "Water and Power: The Moscow Canal and the 'Port of Five Seas'," in Jane Costlow and Arja Rosenholm (eds) *Meanings and Values of Water in Russian Culture* (London & New York, 2017), pp. 175–88.
17. Schama, *Landscape and Memory*, pp. 260–1.
18. The construction of the Panama and Suez Canals bears witness to this process. US water projects in the 1930s, such as the construction of the Hoover Dam, followed a similar pattern. A full discussion of the Panama and Suez Canals, as well as the Hoover Dam project, is beyond the scope of this book chapter. Selected titles include: David McCullough, *The Path Between The Seas: The Creation of the Panama Canal 1870–1914* (New York, 1978); Julie Greene, *The Canal Builders: Making America's Empire at the Panama Canal* (New York, 2009); Zachary Karabell, *Parting the Desert: The Creation of the Suez Canal* (New York, 2009); and Michael Hiltzik, *Colossus* (New York, 2011).
19. Throughout this discussion either "Port of Five Seas" or the acronym PPM from the Russian *Port piati morei* will be used to indicate this trope.
20. For a complementary approach to the idea of Moscow as the "Port of Five Seas," see Eva Binder, "Moskau-Hafen von funf Meeren: Die stalinische 'Wasserkultur' und ihre symbolischen Bedeutungen," in Doris Eibl (ed.), *Wasser und Raum: Beiträge zu einer Kulturtheorie des Wassers* (Göttingen, 2008),

pp. 319–40. Binder focuses on cinematic and literary treatments of Stalinist water culture, and argues that Moscow became a "southern," rather than "northern," center of culture (i.e. St. Petersburg/Leningrad).

21. Растёт под руководством партии и правительства красавец-канал. Растёт не по дням, а по часам. В 1937 году Москва станет портом трёх морей Каспийского, Балтийского и Белого. А через несколько лет, когда будут построен канал Волга-Дон, Москва станет портом пяти морей: Каспийского, Чёрного, Азовского, Балтийского и Белого. *Pravda* 6 January 1935: no page number noted.
22. For broader discussions of the power of language both in the creation of the Soviet state and discussing the Gulag see Michael S. Gorham, *Speaking in Tongues: Language Culture & the Politics of Voice in Revolutionary Russia* (DeKalb, IL, 2003); and Dariusz Tolczyk, *See No Evil: Literary Cover-Ups & Discoveries of the Soviet Camp Experience* (New Haven, 1999).
23. This idea was expounded upon by a Russian blogger known as "Shon," who raised just this issue in a blog entry in the context of the impending Russian Navy Day in 2006. The blogger cites no direct references, but his observations and commentary are well documented in terms of their historical accuracy. See Shon, http://redshon.livejournal.com/1066867.html. Accessed 14 June 2010.
24. "Москва будет портом пяти морей!"
25. То о чём пел народ, что звучало в словах / Стало былью сегодняшних дней. / Он готов, наш канал! / Скоро будет портом пяти морей! "Moskva budet portom piati morei!" in *Stikhi i pesni o Kanale Moskva-Volga k 1 maia 1937 goda* (Dmitrov, 1937), p. 1.
26. "Стало былью сегодняшних дней."
27. For a complete discussion of the *Library of Re-forging*, see Chapter Two.
28. Veniamin Riumin, *PPM. Rasskazy* in *Biblioteka Perekovki*, Vyp. 6 (Dmitrov, 1935), p. 16.
29. Ibid.
30. Sergei Riabonon', "Zavtra," "Zdes', v portu piati morei" in *Novaia Volga. Sbornik stikhov lagerno-stroitelei Kanala Moskva-Volga, Biblioteka Perekovki*, Vyp. 31 (Dmitrov, 1936), p. 55.
31. In his otherwise excellent treatment of the Moscow Canal, Schloegel mistakenly notes that "The building of the canal would turn Moscow, the city at the centre of the interior, into the port of five seas." Karl Schloegel, *Moscow, 1937*, Rodney Livingstone (trans) (Cambridge, UK, 2012), p. 273.
32. *Kanal imeni Moskvy* (Moscow, 1987), Inside cover. "*Москва-Порт Пяти Морей.* Эти крылатые слова появились после создания канала имени Москвы, благодаря которому в европейской части СССР образовалась единая глубоководная речная система. Белоснежные пассажирские лайнеры отправляются из Москвы в Горький, Ленинград, Астрахань и во многие другие города нашей Родины. Грузовые суда … осуществляют международные бесперевалочные грузовые перевозки

по речным и морским путям к портам Европы, Северной Африки и Ближнего Востока." The text was published in 1987 before many Soviet city names reverted to their pre-Soviet titles, in particular Leningrad (now St. Petersburg) and Gorky (now Nizhny Novgorod).

33. For a fuller discussion of the 70th-anniversary celebration of the Moscow Canal see Chapter Four, as well as my article "The 70th Anniversary of the Moscow Canal," *NCEEER Working Papers* http://www.ucis.pitt.edu/nceeer/2009_822-13g_Ruder.pdf.
34. Elena Eremenko, "Moskva-Port piati morei," *Kanal imeni Moskvy 70 let* (Moscow, 2007), p. 8.
35. Ibid., p. 8. The following language also was lifted from the 1987 text with adjustments that reflect the renaming of several Russian cities: "Белоснежные пассажирские лайнеры отправляются из Москвы в Санкт-Петербург, Нижний Новгород, Астрахань, Волгоград, Ростов, Пермь и другие города России."

    The Russian version reads: "Эти крылатые слова появились после того, как в европейской части России после создания Канала имени Москвы образовалась единая глубоководная речная система . . . Канал до сих пор отвечает всем современным техническим требованиям и является глубоководной транспортной магистралью, обеспечивающей соединение столицы с главной рекой России-Волгой и дающей выход столице к пяти морям-Балтийскому, Азовскому, Чёрному, Белому и Каспийскому."
36. http://mosmuseum.ru/exhibitions/p/moskva-port-pyati-morey/. Accessed 23 May 2017.
37. Ibid.
38. P(avel) Lopatin, *Volga idet v Moskvu* (Moscow, 1938), recto p. 76. To date I have been unable to discover the details of Lopatin's biography.
39. Pavel Lopatin, *Moskva-Volga* (Moscow-Leningrad, 1939), p. 9.
40. Ibid., p. 71.
41. Ibid., p. 74.
42. Lopatin, *Kanal Moskva-Volga* (Moscow, 1937), p. 8.
43. Illustration from *The USSR in Construction* 2 (February 1938), p. 34. This issue is richly illustrated with photographs that document not only the construction (with little or no attention paid to the canal's builders) but also the leisure activities that the canal facilitated. Also included are the requisite photographs of the Lenin and Stalin monuments, as well as other architectural and sculptural highlights. This issue can be accessed at these two sites: http://library2.usask.ca/USSRConst/gallery/canal and http://rampageteam.ru/sity19rupo/%D0%A1%D0%A1%D0%A1%D0%A0_%D0%BD%D0%B0_%D1%81%D1%82%D1%80%D0%BE%D0%B9%D0%BA%D0%B5.
44. Sergei Kirov was a prominent Bolshevik, member of the Politburo and the very popular head of the Communist Party in Leningrad. He was assassinated on 1 December 1934. Sergo Ordzhonikidze also was a prominent Bolshevik who

served on the Communist Party Central Committee and as the Commissar of Heavy Industry in the 1930s. He died in 1937 in what many assumed was a suicide.

45. "Pokaianie," *Dmitrovskii vestnik* No. 8 (21) August 2007, no page given. In the late 1990s and early 2000s the Memorial Society published a multi-volume work listing all those who could be documented as victims at the Butovo Shooting Range. Beginning with Book 2, the names of Dmitlag inmates who were executed there are included, as is an article by Nikolai Fedorov about Dmitlag. See *Butovsky poligon. 1937–1938 gg. Kniga Pamiati zhertv politicheskikh repressii*, v. 2 (Moscow, 1998); v.3 (Moscow, 1999); v. 4 (Moscow, 2000); v. 5 (Moscow, 2001); v. 6 (Moscow, 2002). Volume 7 (Moscow, 2003) contains an article by Fedorov about Dmitlag camp director Semyon Firin (pp. 45–52), as well as the reminiscences of Aleksei Komarovsky, who spent time as a free worker at Dmitlag (pp. 53–9).
46. The monument to Lenin still stands, while the monument to Stalin was removed in the early 1960s during de-Stalinization. It lies at the bottom of the Moscow Canal channel at the approach to Lock 1. The dimensions of the two statues are: Lenin Monument: Height: 37 meters (121 ft.); Weight: 450 tons; Stalin monument: Height: 37 meters (121 ft.); Weight: 540 tons. Both monuments were constructed by Dmitlag laborers and designed by renowned sculptor S. D. Merkurov. For more about the monuments see Chapter Four of this study as well as Mikhail Bulanov, *Kanal Moskva-Volga: Khronika Volzhskogo raiona gidrosooruzhenii* (Dubna, 2007), p. 132, N5 p. 135.
47. See *Volga, Kama, Oka, Don. Putevoditel'* (Moscow, 1955), p. 15.
48. The complete Russian lyrics are available at http://www.sovmusic.ru/english/text.php?fname=shstran6. Accessed 13 May 2017.
49. My thanks to Rolf Hellebust for sharing this insight.
50. As Lefebvre notes, "The illusion of a transparent, 'pure' and neutral space ... has permeated Western culture." Henri Lefebvre, *The Production of Space*, Donald Nicholson-Smith (trans) (Oxford, UK, 1991), p. 292.
51. In Russian *Постановление о Генеральном плане развития и реконструкции Москвы.* The resolution was adopted by the Council of People's Commissars and the Central Committee of the Communist Party (СНК и ЦК ВКП(б)) on 10 July 1935. Lazar' Kaganovich supervised plans and labor for the reconstruction of Moscow, and also served as the secretary of the Moscow Region and Moscow City Communist Parties. A staunch Stalin supporter, he likewise served on the Central Committee of the Communist Party. For Kaganovich's recollections of the Moscow Canal project see Lazar' Kaganovich, *Pamiatnye zapiski rabochego, kommunista-bol'shevika, profsoiuznogo, partiinogo i sovetsko-gosudarstvennogo rabotnika* (Moscow, 1996), pp. 442–6.
52. For further discussion of the water supply issue, see M. I. Bulanov, *Kanal Moskva-Volga. Khronika volzhskogo raiona gidrosoorushenii* (Dubna, 2007), pp. 10–11.
53. Cited in V. I. Maslov, *Kanal imeni Moskvy: Stroika vek. Sud'by liudei* (Mytishchi, 2012), p. 197.

54. Ibid., p. 200.
55. Ibid.
56. For a recent treatment of Moscow as "Port of Five Seas," see Phoebe Taplin, *The Moscow News* 15 June 2015 http://themoscownews.com/columnists/20090914/55387704.html.
57. An excellent web site that provides a pictorial tour of the Volga/Moscow Sea junction is https://anashina.com/ivankovskaya-ges-v-dubne/. The site's author explores not only the physical structures at the junction, but the flora found there as well. Site is active as of 13 May 2017.
58. In Russian, "Воля большевиков и вождя повернула Волгу в красную столицу." Maslov, p. 206.
59. Karl Karlovich Kripaitis was a career officer in the OGPU-NKVD. He worked on the construction of the Belomor Canal and from there moved to the construction site of the Volga Junction on the Moscow Canal. He served on the project in 1933–8, first as the head of Sector 2, then as an assistant to the chief of the Volga Region on the MVC, then as the assistant director of that region. For his work on the Moscow Canal he received the Order of the Red Banner of Labor. M. I. Bulanov, *Kanal Moskva-Volga*, p. 18.
60. Ibid., p. 23.
61. Ibid., p. 24.
62. Maslov, *Kanal imeni Moskvy: Stroika veka. Sud'by liudei*, p. 41.
63. V. Zhurin, G. Machtet, and A. Berenzon, *Tekhno-ekonomicheskaia zapiska: Prilozhenie: Skhematicheskii proekt v chertazhakh* (Dmitrov, 1934). These notes cover all the construction efforts to be undertaken in conjunction with the Moscow Canal. Zhurin and Machtet served as assistant engineers under MVC chief engineer Sergei Zhuk, while Berenzon headed the Financial Planning section. MVC construction chief Kogan and chief engineer Zhuk authored the introduction to the *Notes*.
64. Ibid., p. 69.
65. Ibid., pp. 69–70.
66. The Kovrovets excavator was named after the small city in which it was produced, Kovrov.
67. V. Zhurin, G. Machtet, and A. Berenzon, *Tekhno-ekonomicheskaia zapiska: Prilozhenie: Skhematicheskii proekt v chertazhakh*, p. 72.
68. M. I. Bulanov, *Kanal Moskva-Volga*, pp. 18–19.
69. Ibid., pp. 19–20.
70. http://ftp.jinr.ru/dubna-e.htm. Accessed 27 June 2013. This is the official site of the Joint Institute for Nuclear Research and provides additional information on the Institute's research scope, international partners, and current initiatives.
71. For more detailed information on Dubna, see the Joint Institute for Nuclear Research website, http://wwwinfo.jinr.ru/dubna-e.htm, as well as http://www.dubna.ru/, the main site for the city of Dubna. Dubna is the northernmost city in the Moscow region on the banks of the Volga River. It is a sister city of

LaCrosse, WI, as well as a "science city" because of its postwar history as the leading center for nuclear physics research. The city's contemporary significance as a research center belies its history dating back to its founding in the twelfth century. For general histories of the city, see also http://www.russia-ic.com/regions/1724/5149/history/ and http://rusmania.com/central/moscow-region/dubna/history/. Accessed 27 August 2016.

72. The exact English translation of the French *avant-port* is outer harbor or port. However, this was not the case for the Moscow Canal, where rather than being a harbor the *avant-port* was not a geographic feature, but rather a temporary space.
73. http://viktorovich-s.livejournal.com/5474.html. Accessed 13 May 2017.
74. M. I. Bulanov, *Kanal Moskva-Volga*, p. 27.
75. Ibid., pp. 24–5.
76. Anushvan Alekseevich Lazareev was a convicted petty criminal and recidivist. He twice tried to escape from incarceration. He was captured after the second escape attempt and put in solitary confinement. At this point Dmitlag head Firin "had a conversation with him," the result of which was a subsequent sustained record of over-fulfilling work quotas. Lazareev and his 450-member work brigade routinely achieved labor excellence at the Volga Junction site in spite of performing the most back-breaking task: hauling earth-laden wheelbarrows out of excavation sites. For his efforts Lazareev was freed at the conclusion of the MVC construction, only to be arrested as part of the "Firin Affair" (the mass arrest of Semyon Firin and anyone considered to be his close collaborator) and sentenced to death by firing squad. See Bulanov, p. 29. For an official record of Lazareev's career, arrest, and execution see *Rasstrel'nye spiski. Moskva 1935–1953. Donskoe kladbishche {Donskoi krematorii}* (Moscow, 2005), p. 261.
77. For a complete description of the process see Maslov, p. 61. This technology was used all along the canal construction site wherever large amounts of soil needed to be moved. Water cannons (гидромониторы) were likewise deployed in order to blast copious amounts of soil, semi-liquefy it, and then make it more transportable more quickly.
78. Maslov, *Kanal imeni Moskvy: Stroika veka. Sud'by liudei*, p. 57.
79. http://moskva-volga.ru/gallery/picture.php?/1368/category/57. Accessed 13 May 2017.
80. M. I. Bulanov, *Kanal Moskva-Volga*, p. 48.
81. Ibid., p. 59.
82. In spite of her seemingly superhuman efforts, Galina Taraskaya was arrested as part of the "Firin Affair" (see note 72). She was arrested in mid-July 1937 in spite of her well-earned early camp release and various awards for exemplary labor. On 19 August 1937 she was sentenced to death by firing squad, which carried out the execution. For a biography of Taraskaya, see Bulanov, pp. 91–6. For an official record of Taraskaya's career, arrest, and execution see *Rasstrel'nye spiski. Moskva 1935–1953. Donskoe kladbishche {Donskoi krematorii}* (Moscow, 2005), p. 449.

83. https://anashina.com/ivankovskaya-ges-v-dubne/. Accessed 13 May 2017.
84. https://anashina.com/ivankovskaya-ges-v-dubne/#i-3. Accessed 13 May 2017.
85. This process was overseen by Bulanov's great uncle, Grigory Dmitrievich Bulanov, who headed the Bolshevik Collective Farm. Bulanov, pp. 32–3.
86. Ibid., pp. 33–4.
87. Ibid., p. 49.
88. Ibid., pp. 43–4.
89. Various websites, almost exclusively in Russian, provide the best information on the history and destruction of Korcheva. These include http://viktorovich-s.livejournal.com/5474.html, which features many current and historical photographs of the town; https://ru.wikipedia.org/wiki/%D0%9A%D0%BE%D1%80%D1%87%D0%B5%D0%B2%D0%B0 serves as the official site about Korcheva; http://kitowras.livejournal.com/658989.html illustrates in photographs and text a trip the blogger made to the town's remains on the banks of the Moscow Sea; and http://konakovo.ru/city/history/gorod_korcheva_kratkie_svedeniya_o_proshlom/ provides ethnographic information and local lore about Korcheva, as well as some photographs. See also Bulanov, pp. 62–3 and Maslov, p. 65.
90. Bulanov, p. 52.
91. Ibid., p. 63.
92. http://konakovo.ru/city/history/gorod_korcheva_kratkie_svedeniya_o_proshlom/. Accessed 27 August 2016.
93. Maslov, p. 85.
94. http://moskva-volga.ru/gallery/picture.php?/1480/category/44. Accessed 13 May 2017.

Chapter 2 How the Gulag Built the Moscow Canal

1. *Listen, Volga!* Music by G. Gamburg, words by Sergei Alymov. Soundtrack to the film *Moscow-Volga*. There are two versions of the song. One is found at http://www.sovmusic.ru/text.php?from_sam=1&fname=s15999, while the other is available at http://www.sovmusic.ru/text.php?from_sam=1&fname=s16249/. The words and music are available for purchase at https://www.ozon.ru/context/detail/id/7217942/. All accessed 23 June 2017.

   For additional reading on Alymov, see Cynthia A. Ruder, *Making History for Stalin. The Story of the Belomor Canal* (Gainesville, FL, 1998), pp. 54–6 and throughout Chapter Three.
2. *Moscow-Volga. Film-documents about the Greatest Structure of the Stalinist Epoch. 1933–1937*, Rafail Gikov (dir.) (Moscow, 1937). With a running time of 57 minutes, the film is available on YouTube at https://www.youtube.com/watch?v=UozVxoU_dJo.
3. Dmitlag is the acronym for the Dmitrov lager'/Dmitrov camp.
4. Cynthia A. Ruder, *Making History for Stalin*, p. 127.

5. http://www.sovmusic.ru/text.php?from_sam=1&fname=s15999. Accessed 14 May 2017.
6. Steven A. Barnes, *Death and Redemption in the Gulag. The Gulag and the Shaping of Soviet Society* (Princeton, NJ, 2011). This is perhaps the best recent work on the Gulag. Other excellent sources include Lynne Viola, *The Unknown Gulag. The Lost World of Stalin's Special Settlements* (Oxford, UK, 2007); Michael David-Fox (ed.), *The Soviet Gulag. Evidence, Interpretation, and Comparison* (Pittsburgh, PA, 2016); Michael Jakobson, *Origins of the Gulag. The Soviet Prison Camp System 1917–1934* (Lexington, KY, 1993); Oleg V. Khlevniuk, *The History of the Gulag. From Collectivization to the Great Terror* (New Haven, CT, 2004), and *Gulag 1918–1960. Dokumenty* (Moscow, 2002). There is an abundance of more specialized studies that examine the return of Gulag inmates and the repercussions of the closure of the Gulag in its Stalinist incarnation. These include Kathleen (Kelly) Smith, *Remembering Stalin's Victims* (Ithaca, NY, 1996); Golfo Alexopoulos, *Stalin's Outcasts. Aliens, Citizens, and the Soviet State 1926–1936* (Ithaca, NY, 2003); Fyodor Vasilievich Mochulsky, *Gulag Boss. A Soviet Memoir*, Deborah Kaple (ed. & trans) (Oxford, UK, 2011); Nanci Adler, *Gulag Survivor: Beyond the Soviet System* (New Brunswick, NJ, 2002), and *Keeping Faith with the Party: Communist Believers Return from the Gulag* (Bloomington, IN, 2012); Miriam Dobson, *Khrushchev's Cold Summer: Gulag Returnees, Crime, and the Fate of Reform after Stalin* (Ithaca, NY, 2009). Numerous other excellent studies have been and continue to be published on the Gulag; this partial list accounts for only some of those titles.
7. The most contemporary and continually expanding compendium of materials concerning the construction of the Moscow–Volga Canal is the website Moskva-volga.ru, which includes photographs, documents, commentary, and publication reprints. It is a treasure trove of MVC materials that are constantly updated and emended. See http://moskva-volga.ru/.
8. Boris Groys, "The Art of Totality," in Evgeny Dobrenko & Eric Naiman (eds), *The Landscape of Stalinism: The Art & Ideology of Soviet Space* (Seattle, WA, 2003), p. 96.
9. For the classic treatments of space that have informed this study in general see Michel de Certeau, *The Practice of Everyday Life*, Steven F. Rendall (trans) (Berkeley, CA, 1984); Henri LeFebvre, *The Production of Space*, Donald Nicholson-Smith (trans) (Oxford, UK, 1991); and Gaston Bachelard, *The Poetics of Space*, Maria Jolas (trans) (Boston, MA, 1994).
10. http://www.moskva-volga.ru/gallery/picture.php?/1058/category.
11. Throughout this discussion of Dmitlag the acronyms OGPU and NKVD will be used. Prior to 1934 these were two separate organizations that managed policing and state security. They were merged in 1934 into one organization that assumed the name NKVD. For a clear explanation as to how this merger occurred see Paul R. Gregory, *Terror by Quota: State Security from Lenin to Stalin* (New Haven, CT, 2009), pp. 86–90. OGPU is the acronym for the Joint State Political Directorate (*Ob"ediniennoe gosudarstvennoe politicheskoe upravlenie*).

As noted previously, NKVD stands for the People's Commissariat of Internal Affairs (*Narodnyi kommissariat vnutrennykh del*), later known as the MGB and KGB in Soviet times, and currently as the FSB.

12. For the per-year totals for Dmitlag see A. I. Kokurin and Yu. N. Morukov, *Stalinskie stroiki GULAGa 1930–1953* (Moscow, 2005), p. 523. Kokurin and Morukov offer the most concise and concentrated discussion of the Moscow–Volga Canal project and include several important archival documents that discuss key moments in the construction process. The entire volume examines the canals, railroads, and gold fields built during the Stalinist era. The volume by A. I. Kokurin and N. V. Petrov, *GULAG. Glavnoe upravlenie lagerei. 1918–1960* (Moscow, 2002) also offers extensive statistics not only on Dmitlag, but on other camps. See especially pp. 410–14.
13. Boris Groys, "The Art of Totality," p. 96.
14. V. S. Barkovsky, *Tainy Moskva-Volgostroia* (Moscow, 2007), p. 12.
15. Kokurin and Morukov, *Stalinskie stroiki*, pp. 60–1.
16. Ibid., p. 68. For an excellent summary of Articles 35 and 58, those most responsible for the incarceration of prisoners in the Gulag, see Khlevniuk, *The History of the Gulag*, pp. 364–8. In addition, a clear explanation of Article 59, another section of the law applied to some Gulag prisoners, can be found at http://www.cyberussr.com/rus/uk59-e.html. Accessed 30 December 2016.
17. Lazar' Moiseevich Kaganovich,"Kanal Moskva-Volga" in *Pamiatnye zapiski rabochego, kommunista-bol'shevika, profsoiuznogo, partiinogo i sovetskogo gosudarstvennogo rabotnika* (Moscow, 1996), pp. 442–6. This and subsequent quotations are from this edition, published in the series *Moi 20ii vek*. All translations are mine.
18. Ibid., p. 442.
19. For a discussion of the deliberations and details concerning the best canal route see *Kanal Moskva-Volga. 1932–1937* (Moscow, 1940), pp. 46–56. A husband and wife engineering team worked on the canal as well. I. S. Semenov devised the plan for the Dmitrov option, while his wife supervised engineering efforts in Iksha. See N. Fedorov, *Byla li tachka u ministra?* (Dmitrov, 1997), pp. 28–32. Maslov likewise discusses the decision to accept the Dmitrov route. See Maslov, *Kanal imeni Moskvy*, pp. 34–7.
20. Kaganovich, *Pamiatnye zapiski*, p. 443.
21. Ibid., p. 445.
22. Kokurin and Morukov chronicle the bureaucratic steps followed in implementing the Moscow–Volga project. Subsequent page numbers refer to their discussion, *Stalinskie stroiki*, pp. 59–78.
23. Ibid., p. 60.
24. Ibid., pp. 83–4.
25. Bulanov provides brief profiles of each man in his *Kanal Moskva-Volga: Khronika volzhskogo raiona gidrosooruzhenii* (Dubna, 2007), Kogan, pp. 15–16; Firin, p. 19; Zhuk, p. 22.

26. Ibid., p. 64.
27. Ibid., p. 60.
28. Ibid., p. 85.
29. Ibid., p. 99.
30. Ibid.
31. Ibid., p. 95.
32. Ibid., p. 83.
33. Cited in both Kokurin & Morukov, *Stalinskie stroiki*, p. 61 and in V. I. Maslov, *Kanal imeni Moskvy*, p. 39.
34. Maslov, *Kanal imeni Moskvy*, p. 34.
35. Ibid., p. 39.
36. Maslov includes the photographs throughout his narrative, but especially poignant are those on pp. 16, 38–43, 51 and 108.
37. TsGAMO, f. 2589, op. 1, d. 84, l. 31 verso.
38. Maslov, p. 39.
39. The issue of escape was pertinent not only to Dmitlag, although the farther afield a prisoner would find himself, the less chance of escape, especially from the camps in Norilsk, Vorkuta, and Kolyma. A general OGPU order of 21 May 1934 speaks to the issue of escape. See A. I. Kokurin and N. V. Petrov, *GULAG*, pp. 451–2. In a similar vein, the OGPU also issued an order to forbid the distribution of vodka to prisoners (ibid., pp. 450–1).
40. Dan Healey, "'Dramatalogical' Trauma in the Gulag. Malingering, Self-Inflicted Injuries and the Prisoner-Patient," in Felicitas Fischer Von Weikersthal and Karoline Thaidigsmann (eds), *(Hi-)Stories of the Gulag. Fiction and Reality* (Heidelberg, 2016), pp. 37–62, here p. 47.
41. Ibid., p. 47.
42. Ibid., p. 45.
43. Oleg Khlevniuk, "The Gulag and the Non-Gulag as One Interrelated Whole," in Michael David-Fox (ed.), *The Soviet Gulag. Evidence, Interpretation, and Comparison* (Pittsburgh, PA, 2016), p. 34.
44. Ibid.
45. Kokurin & Morukov, *Stalinskie stroiki*, p. 523.
46. Ibid.
47. V. S. Barkovsky, *Tainy Moskva-Volgostroia*, p. 12.
48. This camp population is the subject of a new rubric on the Moskva-volga.ru web site. The site's authors are compiling a "card catalogue" of information on individual prisoners. Currently the catalogue is 28 pages long, with new listings added regularly. As the site's authors note, the information they are culling is from family members of former prisoners. http://moskva-volga.ru/category/kartoteka/. Accessed 19 May 2017.
49. GARF, f. 9489, op. 2, d. 122, ll. 37, 196, 201, 208, 212, 228, and 245.
50. Personal interview with V. S. Barkovsky, 12 August 2004.
51. Kokurin & Morukov, *Stalinskie stroiki*, p. 523.

52. Golfo Alexopoulos, "Destructive Labor Camps: Rethinking Solzhenitsyn's Play on Words," in Michael David-Fox (ed.), *The Soviet Gulag. Evidence, Interpretation, and Comparison* (Pittsburgh, PA, 2016), pp. 42–64, here p. 59.
53. Ibid., pp. 59–64.
54. Barkovsky details how the records of the Dmitlag archive were ordered removed in order to preserve them. However, when the boxes arrived at Ulyanovsk on the Volga River, they were instead tossed into a bonfire by an NKVD official. Upon being questioned as to why this was happening and how it would be explained, the NKVD official replied, "It's none of your business." Hence valuable records and documents were lost forever through the irresponsibility of an NKVD operative. For a full account see Barkovsky, *Tainy Moskva-Volgostroia*, pp. 17–18.
55. Personal interview with V.S. Barkovsky, 12 August 2004.
56. V. S. Barkovsky, *Tainy Moskva-Volgostroia*, pp. 22–3.
57. Kokurin & Morukov, *Stalinskie stroiki*, p. 57.
58. For excellent discussions of the slippage between the boundaries of Gulag camps and the population centers near them see Wilson Bell, "Was the Gulag an Archipelago? De-Convoyed Prisoners and Porous Borders in the Camps of Western Siberia," *The Russian Review*, 72.1 (January 2013), pp. 116–41; Alan Barenberg, *Gulag Town, Company Town: Forced Labor and Its Legacy in Vorkuta* (New Haven, CT, 2014); and Oleg Khlevniuk, "The Gulag and the Non-Gulag as One Interrelated Whole," in Michael David-Fox (ed.), *The Soviet Gulag. Evidence, Interpretation, and Comparison* (Pittsburgh, PA, 2016), pp. 25–41.
59. TsGAMO, f. 2589, op. 1, d. 86, l. 9.
60. *O nagrazhdenii rabotnikov stroitel'stva kanala Moskva-Volga i zavodov-postavshchikov.* 14 July 1937.
61. *O nagrazhdenii i l'gotakh dlia stroitelei kanala Moskva-Volga.* 14 July 1937.
62. Personal archive of Mikhail Bulanov.
63. For an extended discussion of re-forging see A. Vyshinsky, *Introduction* in I. Averbakh, *Ot prestupleniia k trudu* (Moscow, 1936), p. IX. The entire odious Averbakh book discusses re-forging and its achievements during the first half of the 1930s. See also Viktor Shklovsky, "Perekovka na kanale Volga–Moskva," *Bol'shevistskaya pechat'* 1 (1937), pp. 30–3. Also Cynthia A. Ruder, *Making History for Stalin*, pp. 132–4, 143–53, and 163–6; and Julie Draskoczy, *Belomor. Criminality and Creativity in Stalin's Gulag* (Boston, MA, 2014).
64. For an analysis of Firin as the chief instigator of re-forging see N. Fedorov, "Dvigatel' 'Perekovki'," in *Butovsky Poligon. 1937–1938. Kniga Pamiati Zhertv Politicheskikh Repressii*, v. 7 (Moscow, 2003), pp. 45–52.
65. KVO – the *Kul'turno-Vospitatel'nii Otdel/Cultural Education Office* – was charged in the camp with promoting literacy, educational courses, training, and propaganda activities. The director/chief cultural education officer of the KVO, typically an employee of the NKVD, although not necessarily an NKVD officer, recruited staff to help with these initiatives. Staff members could be free workers or prisoners depending on their ability to read and

write, and contingent upon any other skills they might have, such as singing, playing an instrument, drawing, or other talents. KVCh – *Kul'turno-Vospitatel'naia Chast'* – was a sub-division of a KVO. The KVO generally was located at camp headquarters, while a KVCh would be found at each major camp sub-division. The KVCh carried out the programming – from educational work to agitation brigades to propaganda initiatives – at the local level within the camp's sectors.

66. http://moskva-volga.ru/bibliografiya-kvo-dmitlaga/. Accessed 31 December 2016.
67. An excellent source for the editorial boards of Dmitlag publications in general and *Moskva-Volgostroi* in particular is http://moskva-volga.ru/polnyj-putevoditel-po-zhurnalu-moskvavolgostroj-1934-1937/. Accessed 19 May 2017.
68. http://www.litfund.ru/auction/13/471/. Accessed 16 May 2017. See also http://moskva-volga.ru/bibliografiya-kvo-dmitlaga/.
69. Presumably there are copies of the *BP* elsewhere, but to date copies have been located only in the GARF library, Memorial Society archives, and in the Russian State Library. For a relatively complete listing see http://moskva-volga.ru/bibliografiya-kvo-dmitlaga/. Accessed 16 May 2017. It is likely that the closed archive supervised by the administration of the Moscow Canal contains copies as well, although this is impossible to verify in practice.
70. N. Ryzhkova, "Muzyka iz Gulaga," *Neva* 7 (2003). Accessed at http://magazines.russ.ru/neva/2003/7/ryzhk.html. The print version of the article is in *Neva* 7 (2003), pp. 243–50.
71. D. Kabalevsky, "Kanaloarmeiskaia pesnia. Stat'ia," *Na shturm trassy*, No. 11 (26), (November 1936), pp. 16–17. For more information about Kabalevsky, see http://www.kabalevsky.ru/, a site dedicated to his life and works. He was not only a highly regarded Soviet composer, but also a long-time professor at the Moscow Conservatory.
72. See http://www.cyberussr.com/rus/uk24-r.html for this iteration of Article 35, 20 May 1930 (SU No. 26, st. 344). Accessed 3 June 2012.
73. For a fuller discussion of this phenomenon in the early 1930s see Paul Hagenloh, *Stalin's Police: Public Order and the Mass Repression in the USSR, 1926–1941* (Washington, DC, 2009), pp. 114–19.
74. Ibid., p. 118.
75. David R. Shearer, *Policing Stalin's Socialism: Repression and Social Order in the Soviet Union, 1924–1953* (New Haven, CT, 2009), pp. 328–9. Shearer confirmed his understanding of the 35-ers epithet in an e-mail to the author on 31 May 2012.
76. This statement is based on references to *BP* authorship in *Na shturm trassy*, as well as the absence of personnel files in the NKVD card catalogue housed in GARF. Those *BP* authors who were either prisoners assigned to the KVO or serving on the editorial boards of Dmitlag publications or were "free" workers have files in the NKVD card catalogue, among them Zhigul'sky, Mogilianskaya, Kuhn, Sobolevsky, and Kalent'ev.

77. For a detailed explanation of the categories of Gulag inmates prior to 1940 see Steven A. Barnes, *Death and Redemption*, pp. 83–93.
78. *Biblioteka Perekovki*, *Kanaloarmeiskii plakat*, Vyp. 27, p. 14.
79. T. Valentinov, "Stranitsy zhizni i bor'by". Stat'ia, Na shturm trassy, No. 9 (26) (September 1936), pp. 34–5.
80. Indeed, one wonders why there was even a charge for the *BP* releases since the circulation figures were so small and there was, at least in what I have been able to determine, no intention to sell issues outside of Dmitlag. Perhaps the purchase of an issue suggested that the inmate truly was serious about the process of re-forging, provided that the inmate could read?
81. *Na shturm trassy*, No. 1(6), (15 January 1935), Inside back cover.
82. Firin's booklet *The Moscow–Volga Canal* (*Kanal Moskva-Volga*) launched the series in late 1934 and is featured in an advertisement in *Na shturm trassy*. It is not surprising that the Firin booklet disappeared given his own disappearance from the public stage after his arrest in April 1937 and subsequent execution.
83. Many of the titles in the *BP* were highlighted and/or pictured in articles in *Na shturm trassy*. See T. Valentinov, "Stranitsy zhizni i bor'by. Stat'ia," *Na shturm trassy*, No. 9 (26) (September 1936), pp. 34–5; A. Rasstanov, "Dokumenty chuvstva i masterstva," *Na shturm trassy*, No. 1 (18) (January 1936), pp. 38–9.
84. The archive at the Moscow Office of the Memorial organization houses the personal archive of Konstantin Sobolevsky, donated to the organization by his family. Among other items the archive contains some of his drawings, as well as letters to his wife and parents, and letters that his family sent to Soviet officials in order to protest his incarceration and fight for his release.
85. My thanks to a colleague for suggesting this interpretation.
86. The best way to evaluate these compositions would be to hear them. To the best of my knowledge none have been recorded for posterity.
87. Photo featured in an exhibit at the Moscow Canal Museum in Dedenevo.
88. Aleksandra Orlova, "Strannaia kniga," *Zhurnal Vestnik Online*, 5(342), (3 March 2004). Orlova goes on to note mistakenly that these volumes were produced by incarcerated musicians on the Belomor Canal project, which is not true. They are the product of Dmitlag.
89. N. Ryzhkova, "Muzyka iz Gulaga." Print version.
90. Ibid., p. 243.
91. Ibid., p. 246.
92. Ibid., p. 249.
93. Ibid., p. 250. In her article Ryzhkova refers to the *Martirolog* published in the commemorative volumes for the Butovo Shooting Range. *Butovsky poligon 1937–1938. Kniga pamiati zhertv politicheskikh repressii* (Moscow, 1997–2003). Lists of those from Dmitlag who were shot at Butovo appear in volumes 2–7.

94. D. Kabalevsky, "Kanaloarmeiskaia pesnia. Stat'ia," *Na shturm trassy*, No. 11 (26), (November 1936), p. 16.
95. It is unclear exactly what responsibilities were included in the position of "inspector" of the KVO. This probably was a supervisory position that required its holder to promote and organize the use of music on building sites and in agitation brigades, and to ensure that music was composed, performed, and advertised on the pages of Dmitlag publications. According to Ryzhkova, "M. Ia. Chernyak lived a long life, was a member of the Union of Soviet Composers, [and] the author of many compositions published in the fifties and sixties." See http://magazines.russ.ru/neva/2003/7/ryzhk.html.
96. A "navvy" is a laborer engaged in construction and excavation work on roads, canals, and railroads. It is an outdated term.
97. *Muzyka trassy*, pp. 10–11.
98. Ibid., p. 38. The Russian lyrics are as follows:

    И вновь весна, бодря и задирая,
    Кружит башку и плещется в груди.
    Весь мир пройду от края и до края,
    Вся жизнь моя большая впереди.

    Большая жизнь кипеньем бурных строек,
    И ей кипеть в котле горячих дней
    В глухих степях, на фабриках и заводах
    Великой мудрой родины моей.

    Мне ярче всех сегодня солнце всходит,
    И тесно сердцу шалому в груди,
    Всё оттого, что я на что-то годен,
    И жизнь моя большая впереди.

99. With the exception of Brilev, Mogilianskaya, Sobolevsky and Zhigul'sky, it has been difficult to determine whether or not other authors in the *BP* managed to survive their incarceration in Dmitlag. All were executed at the Donskoi cemetery/crematorium. Short biographies are provided for them in *Rasstrel'nie zapiski. Moskva 1935–1953. Donskoe kladbishche {Donskoi krematorii}* (Moscow, 2005). These listings provide arrest records, residences in Dmitrov, and dates of rehabilitation. Brilev's entry is on p. 68, Mogilianskaya's on p. 315, Sobolevsky's on p. 431, and Zhigul'sky's on p. 169.
100. *Kanal askari*, p. 17.
101. Ibid., p. 41.
102. *Records: Poetry of National Minority Prisoners*, p. 38.
103. Ibid., p. 19. The Russian is as follows:

    Мы армия ударного канала.
    Мы – канал-аскари.
    Мы и творцы, и дети канала,
    Мы – канал-аскари.

Мы пришли с Востока
И не уйдём мы на Восток,
Не окончив нашу стройку.
Мы – канал аскари.

Я – узбек, ты – грузин,
А сосед – армянин.
Мы – канал-аскари.
И канал наш один.

104. From 1933–4 Mogilianskaya remained at BelBaltLag as a "free" worker until her assignment at Dmitlag was finalized.
105. Currently the Hunterian Museum at the University of Glasgow is featuring a virtual exhibition entitled "Beauty in Hell: Culture in the Gulag." This exhibition, based on the research of Gulag scholar Andrea Gullotta, offers a wealth of materials regarding cultural life and cultural production at Solovki. Photographs, biographical materials, reference sources and more comprise the presentation and provide a glimpse into the cultural life of the first link in the Gulag chain. Among the cultural practitioners featured is Lidia Mogilianskaya. See https://www.gla.ac.uk/hunterian/visit/exhibitions/virtualexhibitions/beautyinhellcultureinthegulag/#d.en.531100. Accessed 2 November 2017.
106. In terms of the "affirmative action" empire, Mogilianskaya could check two important boxes: she was a woman and an ethnic Ukrainian.
107. Lidia Mogilianskaya, *Dva Kanala: Stikhotvoreniia*, p. 15.
108. I realize this is a rather infelicitous translation of the word *kanaloarmeika*, but the -ette suffix in English captures a bit of the feminine ending in the Russian. Any other translation, such as female canal-soldier, seems cumbersome and not in the spirit of the Russian original.
109. *Canal Soldierette*, p. 30. The Russian is as follows:

На канале мой сыночек
Подрастает дни и ночи, -
Будет честным он рабочим.

Будет он, как все вы – люди,
Воровать совсем не будет,
Кочевую жизнь забудет.

Мы не зря каналы роем-
Для цыган колхоз построим,
Сына сделаем героем.

110. Anatoly Mol'kov, *Spring*, p. 37.
111. Ibid., p. 40. The title's white/black contrast is suggestive. Either the poet's beloved has dark hair, and the optimism of the poem, its whiteness, is in contrast to her. Or the woman is a negative force in opposition to the poem's positive tone. Given the poem's content, the first suggestion seems most plausible.

112. Ibid., p. 40.
113. Ibid., p. 43. The Russian is as follows:

Ты далеко. Легли между нами
По изумрудным лесистым равнинам
Версты гудения синих рельс,
Версты гудения проводов.

Только радостно бьётся сердце:
Мы оба связаны общим делом.
Ты ушла с головой в учёбу,
В страницы мудрых, тяжёлых книг.

И мы с ребятами, точно знамя,
Подняв боевую весёлую песню,
Роем, готовим путь пароходу,
Который ты поведёшь в Москву.

114. Ibid., p. 45. The Russian is as follows:

Весна жасминною порошей
Закружит в теплой синеве,
И я приду – другой, хороший,
Полезный новый человек.

И радость двойная украдкой
Блеснет из глаз твоих глубин.
В моей стране хорошей сладко
Цвести, работать и любить.

115. Ibid., p. 48.
116. N. Fedorov, "Detishche besklassovogo obshchestva," in *Butovsky Poligon. 1937–1938. Kniga Pamiati Zhertv Politicheskikh Repressii*, v. 6 (Moscow, 2002), pp. 30–41.
117. As noted above, Gleb Kuhn, Konstantin Sobolevsky, and Lidia Mogilianskaya were executed after their stints in Dmitlag; all three actively participated in the *BP* project, but Kuhn and Mogilianskaya in particular were tarnished because of their close relationship with Firin.
118. Two important issues related to the notion of producing art on demand are the role of the perpetrator and the role of memory in reconstructing difficult moments in a culture's history, such as inmate cultural production on the Moscow Canal. The most cogent discussion to date regarding the role of the perpetrator and the ramifications of that term is Lynne Viola's work on perpetrators during the Stalinist terror of the 1930s. See her superb article, "The Question of the Perpetrator in Soviet History," *Slavic Review* 75, 1(2013), pp. 1–23, as well as her forthcoming book *Stalinist Perpetrators on Trial. Scenes from the Great Terror in Soviet Ukraine* (Oxford, UK, 2017).

Regarding the problem of cultural memory in relation to Gulag cultural production see Alexander Etkind's recent work, *Warped Mourning: Stories of the Undead in the Land of the Unburied* (Stanford, CA, 2013).

119. Karl Schloegel, *In Space We Read Time* (New York, NY, 2016), p. 417.
120. Ibid.
121. Bettina Greiner, "The Gulag. An Incarnation of the State that Created It," in Michael David-Fox (ed.), *The Soviet Gulag. Evidence, Interpretation, and Comparison* (Pittsburgh, PA, 2016), pp. 314–20, here p. 315.
122. Ibid.

Chapter 3 Creating Metaphorical and Ideological Space: Cultural Production and the Moscow Canal

1. I. Eksler, "The Face of the Canal," GARF, f. 7952, op. 2, d. 122, l. 53.
2. A. V. Kosarev, "The Greatest Structure of the Stalinist Epoch," *Kanal Moskva-Volga*, unpublished manuscript, p. 10.
3. For striking images of the Moscow Canal, including the sculptures discussed here, see http://www.calvertjournal.com/features/show/4180, which features photographs by Olya Ivanova and text by Anastasiia Fedorova. Ivanova photographed the Moscow Canal in the winter, when repairs are conducted on the waterway and recreational areas are deserted until warmer weather arrives. Accessed 20 June 2017.
4. The large monuments to Lenin and Stalin at the confluence of the Moscow Canal with the Volga River will be discussed in detail in Chapter Four.
5. Photographs of these sculptures can be found in *Kanal Moskva-Volga, 1932–1937* (Moscow, 1940), p. 182 and pp. 188–93. Many of these figures will be discussed in Chapter Four, which examines in greater detail the architecture of the Moscow Canal.
6. For additional photographs of these sculptures taken shortly after the Moscow Canal opened, see http://moskva-volga.ru/gallery/index.php?/category/31, images 12–16. Accessed 18 May 2017.
7. Emergency and barrier gates were constructed at various points along the canal in order to cut off the flow of water during a crisis or when structural repairs are necessary.
8. These photos are included in *Arkhitektura kanala Moskva-Volga*, I. G. Sushkevich (ed.) (Moscow, 1939), pp. 103–4.
9. As Keith Blasing points out, "Andrei Platonov's *Happy Moscow* deals with exactly this, but in a tragic mode. The heroine of the story, Moskva Chestnova, is an aerial daredevil, but her parachute catches fire, and her life is a downward spiral from there, including being maimed in the construction of the Moscow Metro. It's an amazingly honest literary treatment of the other side of the issues you talk about in this book – the use of Moscow as a showpiece, technological advancement, and so on. Which, of course, is why it was not published until the 1990s." E-mail correspondence 28 June 2017.

10. For the most recent discussion of the importance of aviation in the Stalinist era see Scott Palmer, *Dictatorship of the Air: Aviation Culture and the Fate of Modern Russia* (Cambridge, UK, 2006).
11. For the most detailed discussion of the presentation of the human body as metaphor, especially in the 1930s, see Keith A. Livers, *Constructing the Stalinist Body: Fictional Representations of Corporeality in the Stalinist 1930s* (Lanham, MD, 2004), as well as Eric Naiman, *Sex in Public: The Incarnation of Early Soviet Ideology* (Princeton, NJ, 1997).
12. My thanks to Keith Blasing for pointing out the motto's origin. E-mail correspondence 28 June 2017.
13. This image parallels that of a 1937 painting by Alexander Samokhvalov, *Female Metro Worker with a Drill*. For a full description see Mike O'Mahony, "The Moscow Metro" in Valerie Kivelson and Joan Neuberger (eds), *Picturing Russia: Explorations in Visual Culture* (New Haven, CT, 2008), pp. 185–8. See especially pp. 187–8.
14. I. Eksler, "The Face of the Canal," GARF, f. 7952, op. 2, d. 122, l. 52.
15. Abram Tertz [Andrei Sinyavsky], "On Socialist Realism," *The Trial Begins and On Socialist Realism*, Max Hayward and George Dennis (trans) (Berkeley & Los Angeles, CA, 1982). Note that some critics in fact trace many of the elements of the socialist realist canon back to the avant-garde. For example Boris Groys contends that socialist realism was more avant-garde than the avant-garde itself. For a full discussion see Boris Groys, *The Total Art of Stalinism: Avant-Garde, Aesthetic Dictatorship, and Beyond*, Charles Rougle (trans) (Princeton, NJ, 1992).
16. Katerina Clark, "Little Heroes and Big Deeds: Literature Responds to the First Five-Year Plan," in Sheila Fitzpatrick (ed.), *Cultural Revolution in Russia, 1928–1931* (Bloomington, IN, 1984), pp. 189–206. Clark's article provides a full and nuanced treatment of this idea.
17. Toby Clark, "The 'New Man's' Body," in Matthew Cullerne Bown and Brandon Taylor (eds), *Art of the Soviets: Painting, Sculpture and Architecture in a One-Party State, 1917–1992* (Manchester, UK & New York, NY, 1993), p. 44.
18. For this and other examples of 'vanishing commissars' see David King's path-breaking work *The Commissar Vanishes: The Falsification of Photographs and Art in Stalin's Russia* (New York, NY, 1997). The images cited here are on pp. 136–7 and 156–7.
19. Recently a number of Modorov's paintings were found in a Voronezh art museum. For one example see https://www.facebook.com/groups/Moskva.Volga.Ru/permalink/970426856428736/
20. Henri Lefebvre, *The Production of Space*, Donald Nicholson-Smith (trans) (Oxford, UK and Cambridge, MA, 1991), pp. 273–4.
21. Ibid., p. 274.
22. Matthew Cullerne Bown, *Socialist Realist Painting* (New Haven, CT, 1998), p. 179.

23. Ibid., p. 179.
24. Very brief biographies of all the artists can be found in Matthew Cullerne Bown, *A Dictionary of Twentieth Century Russian and Soviet Painters: 1900–1980s* (London, 1998), E.V. Egorov, p. 77; F.A. Modorov, p. 211; S.I. Shchelokov, p. 283. After extensive searches I could find no concrete biographical information concerning A. Berezkin.
25. http://kupitkartinu.ru/painters/modorov-fedor-aleksandrovich/. Accessed 15 June 2016.
26. For a sense of Modorov's paintings at auction and the thematic scope of his oeuvre, see http://artinvestment.ru/en/auctions/18760/records.html?work_id=264720; http://artpoisk.info/artist/modorov_fedor_aleksandrovich_1890/gallery/; and especially http://sovcom.ru/index.php?category=painters&painterstype=painter&painter=308, where two of his Moscow Canal paintings, "The Tushino Lock. The Moscow-Volga Canal" (1937) and "The Moscow Volga Canal" (1937) are included with their selling prices. In addition, a number of recently discovered Modorov paintings can be found on the Moskva-volga.ru Facebook page. See https://www.facebook.com/groups/Moskva.Volga.Ru/ for various posts that feature his paintings. Accessed 2 November 2017.
27. Biographical information about Shchelokov is scant. For the most complete information available see http://www.sakharov-center.ru/asfcd/khudozhniki/?t=page&id=291. Accessed 15 June 2016.
28. E-mail correspondence with Natalya Mikhailovna Shumeiko, chief curator of the Saratov Regional Studies Museum, 24 June 2016.
29. Aleksandr Grigorenko, *Gulag, kanal, khudozhnik*, http://moscow.clow.ru/information/1/6/znm2g16.html. Accessed 7 July 2016.
30. Ibid. The location of the painting to which Grigorenko refers is unknown.
31. http://artinvestment.ru/auctions/14330/biography.html. Accessed 7 July 2016. In addition to Egorov's biography this site features a list of his works that have come up for auction. For a more complete discussion of Egorov's art and artistry see Efim Vodonos, "'Groza momental'aia navek': O tvorchestve Evgeniia Egorova," http://magazines.russ.ru/volga21/2007/9/ef14.html. Accessed 16 June 2016.
32. For more biographical information about Satel', as well as illustrations of the paintings featured on Russian art auction sites, see http://sovcom.ru/index.php?category=painters&painterstype=painter&painter=2363; http://rus-gal.ru/author/2057; http://www.artpanorama.su/?category=artist&id=753&show=short&right=no; and http://peresvetovgallery.ru/hudozhniki-sssr/satel-georgij-eduardovich.html. All accessed 16 July 2016.
33. Matthew Cullerne Bown, *Socialist Realist Painting*, p. 182.
34. Ibid., p. 195. In another context Bown refers to Modorov as "an unpopular personality and an inferior painter." Ibid., p. 284.
35. This is in contradistinction to the Belomor Canal, whose locks initially were constructed of wood, only to be replaced later with concrete.

36. Nick Baron, "The Mapping of Illiberal Modernity: Spatial Science, Ideology and the State in Early Twentieth-Century Russia," in Sanna Turoma and Maxim Waldstein (eds), *Empire De/Centered. New Spatial Histories of Russia and the Soviet Union* (Farnham, UK, 2013), pp. 128–9.
37. Ibid., p. 118.
38. Henri Lefebvre, *The Production of Space*, p. 274.
39. For the best examination of this phenomenon see David King, *The Commissar Vanishes*.
40. The illustrators include Gleb Kuhn, Vasily Elkin, and Konstantin Sobolevsky. As noted in Chapter Two, Kuhn and Sobolevsky were Dmitlag inmates who worked in the Dmitlag artist's studio, the source of most of the drawings, posters, and paintings produced for the Moscow Canal. It is regrettable that more information about them cannot be included in the present study because of space and thematic limitations. I hope to prepare an article that focuses on their work and fates after Dmitlag. Elkin's poster "Greetings to the great Stalin. The Moscow Canal is open!" is the illustration used for the cover of this book. In addition, Elkin authored his own booklet in the *Library of Re-forging* series. For further information about Gleb Kuhn see N. A. Fedorov, "Glavnii khudozhnik kanala," in *Byla li tachka u ministra?* . . . , pp. 43–59. In the same publication Fedorov profiles Konstantin Sobolevsky "Khochetsia. Uzhasno khochetsia zhit'," pp. 59–68. Both Kuhn and Sobolevsky were executed in 1937. Vasily Elkin, who was a well-known and well-established artist, was arrested in 1934 and sentenced to three years in the camps under Article 58.10 for supposed "anti-Soviet propaganda." Elkin served his sentence at Dmitlag, where he continued his artistic work. After completing his sentence he remained at Dmitlag voluntarily and then later was permitted to return to Moscow. A superb article about Elkin, as well as many examples of his artistic output both within and outside Dmitlag can be found in Igor Kuvyrkov, "Khudozhnik Dmitlaga Vasily Elkin," http://moskva-volga.ru/hudozhnik-dmitlaga-vasilij-yolkin/. Accessed 19 May 2017.
41. GARF, f. 7952, op. 2, d. 22, ll. 1–4.
42. For a concise, accessible description of the *History of Factories and Plants* series see the online encyclopedia entry at http://enc-dic.com/enc_sie/Istorija-fabrik-i-zavodov-377.html. Accessed 22 October 2016.
43. For a complete discussion of this volume see Cynthia A. Ruder, *Making History for Stalin*, as well as Julie Draskoczy, *Belomor*.
44. For a fuller discussion of the shift from collective to individual acts of worker heroism see Katerina Clark, "Little Heroes and Big Deeds" and Karen Petrone, *Life Has Become More Joyous, Comrades!* (Bloomington, IN, 2000).
45. This and all subsequent references to the text are taken from *Kanal Moskva-Volga*, unpublished manuscript, 1937?, p. 10. All translations are mine. Note that the official title GARF ascribes to the manuscript proofs is *Maket gotovivsheisia k izdaniiu knigi o stroitel'stve kanala Moskva-Volga* (*Maquette of a*

book prepared for publication about the construction of the Moscow–Volga Canal). Presumably this item is still located in the GARF library.

46. Karl Schloegel, *Moscow 1937*, Rodney Livingstone (trans) (Cambridge, UK, 2012), p. 275.
47. Toby Clark, "The 'New Man's' Body," p. 44.
48. The concepts of monuments and monumentalism are valid and important to any examination of Stalinist construction projects and will be discussed in greater detail in Chapter Four. On the issue of monuments and monumentality see William H. Gass, "Monumentality, Mentality," *Oppositions* 25 (1982), pp. 127–44. The notion of monumental texts has been taken up in two fascinating articles: Elaine MacKinnon, "Writing History for Stalin: Isaak Izrailevich Mints and the *Istoriia grazhdanskoi voiny*," *Kritika* v. 6, 1 (Winter 2005), pp. 5–54, and Brian Kassof, "A Book of Socialism: Stalinist Culture and the First Edition of the *Bol'shaia sovetskaia entsiklopedia*," *Kritika* v. 6, 1 (Winter 2005), pp. 55–95.
49. Bulanov and Barkovsky, in conversations with the author, both noted that this museum burnt down. Personal conversations, May 2007.
50. *Kanal Moskva-Volga*, p. 146.
51. Ibid., p. 155.
52. This narrative segment is attributed to "L. Kaganovich. Nachal'nik otdela oborudovaniia sektora montazhnykh rabot." Ibid., p. 213.
53. Ibid., p. 162.
54. Ibid., p. 163.
55. The first poster appears between pp. 222–3 and the second is between pp. 232–3.
56. The majority of inmate authors worked throughout the construction of the Moscow Canal in the print outlets made available to Dmitlag. See Chapter Two for a fuller discussion of this practice.
57. For the full account of Roitenburg's experience on the Belomor Canal see Mikhail Zoshchenko, "Istoriia odnoi perekovki," in M. Gorky, L. Averbakh, S. Firin (eds), *Belomorsko-baltiiskii kanal imeni Stalina. Istoriia stroitel'stva 1931–1934* (Moscow, 1998), pp. 493–524. This edition is a reprint of one of the original versions published in 1934. Who produced this most recent Russian version remains a mystery since the barest of publication details are provided.
58. Karl Schloegel, *Moscow 1937*, p. 291.
59. *Kanal Moskva-Volga*, p. 321.
60. Like many others involved in the Moscow Canal project, Fridliand was arrested and executed on 20 June 1937. Ibid., p. 287.
61. Ibid., p. 334.
62. Ibid.
63. Ibid., p. 348.
64. GARF, f. 7952, op. 2, d. 122, ll. 1–198. Subsequent references refer to this file and are noted only by list' (l., i.e. page) numbers. All translations are mine.

65. Ibid., l. 5.
66. Ibid., ll. 1–4.
67. Vyacheslav Mikhailovich Molotov (Skriabin) was an Old Bolshevik, protégé and confidant of Stalin and important figure in the Soviet government. He held various posts, the most important and lengthy of which was as the Soviet Foreign Minister. He negotiated the Molotov–Ribbentrop pact with Nazi Germany that was supposed to prevent a war with Germany. As we know, the pact failed to prevent the Nazi invasion of the USSR on 21 June 1941.
68. GARF, f. 7952, op. 2, d. 122, l. 6.
69. Mikhail Ivanovich Kalinin was an Old Bolshevik and Soviet statesman, member of Stalin's inner circle and Party member. His posts during his career included being the Chairman of the Presidium of the Supreme Soviet and the Chairman of the Central Executive Committee of the All-Russian Congress of Soviets.
70. Alexander Fedorovich Gorkin was an Old Bolshevik and a Soviet statesman. He served as the Secretary of the Presidium of the Supreme Soviet of the USSR. Later in his career he was the Chairman of the Supreme Court of the USSR.
71. GARF, f. 7952, op. 2, d. 122, ll. 187–9.
72. Ibid., l. 195.
73. It is unclear which Zheleznov this refers to. Two possibilities are Mikhail Zheleznov, a Soviet artist, and Pavel Zheleznov a Soviet poet. They are not related to each other.
74. Ibid., ll. 192–3.
75. Page 194 of the archival file includes the "Explanation" for the scope and contents of the volume. The entry is signed by T. Kovenev, while the printed version of his name is T (superimposed over B) Korenev.
76. Ibid., l. 194.
77. Ibid.
78. The book's length was to be 10–12 printer sheets (*Ob"em sbornika 10–12 pechatnykh listov*), which is approximately 150–75 printed pages. Ibid., l. 194.
79. Ibid., l. 176. This rhetoric is also reminiscent of Jeffrey Brooks' analysis of *Pravda* in his book *Thank you Comrade Stalin!* (Princeton, NJ, 2001).
80. Ibid., l. 187.
81. Ibid., l. 62.
82. Katerina Clark, *Moscow, the Fourth Rome* (Cambridge, MA, 2011), pp. 280–1. For a fuller discussion of this concept see Clark's Chapter Eight, *The Imperial Sublime*.
83. Ibid., p. 286.
84. Ibid., p. 299.
85. Ibid.
86. Ibid.
87. Ibid., p. 290.
88. Ibid., p. 299.
89. *Kanal Moskva-Volga, 1932–1937* (Moscow, 1940). All translations are mine.
90. http://moskva-volga.ru/putevoditel-po-krasnym-knigam/. Accessed 20 May 2017.
91. Ibid.

92. *Kanal Moskva-Volga, 1932–1937* (Moscow, 1940), pp. 5–7.
93. Ibid., pp. 181–93.
94. A. I. Mikhailov, *Arkhitektura Kanala Moskva-Volga* (Moscow, 1939) is the small paperback book, while *Arkhitektura Kanala Moskva-Volga*, I.G. Sushkevich (ed.) (Moscow, 1939) is the more complete, hard-bound, large-format, richly illustrated tome, not ascribed to a specific author.
95. Ibid., p. 181.
96. Ibid., p. 182.
97. GARF, f. 7952, op. 2, d. 122, l. 171.
98. *Kanal Moskva-Volga*, p. 213.
99. *Kanal Moskva-Volga, 1932–1937* (Moscow, 1940), pp. 282–90.
100. Ibid., p. 288.
101. Ibid.
102. Ibid., p. 289.
103. Ibid.
104. Ibid.
105. Ibid.
106. Ibid., p. 11.
107. Ibid., p. 12.
108. Ibid., p. 312.
109. Ibid., p. 314.
110. Ibid.
111. Terje Tvedt, *Water and Society: Changing Perceptions of Societal and Historical Development* (London, 2016), p. 13.

Chapter 4 Monuments, Monumentality, and Memory: Forgetting and Remembering

1. Nick Baron, "The Mapping of Illiberal Modernity: Spatial Science, Ideology and the State in Early Twentieth-century Russia" in Sanna Turoma and Maxim Waldstein (eds), *Empire De/Centered. New Spatial Histories of Russia and the Soviet Union* (Farnham, UK, 2013), pp. 105–34, here p. 133.
2. This document provides an accessible and brief history not only of the WPA, but of the Civilian Conservation Corps and other job-creating initiatives implemented in the 1930s to combat the Great Depression. See https://www.fws.gov/uploadedFiles/Depression%20Era%20Programs%20-%20Region%206.pdf. Accessed 28 December 2016.
3. For an easily accessible history of construction and extensive photographs of the Hoover Dam see https://www.usbr.gov/lc/hooverdam/. Accessed 28 December 2016.
4. Katerina Clark, *Moscow, The Fourth Rome* (Cambridge, MA, 2011), p. 112.
5. Ibid.
6. Ibid.

7. Ibid., pp. 112–13.
8. Ibid., p. 113.
9. Ibid., pp. 113–14.
10. For Lefebvre's complete discussion of monumental space see Henri Lefebvre, *The Production of Space*, Donald Nicholson-Smith (trans) (Oxford, UK, 1991), pp. 220–6. My distinction between memorial and monumental space relies on this and other approaches to the notion of memorials, monuments, and monumentality, as the discussion in this chapter illustrates.
11. I. Eksler, Caption to a photograph of a Moscow Canal lock at night, in *The USSR in Construction* 2 (1938), p. 33.
12. A.I. Mikhailov, *Arkhitektura Kanala Moskva-Volga* (Moscow, 1939), p. 67.
13. https://ru.wikipedia.org/wiki/%D0%9F%D0%B0%D0%BC%D1%8F%D1%82%D0%BD%D0%B8%D0%BA_%D0%9B%D0%B5%D0%BD%D0%B8%D0%BD%D1%83_%D1%83_%D0%B2%D1%85%D0%BE%D0%B4%D0%B0_%D0%B2_%D0%92%D0%BE%D0%BB%D0%B3%D0%BE-%D0%94%D0%BE%D0%BD%D1%81%D0%BA%D0%BE%D0%B9_%D0%BA%D0%B0%D0%BD%D0%B0%D0%BB. Accessed 18 December 2016.
14. S. D. Merkurov, "Monumental'naia skul'ptura na kanale Moskva-Volga," in *Arkhitektura Kanala Moskva-Volga*, I.G. Sushkevich (ed.) (Moscow, 1939), pp. 68–72. Here p. 68.
15. Ibid., p. 70.
16. *Kanal Moskva-Volga. 1932–1937* (Moscow, 1940), p. 88.
17. The most complete narrative of the construction of these monuments can be found in Bulanov's *Kanal Moskva-Volga*, pp. 127–32. The discussion in this chapter is based largely on Bulanov's account.
18. Ibid., p. 128.
19. Ibid., p. 129.
20. Ibid.
21. Ibid., p. 130.
22. Ibid., p. 129.
23. Ibid., p. 130.
24. Ibid., p. 131.
25. Ibid., p. 135.
26. For a report on the dedication ceremony see http://m.dubna.ru/37/10237.html. A virtual tour of the site can be found at http://dubna.navse360.ru/kultura/pamyatnyj-znak-stroitelyam-kanala-moskva-volga. Both sites accessed 23 May 2017.
27. Tyler J. Kelley, "Choke Point of a Nation," *New York Times*, 27 November 2016, Business section, pp. 1 & 6. Here p. 6. This article about dams and locks on the Ohio River reveals that inland water transportation routes remain important not only in regard to the Moscow Canal and Russia, but to any country that depends on rivers to transport goods to consumers.

28. M. Kolentsev, *Monumental'nye sooruzheniia*, in *Kanaloarmeiskii plakat*, *Biblioteka Perekovki*, Vyp. 27 (1936), p. 41. Kolentsev used a quotation from Genrikh Yagoda on the poster.
29. Prof. V. F. Krinsky, "Arkhitektura shliuzov kanala Moskva-Volga," in *Arkhitektura kanala Moskva-Volga*, I.G. Sushkevich (ed.) (Moscow, 1939), pp. 39–57, here p. 52.
30. Ibid., p. 51.
31. Ibid.
32. Ibid., p. 52.
33. V. M. Perlin, "Arkhitektura Kanala Moskva-Volga," in *Arkhitektura kanala Moskva-Volga*, I.G. Sushkevich (ed.) (Moscow, 1939), pp. 9–38, here p. 35.
34. http://moskva-volga.ru/propavshie-freski-bruni/. Accessed 20 December 2016. This article discusses not only the Bruni frescoes at Lock 6, but also the fate of the artist Bruni and the architect Vegman.
35. Cited in http://moskva-volga.ru/propavshie-freski-bruni/.
36. http://map.infoflot.ru/region_europe/central/kim/arhitektura/arhitektura.htm. Accessed 20 December 2016.
37. Prof. V. F. Krinsky, "Arkhitektura shliuzov kanala Moskva-Volga," p. 56.
38. The Northern River Station stands adjacent to the Northern River Port that is still in operation. Cargo is shipped to and from the port, as well as from the Southern River Port located on the Moscow River in the Nagatino region of southern Moscow. In 1932 a wooden Southern River Station was built and remained in use until 1972 when it was dismantled. Only in 1985 was a new Southern River Station constructed that was in service until the building was renovated at some point after 2012, at which time it was converted into a children's store. According to one source a "sculpture of goddesses representing the five seas to which the capital was connected after the construction of the Moscow–Volga Canal" still embellished the structure in 2012, only to disappear after the most recent renovation. See http://www.msk-guide.ru/yurv.htm. Accessed 28 December 2016. Photographs of the original wooden structure designed by the architect R. Ia. Khiger are included on the Wikipedia page for the Southern River Station at https://ru.wikipedia.org/wiki/%D0%AE%D0%B6%D0%BD%D1%8B%D0%B9_%D1%80%D0%B5%D1%87%D0%BD%D0%BE%D0%B9_%D0%B2%D0%BE%D0%BA%D0%B7%D0%B0%D0%BB. Accessed 28 December 2016.
39. Mikhailov, *Arkhitektura Kanala Moskva-Volga*, p. 64.
40. Ibid.
41. http://raskalov-vit.livejournal.com/96996.html. Accessed 27 December 2016. Photograph 15 clearly shows the jewel-encrusted hammer and sickle.
42. Mikhailov, *Arkhitektura Kanala Moskva-Volga*, p. 64.
43. Ibid., p. 62.
44. Ibid.
45. Ibid., p. 64.
46. Ibid.

47. A. M. Rukhliadev, "Arkhitektura rechnogo vokzala v Khimkakh" in *Arkhitektura kanala Moskva-Volga*, I.G. Sushkevich (ed.) (Moscow, 1939), pp. 58–67, here p. 59.
48. Mikhailov, *Arkhitektura Kanala Moskva-Volga*, p. 64.
49. Ibid.
50. A. M. Rukhliadev, "Arkhitektura rechnogo vokzala v Khimkakh" in *Arkhitektura Kanala Moskva-Volga*, p. 67.
51. Here Clark's contention that the main concern of Socialist Realist architecture (pp. 112–3) focused on decorative exteriors falls a bit short in the sense that the architects' design for the interior of the Northern River Station was just as decorative as the building's exterior. Perhaps it would be more appropriate to say that the level of decorative interiors in Stalinist buildings depended heavily on their function, to wit the lavish lobbies, high ceilings, and millwork in many Stalinist apartment buildings, hotels, and even the central building of Moscow State University.
52. A. M. Rukhliadev, "Arkhitektura rechnogo vokzala v Khimkakh" in *Arkhitektura Kanala Moskva-Volga*, p. 67.
53. Ibid.
54. Mikhailov, *Arkhitektura Kanala Moskva-Volga*, p. 64.
55. Ibid., p. 66.
56. A. M. Rukhliadev, "Arkhitektura rechnogo vokzala v Khimkakh" in *Arkhitektura Kanala Moskva-Volga*, p. 58.
57. Ibid.
58. The Dynamo Water Stadium was built in 1935 and designed by the architect G. Ia. Movchan, who also worked as an architect on the Moscow Canal. The water stadium and its adjacent park housed various sport facilities that ranged from swimming areas in the Khimki Reservoir to a multi-level diving platform, to a stadium where spectators could sit and view activities on the water, as well as fields for soccer and other sports. After a renovation for the 1980 Olympics, the Dynamo complex fell into complete disrepair until it was purchased by private investors who restored the original structure and developed the area as a premier athletic center for everything from water polo to fencing. The complex includes a bar and restaurant. It also holds various sports competitions throughout the year. The original water stadium has become the lesser attraction in spite of its architectural significance. For photographs taken in 2004 prior to renovation, see http://www.landscape-design.ru/articlex.php?c=VS. For the new version of the Water Stadium see http://vodnydynamo.ru/. Both sites accessed 27 December 2016.
59. See http://www.colta.ru/news/8171. Accessed 24 May 2017.
60. See http://moskva-volga.ru/vlasti-moskvy-ishhut-podryadchika-dlya-nauchnoj-restavratsii-severnogo-rechnogo-vokzala/ and https://stroi.mos.ru/news/severnyi-rechnoi-vokzal-v-moskve-planiruetsya-otrestavrirovat-husnullin for additional information on this process. Accessed 24 May 2017.

61. http://moskva-volga.ru/opredelilsya-pobeditel-v-konkurse-na-proekt-restavratsii-severnogo-rechnogo-vokzala/. Accessed 24 May 2017.
62. A. I. Mikhailov, "Znachenie kanala Moskva-Volga v razvitii sovetskoi arkhitektury," *Arkhitektura Kanala Moskva-Volga*, I.G. Sushkevich (ed.) (Moscow, 1939), pp. 73–89, here p. 83.
63. Ibid.
64. Ibid.
65. Ibid.
66. Ibid., pp. 83–4.
67. Ibid., p. 84.
68. Ibid.
69. Evgeny Dobrenko, "The Art of Social Navigation. The Cultural Topography of the Stalin Era," in Evgeny Dobrenko and Eric Naiman (eds), *The Landscape of Stalinism. The Art and Ideology of Soviet Space* (Seattle, WA and London, 2003), pp. 163–200, here p. 167.
70. Ibid., p. 175.
71. Ibid., p. 178.
72. Ibid.
73. Ibid., p. 179.
74. My thanks to Keith Blasing for pointing out that "many of these were 'CTO' ('cancelled to order'), meant to be used in collections with a special cancellation, but never postally used. The point is still valid, however, as CTO stamps were meant to travel to people's stamp collections all over the world and serve as propaganda, maybe even more than use on an envelope would entail (because a stamp collection is a space of commemoration even more than a used envelope) ... It's devilishly hard to compile a collection of postally used Soviet stamps." E-mail correspondence 28 June 2017.
75. I am indebted to Valentin Barkovsky for giving me a set of these matchbox covers.
76. *Kanal imeni Moskvy* (Moscow, 1987). This "prospectus," as it is called, was produced by Rechflot's commercial office likely as either a souvenir of a trip along the canal or as an advertisement to induce potential travelers to use the firm for a cruise on the Moscow Canal.
77. P. Volkov, *Moskva-Volga: Kanal imeni Moskvy* (Moscow, 1987).
78. N. A. Fedorov, *Byla li tachka u ministra?*. (Dmitrov, 1997).
79. "Perechen' grazhdanskikh i promyshlennykh zdanii i sooryzhenii postroennykh Dmitlagom GULAG, OGPU-NKVD SSSR v period 1932–1937 gg. Na territorii goroda Dmitrova i v ego okrestnostiakh," *Dmitrovskii vestnik* (27 March 2007), p. 8.
80. For an excellent summary of Fedorov's life and work see http://dmkray.ru/fjodorov-n-a.html. Accessed 14 December 2016. The site also features a bibliography of Fedorov's work and tributes to him.
81. The monastery was re-consecrated in 1993 and since then has been a functioning Russian Orthodox church and complex for the monks who live there.

82. N. A. Fedorov, *Byla li tachka u ministra?*, p. 19.
83. For a complete discussion of Nekrasov, his fate before and after the February and October Revolutions, see Fedorov, *Byla li tachka u ministra*, pp. 32–9.
84. For a complete listing of all the structures see "Perechen' grazhdanskikh i promyshlennykh zdanii i sooryzhenii postroennykh Dmitlagom GULAG, OGPU-NKVD SSSR v period 1932–1937 gg. Na territorii goroda Dmitrova i v ego okrestnostiakh," *Dmitrovskii vestnik* (27 March 2007), p. 8.
85. This definition of memorial space relies heavily on the work of Simon Schama, in particular on his discussion of the memorial at Giby in Poland, the picture of which bears a striking resemblance to the Gulag memorial on the banks of the Moscow Canal. See Simon Schama, *Landscape and Memory*, pp. 24–6 and color illustrations 6 & 7 between pp. 82 and 83.
86. "В память о соотечественниках погибших при строительстве канала Москва-Волга 1932–1937 гг. Прах многих из них лежит в Дмитровской земле."
87. http://anashina.com/ivankovskaya-ges-v-dubne/#i-3. Accessed 18 December 2016. This site features photographs of the Volga/Moscow Canal junction, including the Lenin Sculpture, the Ivan'kovo Hydro-Electric station, the canal's first lock, and other landscapes.
88. For additional information about the *maska skorbi*, as it is known in Russian, see a Russian account http://www.magadangorod.ru/index.php?news id=16428 and http://journals.ed.ac.uk/unfamiliar/article/view/475 for a discussion of the memorial in English. Both sites accessed 24 May 2017.
89. Zuzanna Bogomil, "Stone, Cross and Mask: Searching for [the] Language of Commemoration of the Gulag in the Russian Federation," in *Polish Sociological Review* 177 (2012), pp. 71–90, here p. 90. In this article Bogomil traces how the "soft" memorials of the late 1980s quickly became "hard" memorials (she employs Aleksander Etkind's terminology of hard and soft memory-scapes) of the 1990s and beyond. She examines how the Russian Orthodox Church has assumed an increasing role in the construction of these memorials.
90. According to Mikhail Bulanov there was a museum organized in Dmitrov during the construction of the Moscow Canal, but it is unclear what happened to it or its contents. Bulanov noted that even Fedorov, the leading authority on Dmitlag and Dmitrov, did not know what happened to the museum. In addition, Bulanov reported that a second museum was organized in Khimki dedicated to the Moscow Canal, but a fire in the 1970s or 1980s destroyed it and all its contents. Further research is required in order to adequately document these claims, although Bulanov is a highly reliable source. Personal conversation 2 June 2008.
91. Sekirnaia Hill is located in the Solovetsky Monastery on the Solovetsky Islands. During its use as the Gulag camp Solovki, Sekirnaia Hill, on which the Church of the Ascension is located, was the site of extreme torture, punishment, and confinement for Solovki prisoners.

92. Zusanna Bogomil, "The Solovetski Islands and Butovo as Two 'Russian Golgothas'. New Martyrdom as a Means to Understand Soviet Repression," in Felicitas Fischer von Weikersthal and Karoline Thaidigsmann (eds), *(Hi-) Stories of the Gulag. Fiction and Reality* (Heidelberg, 2016), pp. 133–56, here p. 149.
93. For a good summary of these events see Veronika Dorman, "From the Solovki to Butovo: How the Russian Orthodox Church Appropriates the Memory of the Repressions. Summary," in *Laboratorium* 2 (2010), pp. 431–6. This is an English summary of Dorman's longer article in Russian, "Ot Solovkov do Butovo: Russkaia Pravoslavnaia Tserkov' i Pamiat' o Sovetskikh Repressiiakh v Post-Sovetskoi Rossii," in *Laboratorium* 2 (2010), pp. 327–47. The Russian version provides a much more detailed account of the procession of the Solovki cross to Butovo and also analyzes the increasing role of the Russian Orthodox Church in appropriating the memory of and memorials to the victims of Stalinist Terror.
94. Dorman, English Summary, p. 435.
95. http://www.fgup-KiM.ru/go/present. Accessed 29 March 2009. "Укреплять безопасность и антитеррористическую защищенность не для приезда вышестоящего начальства и комиссий, а для того, чтобы предупредить чрезвычайное происшествие, не допустить прекращения функционирования особо важного стратегического объекта – это наша сегодняшняя задача."
96. https://fgbu-KiM.ru/go/head. Accessed 13 December 2016.
97. An earlier version of this discussion was published as "The 70th Anniversary of the Moscow Canal." Working Paper for the National Council for Eastern Europe, Eurasia and Russia, 2009. http://www.nceeer.org/Papers/papers.php. In addition, segments of the discussion of memorial space appear in "The Moscow Canal and the Creation of Memorial Space," *Gulag Studies* 4 (2011), pp. 59–67.
98. Shvedova had started her job just days before I met her in June 2008; she was neither an engineer, nor a long-time MVC employee, and therefore not a specialist on the waterway. After I made numerous attempts to meet with Sidorov – over the course of almost a year – he told me he would have his secretary call me to set up an appointment. When no such call was forthcoming, I contacted the secretary, only to find out that I had to submit an official letter requesting an interview. I then had to call another office to determine whether my letter had been officially received and recorded, at which time I was given Shvedova's name and told that she, not Sidorov, would see me. The meeting with her almost did not occur because she needed over a week to set up and clear it with the MVC Administration. Literally three days before my departure from Moscow, I met with Shvedova and, in the meantime, requested and received a meeting with Nina Nikolaevna Ermakova, head of the hydro-engineering department.
99. The official Russian name of the entity that oversees operation of the Moscow Canal is FGBU-KiM – Federal'noe gosudarstvennoe biudzhetnoe uchrezhde-

nie-Kanal imeni Moskvy (Federal State Enterprise – The Moscow Canal). This title takes into account that the Moscow Canal system consists not only of the canal itself, but also of the Stalin Waterworks and its supply canal, the Oka and Moscow Rivers, and the Uglich and Rybinsk Reservoirs. https://fgbu-MVC.ru/go/about. Accessed 13 December 2016.

100. http://www.fgup-MVC.ru/news/company/5/. Accessed 6 August 2008. Link is no longer operational.
101. I am indebted to N. N. Ermakova, hydro-engineer on the canal staff, who supplied me with a copy of this song, as well as with a copy of the official Jubilee invitation, the official MVC anthem, the commemorative pin, and the commemorative album.
102. According to informed sources the publication of this volume was fraught with difficulty. The firm originally charged with producing it suffered from financial problems. The woman who compiled the work had no connection to the canal and was viewed as a less-than-adequate writer and editor. The book was not ready in time for the 14 July 2007 celebration. When it did appear, it contained egregious mistakes, including misidentified photographs and factual errors. A revised edition of the book was published only in Spring 2008 with most of the errors corrected. Sources note, however, that the book, with its sparse content and relatively prosaic format, reflected poorly on the MVC Administration. Given that the volume was conceived of as the single celebratory print souvenir of the Moscow Canal's 70th Anniversary, some believed that a more ostentatious volume, worthy of this milestone, should have been produced. *Kanal imeni Moskvy: 70 let* (Moscow, 2007).
103. My thanks to Karen Petrone for providing this important detail.
104. http://www.museum.ru/M448. Accessed 15 December 2016. This site provides the history of the museum, its facilities and services. The material is available in both Russian and English.
105. New Martyrs are those believers who were repressed during the Stalinist Terror. Sites such as http://martyr.ru/ and http://www.hristianstvo.ru/heritage/saints/newmartires/ provide information in Russian and English concerning the definition and development of the New Martyrs. Sites accessed 24 May 2017.
106. Tiagacheva's husband, Leonid Tiagachev, was the President of the Russian Olympic Committee at this time.
107. http://www.fgup-MVC.ru/news/company/3/. Accessed 7 August 2008. Link is no longer operational.
108. "Istoriia bez kupiur," *Zerna* (August 2007), p. 2.
109. http://www.temples.ru/show_picture.php?PictureID=175562. Photographer Yuri Sergeevich Kvasnikov. For an excellent view of the chapel from the water see the site http://river-forum.ru/showthread.php/8133-%D1%82-%D1%85-%D0%98.%D0%90.-%D0%9A%D1%80%D1%8B%D0%BB%D0%BE%D0%B2-%D0%9C%D0%BE%D1%81%D0%BA%D0%B2%D0%B0-%

D0%A1%D0%B0%D0%BD%D0%BA%D1%82-%D0%9F%D0%B5%D1%82%D0%B5%D1%80%D0%B1%D1%83%D1%80%D0%B3-%D0%9C%D0%BE%D1%81%D0%BA%D0%B2%D0%B0-%D1%81-16.08-%D0%BF%D0%BE-28.08.2015. Both sites accessed 24 May 2017.

110. Ibid.

111. Aleksander Etkind, "Post-Soviet Hauntology: Cultural Memory of the Soviet Terror," in *Constellations* 16 (1), pp. 182–200.

112. https://fgbu–kim.ru/go/news. Accessed 15 December 2016.

113. The following discussion on contested space, especially in regard to public and private re-interpretations of historical space, owes much to the following foundational works (among others) on the examination of "space" and "place" as critical constructs: Henri Lefebvre, *The Production of Space*; Simon Schama, *Landscape and Memory*; Edward W. Soja, *Postmodern Geographies: The Reassertion of Space in Critical Social Theory* (London, 2001).

114. From V.S. Barkovsky, *Tainy Moskva-Volgostroiia* (Moscow, 2007), p. 4. While no additional publication information is provided in the booklet, Barkovsky informed me that the production of the book was underwritten by the Memorial organization. Interview with V.S. Barkovsky in Moscow, 17 November 2007.

115. Remember that Firin and Kogan were NKVD officers, while Zhuk was an NKVD civilian employee. Semyon Firin headed Dmitlag 1933–7, Lazar' Kogan supervised Canal construction 1932–6, and Sergei Zhuk served as the chief engineer of Moskva-Volgostroi 1930–7.

116. Anatoly Salutsky, *The Moscow Canal at 80: A First-hand Account of the NKVD Dmitlag* [*Kanaly Moskva-Volga 80 let: pravda o Dmitlage NKVD iz pervykh ruk*] (Moscow, 2017). For additional information see https://www.facebook.com/groups/Moskva.Volga.Ru/permalink/956529544485134/. Accessed 2 November 2017.

117. For additional information see http://moskva-volga.ru/v-mezhdunarodnom-memoriale-otkrylas-vystavka-kanal-imeni/. Accessed 2 November 2017.

118. See https://www.facebook.com/groups/Moskva.Volga.Ru/permalink/985527018252053/. Accessed 2 November 2017.

119. In his article "Monumentality, Mentality," William Gass describes the difference between monuments, which in his argument include everything from gravestones to large architectural structures, and monumentality. See William H. Gass, "Monumentality, Mentality," in *Oppositions* 25 (1982), pp. 127–44, here pp. 129–30.

120. Ibid., pp. 130 and 132.

121. Ibid., p. 138.

122. Zuzanna Bogomil, "Stone, Cross and Mask: Searching for [the] Language of Commemoration of the Gulag in the Russian Federation," in *Polish Sociological Review* v. 177 (2012), pp. 71–90, here pp. 71–2. Etkind's quoted remarks are from Aleksander Etkind, "Post-Soviet Hauntology: Cultural Memory of the Soviet Terror," in *Constellations* 16 (1), pp. 182–200. Etkind fully explicates

these ideas in *Warped Memory: Stories of the Undead in the Land of the Unburied* (Stanford, CA, 2013). See especially pp. 206–11.

123. Alexander Etkind, *Warped Mourning*, p. 207.
124. Zuzanna Bogomil, "Solovetski Islands as 'Russian Golgotha'," p. 152.
125. Ibid., pp. 152–3.
126. Roger Friedland and Richard D. Hecht, "The Powers of Place," in Oren Baruch Stier and J. Shawn Landres (eds), *Religion, Violence, Memory, and Place* (Bloomington, IN, 2006), pp. 17–36, here p. 19.
127. Ibid., p. 29.
128. Ibid., p. 30.
129. Christopher Tilley, *A Phenomenology of Landscape: Places, Paths and Monuments* (London, 1994), p. 33. Also cited in Bogomil, "Solovetski Islands," note 42, p. 146.

Chapter 5 The Present and Future of the Moscow Canal

1. As of this writing a recent (28 May 2017) issue of the *New York Times Book Review* testifies to the ongoing importance of and fascination with water. It featured reviews of three new books, all of which explore the history and environmental problems associated with different bodies of water. See reviews of Jack E. Davis, *The Gulf: The Making of an American Sea* (New York, NY, 2017), p. 11; Dan Egan, *The Death and Life of the Great Lakes* (New York, NY, 2017), p. 12; and David Owen, *Where the Water Goes: Life and Death Along the Colorado River* (New York, NY, 2017), p. 13.
2. Tim Arango, "Turkish Dam Project Threatens to Submerge Thousands of Years of History," *New York Times* (2 September 2016). http://www.nytimes.com/2016/09/02/world/europe/turkey-hasankeyf-ilisu-dam.html?_r=0. Accessed 15 October 2016. The article features stunning photographs of the areas in and around Hasenkeyf that will disappear because of the Ilisu Dam project.
3. Ibid.
4. Ibid. My thanks to Keith Blasing for pointing out that a similar situation exists in the Florida panhandle, which is the ultimate destination of the Chattahoochee River, where the same complaint was made against Georgia/Atlanta for draining the river closer to its source. These examples are not unique and reveal how highly contentious water issues are. E-mail correspondence 28 June 2017.
5. *The Moscow Times* (11 October 2016), https://themoscowtimes.com/news/revolutionary-youth-group-hangs-solzhenitsyn-effigy-on-moscow-gulag-museum-55685. Accessed 15 October 2016. The article includes a photograph of the Solzhenitsyn effigy and the text that was attached to it.
6. Ibid.
7. I refer here to the desecration of unique and priceless sites and relics in Afghanistan, Syria, and elsewhere in the Middle East and Central Asia.

8. http://www.ebay.com/itm/Antique-Vintage-Porcelain-Tea-Pair-Canal-Moscow-Volga-Verbilki-1930-VERY-RARE-/291926561705?hash=item43f82dd3a9:g:yeQAAOSwcL5XNYJG. Accessed 19 November 2016.
9. http://www.ebay.com/itm/Soviet-MOSKVA-VOLGA-CANAL-Builder-Badge-Stalin-GULAG-Best-Worker-Medal-ORIGINAL-/331352752570?hash=item4d2629c1ba:g:-EEAAOSwajVURrIb. Accessed 19 November 2016.
10. For further details concerning the Rechnik brouhaha, see http://rt.com/news/prime-time/rechnik-demolition-moscow-controversy/; http://russiaprofile.org/politics/a1266435093/print_edition/; http://www.scanex.ru/en/news/News_Preview.asp?id=n113544; http://ria.ru/trend/rechnik_house_demolition/; http://www.rg.ru/2010/01/21/rechnik-site.html; http://www.youtube.com/playlist?list=PLE69C6B78BD289D6F. Accessed 27 May 2014. Numerous other sites in English and in Russian describe the history of the conflict in Rechnik and its ultimate resolution.
11. Personal conversation, 24 May 2007.
12. There are numerous reports that detail these efforts and that represent varying views on these initiatives. Regarding statue removal in New Orleans see, among others, https://www.washingtonpost.com/national/new-orleans-begins-removing-monument-to-confederate-gen-robert-e-lee/2017/05/19/c4ed94f6-364d-11e7-99b0-dd6e94e786e5_story.html?utm_term = .b8e9c7f5d319 and https://www.nytimes.com/2017/05/11/us/jefferson-davis-statue.html?_r = 0. Accessed 22 May 2017. For reports on these efforts around the state of Kentucky see http://www.courier-journal.com/story/news/local/2015/06/23/kentucky-hears-calls-removal-jefferson-davis-statue-capitol/29168623/; http://www.foxnews.com/us/2016/05/01/kentucky-confederate-monument-to-be-removed-after-120-years.html; http://www.wkyt.com/home/headlines/Lexington-statue-of-Confederate-leader-Hunt-Morgan-vandalized-310076651.html and most recently http://www.kentucky.com/news/local/counties/fayette-county/article152916439.html. Accessed 27 May 2017.
13. For a compelling discussion of this issue see Alexander Etkind, *Warped Mourning: Stories of the Undead in the Land of the Unburied* (Stanford, CA, 2013). Especially pertinent here are Chapters Nine, "The Hard and the Soft," and Ten, "Post-Soviet Hauntology."
14. https://en.wikipedia.org/wiki/Lost_Worlds_(TV_series). This program aired on 17 October 2007, Season 2, Episode 12.
15. https://russia.tv/brand/show/brand_id/59309/.
16. Their Facebook page can be found at https://www.facebook.com/groups/Moskva.Volga.Ru/.
17. The site's authorial team includes Igor Kuvyrkov, Ilya Rozhdestvensky, Vladimir Rodionov, and Sergei Gaev.
18. http://moskva-volga.ru/o-proekte/. Accessed 2 December 2016.
19. http://moskva-volga.ru/category/kartoteka/. Accessed 22 May 2017.
20. Facebook post from 18 May 2017 on https://www.facebook.com/groups/Moskva.Volga.Ru/.

21. http://hraniteli-nasledia.com/articles/initsiativy/kanal-imeni-moskvy-obekt-yunesko/. Accessed 3 December 2016.
22. http://dolgoprudnymuseum.ru/vr/can/. Accessed 20 June 2017.
23. Facebook post from 18 April 2017 on https://www.facebook.com/groups/Moskva.Volga.Ru/.
24. The conference's full program can be found at http://moskva-volga.ru/programma-mezhregionalnoj-nauchnoj-konferentsii-posvyashhyonnoj-80-letiyu-kanala-imeni-moskvy/. Accessed 27 May 2017. In addition, some of the presentations have been uploaded to this site http://dkraeved.ru/articles.html, as well as to http://ikuv.ru/nerealizovannye-obekty-hlebnikovskogo-uchastka-stroitelstva-kanala-moskva-volga/.
25. http://moskva-volga.ru/volga-techyot-v-moskvu-yubilejnaya-vystavka-v-dubne/. Accessed 18 July 2017.
26. See http://moskva-volga.ru/ as well as the Moskva-Volga.ru Facebook page for articles and broadcasts.
27. See http://www.rbc.ru/rbcfreenews/570329879a794763db501ff7 for a brief description of the case and the suspects, as well for the further disposition of the criminal case. Accessed 3 December 2016.
28. https://lenta.ru/news/2016/08/16/mosvodokanal/. Accessed 3 December 2016.
29. https://fgbu-kim.ru/go/news. Accessed 2 December 2016
30. https://fgbu-kim.ru/go/construction. Accessed 3 December 2016. Rubrics under the "Construction" tab include: The Construction of the Canal; The War Years; The Present Day; Veterans; and the Canal Construction Museum.
31. https://www.litres.ru/anonim/kanal-imeni-moskvy/. Accessed 3 December 2016. There are a number of sites that advertise and review this first book in the series. This site in particular contains both on-line access to the book and information about purchasing the hard copy, plus publication information and some reviews. Access to the on-line text for *The Moscow Canal* can be found at http://www.e-reading.club/book.php?book=1041569. Basic information regarding the series' second book, *Labyrinth*, can be found at https://www.litres.ru/raznoe-8302728/kanal-imeni-moskvy-labirint/. Accessed 3 December 2016.
32. For photographs and the news item about this memorial see: https://www.facebook.com/gulagmuseum/?hc_ref=NEWSFEED&fref=nf. Accessed 31 May 2017. And https://www.novayagazeta.ru/articles/2017/05/31/72649-stena-skorbi. Accessed 1 June 2017.
33. Alexander Etkind, *Warped Mourning*, p. 186.
34. http://www.rferl.org/a/russia-perm-gulag-museum-takeover-contribution-to-victory/27152188.html and http://gulaghistory.org/nps/onlineexhibit/stalin/perm36.php. Both sites provide vital information about the Perm-36 camp and the controversies this space has caused. Accessed 4 December 2016.
35. *Kanal Moskva-Volga 1931–1937* (Moscow, 1940), p. 11.

36. Karl Schloegel, *In Space We Read Time: On the History of Civilization and Geopolitics*, Gerrit Jackson (trans) (New York, NY, 2016), p. 417.
37. James C. Scott, *Seeing Like a State: How Certain Schemes to Improve the Human Condition Have Failed* (New Haven, CT, 1998), p. 195.
38. Ibid., p. 89. Scott defines "high modernism" thusly: "The first is the aspiration to the administrative ordering of nature and society, an aspiration that we have already seen at work in scientific forestry, but one raised to a far more comprehensive and ambitious level. 'High modernism' seems an appropriate term for this aspiration. As a faith, it was shared by many across a wide spectrum of political ideologies. Its main carriers and exponents were the avant-garde among engineers, planners, technocrats, high-level administrators, architects, scientists, and visionaries ... They envisioned a sweeping, rational engineering of all aspects of social life in order to improve the human condition. As a conviction, high modernism was not the exclusive property of any political tendency; it has both right- and left-wing variants, as we shall see. The second element is the unrestrained use of the power of the modern state as an instrument for achieving these designs. The third element is a weakened or prostrate civil society that lacks the capacity to resist these plans. The ideology of high modernism provides, as it were, the desire; the modern state provides the means of acting on that desire; and the incapacitated civil society provides the level terrain on which to build (dis)utopias."
39. Ibid., p. 161.
40. Bettina Greiner, "The Gulag: An Incarnation of the State That Created It" in Michael David-Fox (ed.), *The Soviet Gulag: Evidence, Interpretation, and Comparison* (Pittsburgh, PA, 2016), p. 315.
41. James R. Scott, *Seeing Like a State*, p. 195.
42. Vasily Grossman, *Everything Flows*, Robert and Elizabeth Chandler with Anna Aslanyan (trans) (New York, NY, 2009).
43. http://www.gulagmaps.org/. Accessed 2 June 2017.

BIBLIOGRAPHY

Archival Materials

GARF (State Archive of the Russian Federation)

Biblioteka Perekovki (Dmitrov, 1935–6).
Funds
f. 7952, op. 2, d. 22, ll. 1–4.
f. 7952, op. 2, d. 122, ll. 1–198.
f. 9489, op. 2, d. 122, ll. 37, 196, 201, 208, 212, 228 and 245.
Kanal Moskva-Volga, 1937. *Maket gotovivsheisia k izdaniiu knigi o stroitel'stve kanala Moskva-Volga.*

TsGAMO (Central State Archive of the Moscow Region)

f. 2589, op. 1, d. 1, 20, 24, 29, 30, 32, 43, 54, 64, 67–69, 76–77 and 83–86.

Select Bibliography

Alexopoulos, Golfo, "Destructive Labor Camps: Rethinking Solzhenitsyn's Play on Words," in Michael David-Fox (ed.), *The Soviet Gulag. Evidence, Interpretation, and Comparison* (Pittsburgh, PA, 2016), pp. 42–64.

Anonymous, *Kanal imeni Moskvy* (Moscow, 2014).

——— *Kanal imeni Moskvy. Labirint* (Moscow, 2016).

Arango, Tim, "Turkish Dam Project Threatens to Submerge Thousands of Years of History," *New York Times* (2 September 2016). http://www.nytimes.com/2016/09/02/world/europe/turkey-hasankeyf-ilisudam.html?_r=0.

Averbakh, I., *Ot prestupleniia k trudu* (Moscow, 1936).

Bachelard, Gaston, *The Poetics of Space,* Maria Jolas (trans) (Boston, MA, 1994).

Barkovsky, V. S., *Tainy Moskva–Volgostroia* (Moscow, 2007).

Barnes, Steven A., *Death and Redemption in the Gulag. The Gulag and the Shaping of Soviet Society* (Princeton, NJ, 2011).

Baron, Nick, "The Mapping of Illiberal Modernity: Spatial Science, Ideology and the State in Early Twentieth-century Russia," in Sanna Turoma and Maxim Waldstein (eds), *Empire De/Centered. New Spatial Histories of Russia and the Soviet Union* (Farnham, UK, 2013), pp. 105–34.

Bell, Wilson, "Was the Gulag an Archipelago? De-Convoyed Prisoners and Porous Borders in the Camps of Western Siberia," *The Russian Review*, 72.1 (January 2013), pp. 116–41.

Binder, Eva, "Moskau-Hafen von funf Meeren: Die stalinische 'Wasserkultur' und ihre symbolischen Bedeutungen," in Doris Eibl (ed.), *Wasser und Raum: Beiträge zu einer Kulturtheorie des Wassers* (Göttingen, 2008), pp. 319–40.

Bogomil, Zuzanna, "Stone, Cross and Mask: Searching for [the] Language of Commemoration of the Gulag in the Russian Federation," *Polish Sociological Review*, 177 (2012), pp. 71–90.

——— "The Solovetski Islands and Butovo as Two 'Russian Golgothas.' New Martyrdom as a Means to Understand Soviet Repression," in Felicitas Fischer von Weikersthal and Karoline Thaidigsmann (eds), *(Hi-)Stories of the Gulag. Fiction and Reality* (Heidelberg, 2016), pp. 133–45.

Bown, Matthew Cullerne, *A Dictionary of Twentieth Century Russian and Soviet Painters: 1900–1980s* (London, UK, 1998).

——— *Socialist Realist Painting* (New Haven, CT, 1998).

Bulanov, M. I., *Kanal Moskva-Volga: Khronika volzhskogo raiona gidrosooruzhenii* (Dubna, 2007).

Butovskii poligon. Kniga pamiati zhertv politicheskikh repressii v. 2–7 (Moscow, 1998–2003).

Cheremykh, N. A., *Khochetsia, chtoby znali i drugie ...* (Moscow, 1965).

Clark, Katerina, "Little Heroes and Big Deeds: Literature's Response to the First Five-Year Plan," in Sheila Fitzpatrick (ed.), *Cultural Revolution in Russia, 1928–1931* (Bloomington, IN, 1978), pp. 189–206.

——— *Moscow, the Fourth Rome* (Cambridge, MA, 2011).

Clark, Toby, "The 'New Man's' Body," in Matthew Cullerne Bown and Brandon Taylor (eds), *Art of the Soviets: Painting, Sculpture and Architecture in a One-Party State, 1917–1992* (Manchester, UK, and New York, NY, 1993), pp. 33–50.

Clowes, Edith W., *Russia on the Edge: Imagined Geographies and Post-Soviet Identity* (Ithaca, NY and London, UK, 2011).

Cosgrove, Denis and Stephen Daniels (eds), *The Iconography of Landscape* (Cambridge, UK, 2004).

de Certeau, Michel, *The Practice of Everyday Life*, Steven F. Rendell (trans) (Berkeley, CA, 1984).

Dobrenko, Evgeny, "The Art of Social Navigation: The Cultural Topography of the Stalin Era," in Evgeny Dobrenko and Eric Naiman (eds), *The Landscape of Stalinism: The Art and Ideology of Soviet Space* (Seattle, WA, 2003), pp. 163–200.

Dobrenko, Evgeny, and Eric Naiman (eds), *The Landscape of Stalinism: The Art and Ideology of Soviet Space* (Seattle, WA, 2003).

Dorman, Veronika, "From the Solovki to Butovo: How the Russian Orthodox Church Appropriates the Memory of the Repressions. Summary," *Laboratorium* 2 (2010), pp. 431–6.

——— "Ot Solovkov do Butovo: Russkaia Pravoslavnaia Tserkov' i Pamiat' o Sovetskikh Repressiiakh v Post-Sovetskoi Rossii," *Laboratorium* 2 (2010), pp. 327–47.

Draskoczy, Julie, *Belomor: Criminality and Creativity in Stalin's Gulag* (Boston, MA, 2014).

Eksler, I., "Caption to a Photograph of a Moscow Canal Lock at Night." *The USSR in Construction* 2 (1938), p. 33.

——— "The Face of the Canal," GARF, f. 7952, op. 2, d. 122, ll. 52, 53.

Eremenko, Elena, "Moskva—Port piati morei," *Kanal imeni Moskvy 70 let* (Moscow, 2007).

Etkind, Aleksander, "Post-Soviet Hauntology: Cultural Memory of the Soviet Terror," *Constellations* 16 (1) 2009, pp. 182–200.

——— *Warped Mourning: Stories of the Undead in the Land of the Unburied* (Stanford, CA, 2013).

Fedenko, I., *Kanal imeni Moskvy* (Moscow, 1955).

Fedorov, N. A., *Byla li tachka u ministra?... Ocherki o stroitel'stve kanala Moskva-Volga* (Dmitrov, 1997).

——— "Dmitlag. Iz istorii stroitel'stva kanala Moskva-Volga," *Butovskii poligon. Kniga pamiati zhertv politicheskikh repressii* v.2 (Moscow, 1998).

Friedland, Roger and Richard D. Hecht, "The Powers of Place," in Oren Baruch Stier and J. Shawn Landres (eds), *Religion, Violence, Memory, and Place* (Bloomington, IN, 2006), pp. 17–36.

Gamburg, G. and Sergei Alymov, *Listen, Volga!*, Soundtrack to the film *Moscow–Volga*.

Gass, William H., "Monumentality, Mentality," *Oppositions* 25 (1982), pp. 127–44.

Gikov, Rafail, dir., *Moscow–Volga. Film-documents About the Greatest Structure of the Stalinist Epoch 1933–1937* (Moscow, 1937).

Gregory, Paul R., *Terror by Quota: State Security from Lenin to Stalin* (New Haven, CT, 2009).

Greiner, Bettina, "The Gulag: An Incarnation of the State That Created It," in Michael David-Fox (ed.), *The Soviet Gulag. Evidence, Interpretation, and Comparison* (Pittsburgh, PA, 2016), pp. 314–20.

Grigorenko, Aleksandr, *The Gulag, the Canal, and the Artist* [*Gulag, Kanal i Khudozhnik*], http://moscow.clow.ru/information/1/6/znm2g16.html.

Grossman, Vasily, *Everything Flows*, Robert and Elizabeth Chandler with Anna Aslanyan (trans) (New York, NY, 2009).

Groys, Boris, "The Art of Totality," in Evgeny Dobrenko and Eric Naiman (eds), *The Landscape of Stalinism: The Art & Ideology of Soviet Space* (Seattle, WA, 2003), pp. 96–122.

——— *The Total Art of Stalinism: Avant-Garde, Aesthetic Dictatorship, and Beyond.* Charles Rougle (trans) (Princeton, 1992).

Hagenloh, Paul, *Stalin's Police: Public Order and the Mass Repression in the USSR, 1926–1941* (Washington, DC, 2009).

Hall, Elvajean, *The Volga: The Lifeline of Russia* (New York, 1965).

Healey, Dan, "'Dramatalogical' Trauma in the Gulag. Malingering, Self-Inflicted Injuries and the Prisoner-Patient," in Felicitas Fischer Von Weikersthal and Karoline Thaidigsmann (eds), *(Hi-)Stories of the Gulag. Fiction and Reality* (Heidelberg, 2016), pp. 37–62.

"Istoriia bez kupiur," *Zerna*, August 2007, p. 2.

Jakobson, Michael, *Origins of the Gulag. The Soviet Prison Camp System 1917–1934* (Lexington, KY, 1993).

Josephson, Paul R., *Industrialized Nature: Brute Force Technology and the Transformation of the Natural World* (Washington, DC, 2002).

Kabalevsky, D., "Kanaloarmeiskaia pesnia. Stat'ia," *Na shturm trassy,* No. 11 (26), November 1936, pp. 16–7.

Kaganovich, Lazar' Moiseevich, *Pamiatnye zapiski rabochego, kommunista-bol'shevika, profsoiuznogo, partiinogo i sovetskogo gosudarstvennogo rabotnika* (Moscow, 1996).

Kanal im. Moskvy, http://www.fgbu-kim.ru/.

Kanal imeni Moskvy (Moscow, 1987).

Kanal imeni Moskvy: 70 let (Moscow, 2007).

Kanal Moskva-Volga, 1932–1937 (Moscow, 1940).

Kassof, Brian, "A Book of Socialism: Stalinist Culture and the First Edition of the *Bol'shaia sovetskaia entsiklopediia,*" *Kritika* v.6, 1 (Winter 2005), pp. 55–95.

Kelley, Tyler J., "Choke Point of a Nation," *New York Times*, 27 November 2016: Business section, pp. 1, 6.

Khlevniuk, Oleg V., "The Gulag and the Non-Gulag as One Interrelated Whole," in Michael David-Fox (ed.), *The Soviet Gulag. Evidence, Interpretation, and Comparison* (Pittsburgh, PA, 2016), pp. 25–41.

——— *The History of the Gulag. From Collectivization to the Great Terror* (New Haven, CT, 2004).

King, David, *The Commissar Vanishes: The Falsification of Photographs and Art in Stalin's Russia* (New York, NY, 1997).

Kogan, Lazar', *Pravda* 6 January 1935, npn.

Kokurin, A. I. and N. V. Petrov, comps., *GULAG (Glavnoe upravlenie lagerei): 1918–1960* (Moscow, 2002).

Kokurin, A. I. and Yu. N. Merkurov, comps., *Stalinskie stroiki GULAGA: 1930–1953* (Moscow, 2005).

Komarovsky, A., *The Moscow–Volga Canal* (Moscow, 1939).

Kosarev, A. V., "The Greatest Structure of the Stalinist Epoch," *Kanal Moskva-Volga*, maquette, p. 10.

Krinsky, V. F., "Arkhitektura shliuzov kanala Moskva-Volga," *Arkhitektura kanala Moskva-Volga* (Moscow, 1939), pp. 39–57.

Kunichika, Michael, "Landscape and Vision at the White Sea-Baltic Canal," in Valerie Kivelson and Joan Neuberger (eds), *Picturing Russia: Explorations in Visual Culture* (New Haven, CT, 2008), pp. 254–8.

Lefebvre, Henri, *The Production of Space*, Donald Nicholson-Smith (trans) (Oxford, UK, 1991).

Livers, Keith A., *Constructing the Stalinist Body: Fictional Representations of Corporeality in the Stalinist 1930s* (Lanham, MD, 2004).

Lopatin, P[avel], *Kanal Moskva-Volga* (Moscow, 1937).

——— *Moskva-Volga* (Moscow-Leningrad, 1938).

——— *Volga idet v Moskvu* (Moscow, 1938).

MacKinnon, Elaine, "Writing History for Stalin: Isaak Izrailevich Mints and the *Istoriia grazhdanskoi voiny,*" *Kritika* v.6, 1 (Winter 2005), pp. 5–54.

Maslov, V. I., *Kanal imeni Moskvy: Stroika vek. Sud'by liudei* (Mytishchi, 2012).

Merkurov, S. D., "Monumental'naia skul'ptura na kanale Moskva-Volga," in *Arkhitektura kanala Moskva-Volga* (Moscow, 1939), pp. 68–72.

Mikhailov, A. I., *Arkhitektura Kanala Moskva-Volga* (Moscow, 1939).

——— "Znachenie kanala Moskva-Volga v razvitii sovetskoi arkhitektury," in *Arkhitektura kanala Moskva-Volga* (Moscow, 1939), pp. 73–89.

Mitchell, Don, *Cultural Geography: A Critical Introduction* (Oxford, UK and Cambridge, MA, 2000).

Na shturm trassy, No. 1(6), 15 January 1935.

O'Mahony, Mike, "The Moscow Metro," in Valerie Kivelson and Joan Neuberger (eds), *Picturing Russia: Explorations in Visual Culture* (New Haven, CT, 2008), pp. 185–8.

O nagrazhdenii i l'gotakh dlia stroitelei kanala Moskva-Volga. 14 July 1937. TsGAMO, f. 2589, op. 1, d. 67, l. 1 ob.

O nagrazhdenii rabotnikov stroitel'stva kanala Moskva-Volga i zavodov-postavshchikov (Moscow, 1937) (Russian State Library, R 322/1284).

Orlova, Aleksandra, "Strannaia kniga," in *Vestnik*, 5(342), 3 March 2004.

Palmer, Scott, *Dictatorship of the Air: Aviation Culture and the Fate of Modern Russia* (Cambridge, UK, 2009).

Paperny, Vladimir, *Architecture in the Age of Stalin: Culture Two*, John Hill and Roann Barris (trans) in collaboration with the author (Cambridge, UK, 2002).

——— *Kul'tura dva* (Moscow, 1996).

——— "Men, Women, and the Living Space," in William Craft Brumfield and Blair A. Ruble (eds), *Russian Housing in the Modern Age: Design & Social History* (Cambridge, UK, 1993), pp. 149–70.

"Perechen' grazhdanskikh i promyshlennykh zdanii i sooryzhenii postroennykh Dmitlagom GULAG, OGPU-NKVD SSSR v period 1932–1937 gg. na territorii goroda Dmitrova i v ego okrestnostiakh," *Dmitrovskii vestnik*, 27 March 2007, p. 8.

Perlin, V. M., "Arkhitektura kanala Moskva-Volga," in *Arkhitektura kanala Moskva-Volga* (Moscow, 1939), pp. 9–38.

Petrone, Karen, *Life Has Become More Joyous, Comrades!* (Bloomington, IN, 2000).

"Pokaianie," *Dmitrovskii vestnik*, No. 8 (21) August 2007.

Postanovlenie o general'nom plane razvitiia i rekonstruktsii Moskvy, Council of People's Commissars and the Central Committee of the Communist Party (SNK i TsK VKP(b)), 10 July 1935.

Rasstanov, A., "Dokumenty chuvstva i masterstva," *Na shturm trassy,* No. 1 (18) January 1936, pp. 38–9.

Rasstrel'nie zapiski. Moskva 1935–1953. Donskoe kladbishche {Donskoi krematorii} (Moscow, 2005).

Riabonon', Sergei, *Novaia Volga. Sbornik stikhov lagerno-stroitelei Kanala Moskva-Volga.* Biblioteka Perekovki, Vyp. 31 (Dmitrov, 1936).

Riumin, Veniamin, *PPM. Rasskazy*, Biblioteka Perekovki, Vyp. 6 (Dmitrov, 1935).

Ruder, Cynthia A., *Making History for Stalin. The Story of the Belomor Canal* (Gainesville, FL, 1998).

——— "The Moscow Canal and the Creation of Memorial Space," *Gulag Studies*, 4 (2011), pp. 59–67.

——— "The 70th Anniversary of the Moscow Canal," *Working Paper for the National Council for Eastern Europe, Eurasia and Russia*, 2009, http://www.nceeer.org/Papers/papers.php.

——— "Water and Power: The Moscow Canal and the 'Port of Five Seas'" in Jane Costlow and Arja Rosenholm (eds), *Meanings and Values of Water in Russian Culture* (London & New York, 2017), pp. 175–88.

Rukhliadev, A. M., "Arkhitektura rechnogo vokzala v Khimkakh," in *Arkhitektura kanala Moskva-Volga* (Moscow, 1939), pp. 58–67.

Rukodel'naia reka. GARF f. 7952, op. 2, d. 122, ll. 1–198.
Rusnock, K. Andrea, *Socialist Realist Painting During the Stalinist Era (1934–41): The High Art of Mass Art* (Pittsburgh, 2010).
Ryzhkova, N., "Muzyka iz GULAGa," *Neva* 7 (2003), pp. 243–50. Also available online at http://magazines.russ.ru/neva/2003/7/ryzhk.html.
Schama, Simon, *Landscape and Memory* (New York, NY, 1995).
Schloegel, Karl, *In Space We Read Time: On the History of Civilization and Geopolitics*, Gerrit Jackson (trans) (New York, NY, 2016).
——— *Moscow 1937*, Rodney Livingstone (trans) (Cambridge, UK, 2012).
Scott, James C., *Seeing Like a State: How Certain Schemes to Improve the Human Condition Have Failed* (New Haven, CT, 1998).
Shearer, David R., *Policing Stalin's Socialism: Repression and Social Order in the Soviet Union, 1924–1953* (New Haven, CT, 2009).
Shklovsky, Viktor, "Perekovka na kanale Volga-Moskva," *Bol'shevistskaya pechat'* 1 (1937).
Smith, Jeremy (ed.), *Beyond the Limits: The Concept of Space in Russian History and Culture* (Helsinki, 1999).
Soja, Edward W., *Postmodern Geographies: The Reassertion of Space in Critical Social Theory* (London, UK, 2001).
Stikhi i pesni o Kanale Moskva-Volga k 1 maia 1937 goda (Dmitrov, 1937).
Sushkevich, I. G. (ed.), *Arkhitektura kanala Moskva-Volga* (Moscow, 1939).
Taplin, Phoebe, "Moscow 'Port of Five Seas'," *The Moscow News*, 15 June 2015.
Tekhno-ekonomicheskaia zapiska. Prilozhenie: Skhematicheskii proekt v chertezhakh (Dmitrov, 1934).
Tertz, Abram [Andrei Sinyavsky], "On Socialist Realism," in *The Trial Begins and On Socialist Realism*, Max Hayward and George Dennis (trans) (Berkeley & Los Angeles, CA, 1982).
Tilley, Christopher, *A Phenomenology of Landscape: Places, Paths, and Monuments* (Oxford, UK, 1994).
Tuan, Yi-Fu, *Space and Place: The Perspective of Experience* (Minneapolis, 1977).
Tvedt, Terje, *Water and Society: Changing Perceptions of Societal and Historical Development* (London, 2016).
The USSR in Construction, 2 (February 1938).
Valentinov, T., "Stranitsy zhizni i bor'by. Stat'ia," *Na shturm trassy,* No. 9 (26) September 1936, pp. 34–5.
Viola, Lynne, "The Question of the Perpetrator in Soviet History," *Slavic Review* 75, 1 (2013), pp. 1–23.
——— *The Unknown Gulag. The Lost World of Stalin's Special Settlements* (Oxford, UK, 2007).
Vodonos, Efim, "'Groza momental'naia navek': o tvorchestve Evgeniia Egorova," http://magazines.russ.ru/volga21/2007/9/ef14.html.
Volga, Kama, Oka, Don. Putevoditel' (Moscow, 1955).
Volkov, P., *Moskva-Volga: Kanal imeni Moskvy* (Moscow, 1987).
Von Geldern, James, "The Centre and the Periphery: Cultural and Social Geography in the Mass Culture of the 1930s," in Stephen White (ed.), *New Directions in Soviet History* (Cambridge, UK, 1992), pp. 62–80.
Weiner, Douglas R., *A Little Corner of Freedom: Russian Nature Protection from Stalin to Gorbachev* (Berkeley, CA, 1999).

Widdis, Emma, "Viewed from Below: Subverting the Myths of the Soviet Landscape," in Birgit Beumers (ed.), *Russia on Reels: The Russian Idea in Post-Soviet Cinema* (London, 1999), pp. 66–75.

——— *Visions of a New Land: Soviet Film from the Revolution to the Second World War* (New Haven, CT, 2003).

Wittfogel, Karl A., *Oriental Despotism: A Comparative Study of Total Power* (New Haven, CT, 1957).

Wolf, Erika, "The Visual Economy of Forced Labor: Alexander Rodchenko and the White Sea–Baltic Canal," in Valerie Kivelson and Joan Neuberger (eds), *Picturing Russia: Explorations in Visual Culture* (New Haven, CT, 2008), pp. 168–74.

Zeisler-Vralsted, Dorothy, "The Cultural and Hydrological Development of the Mississippi and Volga Rivers," in C. Mauch and T. Zeller (eds), *Rivers in History: Perspectives on Waterways in Europe and North America* (Pittsburgh, PA, 2008).

——— *Rivers, Memory, and Nation-Building: A History of the Volga and Mississippi Rivers* (New York, NY, 2015).

Zhurin, V., G. Machtet and A. Berenzon, *Tekhno-ekonomicheskaia zapiska: Prilozhenie: Skhematicheskii proekt v chertazhakh* (Dmitrov, 1934).

Zoshchenko, Mikhail, "Istoriia odnoi perekovki," in M. Gorky, L. Averbakh and S. Firin (eds), *Belomorsko–Baltiiskii kanal imeni Stalina. Istoriia stroitel'stva 1931–1934* (Moscow, 1998), pp. 493–524.

INDEX

Page numbers in *italics* indicate figures, PL refers to plates section.